Private Wealth and Public Revenue in Latin America

Inequality and taxation are fundamental problems of modern times. How and when can democracies tax economic elites? This book develops a theoretical framework that refines and integrates the classic concepts of business's instrumental (political) power and structural (investment) power to explain the scope and fate of tax initiatives targeting economic elites in Latin America after economic liberalization. In Chile, business's multiple sources of instrumental power, including cohesion and ties to right parties, kept substantial tax increases off the agenda. In Argentina, weaker business power facilitated significant reform, although specific sectors, including finance and agriculture, occasionally had instrumental and/or structural power to defend their interests. In Bolivia, popular mobilization counterbalanced the power of economic elites, who were much stronger than in Argentina but weaker than in Chile. The book's in-depth, medium-N case analysis and close attention to policy-making processes contribute insights on business power and prospects for redistribution in unequal democracies.

Tasha Fairfield is an Assistant Professor in the Department of International Development at the London School of Economics. She holds a PhD in political science from the University of California, Berkeley, and degrees in physics from Harvard University and Stanford University. Her research interests include democracy and inequality, business politics, policy formulation, and the political economy of development. Prior to her current appointment, she was a Hewlett Fellow at Stanford University's Center on Democracy, Development, and the Rule of Law and a Visiting Fellow at the University of Notre Dame's Kellogg Institute for International Studies. Her research has been supported by the Social Science Research Council, Fulbright-Hays, and the International Centre for Tax and Development.

Private Wealth and Public Revenue in Latin America

Business Power and Tax Politics

TASHA FAIRFIELD

London School of Economics

CAMBRIDGE
UNIVERSITY PRESS

CAMBRIDGE
UNIVERSITY PRESS

32 Avenue of the Americas, New York, NY 10013-2473, USA

Cambridge University Press is part of the University of Cambridge.

It furthers the University's mission by disseminating knowledge in the pursuit of education, learning, and research at the highest international levels of excellence.

www.cambridge.org
Information on this title: www.cambridge.org/9781107088375

First published 2015

A catalog record for this publication is available from the British Library.

Library of Congress Cataloging in Publication data
Fairfield, Tasha, 1973–
Private wealth and public revenue in Latin America: business power and tax politics / Tasha Fairfield.
    pages cm
Includes bibliographical references and index.
ISBN 978-1-107-08837-5 (hardback)
1. Fiscal policy – Latin America.   2. Taxation – Political aspects – Latin America.
3. Corporations – Taxation – Latin America.   4. Business and politics – Latin America.   5. Wealth – Political aspects – Latin America.   6. Economic development – Latin America.   I. Title.
HJ799.53.F35   2015
339.5'25098–dc23   2014032251

ISBN 978-1-107-08837-5 Hardback

Contents

Figures and Tables

TABLES

Acronyms

ABA	Asociación de Bancos de la Argentina (Bank Association of Argentina)
ABIF	Asociación de Bancos e Instituciones Financieras, Chile (Chilean Association of Banks and Financial Institutions)
ADEBA	Asociación de Bancos Argentinos (Argentine Bank Association)
ADN	Acción Democrática y Nacionalista, Bolivia (Democratic Nationalist Action Party)
AEA	Asociación Empresaria Argentina (Argentine Business Association)
AFIP	Administración Federal de Ingresos Públicos, Argentina (Federal Administration of Public Revenue)
ASOBAN	Asociación de Bancos Privados de Bolivia (Bolivian Private Bank Association)
CADEX	Cámara de Exportadores de Santa Cruz, Bolivia (Santa Cruz Chamber of Exporters)
CAINCO	Cámara de Industria y Comercio de Santa Cruz, Bolivia (Santa Cruz Chamber of Industry and Commerce)
CAO	Cámara Agropecuaria del Oriente, Santa Cruz, Bolivia (Eastern Chamber of Agriculture)
CChC	Cámara Chilena de la Construcción (Chilean Chamber of Construction)
CEP	Centro de Estudios Públicos, Chile (Center for Public Studies)
CEPAL	Comisión Económica para América Latina y el Caribe (Economic Commission for Latin America and the Caribbean)

CEPB	Confederación de Empresarios Privados de Bolivia (Bolivian Confederation of Private Entrepreneurs)
CERC	Centro de Estudios de la Realidad Contemporánea, Chile (Center for the Study of Contemporary Reality)
CGT	Confederación General del Trabajo (General Confederation of Workers)
CIARA	Cámara de la Industria Aceitera de la República Argentina (Argentine Oil Industry Chamber)
CNCB	Cámara Nacional de Comercio, Bolivia (Bolivian National Chamber of Commerce)
CNCC	Cámara Nacional de Comercio, Chile (Chilean National Chamber of Commerce)
CNI	Cámara Nacional de Industrias, Bolivia (Bolivian National Chamber of Industry)
COB	Central Obrera Bolivia (Bolivian Workers Confederation)
CODELCO	Corporación Nacional del Cobre, Chile (Chilean National Copper Corporation)
CONINAGRO	Confederación Intercooperativa Agropecuaria, Argentina (Inter-Cooperative Agricultural Cooperative)
COPAL	Coordinadora de las Industrias de Productos Alimenticios, Argentina (Coordinator of Argentine Food Product Industries)
CPC	Confederación de la Producción y del Comercio, Chile (Chilean Confederation of Production and Commerce)
CRA	Confederaciones Rurales Argentinas (Argentina Rural Confederations)
CT	Corporate tax
DNIAF	Dirección Nacional de Investigaciones y Análisis Fiscal, Argentina (Argentine National Directorate of Fiscal Research and Analysis)
ECTCU	European Commission Taxation and Customs Union
FAA	Federación Agraria Argentina (Argentine Agricultural Federation)
FEPB-LP	Federación de Empresarios Privados de Bolivia, La Paz (La Paz Federation of Private Entrepreneurs)
FEPB-SC	Federación de Empresarios Privados de Bolivia, Santa Cruz (Santa Cruz Federation of Private Entrepreneurs)
FIEL	Fundación de Investigaciones Económicas Latinoamericanas, Argentina (Latin American Economic Research Foundation)
FPV	Frente para la Victoria, Argentina (Victory Front)
FUT	Fondo de Utilidades Tributarias, Chile (Taxable Profits Fund)

INE	Instituto Nacional de Estadística de Bolivia (Bolivian National Statistics Institute)
MAS	Movimiento al Socialismo, Bolivia (Movement for Socialism)
MECON	Ministerio de Economía y Producción, Argentina (Argentine Ministry of Economy and Production)
MIR	Movimiento de Izquierda Revolucionaria, Bolivia (Movement of the Revolutionary Left)
MNR	Movimiento Nacionalista Revolucionario, Bolivia (National Revolutionary Movement)
PDC	Partido Demócrata Cristiano, Chile (Christian Democratic Party)
PIT	Personal income tax
PJ	Partido Justicialista, Argentina (Peronist Party)
PODEMOS	Poder Democrática Social, Bolivia (Social and Democratic Power Party)
PPD	Partido Por La Democracia, Chile (Party for Democracy)
PRDS	Partido Radical Social Demócrata, Chile (Radical Social Democratic Party)
PS	Partido Socialista, Chile (Socialist Party)
RC-IVA	Régimen Complementario al Impuesto al Valor Agregado, Bolivia (Complementary VAT Regime)
RN	Renovación Nacional, Chile (National Renovation Party)
SBIF	Superintendencia de Banco e Instituciones Financieras, Chile (Superintendency of Banks and Financial Institutions)
SII	Servicio de Impuestos Internos, Chile (Chilean Internal Revenue Service)
SIN	Servicio de Impuestos Nacionales, Bolivia (Bolivian National Revenue Service)
SNA	Sociedad Nacional de Agricultura, Chile (Chilean National Agricultural Society)
SOFOFA	Sociedad de Fomento Fabril, Chile (Chilean Industrial Society)
SONAMI	Sociedad Nacional de Minería, Chile (Chilean National Mining Society)
SRA	Sociedad Rural Argentina (Argentine Rural Society)
UCR	Unión Cívica Radical, Argentina (Radical Civic Union Party)
UDI	Unión Democrática Independiente, Chile (Independent Democratic Union Party)
UIA	Unión Industrial Argentina (Argentine Industrial Union)

Acknowledgments

Contrary to its somewhat dry reputation, tax policy making showcases gripping power politics, strategic calculations, and sometimes even dramatic political battles that capture world headlines. *Private Wealth and Public Revenue in Latin America* endeavors to bring these fascinating policy processes to life while addressing key political economy questions of who gets what, when, and how. To that end, I am indebted to hundreds of informants who shared their expertise, strongly held convictions, political insights, and colorful narratives of policy processes in Chile, Argentina, and Bolivia. The ample quotations included in this book not only provide critical evidence to substantiate my arguments but also aim to convey elements of the captivating conversations that have sparked and sustained my own interest in Latin American tax politics.

I am particularly grateful to the many informants who generously met with me on multiple occasions, including two Argentine tax-agency informants and a Chilean financial-sector expert, whose identities are confidential, as well as Fernando Cossio, Juan Carlos Gómez-Sabaini, Pablo Guidotti, Michael Jorratt, Mario Marcel, Manuel Marfán, Carlos Montes, and José Antonio Nogales, among many others. I would like to give special thanks to former presidents Ricardo Lagos, Gonzalo Sánchez de Lozada, and Carlos Mesa. I also wish to acknowledge three prominent public servants and thoughtful informants who passed away before this book was completed: Edgardo Boeninger, Jaime Crispi, and Guillermo Justiniano.

This research would not have been possible without extensive fieldwork generously supported by the Social Science Research Council and Fulbright-Hays as well as funding for follow-up research provided by the Center for Latin American Studies (CLAS) at the University of California, Berkeley, and the International Centre for Tax and Development (ICTD). A Phi Beta Kappa

Northern California Association graduate scholarship, a Hewlett fellowship at Stanford University's Center on Democracy, Development, and the Rule of Law (CDDRL), and a postdoctoral fellowship at the University of Notre Dame's Kellogg Institute for International Studies provided critical support during the early analysis and writing stages. I thank Larry Diamond, Scott Mainwaring, Harley Shaiken, Mick Moore, and the academic communities at CDDRL, Kellogg, CLAS, and ICTD for their support and engagement with my research. I am also grateful to Cynthia Arnson, Marcelo Bergman, and James Mahon for the opportunity to present and develop aspects of my research as part of the Woodrow Wilson Center initiative Taxation and Equality in Latin America.

I thank my dissertation advisors, Ruth Berins Collier, David Collier, and Kent Eaton, for their wonderful support, mentoring, and guidance at every stage of the project. They provided a wealth of assistance with conceptual, analytical, methodological, substantive, and logistical issues during many hours of engaging conversations, which I am fortunate to still enjoy today. I am also grateful to my outside committee member, Emmanuel Saez, who provided valuable guidance on technical aspects of taxation. I express special thanks to Ben Ross Schneider as well for his long-standing interest in and unwavering support for my research, his expert suggestions and astute critiques that helped me hone my analysis, and his advice and assistance on numerous professional matters.

Fellow participants in the Latin American Politics workshop at UC Berkeley read and commented on numerous drafts during the dissertation stage of this research. I am particularly grateful to Mauricio Benitez, Taylor Boas, Adam Cohen, Candelaria Garay, Maiah Jaskoski, Diana Kapiszewski, Lindsay Mayka, and Jessica Rich, who have continued to provide input and suggestions long after our Berkeley days.

This book has benefited greatly from the insightful comments of many comparative politics scholars. I am especially grateful to Matthew Carnes, Matthew Cleary, Kent Eaton, Pepper Culpepper, Jacob Hacker, Stephen Kaplan, Evan Lieberman, Juan Pablo Luna, Scott Mainwaring, Aaron Schneider, Andrew Schrank, and Ken Shadlen for incisive feedback on various chapters, and to Ben Ross Schneider, Eric Hershberg, and Renato Boschi for generously reading and providing comments on the entire manuscript. I likewise thank three anonymous readers who carefully reviewed the manuscript for Cambridge University Press.

Numerous other colleagues contributed to the development of this research. I owe thanks to Laura Enríquez and Terry Karl for encouraging me to study Latin American politics and to Delia Boylan for first sparking my interest in inequality and taxation in Latin America. Marcelo Bergman, David Doyle, Sebastián Etchemendy, Robert Fishman, Gustavo Flores-Macías, Carlos Freytes, Stephan Haggard, Evelyne Huber, Robert Kaufman, Peter Kingstone, Marcus Kurtz, David Leonard, James Mahon, James McGuire, Andrés Mejía

Acosta, Paul Pierson, Alison Post, Wilson Prichard, Timothy Scully, Eduardo Silva, John Stephens, Kurt Weyland, and Nicholas Ziegler offered valuable input at various stages of my research.

My colleagues in International Development and beyond at the LSE provided an excellent support network as I revised the manuscript and gave helpful advice on the publication process. Among others, I am grateful to Tim Allen, Catherine Boone, Lloyd Gruber, Jean Paul Faguet, Jonathan Hopkin, Stephanie Rickard, and Ken Shadlen.

At Cambridge University Press, I thank Lewis Bateman, Shaun Vigil, and the production team for their efforts on behalf of this book. Portions of some chapters appeared previously in *Latin American Politics and Society, Studies in Comparative International Development,* and *World Development.* I thank Wiley, Springer, and Elsevier for permission to include excerpts from these articles.

Many friends and colleagues have provided multifaceted support, encouragement, inspiration, and sage advice. I am indebted to Diana Kapiszewski in all of these regards beyond what I can express with words. Taylor Boas unfailingly addressed and helped me resolve endless *consultas.* Kent Eaton's unwavering enthusiasm and positive energy helped pull me out of inevitable mental and emotional potential wells along the way. Matthew Carnes's appreciation for the nuances in my research also helped me push through tough times. Heartfelt thanks as well to Leonardo Arriola, Natalia Ferretti, Candelaria Garay, Alisa Gaunder, Maiah Jaskoski, Stephanie McNulty, Berkay Ozcan, and Wendy Sinek.

I could not have completed this book without Andrew Charman and Leyli, who have lovingly accompanied me (virtually if not always in person) throughout this odyssey. Andy has been my emotional and intellectual anchor.

Last but not least, I express deep gratitude to my very special parents Ann and Ken for the sacrifices they made to give me opportunities they never had. Beyond their enduring love and support, my father also generously devoted numerous hours to provide invaluable editing assistance that greatly improved the manuscript.

I

Tax Policy and Economic Elites
Going Where the Money Is

Policymakers around the globe have faced contentious debates and high-stakes political battles over tax policy as they struggle to satisfy a wide range of pressing revenue needs, from closing gaping budget deficits that threaten macroeconomic stability to securing sustainable funding for welfare state maintenance or expansion. In Latin America, tax reforms that target economic elites are an obvious option – this region is home to some of the world's most unequal democracies, yet the rich generally pay very low taxes. Although at first glance, many readers might expect democracy to empower average citizens at the expense of the rich, policymakers often have either avoided initiatives to tax economic elites or failed in their efforts to do so. Others might anticipate that economic elites enjoy inherent advantages that privilege their interests over those of average citizens. Yet economic elites are not always able to secure the policies they prefer. In some cases, governments have proposed and successfully enacted reforms that increase taxation of economic elites. Through comparative analysis of tax policy reforms in Latin America, this book develops a broad theoretical framework for explaining how and when economic elites' interests prevail in market democracies and how much scope policymakers can create for equity-enhancing reforms.

To meet revenue needs during the decades following economic liberalization and structural adjustment, governments in Argentina, Chile, and Bolivia all considered initiatives to tax the extensive income, profits, and wealth concentrated in the hands of economic elites, be they capital owners, big businesses, landowners, or high-income professionals. Yet the scope and fate of these initiatives varied across the countries. Whereas Argentina enacted significant tax increases on economic elites, reforms were marginal in Chile and Bolivia. Closer scrutiny reveals that reforms also varied across distinct tax policy areas and over time, particularly in Argentina and Bolivia. Leading theories, including those that attribute progressive tax increases to elite cohesion or to median voter preferences, as well as those that associate lack of reform with capital mobility or the overwhelming influence of money and wealth, cannot explain this variation.

The framework I develop to explain the scope of tax policy proposals, legislative outcomes, and the timing of reform focuses on the power of economic elites, especially business actors. Business – whether as individual firms and investors or as organized political actors – plays a central role in tax politics and economic policymaking more broadly, particularly in Latin America's highly unequal democracies. I draw on the classic concepts of structural power and instrumental power from early business politics literature. Structural power can be thought of as "investment power," while instrumental power can be thought of as "political power." I argue that when economic elites have strong power of either type, their interests shape policy outcomes.

Structural power arises from the profit-maximizing behavior of individual firms and capital owners. If policymakers anticipate that a reform will provoke reduced investment or capital flight, they may rule it out for fear of harming growth and employment. Structural power requires no organization or political action on the part of economic elites; instead, market signals coordinate their behavior in the economic arena. In contrast, instrumental power entails engagement within the political arena and deliberate actions to influence policy, such as lobbying. I identify sources of instrumental power that fall under two categories: relationships with decision makers that provide access and may create bias in favor of economic elites, and other resources, including cohesion, that help economic elites pressure policymakers more effectively. Both structural power and instrumental power vary over space and time. Instrumental power may also vary across sectors or subtypes of economic elites within a given country. Structural power, meanwhile, is highly context-specific; it cannot be reduced to capital mobility or a sector's economic importance, but also depends on the incentives a particular policy creates and ultimately on policymakers' expectations about the aggregate economic outcomes of multiple individual investment decisions.

The power of economic elites is a critical and often underemphasized variable in political economy,[1] and it is particularly important for taxation, a policy area that affects elites' core material interests. Whereas business politics literature historically posed a dichotomy between structural and instrumental approaches, I treat structural power and instrumental power as complementary. I argue that taxing economic elites will be difficult when either their instrumental power or their structural power is strong – policymakers may even eliminate tax increases from their agenda in anticipation of costly political battles and/or disinvestment. The more types and sources of power economic elites enjoy, and the more institutionalized their sources of power, the more

---

[1] Likewise, Schrank (2007: 191) calls for a return to "old-fashioned power politics" in political economy.

significant and consistent their influence will be: their interests will prevail to a greater extent in policymaking. Popular mobilization can occasionally counterbalance or even overwhelm the power of economic elites. And strategies that cultivate favorable public opinion or temper elite antagonism can help governments legislate incremental tax increases. However, governments have much more scope to tax economic elites whose structural power and instrumental power are both weak.

To briefly sketch how this framework applies to the country cases, economic elites in Chile had multiple, strong, and institutionalized sources of instrumental power, including cohesion and ties to right parties, that discouraged governments from attempting to legislate anything but marginal tax increases. In Argentina, economic elites lacked these sources of power and tended to be much weaker; governments therefore were able to legislate more significant tax increases. However, certain sectors did have other sources of power (instrumental and/or structural) during specific periods that allowed them to defend their own particular interests. Bolivia in the early 2000s is an intermediate case; economic elites' instrumental power was weaker than in Chile but stronger than in Argentina. During this period of extreme social unrest, economic elites were not able to keep reforms they disliked off the agenda as in Chile, but they were more successful than their Argentine counterparts at defeating initiatives later in the policy process – unless popular sectors mobilized in favor of reform.

By carefully examining tax policymaking processes, including the critical but often overlooked stages of agenda formulation and proposal design, this book yields insights about the mechanisms through which economic elites exert influence in market democracies. These insights contribute to a reemerging literature on business power and inform ongoing theoretical debates on the relationship between democracy, inequality, and redistribution. The book further contributes to research on state-society fiscal bargaining by providing a systematic basis for assessing elite taxpayers' bargaining power and by offering a distinct perspective on the causal effects of elite cohesion on extractive capacity.

In addition, this book helps fill major empirical gaps in two important literatures: research on welfare provision in developing countries, and research on economic reforms in Latin America. Many authors argue that sustainable and inclusive social protection requires tax capacity, yet this aspect of welfare state development has received much less attention than the politics of social spending (Haggard and Kaufman 2008; Huber and Stephens 2012).[2] In some cases, major political constraints to expanding social protection lie on the tax policy side of the fiscal equation. Likewise, despite the fundamental importance of taxation – which is critical for political and economic

---

[2] Others note that reallocation can finance welfare expansion despite tax constraints (McGuire 2010, Garay 2014).

development – political scientists studying Latin America's far-reaching economic reforms have paid much more attention to policy areas such as trade liberalization and privatization.[3]

Finally, although business's importance for economic development is widely acknowledged, business actors in Latin America remain understudied (Ames et al. 2012, Karcher and Schneider 2012). Conducting research on business politics is a difficult and labor-intensive endeavor. Business's political engagement often takes place out of the public eye, and accessible, quantifiable indicators of business influence are rarely available (Karcher and Schneider 2012: 281).[4] By drawing on extensive fieldwork, hundreds of interviews, and documents unavailable outside the studied countries, this book advances our empirical knowledge and understanding of business's potentially far-reaching role in policymaking.

1.1 DIVERGENT REFORM EXPERIENCES

Argentina, Chile, and Bolivia stand out as leading Latin American cases of economic liberalization and market-oriented tax reform in the 1980s and 1990s. Value-added taxes (VATs) with broad bases and relatively high rates were established, and VAT revenue as a percentage of GDP reached European averages by the mid-1990s – around 7 percent of GDP.[5] Despite this success, each country experienced recurrent revenue needs during subsequent decades. Whereas consumption was heavily taxed, income and profits were under-taxed by roughly 6 percentage points of GDP in Chile and Argentina and 3 percentage points of GDP in Bolivia, given these countries' level of development (Perry et al. 2006: 96; Appendix 1.1). Accordingly, governments in each country contemplated "going where the money is" by increasing direct taxes on economic elites' income, profits, and/or wealth. Yet the reforms they enacted varied substantially.

Argentina enacted noteworthy direct tax policy reforms after currency stabilization in 1991. The country's corporate tax rate increased gradually from 20 percent to 35 percent, the highest in the region. Additional reforms closed loopholes and helped control corporate tax avoidance and evasion. Meanwhile, personal income tax modifications increased the burden on individuals in the top brackets. A modest national wealth tax was created and gradually increased. And the tax agency gained essentially unrestricted access to bank information. Bank information is critical for fighting tax evasion because it

---

[3] Exceptions include Weyland (1996), Eaton (2002), Mahon (2004), and Arce (2005).

[4] Accordingly, even scholars in the quantitative tradition recognize the need for intensive qualitative research (Ames et al. 2012).

[5] Consumption taxation in Chile and Bolivia exceeded expectations for countries of their GPD per capita (Appendix 1.1).

facilitates detection of assets that taxpayers have underreported or neglected to declare on their income tax returns.

In contrast, Chile and Bolivia enacted at most marginal direct tax policy reforms. In Chile, increasing the very low corporate tax rate was arguably one of the most important revenue-raising reforms, given the design of the country's integrated income tax system. Little progress was made on this key front; in 2009 Chile's 17 percent corporate tax rate remained the lowest in the region, aside from Paraguay. Meanwhile, reforms to close loopholes and fight evasion emphasized consumption taxes rather than income taxes, and tax agency access to bank information remained highly restricted. In Bolivia, legislating an individual income tax is critical for increasing taxation of economic elites. This tax was eliminated in 1986 because technocrats believed the tax agency was too weak to actually collect it, but tax agency capacity improved dramatically in the 1990s. A 2003 initiative to reinstate the income tax failed; to date, Bolivia still has no personal income tax. A wealth tax initiative was also defeated, and little progress was made in other direct tax policy areas like closing corporate tax loopholes.

These policy differences were not merely cosmetic. Argentina's reforms contributed to a notable increase in direct tax revenue. While direct tax collections held basically constant in Chile and Bolivia at averages of 4.3 percent and 2.3 percent, respectively, Argentine collections grew from less than 2 percent of GDP in 1992 to almost 6 percent of GDP in 2005 (Figure 1.1),[6] the largest increase in Latin America (Sabaini 2005: 32). Argentina enacted revenue-raising reforms in other tax policy areas as well. Thanks to these reforms, as well as improvements in tax administration, overall tax revenue in Argentina grew by almost 8 percent of GDP from 1995 to 2004, again the largest increase in Latin America; the region's average revenue increase during this period was only 2 percent of GDP (Sabaini 2005: 7). In fact, Argentina's tax revenue in 2008 was second in the region only to Brazil and exceeded expectations based on its level of development by a remarkable 5.5 percentage points of GDP (Jiménez et al. 2010: 26).[7]

This cross-national variation is striking, especially considering that Chile has been portrayed as a regional success case for progressive tax reform (Weyland 1997) and for development more broadly, whereas Argentina is often considered to have a weak state, volatile economic governance, and limited extractive capacity (Levitsky and Murillo 2005, Melo 2007, Kurtz 2013). Yet cross-national variation is not the only aspect of tax policy in Latin America that

---

[6] The dip corresponds to Argentina's 2001 economic crisis. Figure 1.1 shows revenue collected by the central state, before transfers to provinces.

[7] Direct tax revenue in Chile and Bolivia increased substantially after 2005, but gains resulted primarily from exogenous commodity booms affecting mineral exports (Appendix 1.2). Total tax revenue in Chile nevertheless remained almost 4 percentage points of GDP below expectations based on per capita GDP (PPP).

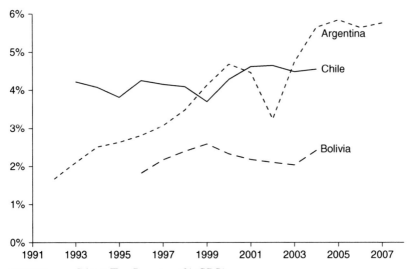

FIGURE 1.1. Direct Tax Revenue (% GDP).
Sources: SII 2009; SIN 2006; DNIAF 2012.

requires explanation. Outcomes also varied within countries, both across tax policy areas and over time. For example, despite Argentina's many successes, governments were not able to eliminate a costly income tax exemption for interest earnings that benefited upper-income individuals, and expanding tax agency access to bank information proved impossible until after the 2001 economic crisis. Further, whereas governments were able to repeatedly increase agricultural export taxes from 2001 through 2007, a 2008 tax increase had to be revoked due to sustained producers' protests. Turning to Bolivia, although efforts to tax domestic elites failed, the country dramatically increased taxation of foreign elites, namely multinational hydrocarbon firms.[8]

The range of policy variation across and within these Latin American countries poses challenges for several well-known theories of taxation (Table 1.1). Approaches treating direct taxation as a collective-action problem resolved through elite cohesion predict incorrect cross-national outcomes for the countries I examine. Economic elites were far more fragmented in Argentina than in Chile or Bolivia, yet Argentina legislated the most significant direct tax increases, contrary to the theoretical expectation. These collective-action approaches emphasize that organization and cohesion encourage elites to focus on shared long-term interests in fiscal stability and other benefits that strong tax capacity affords, thereby making elites more willing to pay direct

---

[8] See Appendix 1.2 on commodity taxation.

TABLE 1.1. *Theoretical Predictions and Latin American Anomalies*

Prediction	Unexpected or Unexplained Outcomes*
Elite cohesion facilitates direct taxation (Weyland 1997, Lieberman 2003, Slater 2010)	Chile (1991–2009), Bolivia / *Argentina*
Capital mobility discourages corporate tax increases (e.g., Rodrik 1997, Williams and Collins 1997, Appel 2011, Swank 2006, Hart 2009)	Argentina (1990s)
Economic importance or wealth confers influence (e.g., Handley 2008, Winters 2011, Gilens 2012)	Argentina, esp. agro-export taxes (post-2002)
Public opinion trumps business interests on high-salience issues (e.g., Smith 2000, Culpepper 2011)[a]	Chile, esp. failed 2004 copper royalty initiative
Benefits for economic elites are necessary for increasing their taxes (e.g., Timmons 2005, 2010)	Argentina, esp. agro-export taxes (post-2002)
Instability discourages policymakers from increasing direct taxes[b] (Melo 2007 drawing on Spiller and Tommasi 2000, Levitsky and Murillo 2005)	Argentina, Bolivia (2003–04) / *Chile (1991–2009)*
Dire macroeconomic need facilitates direct tax increases[c]	Bolivia 2003–04

* Normal type indicates the cause is present but not the outcome; italics indicate the cause is absent but the outcome is present.

[a] See also Murillo (2009).

[b] Melo (2007) links instability to short time horizons and hence policymaker preferences for easily collected indirect taxes rather than direct taxes. Argentina has been plagued by instability – institutional, economic, and political – yet direct tax increases were more significant and had a greater cumulative effect than in Chile, its enviably stable neighbor. Likewise, policymakers proposed taxes on income and wealth in Bolivia during the early 2000s, a period of extreme political instability associated with radical threats to the status quo from mobilized popular sectors.

[c] This argument cannot explain variation across the two countries in this study that were afflicted with economic crises. Argentina legislated direct tax increases in the run-up to the 2001 crisis, but Bolivia's efforts to tax income and wealth failed despite perilous budget deficits.

taxes (Weyland 1997, Lieberman 2003). Yet this logic does not always operate; elites may or may not perceive strong incentives to accept tax increases independently of whether they are cohesive or fragmented. And when they do not perceive incentives to accept tax increases, I argue that cohesion is a source of power that enhances their ability to resist reform. This view agrees with earlier literature that emphasized the potential for cohesive elites to mount collective action *against* progressive reforms.

Explanations focusing on capital mobility as a determinant of direct taxation are incomplete. Many authors have argued that international capital mobility forces governments to compete for investment by reducing corporate taxes.[9] Yet governments increased corporate taxes in Argentina in the 1990s, despite high levels of capital mobility. And although outcomes in Chile agree with the capital-mobility prediction, I will argue that this variable plays at most a secondary role in the explanation. Capital mobility can be a key component of business's structural power, but tax competition arguments often fall short because they are not sensitive to the context specificity of structural power.

Innovative recent research on wealthy individuals and business, discussed further in Section 1.4, leaves important cases unexplained. Theories emphasizing the power of money, wealth, or a sector's economic importance overpredict elite influence in my cases. Argentine elites were often unable to thwart initiatives to tax their income and profits, and economically important sectors were occasionally subjected to heavy tax increases against their wishes. In contrast, theories emphasizing that issue salience and public opinion moderate business influence tend to underestimate economic elites' ability to resist taxation and redistribution. In many cases, tax policy decisions reflected the interests of economic elites much more closely than those of median or marginal voters, despite intense media coverage. Issue salience theories predict instead that when citizens pay attention to an issue, politicians pay attention to public opinion rather than to economic elites (Culpepper 2011: 6).

Arguments that the distribution of the tax burden mirrors the allocation of spending elaborated in literature on fiscal contracts and credible commitments are also incomplete. This perspective cannot account for variation across the cases in which left governments pursued redistributive taxation. In accord with this literature's expectation that states must provide benefits for economic elites in exchange for their tax dollars, Chile's left governments were able to legislate only minor direct tax increases to finance social spending for the poor. Yet left governments in Argentina were able to tax agricultural elites heavily after 2001, even though spending favored urban sectors. This anomaly arises because fiscal-bargaining approaches often do not adequately specify the sources of power that necessitate providing benefits to win elite acquiescence; elite opposition to tax increases is politically irrelevant if elites lack strong sources of power. Political resources in particular often receive insufficient attention.

Table 1.1 includes two additional perspectives that leave Latin American cases unexplained: arguments focusing on instability and on economic need.

One final plausible hypothesis proves unconvincing upon closer scrutiny: that tax increases are easier to legislate in countries with low compliance because economic elites ignore policy initiatives in anticipation that tax increases can be evaded. Contrary to common perceptions, direct-tax evasion in Chile is

---

[9] Others disagree (Inclán et al. 2001, Gelleny and McCoy 2001, Basinger and Hallerberg 2004) or find mixed results (Wibbels and Arce 2003).

essentially as high as in Argentina: around 50 percent (Jiménez et al. 2010: 58, Jorratt 2009: 47–56). Arguments based on evasion levels therefore do not provide traction for explaining Argentina's more significant direct tax policy reforms. Furthermore, my interview data indicate that economic elites do care about statutory tax laws, irrespective of aggregate evasion levels. Tax increases are often designed in ways that curtail or eliminate opportunities for evasion – by implementing withholding regimes, by eliminating loopholes and exemptions, thereby simplifying the tax code and making it easier to detect evasion, or by strengthening the tax agency's auditing powers – for example, through access to information about taxpayers' bank accounts and financial transactions. During the studied period, experts considered tax agencies in Chile, Argentina, and Bolivia to be highly professional with similar levels of institutional capacity and technical competence (Bergman 2009: 76–83, Bolivian Finance Ministry-D 2007: interview),[10] and economic elites recognized that administrative improvements could lead to effective implementation of tax increases in the future, if not the immediate present. Moreover, the large firms and wealthy individuals who are most closely monitored by large-taxpayer units prefer to lower their tax burden through avoidance, which entails use of legal loopholes, rather than through evasion, which is illegal. Accordingly, reforms that close loopholes directly affect their tax burden.

This discussion highlights the need for "middle-range" theory that can account for broad tax policy variation without sacrificing explanatory leverage for parsimony or generality. The instrumental and structural power framework accomplishes this goal by examining multiple potential sources of power rather than focusing on a single causal factor and by recognizing that these sources of power will vary in kind and in strength across different contexts. Moreover, this framework clarifies the need to distinguish between actors' preferences and their ability to obtain the policies they prefer, which is a necessary step in accounting for several of the theoretical anomalies highlighted in Table 1.1. Although my analytical approach introduces complexity, this complexity is structured within a clear overarching conceptual framework that can be broadly applied in political economy beyond the specific issue of taxation.

1.2 AGENDA FORMULATION AND PROPOSAL OUTCOMES

This book systematically examines the tax policymaking process, from agenda formulation to the fate of reform initiatives – how they are modified and whether they are enacted. Close attention to agenda formulation is imperative for assessing to what extent economic elites influence policy decisions because they may be able to shift the set of options under consideration

---

[10] High evasion reflected problems with tax legislation that made administration difficult and noncompliance equilibriums that are hard to alter even when tax administration follows best practices (Bergman 2009).

toward their own policy preferences. Influence over the agenda may in fact be much more significant than influence after the government has initiated a reform proposal.[11] Some authors are pessimistic about prospects for analyzing agenda formulation given the challenges it poses for empirical research (Smith 2000: 149, 159, Fuchs 2007: 59, Falkner 2009: 120, Culpepper and Reinke 2014: 12–13) – alternative reform options that policymakers consider but discard often are not publicly discussed. Baumgartner et al. (2009) tackle the agenda-formulation problem in U.S. politics through interviews with interest groups that reveal which policies they advocate, regardless of whether those issues are a matter of public debate or have entered the legislative agenda. My approach is similar, but I bring the policymakers who actually make decisions about reform initiatives to the forefront of analysis.[12] In-depth interviews conducted for this project with high-level executive-branch officials in charge of tax policy, including three former presidents and twelve former finance ministers, yielded extensive information about their actual policy preferences and the reasons that compelled them to rule out certain reform options.

Agenda formulation can be divided into five idealized stages, in which distinct considerations delineate increasingly restricted subsets of reform options (Figure 1.2). Although policymakers do not explicitly follow these steps, these stages serve as useful heuristics. The first stages involve technical and administrative considerations that shape how policymakers select appropriate tools to tax elites. I briefly discuss these considerations and then focus on the third and fourth stages, in which structural power and instrumental power – the main explanatory factors in this study – lead policymakers to rule out appropriate options. The third and fourth stages of agenda formulation constitute the primary emphasis of this book.

I treat the existing tax system and the relative importance of different types of income and assets as initial conditions that determine the set of relevant revenue-raising reforms. Under-tapped revenue bases are associated with different kinds of investments, wealth, or income flows in different countries and at different times. The nature of under-tapped revenue bases will not only vary across tax systems but may also shift with international economic trends, changes in national development models, or economic crisis. Together, the prevailing tax system and the structure of income and assets determine whether new taxes are needed, which exemptions or loopholes could be most lucratively eliminated, whether rates should be increased, and what additional powers would best help the tax agency fight evasion.[13]

---

[11] For excellent discussion on these points, see Hacker and Pierson (2002: 284).

[12] Baumgartner et al. (2009) interview only policymakers identified as advocates on issues advanced by interest groups. Their study is not designed to analyze policymakers' decision-making processes.

[13] Examples include broader access to bank information and authority to regulate transfer prices.

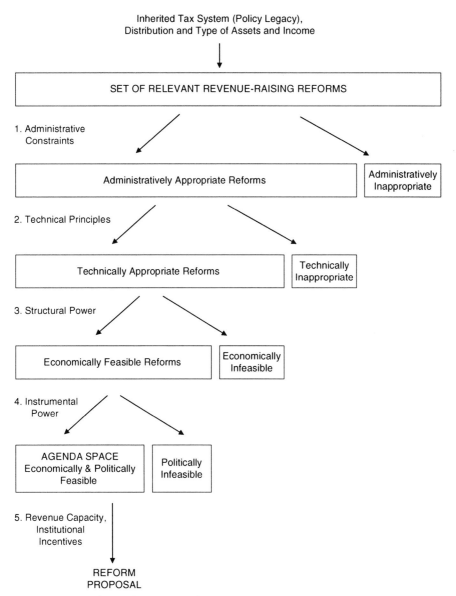

FIGURE 1.2. Defining the Tax Agenda.

Administrative constraints may lead policymakers to rule out some revenue-raising reform options (Stage 1). Where the tax agency's administrative capacity is weak, or where tax agencies face low-compliance environments (Bergman 2009), policymakers may avoid reforms that are comparatively easy to evade, that increase the number of taxpayers to be monitored, or that place greater demands on the tax agency for gathering and processing information.

However, even where administration is weak, reforms targeting economic elites' income, assets, and profits can often be designed to limit opportunities for evasion and place minimal additional demands on the tax agency. For example, taxes on previously exempt forms of income accruing primarily to upper-income groups can be collected through withholding regimes, which essentially preclude evasion, rather than relying on taxpayers to voluntarily declare these income sources on tax returns. In addition, eliminating exemptions and loopholes simplifies tax administration and facilitates detecting evasion. Given these evasion-curtailing options, theories that attribute taxpayers' bargaining power exclusively or primarily to their ability to reduce compliance or hide assets (Timmons 2005, Gehlbach 2008) have limited explanatory scope.

Policymakers may also rule out revenue-raising reforms that are inconsistent with technical principles and economic ideas that they or their advisors espouse (Stage 2). Some economists reject high marginal income tax rates on the assumption that they create work disincentives; others do not ascribe significant efficiency costs to progressive direct taxation or treat the matter as an empirical question.[14] Orthodox economists may rule out sector-specific taxes as inherently distortionary; heterodox economists may view sector-specific taxes as appropriate for both revenue raising and industrial policy. The subset of technically appropriate reforms defined at this stage will thus vary according to policymakers' economic ideology and training.

Regardless of policymakers' technical views, some tax initiatives that target economic elites usually remain on the agenda after Stages 1 and 2. For example, many reforms that eliminate exemptions or loopholes both target economic elites and promote efficiency; orthodox and heterodox economists alike often view these reforms favorably. Furthermore, technocrats of all backgrounds tend to advocate reducing tax evasion and may therefore consider broadening the tax agency's purview for auditing upper-income taxpayers or large businesses.

In sum, administrative and technical considerations, along with the structure of the tax system and the configuration of income and assets, tend to affect *how* policymakers propose to tax economic elites, but not necessarily *whether* they propose to tax economic elites. The critical decisions of whether to propose such reforms, given real-world economic constraints and political considerations, are made during the subsequent two stages of agenda formulation that are the focus of this book.

Economic elites' structural power may compel policymakers to eliminate additional reforms for fear of provoking reduced investment or other negative economic outcomes (Stage 3). In practice, this stage may be intertwined with

---

[14] See Saez et al. (2012) on estimating behavioral responses to tax increases.

Stage 2, in that policymakers' technical training may affect how they model the private sector's reactions to a given reform and hence how they assess structural power. However, reforms considered technically appropriate in theory may be ruled out in practice due to structural power considerations that arise in real-world situations. I have separated Stage 2 and Stage 3 analytically to emphasize these practical considerations and the context specificity of structural power, elaborated in Chapter 2.

Instrumental power shapes a final subset of revenue-raising reforms that policymakers view as not only administratively and technically appropriate and economically feasible but also politically desirable and/or feasible (Stage 4). Where economic elites have strong instrumental power, reforms they oppose may be stricken from the agenda given anticipations that the ensuing political battles will be too costly or will end in defeat. Alternatively, instrumental power arising from favorable relationships with policymakers may lead the latter to prioritize elite interests and refrain from proposing reforms that elites oppose. I subsequently refer to this final subset of reforms as the tax agenda space.[15]

Once the agenda space has been delineated, institutional incentives and potential revenue capacity help determine which reform options policymakers choose to initiate (Stage 5). Institutional incentives, created for example by exclusive executive authority in a particular tax policy domain or by rules governing the distribution of tax revenue between the central government and subnational units, may motivate the executive to favor some tax reforms over others. All else equal, policymakers facing revenue needs will choose reforms with greater revenue-raising capacity. Where the tax agenda space includes more than one feasible option, they may be bundled together into a single reform package.

The fate of reform initiatives – whether they are enacted and the extent to which their original content is modified – depends once again on the power of economic elites. Where reforms require congressional approval, both structural power and instrumental power may influence legislators' votes. Where initiatives take the form of executive or administrative decrees that do not require congressional approval, economic elites may still be able to block enactment or extract concessions from the authorities in charge by deploying their instrumental power.

Government reform strategies can also affect both agenda formulation and proposal outcomes, although they play a less significant causal role. Strategies that rely on astute reform design may circumvent structural power by reducing concerns over disinvestment. Strategies that cultivate public support or temper

---

[15] Economic elites' power in previous time periods may have shaped the prevailing tax system and hence the set of relevant revenue-raising reforms, or administrative capacity, thereby constraining reform choices made during Stage 1. However, explaining the origins of tax systems and administrative capacity lies outside the scope of this book.

elite antagonism may also enhance the political feasibility of reforms that might otherwise run aground due to economic elites' instrumental power.

1.3 OUTLINE OF THE ARGUMENT

The power of economic elites, and their instrumental power in particular, explains most of the variation in tax policy outcomes across the countries examined in this study. Where economic elites' power was strong, governments were able to enact only minor tax increases, even when they skillfully applied multiple reform strategies. In contrast, governments had leeway to enact much more substantial tax increases when economic elites' power was weak. However, governments' strategic errors occasionally contributed to the defeat of tax initiatives in contexts of comparatively weak elite power, and in extraordinary cases, popular mobilization prevailed over economic elites' power.[16]

The following chapters develop this argument in detail. Chapter 2 further elaborates my conceptualization of the power of economic elites, identifies and operationalizes the sources of instrumental power and structural power, and expounds the logic of the causal model. The second part of the chapter identifies and analyzes six strategies for mobilizing public support and/or tempering elite antagonism that can facilitate incremental tax increases in contexts where economic elites have strong sources of power.

Chapters 3 and 4 examine tax reform in Chile, where organized business's strong instrumental power precluded all but modest tax increases while the center-left governed from 1990 to 2010.[17] Chapter 3 focuses on the politics of increasing the corporate tax rate, an important way to raise revenue from economic elites due to unique features of Chile's income tax system. Chapter 4 analyzes alternative revenue-raising and equity-enhancing reforms that governments initiated in other tax policy areas.

Chapter 3 argues that three sources of instrumental power – linkages to right-wing opposition parties (partisan linkages), cohesion, and informally institutionalized government-business consultation – allowed business to keep significant corporate tax increases, and direct tax increases more broadly, off of the government's agenda, even when structural power was weak. Partisan linkages gave business the ability to block reforms in Congress with the help of the right parties, and cohesion allowed business to effectively mobilize against tax increases. Meanwhile, government-business consultation on all aspects of economic policy created incentives for the government to avoid conflict with business on taxation. I argue that strong instrumental power constrained direct tax policy throughout the center-left's tenure in power,

---

[16] The former dynamics are important in two cases and the latter in two distinct cases among the twenty-eight aggregate reform proposals analyzed. See Appendix 1.3.
[17] Chile's well-known 1990 reform is a partial exception.

although additional factors including large fiscal surpluses associated with high international copper prices also contributed to lack of reform during the late 2000s.

Although strong instrumental power discouraged corporate tax increases, Chile's center-left coalition developed a broad repertoire of strategies to facilitate incremental revenue-raising reforms in other tax policy areas. Chapter 4 examines the tax reform agenda and explains the fate of proposals initiated to address three policy goals: controlling tax evasion, eliminating technically unjustified and regressive tax benefits, and strengthening mineral-resource taxation. The case studies demonstrate the key role played by business's instrumental power in restricting the reform agenda; concerns over structural power and other constraints occasionally contributed as well. The case studies also elucidate the potential and the limitations of reform strategies. Overall, while these strategies were critical for increasing taxation, the political space they created for reform proved narrow, given business's strong instrumental power.

The next three chapters analyze tax policy in Argentina. Overall, economic elites in Argentina were much weaker than in Chile, and governments therefore had more leeway to increase taxes on income, profits, and wealth, as expounded in Chapter 5. Business and wealthy individuals lacked reliable allies in Congress, given the absence of a traditional right party in Argentina. Business cohesion was weak at the cross-sectoral level; sectoral divisions and organizational fragmentation made it difficult for business to stage collective action against corporate tax increases. Meanwhile, relationships between business and executive-branch policymakers created instrumental power only at the sectoral level or lower. Given very weak business cohesion, those sectors and firms that did enjoy favorable relationships with the executive pursued their own particular interests rather than defending the interests of the business community at large.

Despite economic elites' weakness at the aggregate level, some sectors in Argentina did have strong instrumental and/or structural power during delimited time periods that allowed them to block tax increases with sector-specific impact. In fact, business power varied not only across sectors, but also across time and across specific policy areas in Argentina, in contrast to the uniformity and stability that prevailed in Chile. Chapters 6 and 7 examine tax reforms affecting two major economic sectors – finance and agriculture – and explain when and why reform proposals succeeded or failed by analyzing changes in business power. The case studies illustrate the mechanisms through which turnover within the executive branch, economic crisis, and change in economic development models can alter business power, facilitating reforms that had been impossible during prior periods.

Chapter 8 turns to Bolivia, a case of intermediate elite power and extreme popular mobilization. From 2003 to 2006, economic elites' instrumental power was significant – much stronger than in Argentina though weaker than in Chile – thanks to cohesion and informal ties to policymakers. However, the threat of mass protest against policies perceived as regressive in a context of massive social unrest compelled cash-strapped governments to propose tax increases that targeted economic elites. And popular sectors could overwhelm opposition from economic elites if they mobilized in favor of reform. Tax policy became a high-stakes balancing act for governments seeking to walk the line between antagonizing the mobilized masses and antagonizing organized business and economic elites. The results were unsuccessful initiatives to tax the income and wealth of national elites, but major tax increases on foreign hydrocarbons companies.

Chapter 9 briefly addresses tax policy developments after elections that brought new political actors to power in Bolivia (2006) and Chile (2010). The rise of Bolivia's heterodox left ironically ended efforts to tax domestic elites, whereas Chile's new center-right government confounded expectations by increasing the corporate tax. The problematic legacy of Bolivia's prior income tax initiatives, along with the government's interest in natural-resource revenue and a broader transformative agenda, explain the first outcome. A new development in Chilean politics – sustained popular mobilization that altered business's strategic calculations – plays an important role in explaining the second outcome and endows this case with similarities to tax politics in Bolivia six years earlier.

1.4 BUSINESS POWER, FISCAL BARGAINING, AND REDISTRIBUTION IN DEMOCRACIES

Analyzing tax policy with close attention to the power of economic elites advances our understanding of business politics and business power, state-society fiscal bargaining, and the relationship between democracy and inequality. These areas have sustained growing interest within comparative politics in recent years, yet much research remains to be done.

Business power was a critical concern for political scientists from the mid-1950s through the 1980s. Scholars including Mills (1956) and Miliband (1969) emphasized business's extensive power based on "instrumental" means, especially connections to state officials. In contrast, Dahl (1961) and other pluralists asserted that nonbusiness actors were equally likely to achieve influence by participating in politics. Other authors subsequently questioned the approach of assessing influence based on active political participation alone. Lindblom (1977) and Block (1977) posited that the "structural dependence of the state on capital"[18] afforded business an automatic veto over a wide range of policies that might affect growth and employment. Since market

---

[18] The phrase is Przeworski and Wallerstein's (1988).

democracies rely on the private sector to create wealth and prosperity, they must enact policies that create incentives for productive investment, or else face economic decline and unhappy voters. But other scholars objected that empirically speaking, the market did not appear to be a prison – as Lindblom (1982) portrayed it – and argued that business interests were sufficiently heterogeneous to give state officials significant leeway for crafting policy coalitions (Vogel 1987).

Despite or perhaps because of these unresolved debates on the nature and extent of business power, political economy turned away from the concept of power in recent decades and focused instead on business interests and policy coalitions. Ensuing research on rich democracies contributed valuable insights on varieties of capitalism, highlighted the importance of business actors in welfare-state development, and called attention to significant variation in employers' interests and preferences across countries and across sectors.[19] Yet this research has not paid sufficient attention to the key questions of how, why, and when business actors influence policy in market democracies.[20] Understanding the preferences of firms and employer associations is certainly critical,[21] but this step is insufficient for explaining policy decisions and assessing business influence. Literature on economic liberalization in Latin America contains many insights on the means and mechanisms of business influence, and I build on these insights in the following chapters. Yet business reactions to reform and policy outcomes have often been analyzed without systematic attention to sources of power.[22] This omission is problematic because strategic calculations based on assessments of business power may affect both the initiatives policymakers propose and business responses to those proposals.

Recent literature begins to remedy this deficit of attention to business power and the means and mechanisms of influence, yet further theorizing is needed. Hacker and Pierson (2002) convincingly illustrate that instrumental power and structural power can be analyzed together to explain variation in the extent to which business interests shape policy outcomes. However, they stop short of systematically specifying concrete sources of instrumental power or theorizing the ways in which instrumental power and structural power can reinforce each other and augment business influence.[23] Within the international relations

---

[19] Hall and Soskice 2001, Estevez-Abe, Iverson, and Soskice 2001, Swenson 2002, Mares 2003, Thelen 2004: 32–3, Iversen 2005, among others. See Schneider 2013 for an important extension of varieties of capitalism to Latin America.

[20] Within varieties of capitalism, Iveren and Soskice (2009) and Schneider and Soskice (2009) call attention to the importance of business's "political representation" and "permeation of politics," yet their analyses still focus on business preferences.

[21] The empirical chapters of this book carefully establish business actors' tax policy preferences based on interviews and written documents.

[22] Exceptions include Schneider (1997) and Thacker (2000), who discuss structural power, and Etchemendy (2011), who focuses primarily on material resources and to some extent collective action.

[23] Hacker and Pierson do not employ the classic business power concepts in subsequent work.

literature, Falkner (2009) also advocates a multidimensional treatment of power, but he leaves open critical questions about operationalizing and measuring business power.[24] Culpepper (2011) argues persuasively that technical expertise affords business strong and largely unvarying influence on low-salience issues, whereas public opinion prevails on high-salience issues. Yet the sources of business power and the extent to which business interests prevail, regardless of issue salience, vary more widely than his argument anticipates.

With the conceptual refinements, guidelines for operationalization, and additional causal specifications I elaborate, the instrumental and structural power framework provides strong leverage for causal inference in comparative political economy. My emphasis on multiple sources of power that may vary over time, across space, and across policy areas redresses problems with earlier treatments of business power that tended to either overestimate or underestimate the extent to which business interests prevail in policymaking.[25]

This framework also contributes to research on taxation and state-society bargaining by systematically specifying sources of taxpayers' bargaining power. Classic studies in this literature, including Bates and Lien (1985) and Levi (1988), provided enduring insights about strategic interactions between states and taxpayers, but they did not adequately theorize taxpayers' political power. Bates and Lien (1985) focus on asset mobility to explain the extent to which taxpayers can shape government policies, without considering political factors.[26] Their research can be seen as part of the reaction against pluralist approaches that focused narrowly on active political participation without considering that owners of mobile assets could influence policy through anticipations of their ability to exit or to evade taxes (Winters 1996). Yet neglecting other sources of power is also problematic. As this book will demonstrate, instrumental power can be as or more important than asset mobility (whether in relation to structural power or to compliance). Levi (1988) considers political resources, along with coercive and economic resources that can underpin bargaining power. Yet she discusses these resources at a very general level, without delineating a concrete set of factors to be observed across cases, independently of policy outcomes. As other authors have noted, this under-specification opens the analysis to potential problems of post hoc assessment (Lieberman 2003: 25). These problems are more pronounced in recent literature on tax bargaining in developing countries. Few studies elaborate a clear, systematic basis for explaining taxpayer influence on state policies, and hence many provide largely

[24] For example, Falkner (2009: 20) describes structural power as an "elusive category" that remains "difficult to pin down."
[25] See also Hacker and Pierson 2002.
[26] A similar critique applies to Timmons (2005); his model focuses exclusively on quasi-voluntary taxpayer compliance without considering any other means through which societal groups might influence fiscal policy.

descriptive accounts of bargaining episodes and outcomes.[27] My framework maintains the emphasis on strategic state-society interactions advocated in the classic fiscal bargaining studies, while also identifying observable sources of power that strengthen economic elites' bargaining position and indicate how and when they are likely to shape policy outcomes.

This book also advances our understanding of redistributive politics and the relationship between democracy and inequality. This literature encompasses diverse approaches ranging from theories emphasizing median voter control to theories emphasizing the materially based influence of the rich. My analysis of tax politics suggests that the former theories tend to underpredict economic elites' ability to resist redistribution, whereas the later approach tends toward the opposite extreme.

The fact that Latin America's economic elites are often able to stymie efforts to tax their income, profits, and assets may not be surprising, yet it poses challenges for a large body of research on democracy and inequality that builds from the premise of median voter control.[28] Works within this literature advance a variety of explanations for the apparent paradox of stable, highly unequal democracies that effect little redistribution, contrary to the material interests of the poor median voter. Authors attribute limited redistribution to skewed voter turnout or restrictions imposed by asset mobility (Boix 2003), voter myopia or ignorance (Bartels 2008), and unclear relationships between voters' views on inequality, their socioeconomic class, and the extent to which they favor redistribution (Kaufman 2009). However, ample research on political representation suggests that there is little a priori basis for expecting a clear link between median voter preferences and policy outcomes. Strong partisan identities (Campbell et al. 1960), cross-cutting voter preferences, multiple issues dimensions that can be exploited (Jacobs and Soss 2010), nonprogrammatic linkages, and segmented electoral strategies (Luna 2014) may allow politicians to escape punishment at the polls when their policy positions deviate from median voter preferences. Moreover, designing policies in ways that weaken voters' ability to ascertain negative consequences or identify who is responsible can free politicians from the constraints of public opinion (Pierson 1994, Hacker and Pierson 2005, 2010), even on high-salience issues. Reformers who

---

[27] Gallo (2008: 163) notes the "ability of taxed groups to mobilize allies and political resources" with little further specification and no systematic scoring across cases. Easter's (2008) interesting discussion of revenue bargains does not fully explain how and why they emerged; Easter (2012) provides a more complete analysis, but taxpayers' sources of bargaining power remain more implicit than explicit. Gehlbach's (2008) systematic analysis of fiscal bargaining focuses on economic sectors' organization and their ability to hide taxable assets, yet his model omits sources of power that I find are as or more important, particularly when reforms by design curtail opportunities for evasion.

[28] For instance, Meltzer and Richard (1981), Boix (2003), Acemoglu and Robinson (2006), McCarty et al. (2008).

wish to tax economic elites can strategically design policies to cultivate popular support. Nevertheless, I maintain that in order to explain varying levels of taxation and redistribution in democracies, we need to look beyond voters and pay much closer attention to economic elites.[29]

My view that the power of economic elites matters more than voter preferences for tax policymaking falls closer to Winters's (2011) innovative work on oligarchy – a radical departure from median-voter approaches that identifies wealth as the ultimate source of power. Winters (2011) emphasizes the ease with which the super-rich convert their wealth into political influence and argues that concentrated wealth overwhelms all other sources of political power that are more equitably distributed. Accordingly, ordinary citizens have little if any say on policies that affect oligarchs' income and assets; the only force that can challenge their power is sustained mobilization from below, which is rare.

Winters's theory emphasizes the uniformity of oligarchic influence in core policy areas like taxation, yet I find substantial variation in Latin American elites' ability to block reforms that increase their tax burden, even in the absence of popular mobilization. I also find that sources of power beyond raw money and wealth, including cohesion and partisan linkages, play an important role in explaining the extent of elite influence. These differences arise partly because the economic elites examined in this book are a broader group than Winters's (2011: 19) oligarchs. Winters argues that oligarchs – extraordinarily wealthy individuals located roughly within the top 0.01 percent of the income distribution – generally do not have collective-action problems when their wealth is threatened because their material interests are automatically aligned. The economic elites relevant for tax policy dynamics and revenue generation in Latin America include domestic businesses and multinational firms, along with high-income professionals and capital owners who belong to the ranks of the "merely wealthy." Though still a tiny elite, these actors may have collective-action problems, even when initiatives to tax income and profits are at stake.[30]

---

[29] Within the formal literature, Acemoglu and Robinson's (2006, 2008: 268) work on elites' "de facto power," arising from "wealth, weapons, or ability to solve the collective action problem," is a step in the right direction. While they begin from the median-voter assumption that "in a democracy, policies are determined by majority voting," they add that elites' de facto power can subvert the majority will. However, this conceptualization of elite power remains underspecified. In practice, it lumps together all means and mechanisms beyond voting through which economic elites exert influence. Political parties, interest organization, and the dynamics of collective action remain largely absent from the analysis.

[30] Regarding my finding of significant variation in tax policy outcomes, it is possible that some direct tax increases left oligarchs relatively unscathed, in line with Winters's emphasis on the ability of the superrich to deflect the burden of redistribution onto the "merely wealthy" strata beneath them. For instance, the actual incidence of corporate tax increases is difficult to assess, since firms may pass some of the burden on to consumers and workers. Additionally, I analyze policy change, whereas Winters (2011: 211–54) analyzes effective tax burdens that oligarchs actually pay; these are distinct dependent variables. However, it is important to emphasize that

Material resources by definition set economic elites apart from other political actors, and their wealth may underpin or facilitate acquisition of other relevant sources of power. As "anti-pluralists" argue, economic advantages do generate major political advantages (Jacobs and Soss 2010: 352). In practice, however, these other sources of power – like cohesion and partisan linkages – vary extensively throughout Latin America's unequal democracies, and they provide significant causal leverage for explaining when and to what extent elite interests prevail; an emphasis on money and wealth alone would overpredict the influence of the economic elites studied in the following chapters. Furthermore, examining other sources of power elucidates the wide range of means and mechanisms through which economic elites influence policy decisions.

My emphasis on elite cohesion and ties to political parties builds on recent work by Hacker and Pierson (2010) as well as research on power resource theory in welfare state literature (Korpi 2006, Huber and Stephens 2012). In Hacker and Pierson's (2010) view, levels of redistribution and inequality in democracies depend not just on the money economic elites bring to bear on politics, but also on the extent to which interests, including business, are organized; in my framework, organization is a key indicator of elite cohesion. Power resource theory also emphasizes organization and ties to parties, but it tends to focus on labor and left parties. The instrumental and structural power framework complements that approach by specifying a comprehensive set of power resources for economic elites.

The concluding chapter of this book explores further theoretical implications regarding business politics, the public good, and the politics of policy change. Whereas leading literature views strong business associations and institutionalized government-business consultation as promoting socially desirable outcomes, I emphasize that these factors can hinder efforts to promote equitable development in highly unequal societies. I revisit arguments that elite cohesion facilitates progressive taxation and analyze why previous research arrived at different conclusions from those presented in this book. Finally, in accord with literature on policy feedback, I illustrate that the politics of policy change can be much more variable than is often assumed in literature on economic reforms and business politics.

1.5 RESEARCH STRATEGY

This book's theoretical insights emerge from systematic qualitative research that combines multilevel comparisons with process tracing. At the highest level of analysis, I contrast characteristic national tax-politics dynamics and policy

---

many reforms I examine were explicitly designed to curtail evasion and avoidance and therefore likely did affect oligarchs along with other upper-income taxpayers. Unfortunately, reliable, comparable data on effective tax rates paid by adults within the top 1 percent are not available for the countries I examine and are unlikely to exist in the near future.

outcomes across the three countries examined. In addition, I conduct multiple structured, focused comparisons (George and Bennett 2005) of tax proposals. At the cross-national level, I compare outcomes in analytically equivalent policy areas. At the national level, I compare successive initiatives designed to address persistent tax issues within each country in order to identify factors that contributed to eventual success or repeated failure. For Argentina, my comparisons follow a sectoral logic, in accord with the nature of variation in business power in that country. I compare reform proposals in different tax policy areas affecting a single sector and also contrast tax politics across sectors. These multiple cross-national and within-country comparisons help highlight the role played by different causal factors while holding others relatively constant.

Process tracing complements these cross-case comparisons by providing a distinct source of causal leverage. Whereas cross-case comparisons give rise to correlation-based inference, process tracing entails inference based on within-case analysis (Collier, Brady, and Seawright 2010). Methodologists have elaborated distinct types of hypothesis tests, loosely based on the logic of necessary and sufficient conditions, that underpin causal inference in process tracing (Ven Evera 1997, Bennett 2010, Collier 2011, Goertz and Mahoney 2012).[31] These tests adjudicate between plausible alternative explanations and lend varying degrees of support to hypotheses by using key diagnostic pieces of evidence to evaluate their likelihood. Recent methodological research explicates the Bayesian logic underpinning inference in process tracing (Bennett and Checkel 2014, Humphreys and Jacobs 2014). Process tracing is ideally suited for theory generation and identification of causal mechanisms, which are major goals of this book. Through careful analysis of multiple within-case observations, I establish the sequences of events through which economic elites succeeded or failed to influence tax policy decisions and identify the sources of power that were most relevant.[32]

My analysis draws on a large body of new data gathered during twenty months of field research in Chile, Argentina, and Bolivia.[33] I conducted 446 in-depth, semi-structured interviews with 358 informants: top-level government officials including three former presidents and almost every finance minister who served in each country during the studied period, tax agency experts, politicians from all major political parties, business leaders and tax advisors, and other actors who participated in policymaking. Interviews with high-level government policymakers provided unique information about decision-

---

[31] See Fairfield (2013: Appendix 1) for explicit applications of process-tracing tests.

[32] Beyond causal inference, process tracing is critical for assessing tax reforms, given the multiple modifications that bills undergo and the significant ways in which seemingly small changes can affect their substantive content and potential impact.

[33] Primary fieldwork was conducted from 2005 to 2007, with follow-up trips in 2008, 2011, and 2012.

making processes, reform options that were considered but discarded, and negotiations with business associations and political parties that shaped reform outcomes. I obtained multiple interviews over extended time periods with key informants, which allowed me to pursue new lines of inquiry that developed as my research progressed. These informants often shared information that was not part of the public record; several informants provided access to internal government documents. I detected and resolved factual inconsistencies that occasionally arose by triangulating between multiple informants and written records. In addition to interviews, I draw on congressional documents, newspaper articles, business publications, tax agency reports, and tax return data.

When working with interviews, care must also be taken to evaluate whether informants have incentives to dissemble or misrepresent motives for past actions (Bennett and Checkel 2014). I address these issues in the empirical chapters where relevant and explain my rationale for the conclusions drawn. Various informants, including politicians interested in self-promotion and businesspeople concerned with portraying their actions in a socially acceptable light, offered candid responses that ran against the expected direction of bias. In addition, the technocrats who often served as key informants had fewer incentives to skew their accounts for political ends. While technocrats may have clear partisan commitments, they do not face the same pressures that elected politicians and party officials experience.

It bears emphasis that this book aims to explain tax policy change, not revenue collection, but with the understanding that the former has important implications for the latter. Building tax capacity in Latin America is no longer simply a matter of administrative or bureaucratic capacity but requires legislative reforms to increase tax burdens, curtail avoidance, and reduce opportunities for evasion. To assess and compare the relative revenue-raising capacity of tax policy changes across countries, I triangulate between my own analysis and expert opinions of reform content and importance, expected revenue estimates available to policymakers while reforms were under debate, and actual revenue-collection trends. Qualitative analysis of reform content is critical for cross-country comparisons, but statutory changes alone do not necessarily establish relative revenue capacity (for example, increasing the corporate tax rate by two points may have a distinct impact in different countries). Expected revenue estimates shape actors' evaluations of reform proposals and are critical to the policymaking process. They provide an important basis for comparison, although estimates may diverge from true revenue yield. Actual revenue changes effected by policy reforms are at best difficult to assess, since revenue collection depends on multiple factors beyond tax policy (including effectiveness of implementation and administration, evasion, and economic variables). However, revenue trends serve as a rough but useful check on whether the other indicators employed capture the relative extent to which governments were able to legislate revenue-raising tax policy reforms.

I chose to analyze Chile, Argentina, and Bolivia based on several criteria. First, these countries encompassed significant variation in the strength and type of economic elites' sources of power, the primary explanatory factors in my theoretical framework. For example, national-level sources of instrumental power like elite cohesion and ties to right parties were strong in Chile, weaker in Bolivia, and largely absent in Argentina. Second, these countries are leading Latin American cases of market-oriented tax reform and economic liberalization more generally. By the early 1990s, VAT revenue in Chile, Argentina, and Bolivia reached European averages. Taxing under-tapped income and profits was therefore a logical and highly salient option for governments facing revenue needs, given that the alternative tax base – consumption – was already heavily tapped. Accordingly, these countries served as "most-likely cases" for initiatives to tax economic elites. This criterion was of practical importance given the infeasibility of obtaining comprehensive information on tax proposals prior to field research.

Third, a paired comparison of Chile and Argentina holds constant several background conditions and institutional factors that are not central to my theoretical framework. These countries share similar levels of economic development, and the central government, which is the focus of my research, collects the great majority of total tax revenue in both countries, despite the fact that Chile is a unitary state whereas Argentina is a federation.[34] These countries' tax agencies were both highly professional and had similar enforcement capacity during the studied periods (Bergman 2009). Fiscal policymaking authority is concentrated within a single ministry, and executives have strong formal legislative powers – the Argentine and Chilean executives are among the strongest in Latin America in terms of formal policymaking powers (Mainwaring and Shugart 1997, Eaton 2002). Chile and Argentina have comparatively stable party systems consisting of two major blocks (*Concertación de Partidos por la Democracia* vs. *Alianza por la Democracia* in Chile; Peronists vs. Radicals in Argentina) with high levels of party discipline.[35] While the Radical Party has fragmented in recent years, Argentina has avoided the party system collapse characteristic of other Latin American party systems with labor-mobilizing parties (Venezuela and Peru). Where party systems are volatile, highly fragmented, and/or party discipline is low, multiple veto players and weak support for the executive in Congress may make government reform proposals difficult to pass regardless of content.[36]

---

[34] The central government collects 96 percent of tax revenue in Chile and 85 percent in Argentina (Cetrángolo 2007: 33).
[35] See, for example, Mainwaring and Scully (1995), Carey (2002), Jones (2002), Eaton (2002), and Luna (2010).
[36] See Carey and Shugart (1998), Mainwaring (1999), Mainwaring and Shugart (1997), Weyland (2002).

Including Bolivia extends the scope of analysis to a country with a lower level of economic development and a very different party system. Bolivia's historically patronage-based party system (Gamarra and Malloy 1995) experienced dramatic change with the emergence of an electorally successful indigenous-left party and the partial demise of the more conservative traditional parties. The Bolivian case also provides an opportunity to apply my theoretical framework to a context in which organized and highly mobilized popular sectors played a far more substantial role in influencing the tax agenda and proposal outcomes than in Chile or Argentina. Indeed, the fact that Bolivia differs from the other two countries on so many dimensions, including strong regional conflict and ethic politics in addition to the factors already mentioned, provides grounds for contending that my framework travels across very different national contexts.

The time period analyzed for each country commences with the advent of revenue-raising initiatives subsequent to the completion of market-oriented tax reforms that accompanied economic liberalization. The relevant periods are 1990–2010 for Chile, 1992–2010 for Argentina, and 2003–06 for Bolivia.[37] In Bolivia, other issues superseded taxation on the national agenda after Evo Morales's election in 2006. Chapter 9 briefly analyzes these dynamics as well as new tax policy developments in Chile after the 2010 election that brought the right to power. The primary time periods analyzed span five major presidential administrations in Argentina, four in Chile, and two in Bolivia, supplemented with two additional administrations in Chapter 9. This breadth allows me to identify changes in business power over the medium term as well as the short term and to assess the impact on the tax agenda and the fate of reform proposals.

I identified all major revenue-raising reform proposals, as well as proposals with more minor revenue capacity that targeted economic elites, through expert interviews and review of legislative records and newspapers. I gathered data on a case universe of more than eighty tax measures embedded within fifty-four reform packages across the three countries. Although my arguments are informed by and incorporate examples from this full set of proposals, the empirical chapters emphasize direct tax proposals designed to tap economic elites' income, wealth, and profits, which are of primary theoretical interest for my research.

The following chapters include case studies of forty-three proposed tax measures embedded in twenty-eight reform packages, along with six instances of "non-reform," in which policymakers considered but decided against

---

[37] In Argentina, VAT base-broadening reforms were enacted in 1990 and 1991, and currency stabilization, a key objective of structural reforms, was achieved in 1992; I begin analysis from this year. In Chile, market-oriented tax reforms occurred under the Pinochet dictatorship; subsequent initiatives to increase taxes occurred after the 1990 democratic transition. Bolivia overhauled its tax system in 1986; significant subsequent revenue-raising reforms did not arise until 2003.

proposing initiatives they felt were important.[38] When the tax measure of primary interest is bundled with other measures in a broader tax reform package, I treat the reform package as a contextual factor with implications for government reform strategies and the fate of the measure of primary interest. When political dynamics and outcomes did not vary across a set of measures bundled into a single reform package, I treat that aggregate set of proposals as the unit of analysis. Through this qualitative, medium-N analysis, I substantiate my argument regarding the importance of business power across multiple cases and contexts.

---

[38] See Appendix 1.3 for further discussion of case selection.

2

The Power of Economic Elites

Economic elites tend to have strong, well-formed preferences regarding tax policy. Other policy areas like trade liberalization and privatization may have multiple and unpredictable distributional effects that make it difficult for business actors to discern their true interests, in which case their reform preferences may vary widely (Schneider 2004b: 460, 475). In contrast, tax increases usually impose clear, predictable, and immediate losses that economic elites can easily identify. Although there can be some variation in attitudes, economic elites generally dislike tax increases affecting their income, profits, or assets. Such reforms inherently threaten their core interest in protecting their wealth (Winters 2011).

To understand how and when economic elites exert influence – not only on taxation but much more generally – we must look beyond their underlying preferences and think seriously about power. In common parlance and even in academic writing, the terms power and influence are often used synonymously. In this book, however, I treat power as a cause and influence as an effect. This distinction helps eliminate the tendency to conflate power with outcomes; assertions that policies reflect the preferences of powerful actors are often tautological in practice. In contrast, the theoretical framework elaborated in this chapter provides explicit guidelines for assessing economic elites' power independently of policy outcomes, identifies the mechanisms connecting sources of power to influence over policy, and elucidates the conditions under which elites' power may increase or decline. In doing so, this chapter contributes to recent efforts to revive the concept of power and hone it into an effective causal variable for comparative political analysis (Hacker and Pierson 2002, Culpepper 2011).

This chapter begins by explicating the classic concepts of instrumental (political) power (Section 2.1) and structural (investment) power (Section 2.2) with clarifications and specifications that build on and move beyond earlier work in comparative politics, American politics, and international relations. In the causal model I advance, either instrumental or structural power can allow economic elites to thwart policies they oppose. However, elites will have more consistent and systematic influence when they possess both types of power; instrumental and structural power can even be mutually reinforcing (Section 2.3). Section 2.4 addresses the oft-asked but elusive question – "How do you get rich people to pay tax?" (Schneider 2012: 202) – an especially salient conundrum where economic elites have strong sources of power. I discuss six strategies for circumventing elite power that can be used to implement incremental tax increases that might otherwise be infeasible. Distinguishing between instrumental power and structural power is critical for identifying these reform strategies and assessing which will be most effective in a given context. Economic elites' instrumental and structural power, and to a lesser extent government reform strategies, serve as the primary independent variables for explaining the scope of the tax agenda and the fate of reform proposals in the following empirical chapters. However, popular mobilization also influenced tax policy in some cases. Section 2.5 elaborates how mobilized popular actors may counteract – or occasionally even reinforce – the power of economic elites.

2.1 INSTRUMENTAL POWER

Instrumental power, first theorized by authors including Mills (1956) and Miliband (1969), entails capacity for deliberate political actions. These actions may include lobbying, direct participation in policymaking, financing electoral campaigns, editorializing in the press, or engaging in various types of collective action. Although the term instrumental power is not used as commonly today, the activities that fall within its domain, especially lobbying and campaign finance, remain major topics in research on business politics. Economic elites may undertake political actions within formal policymaking arenas, of which the most relevant for this book are the executive branch and the legislature.[1] In rare cases, economic elites may also undertake collective action outside of formal policymaking arenas by engaging in protest. As discussed below, instrumental power can be wielded overtly, when economic elites actually undertake political actions, but it can also act indirectly, when policymakers anticipate the reactions of economic elites, or implicitly, when policymakers share common goals with economic elites.

I identify observable sources of instrumental power that make policymakers more responsive to economic elites. These sources of power can be classified as *relationships* with policymakers and *resources* (Table 2.1). Relationships include partisan linkages, whereby economic elites form a party's core constituency (the

---

[1] The judicial branch may also be relevant; see Schneider (2012) on courts and tax policy in Guatemala and Kapiszewski and Taylor (2008) on courts and policymaking more generally. On venue choice for lobbying and policy contestation, see Yadav (2011) and Hacker et al. (2013).

TABLE 2.1. *Sources of Instrumental Power*

Relationships with Policymakers	Partisan Linkages
	Institutionalized Consultation
	Recruitment into Government
	Election to Public Office
	Informal Ties
Resources	Cohesion
	Expertise
	Media Access
	Money

sector most important to the party's political agenda and resources, following Gibson [1992]); institutionalized consultation between the government and business associations; recruitment into government, whereby economic elites hold executive branch appointments; election to public office; and informal ties to policymakers. These relationships afford instrumental power in formal decision-making arenas by enhancing access to policymakers, facilitating participation in policymaking, and creating bias in favor of economic elites' interests. Resources include cohesion, expertise, media access, and money, all of which can help economic elites more effectively lobby or pursue their interests through any of the actions described above.[2]

These sources of power are conceptually distinct, yet they may be mutually reinforcing. For example, business actors with technical expertise may be more likely to receive government appointments, and partisan linkages may strengthen cohesion by fostering a shared identity among economic elites.[3] Resources may strengthen or underpin economic elites' relationships with legislators. And of course money facilitates acquisition of the other resources as well.

Different categories of economic elites may have different sources of instrumental power, and these sources of power vary across countries and over time. In a given country, economic elites in a particular sector (e.g., construction or agriculture) may have strong sources of instrumental power, whereas those in other sectors may not. In some cases, economic elites may have strong instrumental power at the cross-sectoral level that can be mobilized to defend common interests or even the specific interests of a given sector. The arenas in which economic elites enjoy instrumental power can vary across space and time as well; relationships with the executive branch may be strong during some periods whereas relationships with legislators may be more relevant during other periods. Institutionalized relationships with policymakers, like partisan linkages and government-business consultation, tend to be more stable

[2] In conflict-ridden democracies, weapons or ties to militaries may also be relevant.
[3] I thank Timothy Scully for the latter point.

sources of power than noninstitutionalized relationships like recruitment into government and informal ties. Whereas the former sources of power may persist for decades, the latter may vary with electoral cycles or even during a single presidential term.

Economic elites will achieve more significant and more consistent influence when they possess strong and multiple sources of instrumental power. The more resources economic elites have at their disposal, the more numerous, advantageous, and institutionalized their relationships with policymakers, and the more decision-making arenas in which these relationships operate, then the more effectively economic elites can lobby or mobilize in other ways, and the more available channels through which their influence can flow. However, a single strong source of instrumental power may be sufficient for economic elites to block a reform they oppose. Nor does instrumental power operate deterministically;[4] economic elites may fail to obtain their preferred outcome in a particular instance despite strong instrumental power. For example, advancing the interests of powerful economic actors may occasionally become an electoral liability for politicians, in which case pleasing voters may take precedence; alternatively, popular sectors may wield strong countervailing power. Yet identifying sources of instrumental power helps us assess when and where economic elites are more likely to exert influence, as well as the mechanisms through which they obtain influence.

This explanatory framework facilitates analysis of economic elites' influence by drawing clear distinctions between actions, sources of instrumental power, and underlying preferences.[5] Distinguishing between actions and sources of power admits the possibility that economic elites with strong sources of instrumental power may not need to actually undertake any overt political action in order to wield influence. In other words, economic elites may not need to "activate" their sources of power; influence may flow instead through anticipated reactions. In this regard, my framework follows insights from power resources theory, which was developed to resolve conceptual difficulties inherent in approaches that focused on the visible "exercise of power" (Korpi 1985: 33).[6]

Furthermore, distinguishing between actions and underlying preferences clarifies that the strategic context can influence actors' behavior and the choices they make (Frieden 1999, Hacker and Pierson 2002). Weak economic elites who lack sources of power may accept a reform in anticipation that resistance will be futile, yet the absence of active opposition does not necessarily imply that they view the reform favorably. Even strong economic elites

---

[4] Korpi (1985: 34) similarly asserts: "The relationship between the distribution of power resources and the outcomes of conflicts must ... be seen as a probabilistic one."

[5] These distinctions are roughly analogous to those made in game theory between strategies (choices), strategic setting (environment), and utilities (e.g. Frieden 1999, Morrow 1999).

[6] Korpi's critique includes "second" and "third dimensions" of power (Bachrach and Baratz 1970, Lukes 1974).

may accept tax increases under some circumstances, in which case they will not marshal their sources of power to resist. As discussed later in this chapter, popular mobilization and government reform strategies can influence how economic elites react to tax increases by altering the perceived or actual costs and associated benefits of accepting or opposing reform.

Despite these analytical advantages, leading literature on business politics does not always distinguish clearly between actions and sources of power. Schneider (2010: 8), for example, elaborates "a portfolio of business investment in politics" that entails "a range of activities including associations, consultative councils, legislative lobbying, campaign finance, networking, and corruption." Lobbying and corrupt activities like bribery are clearly actions that business may undertake to influence policy; the latter is one of many ways to deploy monetary resources. However, for the purpose of analyzing business influence, the other "activities" are better treated as sources of instrumental power: associations contribute to cohesion, consultative councils are a form of institutionalized government-business consultation, and networks are often built around informal ties to policymakers or recruitment into government.[7] Likewise, Culpepper (2011: 8–9, 188) does not distinguish clearly between political actions and sources of power when he identifies "lobbying capacity, the use of private interest committees, and influencing the tenor of press coverage" as "resources" that managers can deploy to influence policymaking. Yadav's (2011: 12) statement that "Special interest groups can employ a variety of resources, including electoral campaign contributions and legislative lobbying … using money, information, media campaigns, and demonstrations" provides a third example of the tendency to conflate actions and sources of power.[8] While these problems may seem purely semantic, using precise terms and clear concepts is essential for avoiding inferential problems that have often plagued analysis of business power and influence.

Moreover, sources of power and/or actions are often conflated with influence over policy outcomes. Culpepper's (2011: 182) definition of "lobbying capacity" as the "ability to convince politicians and bureaucrats" risks conflating cause and effect; without further specification, this definition confuses assessment of power with policy outcomes.[9] Lobbying is best treated instead

---

[7] It should be noted that Schneider's goal is characterizing patterns of business participation in policymaking, not analyzing business influence.

[8] Demonstrations for instance are actions that will be more effective when business possesses resources like cohesion and money.

[9] Culpepper subsequently argues that expertise – an observable source of power – underpins lobbying capacity (and the aforementioned "use of private interest committees" and "influencing the tenor of press coverage"). In other words, expertise is the key source of power that explains business influence in his cases. Elsewhere, however, expertise and lobbying capacity become decoupled; Culpepper (2011: 188) writes: "expertise and lobbying capacity are the key resources" that afford business influence in low-salience issue areas. The "lobbying capacity" under-specification problem thus reemerges.

as an action that is more likely to succeed when economic elites possess one or more of the sources of power in Table 2.1. This point also applies to Frieden's (1991: 33) postulate that more intense lobbying leads to greater influence.[10] This logic holds when business actors have strong sources of power that dispose policymakers to respond to lobbying. But if business lacks sources of power, lobbying – however intensive – may not achieve any influence, as the case of agricultural producers and export taxes in Argentina will illustrate (Chapter 7). In other words, we should not expect lobbying from a position of weakness to bear results. Clearly specifying and assessing sources of power is therefore critical for analyzing influence.

In addition, literature on business politics often overlooks the role that instrumental power can play in shaping agenda formulation. Instrumental power is usually viewed as influencing policy through "direct" or "overt" means – for example, through lobbying or other observable political actions – after a proposal has been initiated. However, instrumental power can also indirectly influence the reform agenda, a possibility that many authors do not consider (Smith 2000: 115–41, Hacker and Pierson 2002: 279–86, Fuchs 2007: 56–58, 71–95, Falkner 2009: 19).[11] When economic elites have strong and multiple sources of instrumental power, policymakers may anticipate that attempting a given reform will entail major political conflict, and they may rule it out as infeasible or not worth the costs. In these cases, as noted above, the mere anticipation that elites will undertake concerted action against a reform may keep that reform off the agenda[12]; economic elites need not mobilize their sources of power or engage in any direct action to achieve influence. In other cases, recruitment into government or other strong relationship-based sources of power may result in such pervasive convergence of preferences between policymakers and economic elites that policies elites oppose are excluded from the agenda automatically.[13]

Baumgartner et al.'s (2009) innovative research on lobbying in the United States is a partial exception to the tendency of overlooking how instrumental power shapes agenda formulation. They analyze what I describe as the direct role that instrumental power (although they do not use the term) can play in agenda formulation, but they leave its indirect role largely unaddressed. The authors examine how lobbying by business and other interest

---

[10] "Sectors with more specific assets ... exert more pressure on policymakers and obtain more favorable policies."

[11] Most authors treat structural power as the means through which business exerts "indirect" influence over the agenda.

[12] In early business politics literature, Bachrach and Baratz (1970) made similar points about anticipated reactions.

[13] Here the deliberate political actions that are the hallmark of instrumental power may have occurred earlier (e.g., donations that helped elect policymakers), or if economic elites themselves are the policymakers, these actions are their policy decisions. Note however that economic elites often need to actively engage with friends in office to ensure policy influence.

groups can place issues on the legislative agenda that policymakers might otherwise ignore, or prevent other groups from introducing opposing issues. They acknowledge that whether interest groups raise an issue at all depends on assessments of the potential for success and the actions of rival groups (Baumgartner et al. 2009: 201, 214). However, their empirical focus on active lobbying precludes in-depth analysis of how anticipated reactions shape agenda formulation.[14] Additionally, they do not examine the possibility of anticipated interest-group reactions discouraging policymakers from raising issues they care about, given the authors' much greater attention to the goals of interest groups.

Relationships

This section discusses relationship-based sources of instrumental power in greater detail, with attention to corresponding mechanisms of influence, assessment or measurement, and potential variation over time and space. In general, more institutionalized relationships (partisan linkages and institutionalized consultation) will give economic elites more consistent influence than less institutionalized relationships.

Partisan Linkages

I use this term to describe the core constituency relationship between economic elites and conservative parties (Gibson 1992, 1996). Following Gibson (1992: 15): "A party's core constituencies are those sectors of society that are most important to its political agenda and resources. Their importance lies not necessarily in the number of votes they represent, but in their influence on the party's agenda and capacities for political action." Conservative parties necessarily pursue multi-class coalitions in order to construct electoral majorities. However, economic elites are located at the top of the coalitional hierarchy, and they are by far the most important sectors for shaping conservative parties' positions on high-stakes issues (Gibson 1996: 10).[15]

One can identify economic elites as a party's core constituency when the party receives consistently high levels of electoral support or public endorsement from the economic elites in question, when they contribute significant financial resources to the party, and/or when there is "programmatic convergence" between the party's policy positions and the preferences of economic elites (Gibson 1996: 13–14). In this study, I identify partisan linkages by drawing on literature on Latin America's conservative and right parties, as well as my own interviews with country experts, business leaders, and politicians.

---

[14] They analyze a random sample of issues on which interest groups are actively lobbying.
[15] Miliband (1969: 187) similarly described right parties: "For all their rhetoric of classlessness, [they] remain primarily the defense organizations, in the political field, of business and property."

I also examine campaign finance data where available and public political statements made by economic elites.

Partisan linkages afford economic elites influence through representation of their interests, in the executive branch and/or the legislature. Since instrumental power based on partisan linkages depends on the electoral fortunes of conservative parties, it may vary over the medium term. Instrumental power in the legislature arising from partisan linkages will be stronger when conservative parties hold more seats. Accordingly, electoral rules or district malapportionment[16] that favor conservative parties augment instrumental power based on partisan linkages. Legislative institutions requiring supermajorities to approve particular reforms can have the same effect.

Although conservative party politicians usually have informal ties to economic elites, partisan linkages are a more institutionalized relationship than informal ties. Partisan linkages therefore give economic elites more systematic influence than purely informal ties to legislators. However, electoral considerations at times may compel conservative parties to stray from the preferences of their core constituencies such that partisan linkages do not guarantee economic elites influence on all issues at all times. Various government strategies discussed later in this chapter aim to provoke conservative-party legislators to deviate from economic elites' tax policy preferences. Such deviations are more likely during electoral periods in which conservative parties face strong competition for nonelite voters.

Institutionalized Consultation

Formal or informally institutionalized consultation, or *concertation*, as it is often called in literature on Latin America (Schneider 1997: 200), entails regular meetings between government officials and business association leaders. Concertation is similar to tripartite bargaining between government, business, and labor in European corporatism, except that labor need not participate – consultation or concertation in this study describes only the relationship between government and business. Institutionalized government-business consultation may take place in councils or other formal bodies, or it may proceed more informally through regular interactions between high-level policymakers and business association leaders (Silva 1996, Schneider 2004a, 2010). Widely held expectations that consultation with business will precede or accompany major policy initiatives affecting the private sector and an established empirical record of such practices are indicators of informally institutionalized consultation. I draw on interviews with government officials and business informants, as well as literature on government-business relations in Latin America, news articles, and records

---

[16] Snyder and Samuels (2004), Gibson et al. (2004), Adranaz and Scartasini (2011).

from business association Web pages, to establish in which cases this source of instrumental power is present.

Beyond granting business regular access to policymakers, institutionalized consultation can create incentives for governments to cede on issues affecting core business interests. In general, institutionalized consultation may also create incentives for business to compromise with the government; as Schneider (1997: 214) notes, concertation "does not mean simply a zero-sum loss of state autonomy or power to business." However, when consultation is well established in multiple domains, conflict with business over its core interests may create unwanted tension or potentially disrupt mutually beneficial collaboration in other policy areas. Since concertation can improve economic governance and contribute to successful policy implementation (Schneider 1997: 200–12; 2004a: 210–34), governments may have strong incentives to avoid reforms that threaten business's core interests.

Institutionalized consultation requires a well-organized business sector with strong peak associations (Schneider 1997: 201). Accordingly, institutionalized consultation tends to generate instrumental power at the sectoral level or higher if there is a strong economy-wide business association. Furthermore, institutionalized consultation develops over fairly long time periods and is a relatively stable source of instrumental power, although it may be disrupted by the rise of new political actors or other destabilizing factors.

Institutionalized consultation can take place not just between business associations and the executive branch but also with the legislative branch. In the countries examined here, congressional finance committees regularly invited business representatives to present their positions on tax bills, and, in some cases, committee hearings became a key venue of political struggle. However, when the executive's legislative powers and/or de facto authority over economic policy formulation are much stronger than those of Congress, institutionalized consultation with committees is a much weaker source of instrumental power than institutionalized consultation with the executive branch. Business-committee consultation in the studied countries in and of itself did not create incentives for legislators to cede on core business interests, in part because legislators' initiative on economic policy and the scope of their participation in policymaking was much more limited than that of the executive. Instead, consultation with congressional committees served primarily as a formal channel for business access to legislators, and other sources of power like partisan linkages were more relevant in this arena.

Recruitment into Government, Election to Public Office, and Informal Ties

Recruitment into government, through appointments to state ministries or executive-branch positions, enables direct participation by economic elites in policymaking. Recruitment is a classic source of instrumental power discussed

by original authors of the concept (Miliband 1969: 54–57). Contemporary
scholars have noted the importance of government appointments for business
influence in Latin America (Schneider 2010, Arce 2005, Schamis 2002) and
beyond.[17]
  Election to public office also affords direct participation in policymaking.
Various wealthy businessmen have been elected to the presidency in Latin
America in recent years, including Bolivia's Gonzalo Sánchez de Lozada (1993–
97, 2002–03) and Chile's Sebastián Piñera (2010–present), and businesspeople,
large landowners, and other economic elites may hold seats in Congress, even
where partisan linkages are absent.
  Informal ties to government officials or legislators constitute a similar
source of power; however, the nexus of linkages between economic elites and
policymakers is one step further removed. In this case, economic elites are not
policymakers themselves; rather, they may enjoy easy access to and sympathy from executive-branch officials or legislators with whom they have informal ties. These decision makers may in turn advocate policies that economic
elites favor. Theorists including Mills (1956: 278), Miliband (1969: 59), and
Domhoff (1967, 1990) argued that informal ties based on extraction from a
common social circle or socioeconomic class could afford business influence
over members of government and state institutions, even in the absence of
direct participation in policymaking arenas. Common educational or professional experiences and family ties may also serve this purpose. Many authors
have subsequently associated informal ties with business influence in Latin
America.[18]
  Influence arising from these three sources of power tends to be highly contingent and depends on particular characteristics of the policymakers involved
and the institutional environment. Businesspeople elected to the presidency
may pursue agendas that deviate from the interests of other economic elites,
with an eye toward establishing their legacies or boosting their popularity to
maintain power. Likewise, policymakers may have strong personal loyalties
to a political leader that take precedence over informal ties to economic elites
when conflicts of interest arise.[19] Furthermore, state institutions can augment
or temper the effectiveness of informal ties and recruitment. If the state is characterized by a Weberian bureaucracy, associated incentives for policymakers
and bureaucrats to pursue common developmental goals may make them less
responsive to business demands that are inconsistent with those goals, regardless of informal ties. Following Evans (1995, 1997), informal ties to business

---

[17] In Russia, Easter (2012: 68) describes how tycoons in Yeltsin's government gave their own busi-
    nesses tax benefits.
[18] E.g., Silva 1996, Weyland 1996: 59, Teichman 2001, Arce 2005, Schneider 2010.
[19] Conaghan and Malloy (1994: 67) make this point regarding Banzer's authoritarian government
    in Bolivia.

in these circumstances can even empower state officials to better implement developmental agendas. In the absence of a Weberian bureaucracy, however, informal ties may lead to state capture: "When the state lacks the capacity to monitor and discipline individual incumbents, every relationship between a state official and a businessperson is another opportunity to generate rents for the individuals involved" (Evans 1997: 66). Turning to the legislature, the degree to which informal ties serve as effective sources of instrumental power for economic elites depends on characteristics of the country's electoral system. Eaton (2002) argues that where electoral institutions create career-based incentives for legislators to demonstrate loyalty to party leaders, legislators are less receptive to interest-group pressures that run counter to their party's major policy initiatives. In contrast, where electoral institutions "encourage legislators to cultivate personal reputations" (Eaton 2002: 15), legislators have leeway to be much more responsive to business demands. Accordingly, informal ties to legislators are a less effective source of instrumental power in party-centered electoral systems compared to candidate-centered electoral systems. Recognizing the contingent nature of influence derived from informal ties and the importance of institutional environments helps overcome problems inherent in "power elite" approaches, which tend to overestimate the extent to which informal ties or common backgrounds align public policies with business interests.[20]

The degree to which these sources of power afford influence in a given policy area also depends in part on the purview of the relevant policymakers. The higher ranking the officials and the more authority they wield in the policy domain, the more valuable economic elites' informal ties or appointments will be. For economic elites seeking to influence tax policy, appointments or ties to the Finance Ministry tend to be more consequential than appointments or ties to sectoral ministries. Further, the more pervasive economic elites' appointments or connections, the stronger their corresponding instrumental power will be.

Informal ties, election to public office, and/or recruitment may be highly variable over relatively short time periods. Elections can bring economic elites into office or turn them out, and cabinet appointments usually change when a new administration assumes office, if not more frequently.

These sources of power can be identified by examining the professional and personal backgrounds of the policymakers in question and using evidence from interviews and news sources. Assessing these sources of power becomes more important when economic elites lack institutionalized sources of power that afford more systematic influence.

---

[20] Power elite literature is also criticized for overestimating the homogeneity of interests within the business community and between business and state actors (Polsby 1968, Hacker and Pierson 2002).

Resources

Among the resources in Table 2.1, this study emphasizes cohesion, which is most important for explaining variation in tax policy outcomes in the cases examined. For completeness, this section includes brief discussions of all four resources.

Cohesion

Cohesion describes economic elites' capacity to form and sustain a united front and engage in collective action. When economic elites can present a united opposition front, prospects for influencing policy are stronger than if opposition is uncoordinated, or if only certain sectors or subgroups resist.

Cohesion enhances the effectiveness of lobbying or other forms of mobilization through two mechanisms. First, cohesion strengthens economic elites' bargaining position by increasing the cost of divide-and-conquer strategies. If cohesion is weak, policymakers may be able to negotiate acceptance from particular sectors or subgroups by offering only marginal concessions. This logic applies to business elites at both the cross-sectoral and sectoral levels. Economy-wide cohesion strengthens business's bargaining position on issues of cross-sectoral concern, whereas sectoral cohesion strengthens a sector's bargaining position on issues that affect its own special interests. Second, cohesion helps confer legitimacy on economic elites' demands. In contrast, when opposition is uncoordinated or where no united front exists, the demands of any particular group may be dismissed as narrow and self-serving (Silva 1997: 246). This dynamic is especially relevant regarding cross-sectoral taxes; in the absence of elite cohesion, the government can portray each sector as demanding special treatment and unfairly seeking to shift the tax burden onto others. For taxes affecting a single sector, solidarity from economic elites more broadly can legitimate and amplify that sector's opposition.

The commonsense view that unity enhances business power appears frequently in literature on business, elites, and economic reforms. In his classic study of redistribution in Latin America, Ascher (1984: 40) finds that "if a coalition of the wealthy is allowed to form, the results are likely to be devastating" for progressive reform. In contrast, he observes that redistribution is more feasible when elites are regionally or sectorally divided because such divisions can be exploited to impede formation of a united elite-opposition front. Frieden (1991: 33) makes a similar argument at the sectoral level: "The more successful a sector is in coming together to make common demands on policymakers, the more powerful will be the pressure it can exert."[21] Literature on regulation and taxation in the United States reaches similar con-

---

[21] Cooperation among capitalists is an important aspect of sectoral cohesion, along with capital-labor cooperation.

clusions (Vogel 1987: 395, Akard 1992), as does recent research on global environmental politics (Falkner 2009).

I treat encompassing organization as the most important of various factors that contribute to cohesion. Strong economy-wide business associations foster cross-sectoral cohesion by forging consensus among their members (Schneider 2004a) and acting with authority on their behalf. Business associations may also defend the interests of economic elites much more broadly, including upper-income earners and business owners as well as firms and corporations. Economy-wide associations can serve as key interlocutors between the government and economic elites, coordinating lobbying or other forms of collective action including protest. Likewise, strong sectoral business peak associations can contribute to sectoral cohesion. Although collective action can take place in the absence of encompassing organization, it will be much easier to sustain a united front when such an organization exists. In short, organization provides an institutional backbone for cohesion.

Several additional factors may contribute to cohesion. A strong common identity that distinguishes economic elites from other socially constructed groups contributes to cohesion (Lieberman 2003: 16) by promoting elite solidarity. Likewise, shared ideology can promote cohesion (Frieden 1991: 40, Levi 1988: 21)[22] by helping define a common identity or common interests.[23] Finally, homogeneity and concentration (a relatively small number of dominant economic actors) are oft-cited factors that promote business cohesion and facilitate collective action (Olson 1965, Frieden 1991, Etchemendy 2011).

Expertise

Technical expertise may confer instrumental power through several mechanisms. First, it may be a prerequisite for business actors to obtain access to policymakers. The executive branch may have little interest in consulting with business associations unless they bring technical expertise to the table. Second, expertise can enhance the effectiveness of lobbying by legitimating economic elites' demands and making their arguments more persuasive. Command of technical criteria can help business actors frame their interests as congruent with the country's developmental goals, whereas they might otherwise be perceived as purely self-interested.[24] And instead of simply rejecting increased taxation as an unwanted burden, business may be able to present its opposition

---

[22] In a similar vein, Blyth (2002: 38) holds that ideas are "crucial resources in the promotion of collective action."

[23] Note that while common interests may facilitate collective action, cohesion is not simply a function of the distribution of underlying preferences. Chapters 5 and 7 analyze cases where weak cohesion created collective action problems that limited elite influence despite broad opposition to tax increases. Note also that the content and/or nature of elite preferences remain analytically independent from power in this formulation.

[24] Conaghan and Malloy (1994: 73) and Silva (1997: 176) make similar observations.

in terms of technical concerns that policymakers share. Legislators may also be more easily swayed when business lobbyists have strong technical credentials. Investing in business association research divisions or financing think tanks that produce policy recommendations are two ways that business can seek to acquire and broadcast technical expertise.[25]

The degree to which business's technical expertise helps legitimate demands and craft persuasive arguments depends on how much expertise policymakers command. As Culpepper (2011) argues, when business actors possess greater expertise than policymakers on highly complex, obscure policy issues, policymakers tend to defer to lobbyists. In some such cases, policymakers may even delegate rule making to business actors (Culpepper 2011: 178). In contrast, policymakers with extensive expertise on the issue in question are unlikely to accept business assessments without scrutiny, and they may quickly detect flaws in purportedly technical arguments crafted to legitimate business demands.

The extent to which expertise confers instrumental power also depends on whether the policymakers and economic elites in question are trained in similar schools of economic thought. Orthodox policymakers are unlikely to be convinced by heterodox economic arguments, and vice versa. For example, arguments that eliminating tax credits entails technically inappropriate double taxation may resonate with highly orthodox economists, but heterodox policymakers may not be persuaded.

Despite the potential importance of technical expertise, it does not play a central role in explaining variation in tax policy outcomes in the cases examined in this book. Most relevant business associations enjoyed significant technical capacity, yet they sometimes obtained concessions from policymakers and sometimes did not, even when both sides espoused orthodox economic principles. This source of power does not play a strong causal role primarily because executive-branch officials in charge of tax policy all had extensive technical training; there simply was no significant gap in expertise between government and business on tax issues.

Media Access

Preferential media access may help economic elites influence policy through an indirect mechanism: shaping public opinion. Editorials, biased reports, and extensive coverage of economic elites' positions may persuade voters to adopt those views and thereby encourage politicians to implement congruent policies. To the extent that politicians respond to public opinion, media access may thereby affect the executive's reform agenda and/or influence legislators' votes. Preferential media access can also give conservative parties an advantage in electoral campaigns (Gibson 1992: 31) and may thus help economic elites obtain partisan representation. Business may also use media access as part of

---

[25] See Schneider (2013: 147) on Latin American think tanks.

longer-term strategies to shift the terms of public debate and define the scope of policy options considered appropriate.[26]

Authors dating back to Mills (1956: 315) and Miliband (1969: 182, 221) have identified media access as a key source of instrumental power, and much contemporary research concurs.[27] In Latin America, heavy concentration of media ownership and strong financial incentives to cater to advertisers[28] suggest that this source of power could be particularly important. Indeed, many large business groups in Latin America have diversified into media holdings.[29] However, given that links between public opinion and policy are often tenuous, as discussed in Chapter 1, the role of media access as a source of power should not be overemphasized. Opinion polls and survey data on tax reforms in Latin America are rare, making systematic analysis of media effects difficult. Yet this lack of data in and of itself suggests that public opinion, and hence media access, tended to play a modest role in tax politics. In Chile, where business is widely perceived to enjoy preferential media access, I argue that other sources of instrumental power were much more important for influencing tax policy. Where business enjoyed favorable media coverage but did not have other sources of power, it achieved little influence, as in the case of Argentina's industrial sector during the 1990s and agricultural producers in the 2000s.[30] And where business received neither preferential access nor favorable coverage, other sources of instrumental power conferred influence, as in the case of finance in Argentina during the 1990s.

Money

Money enhances economic elites' ability to organize, invest in technical expertise, hire lobbyists,[31] and procure media access. Three additional mechanisms linking money and influence that have been much studied are worth noting. First, financial contributions may sway legislators' votes, although authors disagree regarding to what extent.[32] Second, financial donations may mobilize bias in Congress and shape the legislative agenda (Hall and Wayman 1990). Third,

---

[26] See additional discussion in the subsequent section on "discursive power."

[27] In the United States, Smith (2000) argues that business achieves influence by funding think tanks, whose spokespeople receive extensive media attention based on technical credentials.

[28] Fox and Waisbord (2002), Hughes and Lawson (2004), Wolf (2009), Becerra and Mastrini (2009), Boas (2013).

[29] I think Ben Ross Schneider for this point. Brazil's Globo is a prominent example.

[30] Schneider (2004a: 193) observes that the Argentine industrial association's "greatest strength was its visibility in the press" in the 1990s; however, it achieved little influence on tax policy (Chapter 5). Likewise, farmers' concerns received ample coverage in the Argentine newspaper *La Nación* but failed to influence export tax policy for many years (Chapter 7).

[31] Etchemendy (2011: 67–68) emphasizes the importance of material resources for business lobbying during structural adjustment in Argentina.

[32] Some contend that this hypothesis is not strongly supported for the United States (Hall and Wayman 1990: 798, Baumgartner et al. 2009); evidence from Brazil suggests that campaign contributions do lead to "quid pro quos" (Samuels 2001: 35).

campaign contributions may give conservative parties an electoral advantage. While business usually donates to all major candidates, contributions to conservative parties tend to be much more substantial; as Gibson (1992) notes, campaign contributions are an important component of the core constituency relationship between economic elites and conservative parties.[33]

In general, the extent to which money procures political influence is hotly contested, with some authors arguing that it makes little difference,[34] others calling for greater attention to this resource,[35] and some placing it above all other sources of power (Winters 2011). Given the difficulty of obtaining relevant data in Latin America, systematic analysis of money as a direct source of power lies outside the scope of this book.[36] While my view is that money does matter, I find that other sources of power (which money may in part underpin) explain most of the observed policy variation in this study.

2.2 STRUCTURAL POWER

Structural power stems from the profit-maximizing behavior of private-sector actors and policymakers' expectations about the aggregate economic consequences of myriad individual investment decisions made in response to policy decisions. Block (1977) and Lindblom (1977, 1982), who originally theorized this concept,[37] stressed that governments in market societies depend on business to invest and produce in ways that foster collective prosperity. Accordingly, structural power arises from concerns that a policy will provoke reduced investment, capital flight, or declining production, because of the market incentives the policy creates for firms, capital owners, or producers. Reduced investment or production may in turn lead to slow or declining growth, unemployment, or other macroeconomic problems. If policymakers anticipate such negative aggregate outcomes, they may refrain from initiating the policy in question for the sake of attaining developmental goals or to avoid punishment at the polls for declining prosperity. The defining feature of structural power is that it requires no organization or capacity for political action; instead, market signals coordinate reactions in the economic arena. As summarized by Hacker and Pierson (2002: 281): "The pressure to protect business interests is generated automatically and apolitically. It results from private, individual investment

---

[33] Samuels (2001) finds that in Brazil, left parties receive less corporate funding, and campaign contributions have a large effect on elections. On business contributions helping Yeltsin defeat left-wing competitors in Russia, see Easter (2012: 68). More generally, see Yadav (2011: 26–29) on the growing importance of business funds for campaign finance in developing democracies and Arriola on business financing African opposition campaigns.

[34] Baumgartner et al. (2009) and Culpepper (2010) tend toward this view.

[35] Graetz and Shapiro (2005), Hacker and Pierson (2010), Gilens (2012).

[36] More extensive information is available for Brazil (Samuels 2001). On campaign finance in Latin America, see Posada-Carbó and Malamud (2005).

[37] See also Przeworski and Wallerstein (1988) and Winters (1996).

decisions taken in thousands of enterprises, rather than from any organized effort to influence policymakers."

To better understand this concept, I operationalize structural power as a credible and economically significant *disinvestment threat*. In some cases, the disinvestment threat may take the form of an *exit threat*, whereby policymakers anticipate that domestic or foreign economic elites will remove their capital from the country in pursuit of higher returns elsewhere. In other cases, the disinvestment threat may take the form of a *withholding threat*, whereby policymakers anticipate that economic elites will cancel or postpone productive investment.[38] For example, a company might distribute profits to shareholders instead of reinvesting. Beyond disinvestment threats, structural power may also entail threats that a policy will merely cause investment to stagnate at prevailing levels, or prevent investment from increasing to the desired extent. Even more broadly, structural power may entail a threat that a reform will disrupt normal economic activities other than investment; for example, unfavorable market signals might lead business owners to scale back or halt production, or to hold their goods off of the market until more favorable conditions prevail.[39] For simplicity, I use the term disinvestment throughout the following discussion.

What makes a disinvestment threat credible? First and foremost, private sector agents must have significant and concrete incentives to actually withhold or relocate investment; many policies create no such incentives, even if economic elites dislike them. In addition, for exit threats, capital must be mobile. However, structural power more generally does not require capital mobility. For example, extractive industries with large sunken investments may be unlikely to close their operations, but structural power may still arise from concerns that a policy will discourage new investment.[40] Nor does capital mobility necessarily confer structural power; the policy must actually create negative investment incentives.

Turning to significance, a credible disinvestment threat will generate stronger structural power if the sector or class of investors in question plays an important role in the country's economy. For example, a sector that constitutes a large proportion of GDP, serves as a growth engine, drives job creation, or plays a critical role in ensuring that the broader economy functions smoothly

---

[38] This distinction between withholding and exit threats builds on Winters (1996: 22), who differentiates between withdrawing investment, an option available to all investors, and relocating investment, which is possible only when capital is mobile. Of withdrawing investment, he observes: "At its most dramatic a plant can be closed…. At a much more subtle level an expansion, a new investment, or some kind of reinvestment can be postponed or cancelled."

[39] See Chapter 7 on grain export companies periodically suspending operations during Argentina's 2001 crisis.

[40] See Winters (1996: 23) for further discussion of this point. See also Chapter 8 on the Bolivian hydrocarbons sector's structural power.

(e.g., the financial sector[41]) has the potential to generate stronger structural power than a sector lacking such characteristics. Even substantial disinvestment within a weak or economically insignificant sector may cause little concern. It is worth stressing, however, that economic importance and structural power are not synonymous, although authors sometimes treat them as such (Handley 2008: 10).[42]

Predicting investor behavior and the aggregate effects of myriad individual investment decisions is not an exact science. Rational observers, including highly trained economists, may disagree on the likely consequences of a reform, especially in real-world situations where numerous other variables may affect investment. Incomplete information and uncertainty during periods of instability can also make it difficult to predict how a policy will affect investment trends.

Structural power therefore depends on policymakers' perceptions in the following sense: if policymakers perceive significant disinvestment incentives and a substantial associated economic impact, these concerns will influence agenda formulation regardless of the actual impact the reform would have, which is unobservable at this stage of policymaking (Table 2.2, quadrants a, b). If policymakers do not anticipate disinvestment, or if they believe its economic consequences will be negligible, then structural power – whether weak or simply perceived as such – will have no effect on whether or not a reform is proposed (Table 2.2, quadrants c, d), regardless of whether that reform would have, or ultimately does, stimulate disinvestment. In other words, what matters for policymaking is the anticipated disinvestment threat, not the unobservable "objective" disinvestment threat.

Disjunctures can arise between policymakers' anticipations regarding a reform's likely impact on investment and the actual economic consequences of reform. On the one hand, policymakers might anticipate significant disinvestment even if a reform is in fact unlikely to alter investors' behavior (Table 2.2, quadrant b). On the other hand, policymakers might not anticipate disinvestment in cases where investors will respond negatively to a reform (Table 2.2, quadrant c). As Hacker and Pierson (2002: 282) point out: "structural power is a signaling device; by itself it does not dictate policy choices." Under some conditions, policymakers may misread or simply fail to detect the signal. Retrospectively, it is sometimes possible to identify misperceptions, especially when enacted reforms appear to produce subsequent disinvestment,[43] or when

---

[41] Woll (2014: 101–02) emphasizes the sheer size of the financial sector and the intricate ways in which it is integrated with and supports the real economy in developed democracies.

[42] Etchemendy (2011: 79) uses "structural power" to describe "the value that industrial sectors generate in relation to their degree of concentration," which combines indicators of economic importance (value generated) and collective-action capacity (number of firms in the sector); the latter introduces aspects of instrumental power.

[43] Apropos, Ambroce Bierce's _The Lacking Factor_: "'Your act was unwise,' I exclaimed 'as you see / by the outcome.' He solemnly eyed me. / 'When choosing the course of my action,' said he, / 'I had not the outcome to guide me.'"

TABLE 2.2. *Structural Power and Disinvestment Threats*

		"Objective" Disinvestment Threat	
		High	Low
Anticipated Disinvestment Threat	High	a) Strong Structural Power Keeps reform off agenda, unless other priorities prevail	b) Strong (Perceived) Structural Power Keeps reform off agenda, unless other priorities prevail
	Low	c) Weak (Perceived) Structural Power No effect on reform agenda **Realized Disinvestment Threat** May affect fate of proposal or duration of enacted reform	d) Weak Structural Power No effect on policy decisions

reforms implemented despite perceived structural power do not appear to alter investment trends.[44] Where concerns over investment kept reforms off the agenda, however, it is impossible to know definitively how investment would actually have responded; the "objective" disinvestment threat remains unobservable. Accordingly, in cases where quadrants a) and b) (Table 2.2) cannot reasonably be distinguished, I simply score structural power as strong.

This discussion so far has treated structural power as influencing agenda formulation, in accord with most literature on the concept.[45] However, structural power may also affect the fate of reform initiatives after they have been proposed. For example, where executive initiatives require congressional approval, legislators' concerns over reduced investment may compel them to vote against a reform, even if executive-branch policymakers believe the reform will provoke no negative economic consequences. In other words, structural power may be deemed strong in the legislative arena but weak in the executive arena (or vice-versa).

Alternatively, policymakers may ascertain post facto that the mere announcement or initiation of a proposal actually precipitates disinvestment.[46] They may accordingly rescind or reject the proposal. Likewise, actual disinvestment after a reform is implemented may lead policymakers to subsequently amend or

---

[44] See Chapter 8 on Bolivia's 2005 hydrocarbons reform.

[45] For example, Hacker and Pierson (2002), Fuchs (2007), and Falkner (2009) implicitly equate structural power with "indirect" influence or "agenda-setting power." Smith (2000) is an exception.

[46] Przeworski and Wallerstein (1988) find that capitalists' anticipation of tax increases can lead to reduced investment before implementation.

repeal the offending reform. In these cases, structural power takes the form of a *realized disinvestment threat* (Table 2.2, quadrant c).

Competing priorities can attenuate the causal impact of structural power. Policymakers may have other goals that trump concerns over investment, even if they do anticipate that a reform will provoke disinvestment. For example, a left government might prioritize redistribution over growth, reestablishing fiscal discipline or solvency might take precedence over stimulating investment, and pacifying mobilized popular sectors might preempt concerns over a policy's longer-term economic consequences. However, other priorities will become less relevant as the perceived credibility and impact of the disinvestment threat increases.

As the above discussion illustrates, identifying policymakers' perceptions regarding the anticipated consequences of reform options, as well as additional factors they take into account when making policy decisions, is essential for assessing whether or not structural power influences policy.[47] Accordingly, I draw on interviews with high-level government officials as well as written records to establish whether certain reforms were ruled out for fear of reduced investment and to explain why policymakers perceived structural power to be weak or strong. Where possible, I also examine relevant economic data to assess whether policymakers' anticipations represented an accurate reading of the "objective" disinvestment threat.

Many authors emphasize that macroeconomic factors, including the relative weight of the state versus the private sector in economic activity and levels of international economic integration and global capital mobility, shape structural power.[48] Seismic shifts toward private ownership and global capital mobility in the 1980s and early 1990s paved the way for structural power to play a much more important constraining role in Latin America and other developing regions compared to earlier decades.

Against this macroeconomic backdrop, however, structural power is in fact highly context-specific; it varies across countries, policy areas, and even specific reform proposals. National-level contextual factors such as the broader policy environment (Hacker and Pierson 2002: 282, Gelleny and McCoy 2001, Garrett and Mitchell 2001), or a history of economic instability or

---

[47] Perceptions are indispensible when analyzing anticipated reactions. As such, the importance of perceptions is implicit in the classic formulations of structural power. Both Winters (1996: xv) and Hacker and Pierson (2002: 282) anticipate this point; the former notes that "issues of perception and anticipation are … critical to the actions of both investors and state leaders"; the latter observe: "If influence depends on fear of disinvestment, then it will vary depending on how credible policy makers believe that threat to be." Constructivists in international relations (Bell 2012, Bell and Hindmoor 2014) are developing points about perceptions similar to those I make here and in previous work (Fairfield 2010, 2011), but they venture into relational notions of power and questions of agency that I find less promising for honing structural power into an empirically useful causal variable that is conceptually distinct from instrumental power.

[48] See Winters (1996) on commodity booms and capital mobility.

extensive government intervention can affect the likelihood that a particular reform will provoke reduced investment or capital flight. Structural power may even have a cultural component, to the extent that common national experiences create shared expectations about how investors will respond to particular reforms.[49] Furthermore, the broader structure of the tax system may affect the incentives that a specific tax increase creates. For these reasons, similar reforms may provoke a disinvestment threat in one country but no such threat in another country. In addition, reforms in different policy areas can affect or convey different signals to investors with different types of assets (Maxfield 1997: 38–39). For example, investment in certain sectors or asset classes may be highly sensitive to reforms with a relatively small impact on profits, whereas investment in other sectors or asset classes may be so profitable compared to other options that even substantial tax increases would not deter investment.[50] High commodity prices may contribute to the latter situation with regard to mineral and agricultural export sectors. In general, the extent to which a particular reform creates disinvestment incentives depends not only on how much it affects profits, but also on expected returns to alternative investment options and associated transaction costs (Mahon 1996: 21). Moreover, investors may interpret some reforms as signals that their assets are no longer secure, whereas other reforms may not trigger any such concerns.[51]

Structural power also varies over time. The state of the economy is one factor that can drive fluctuations in structural power. Some authors have observed that structural power should be at it strongest during recessions, when policymakers tend to prioritize investment and job creation (Smith 2000: 148–49). In such contexts, even marginal investment losses may matter, whereas economic boom may make moderate (or even significant) changes in investment levels inconsequential.[52] However, economic crisis can reduce structural power (Block 1979, Akard 1992: 609, Hacker and Pierson 2002). If investment has already fallen dramatically, as occurred during the Great Depression, additional disinvestment may create little cause for concern. Vogel (1987: 394) builds on a synthesis of these views. He argues that structural power will be weak when the economy is either in boom or in bust, but strong when intermediate conditions prevail. Although this relationship between structural power and economic conditions holds across several cases examined in this book, it is not a generalizable rule. Disinvestment threats may persist even during times of strong

---

[49] I thank Peter Evans for this insight. See Chapter 6 on interest earnings in Argentina.
[50] In Argentina, fixed-time deposits illustrate the former case (Chapter 6); soy production illustrates the latter case (Chapter 7).
[51] Chapter 6 illustrates this point for tax reforms affecting Argentina's financial sector.
[52] For a similar view, see Campello (forthcoming) on financial investors' reduced ability to influence economic policy in Latin America during periods characterized by low international interest rates and high commodity prices.

economic growth,[53] and economic crises may enhance rather than diminish structural power, depending on how they alter investors' incentives and the relative economic importance of the sector(s) in question. Given the specificity of structural power to particular contexts and reforms, structural power must be carefully evaluated on a case-by-case basis.

Because experts may disagree on the likelihood that a reform will stimulate reduced investment, turnover in government is another factor that can drive temporal fluctuations in (perceived) structural power. If new authorities espouse different economic principles than their predecessors, they may view a given reform as either more or less deleterious to investment than previous incumbents assumed. Even policymakers and technocrats with similar economic training may predict different consequences to a given reform and have different views regarding the credibility of disinvestment threats.[54]

Identifying these multiple sources of variation helps to reclaim structural power as a useful analytical concept. Early literature, particularly Lindblom's (1982) formulation of "the market as prison," viewed structural power as extremely constraining and could not account for broad cross-national variation in economic policy regimes.[55] But careful analysis of how structural power varies over time, across policy areas, and across countries, in conjunction with attention to instrumental power, provides strong leverage for explaining policy change.[56]

2.3 INTEGRATING ANALYSIS OF INSTRUMENTAL AND STRUCTURAL POWER

Historically, the concept of structural power emerged partly as a reaction against both instrumental definitions of power and its pluralist critics, who

---

[53] See Chapter 6 on taxation of interest earnings in Argentina. More generally, even during economic booms when it might seem that policymakers have little to fear, concerns that a policy may disincentivize investment and deflect the positive economic trajectory may prevail.

[54] For example, orthodox center-left Chilean finance ministers Eyzaguirre and Velasco disagreed on how corporate tax increases would affect investment (Chapter 3).

[55] Lindblom (1982: 326) asserts: "One line of reform after another is blocked by prospective punishment. An enormous variety of reforms do in fact undercut business expectations of profitability and do therefore reduce employment." For additional critiques, see Vogel (1987) and Hacker and Pierson (2002), the latter offer an insightful review of changing perspectives on constraints imposed by structural power.

[56] Lindblom's failure to problematize the credibility of disinvestment threats helps explain why he portrays structural power as monolithic and invariant. Lindblom (1977: 185) writes: "Prophecies of some kinds tend to be self-fulfilling. If spokesmen for businessmen predict that new investment will lag without tax relief, it is only one short step to corporate decisions that put off investment until tax relief is granted." However, a policy's effect on investment behavior may not be clear-cut, and when many investors are involved, business leaders' predictions may not automatically ensue (although signaling effects could be important). Moreover, policymakers do not always unquestioningly accept business actors' evaluations.

argued that divisions and differences of interest within the business community undermined early notions of a power elite. Analysts tended to advocate one type of power or the other instead of adopting an integrated view in which economic elites can possess either or both types of power in any given context. As Hacker and Pierson (2002) recount, the failure to incorporate both instrumental and structural power into a single analytical framework contributed to an impasse in the literature and declining interest in the concept of power within comparative politics. However, examining both types of power is critical for understanding the means and extent to which economic elites exert influence in market democracies. This section explicates how the two types of power can aggregate and interact, although they remain conceptually distinct.

When economic elites enjoy both structural power and instrumental power, they can achieve more consistent and more substantial influence. In these cases, they can exert influence through multiple channels; when one means fails to achieve the goal, another may succeed. For example, if structural power does not deter policymakers from proposing a reform that economic elites oppose, instrumental power may help them obtain concessions later in the policymaking process.

Moreover, instrumental power and structural power can be mutually reinforcing – each may be stronger in the presence of the other. On the one hand, instrumental power can augment structural power. For example, lobbying from a position of strong instrumental power can exacerbate policymakers' concerns that a reform will provoke disinvestment – in other words, structural power can be instrumentally enhanced.[57] Economic elites regularly assert that failure to heed their policy recommendations will lead to grave economic consequences, and these warnings will be taken more seriously when they have strong relationships with policymakers and resources like technical expertise. It is even possible that lobbying could convince policymakers that there is a credible threat of disinvestment when they harbor no preexisting concerns regarding a reform's economic impact. This situation might arise when policymakers lack sufficient expertise to independently evaluate economic elites' claims that a reform will deter investment and growth. Culpepper's (2011: 178) argument that expertise is the key to business influence on low-salience issues draws largely on this logic (although he does not refer to either instrumental or structural power): politicians with little knowledge of policy areas like corporate takeover regulations respond to mangers' demands because "they do not want to risk messing up the economy."

Another scenario involving instrumental enhancement of structural power could occur where business's instrumental power motivates the appointment of key government officials (e.g., the finance minister) whose technical training predisposes them to be highly concerned about the economic consequences of a policy that runs against business preferences. In this example, concerns over

---

[57] See Chapter 6 on bank-information access in Argentina during the 1990s.

structural power are particularly strong because instrumental power influenced the economic tenets prevailing within the government. If the officials in question discard the policy due to anticipated disinvestment, then structural power is the direct cause, yet this structural power has been enhanced by business's prior exercise of instrumental power.[58]

On the other hand, structural power can augment instrumental power. When decision makers worry that a reform or a broader policy agenda may affect investment, they may grant business more extensive access and participation than would otherwise be expected given their existing sources of instrumental power.[59] At one extreme, businesspeople might be recruited into government – thereby acquiring a new source of instrumental power – in order to reestablish investor confidence and thus diminish threats of disinvestment associated with business expectations about an administration's preferred policy agenda.[60] Lindblom's (1977: 170–88) discussion of the privileged position of business is consistent with this view. He argues that public officials grant business privileged access to decision-making arenas – conferring instrumental power – because business makes the decisions that determine growth and employment – in other words, because capital wields structural power.

Despite the fact that instrumental and structural power may interact in mutually reinforcing ways, it is important to recognize that they are nevertheless conceptually distinct. Instrumental power involves capacity for deliberate and often collective action in the political arena, whereas structural power entails apolitical, market-coordinated decisions in the economic arena. Accordingly, structural power and instrumental power need not covary. Structural power may be strong even if instrumental power is weak, and instrumental power can be strong in the absence of structural power. The empirical chapters include cases exemplifying all four combinations of weak and strong scores on these two variables.

Particular care must be taken to distinguish instrumental power from structural power in cases where disinvestment or other forms of economic disruption do occur in response to reform. If these outcomes result from individually rational profit-maximizing decisions, structural power is at work. However, on rare occasion, these outcomes may result from economic protest, which falls within the realm of instrumental power.

---

[58] Thacker's (2000: 36) observation that business's political participation can help decision makers understand which among multiple policies have motivated reduced investment suggests yet another complementarity between instrumental and structural power: the former may clarify signals sent by the latter.

[59] Following this logic, Silva (1997) argues that the Chilean government's concern over investment after the democratic transition motivated close consultation with business.

[60] For example, Ecuadorian president Gutierrez campaigned on a leftist platform but appointed an orthodox economist supported by business as finance minister to quell concerns over potential disinvestment (Campello 2009). Peruvian president Humala reportedly followed a similar strategy.

Economic protest entails deliberate, politically coordinated decisions to relocate or withhold investment (investment strikes),[61] halt production (lockouts or production strikes), or disrupt the sale or distribution of goods (commercialization strikes) in order to exert influence, when individual participants have market-based incentives to continue their normal economic activities. In contrast to market-coordinated disinvestment or disruption of production, economic protest entails short-term costs for participants, and long-run gains depend on whether the actions undertaken influence policy choices and/or politics more broadly.[62] Business strikes, like labor strikes, therefore require collective action, and they are more likely to arise when cohesion among the relevant economic elites is strong.[63] However, Chapter 7 examines an unusual case in which a tax increase catalyzed business strikes despite the participants' prior lack of cohesion.

Many authors do not explicitly consider the possibility that disinvestment can be politically coordinated (Winters 1996: 21–22, Hacker and Pierson 2002: 297, Campello 2009: 2).[64] Yet distinguishing between market coordination and political coordination is important because the logic of disinvestment may affect policymakers' subsequent reactions. For example, if a policy does not significantly alter market incentives but does provoke politically coordinated disinvestment, governments may attempt to ride out the economic protest and wait for the logic of individual short-term profitability to preempt the logic of collective action.

Although the primary case of economic disruption examined in this study was strictly politically coordinated (Argentina's agricultural producers protest, Chapter 7), other instances may involve elements of both structural power and instrumental power. Economic elites may attempt to organize investment strikes to augment their influence even if market-coordinated disinvestment is also taking place. For example, business staged politically coordinated investment strikes in Chile in 1972 to destabilize the Allende government, even though substantial disinvestment had already occurred in response to the government's transformative, redistributive agenda (Ascher 1984: 256).[65] Likewise, business leaders in India attempted to orchestrate an investment strike in the 1940s

---

[61] In contrast to my usage, the term investment strike (or capital strike) is often applied to cases of market-coordinated disinvestment or disruption of production.

[62] This treatment is consistent with Mahon (1996: 20–21), who views capital strikes as "a class of political capital flows" that act as "a *deliberate* tool of pressure, as opposed to a method of increasing expected return."

[63] See Fairfield (2011) for further discussion of business strikes and protests.

[64] Winters (1996: 21–22) and Vogel (1987: 393–94) associate capital strikes with all cases of disinvestment, except those involving relocation of mobile capital. However, relocation and withholding of investment can both result from deliberate, coordinated efforts to effect policy or political change. Conversely, both relocation and withholding can be economically rational responses to market signals.

[65] See also Sigmund 1977, Stallings 1978, and Silva 1996.

against proposed regulatory reforms; this initiative also took place in a context of market-coordinated disinvestment (Chibber 2003: 142–45).

A Note on "Discursive Power"

In recent years, international relations scholars have advanced the concept of "discursive power" to understand business influence in global governance and policymaking (Fuchs 2007, Newell 2009, Falkner 2009).[66] These authors define discursive power as business's ability to exert influence by shaping norms and ideas. As Fuchs (2007: 61) elaborates, the notion of discursive power is related to the "third dimension" of power conceptualized by Lukes (1974: 23), whereby "*A* may exercise power over *B* ... by influencing, shaping, or determining his very wants." While this dimension of power is a well-established concept, I argue that the ideas these authors discuss are already incorporated within the instrumental and structural power framework. As such, discursive power does not add analytical leverage but can instead create conceptual confusion.

To the extent that shaping norms and ideas entails deliberate, strategic actions designed to influence policy outcomes (Fuchs 2007: 60–61, Falkner 2009: 20), discursive power is no different from instrumental power. Early instrumentalists like Mills (1956: 314–15) and Miliband (1969: 182, 211) discuss similar ideas about power as those expounded by Lukes. For example, while Lukes (1974: 23) emphasizes that an actor can "secure ... compliance by controlling ... thoughts and desires," Miliband (1969: 211) discusses "effort[s] business makes to persuade society not merely to accept the policies it advocates but also the ... values and the goals which are its own." Three sources of instrumental power – media access, technical expertise, and informal ties to policymakers – are particularly relevant for the socialization and indoctrination processes these authors discuss. Media access (or control over mass media, as discussed by all three authors) helps business define and disseminate norms. Technical expertise and informal ties may play a role in convincing policymakers that certain policies are appropriate or inappropriate and/ or socializing them into particular schools of economic thought, which may in turn have implications for how they perceive structural power and disinvestment threats – as discussed in the previous section, structural power may thus be instrumentally enhanced. Business-financed think tanks, which may leverage media access and technical expertise, are often particularly active in these regards, aiming to shape policy discourse and restrict the scope of the reform agenda.[67] While Fuchs (2007) identifies seemingly distinct sources

---

[66] See Barnett and Duvall (2005) and Woll (2014) on the related but more nebulous concept of "productive power," to which the following critique also applies.

[67] See Smith (2000) among others.

of discursive power – legitimacy and authority – these attributes can also be related to sources of instrumental power that are more analytically tractable.[68] For example, technical expertise, media access, and cohesion can establish business groups as authoritative actors with legitimate positions and demands.

Notions of discursive power are closely related to framing strategies (Fuchs 2007: 60–61), whereby actors craft appeals using widely shared norms. Government framing strategies to promote tax reform and business counterstrategies are discussed in Section 2.4. There is no need to identify a distinct type of power corresponding to discursive strategies to incorporate the latter into the analysis. Moreover, equating discursive power with discursive strategies (Falkner 2009: 31–32)[69] conflates sources of power, actions, and influence. We cannot conclude that an actor who employs a discursive strategy is necessarily powerful, or that employing a discursive strategy will ensure that the actor's preferences shape policy outcomes. Framing strategies crafted by business actors will be more likely to succeed when sources of instrumental power lend greater weight, attention, and credibility to their arguments.[70]

Finally, whether or not one introduces a concept of discursive power, assessing business influence over policymakers' *a priori* views of what reforms are appropriate and desirable, as per the third dimension of power, poses challenging analytical problems, as many authors (including those critiqued in the preceding paragraphs) have noted (Shapiro 2006). Such endeavors lie beyond the scope of this book.

2.4 REFORM STRATEGIES: CIRCUMVENTING ELITES' POWER

When economic elites have strong instrumental and/or structural power, increasing taxes on income and wealth is difficult. However, astute governments can legislate incremental tax increases that might not otherwise be possible when economic elites are powerful by using strategies that temper

---

[68] Levi (1988: 17) similarly treats legitimacy and authority as derivative of other sources of power.

[69] "In trying to shape social understandings of the problems … and the ideas and norms that should guide policymaking, actors employ discursive strategies and can be said to possess discursive power."

[70] Blyth's (2002) research on ideas and institutional change is instructive in these regards. While his analysis of business's onslaught against "embedded liberalism" in the United States during the 1970s emphasizes the ideas business marshaled, his simultaneous attention to business efforts to rebuild "muscle" by organizing, financing think tanks, and bankrolling campaigns illustrates the underlying importance of instrumental power. Consistent with the theoretical perspective I present above, Blyth (2002: 154) describes the "production and dissemination" of ideas as a deliberate business strategy for pursuing policy change. To a significant extent, his narrative suggests that organization, money, and relationship-based sources of power played an important role in helping business establish the dominance of its new economic ideas.

TABLE 2.3. *Reform Strategies*

		Mechanism	
		Tempering Elite Antagonism	Mobilizing Public Support
Fiscal Policy Domain	Tax-Side	Attenuating Impact Obfuscating Incidence Legitimating Appeals (horizontal equity)	Legitimating Appeals (equity & nationalism)
	Benefit-Side	Compensation Emphasizing Stabilization	Linking to Popular Benefits

Source: Fairfield 2013, reprinted with permission from Elsevier publications.

elite antagonism and/or mobilize public support. Most of these strategies are intimately related to reform design. At the same time, many require concerted framing efforts.[71]

I identify six reform strategies that can be classified according to their "fiscal policy domain." *Tax-side* strategies – attenuating impact, obfuscating incidence, and legitimating appeals – exploit characteristics of the chosen tax instrument(s). *Benefit-side* strategies – compensation, emphasizing stabilization, and linking to popular benefits – deflect debate away from taxation by focusing attention on benefits associated with the tax increase, the reform package in which it is nested, or a broader policy agenda. Many of these strategies have analogs in literature on fiscal bargaining, "reform mongering" in Latin America, welfare state development and retrenchment in advanced industrial democracies, and coalitions for market reform in developing and postcommunist countries. However, tax reform strategies have not been analyzed systematically and comparatively.

The typology in Table 2.3 locates reform strategies according to their fiscal policy domain and the primary mechanism through which they act.[72] Strategies that temper antagonism make economic elites less inclined to use their instrumental power to resist reform. Tempering antagonism can also circumvent structural power by reducing the likelihood that economic elites will disinvest. Strategies that mobilize public support can counterbalance economic elites' instrumental power by creating electoral incentives for politicians to be less responsive to elite interests.

---

[71] The relative importance of policy design versus "crafted talk" has been debated (Jacobs and Shapiro 2000, Hacker and Pierson 2005); I find that both elements can be important and mutually reinforcing.

[72] Following Collier et al. (2012), this typology organizes theory and concepts, draws together multiple lines of investigation, and maps variation in the independent variable.

As Pierson (1993: 625) observes, "Individual policies may have a number of politically relevant characteristics, and these characteristics may have a multiplicity of consequences." The same holds for reform strategies. For instance, a given strategy may have the desired effect on public opinion but undesirable consequences in terms of business reactions. How these multiple political effects play out in particular instances will depend on context-specific factors.[73] I discuss the most salient trade-offs that can arise for each of the strategies with reference to cases examined in the empirical chapters.

Tax-Side Strategies

The three tax-side strategies act through different means. Attenuating impact and obfuscating incidence temper elite antagonism. Legitimating appeals – based on vertical equity, horizontal equity, or nationalism – mobilize public support; horizontal equity appeals can also temper elite antagonism.

Attenuating Impact

This strategy draws on the commonsense observation that economic elites are less likely to mobilize their instrumental power against, or reduce investment in response to, a tax increase, the smaller its impact on their profits or pocketbooks. Various temporal techniques attenuate impact. A tax increase can be phased in gradually, giving firms a transition period to adjust. Reformers can enact a series of incremental tax increases rather than proposing a single more substantial reform. Tax increases can also be legislated to hold effect for a limited time period. These attenuation techniques can be viewed as "foot in the door" strategies (Ascher 1984: 131). For example, renewing temporary tax increases may incur less resistance than passing the initial reform, to the extent that taxpayers become accustomed to the increase and/or the government can demonstrate that it has not harmed growth and investment. However, repeated recourse to temporary increases undermines this technique, as taxpayers learn that such measures will either be renewed or replaced with additional temporary tax increases and therefore press to keep the "door" closed.[74]

Obfuscating Incidence

Obfuscating tax incidence[75] reduces taxpayers' awareness of paying the burden. Economic elites will not react against a tax increase by activating their instrumental or structural power (i.e., disinvesting) if they are not conscious of its impact. Obfuscation entails selecting taxes with low *visibility* (Steinmo 1993,

---

[73] See also Falleti and Lynch (2009) on how context shapes outcomes of causal mechanisms.

[74] This problem occurred in Chile, where temporary tax increases were consistently extended; promises that taxes increases would be temporary lost credibility by the mid 2000s.

[75] I borrow the term obfuscation from Pierson (1994: 19–22), who elaborates analogous strategies for welfare retrenchment.

Wilensky 2002). Direct taxes on income or assets tend to be highly visible. When individuals file income tax returns, they are acutely aware of the tax burden imposed upon them. In contrast, employers' social security contributions have low visibility (Steinmo 1993: 19). Employers pass on the cost of these taxes to employees through lower wages. But because these taxes are collected from employers, wage earners generally are unaware that they bear the burden. This example illustrates a technique for reducing tax visibility: exploiting the phenomenon of burden shifting, which stems from "the difference between the *de jure* and *de facto* incidence of taxes" (Pierson 1994: 21).

Obfuscating techniques have several limitations and drawbacks. First, they can introduce actual uncertainty regarding tax incidence. It may not be clear whether the assumptions required to successfully exploit burden shifting actually hold, in which case, taxpayers other than those intended may be affected.[76] Further, if a reform's incidence becomes too uncertain, business actors may strongly resist because of the difficulties it creates for anticipating costs and planning investments (Ascher 1989: 464).

Second, reducing the visibility of a tax increase intended to raise revenue from economic elites is rarely feasible. Unlike average citizens, elites have the motivation and the resources to ascertain exactly how tax reforms affect their pocketbooks. As Hacker and Pierson (2005: 37) observe: "F. Scott Fitzgerald was right: The very rich *are* different – not just in their preferences regarding tax policy but, crucially, in their level of knowledge with respect to various dimensions of this complex issue."[77]

Legitimating Appeals
Legitimating appeals draw on widely held norms that can mobilize public support and thereby pressure politicians who might otherwise defend elite interests to accept reform. Wilson (1980: 370) envisages these strategies when discussing policies that impose costs on small groups but confer broad benefits, for which success "requires the efforts of a skilled entrepreneur who can mobilize latent public sentiment ... put the opponents of the plan publicly on the defensive ... and associate the legislation with widely shared values."

Legitimating appeals are more likely to succeed when political competition is strong and issue salience is high, such that politicians have electoral incentives to cater to marginal voters (Murillo 2009), and when major elections are

---

[76] See Chapter 6 on Argentina's tax on debt.

[77] The superior resources and information available to economic elites creates inherent asymmetry between the politics of progressive direct taxation and the politics of increasing broad-based taxes or reducing elite taxation. Policymakers pursuing the latter objectives strive to reduce the *public's* awareness of these reforms. There are numerous ways that tax cuts for elites or tax increases affecting the broader public can be designed to achieve that goal (Hacker and Pierson 2005, Wilensky 2002, Steinmo 1993). In contrast, policymakers seeking to raise revenue in highly unequal societies face the far greater challenge of reducing *economic elites'* awareness of tax increases.

approaching, so that citizens are more likely to remember politicians' policy positions when they cast their votes (Jacobs and Shapiro 2000, Gilens 2012). In these circumstances, politicians may prioritize attracting voters over responding to pressure from economic elites. However, the nature of political competition and voter-party linkages conditions the effectiveness of legitimating appeals. Strong partisan identities, cross-cutting voter preferences, clientelism, and charismatic linkages provide ample opportunities for politicians to win votes even if their policy positions deviate from median-voter preferences.[78] For these reasons, strategies that cultivate public support influence tax politics only at the margins when economic elites enjoy strong instrumental power.

VERTICAL EQUITY. Vertical equity entails that the rich should bear a larger share of the tax burden – that is, progressive taxation. Reforms that are not only progressive but also highly targeted at elites are especially well suited for vertical equity appeals. By targeting I refer to how exclusively a tax increase affects upper-income sectors as opposed to middle- or lower-income sectors. Increasing the top marginal income tax rate targets elites more than reducing minimum allowances for all income tax payers. Likewise, excise taxes on luxury goods are more elite-targeted than VAT increases, which affect consumers more broadly. While elite-targeted tax increases are inherently progressive, not all progressive tax increases are elite-targeted.

Vertical equity appeals are more effective when tax increases narrowly target elites. In highly unequal societies, the top income decile includes individuals who can be construed as "middle class," usually professionals who are not manifestly rich according to cultural norms or international comparison. Economic elites and their political allies often frame tax increases as affecting the "middle class" to justify opposition. Such assertions are harder to sustain the more elite-targeted the reform.

However, economic elites may be able to shape public opinion to their own ends by invoking principles other than vertical equity. For example, proponents of estate tax repeal in the United States secured support from ordinary citizens by framing the tax as a "death tax," connoting moral inappropriateness, rather than a tax on extraordinary wealth (Graetz and Shapiro 2005).[79]

Further, while vertical equity appeals can mobilize public support, they pose the potential drawback of provoking intense elite opposition. Although targeting and visibility need not covary, elite-targeted taxes are often highly visible and may thus exacerbate elite antagonism.[80]

---

[78] See, for example, Campbell et al. 1960, Roemer 1999, Luna 2014.

[79] See Chapter 7 on agroexport taxes for similar dynamics. Soy producers framed their opposition as a struggle for provincial rights to counter the central government's portrayal of the taxes as a redistributive tool.

[80] Bolivia's proposed wealth tax illustrates this dynamic (Chapter 8).

HORIZONTAL EQUITY. This principle implies that taxpayers of similar economic means should bear similar tax burdens, regardless of their income sources. Examples of reforms that improve horizontal equity include eliminating sector-specific corporate tax benefits and broadening personal income tax bases to include nonwage income. Anti-evasion reforms also improve horizontal equity by ensuring that all taxpayers pay their due burden.

Because many reforms that enhance horizontal equity also enhance vertical equity, appeals to both principles can often be used simultaneously. Further, in situations where vertical equity appeals might antagonize economic elites, horizontal equity appeals may be used to promote redistributive reforms instead (Ascher 1989: 419). Anti-evasion measures are a prominent example of reforms that facilitate both types of appeals. Middle or lower-income sectors have little opportunity for income tax evasion since taxes are withheld directly from their wages, whereas upper-income sectors receive substantial nonwage income and can under-declare those earnings on tax returns. Similarly, eliminating exemptions for sources of income accruing disproportionately to the wealthy, including rents, interest, and capital gains, enhances both horizontal and vertical equity.

In addition to mobilizing popular support, horizontal equity appeals can temper elite antagonism. By definition, reforms that improve horizontal equity affect some sectors but not others and may hence avoid provoking broad elite opposition. Moreover, horizontal equity appeals are one of the few strategies that can generate support from economic elites. Anti-evasion reforms involving corporate taxes often elicit support from law-abiding firms, which view tax evasion as unfair competition. Eliminating sectoral tax benefits can generate support from sectors that do not receive such privileges. However, where business is highly cohesive, support for eliminating sector-specific benefits tends to be passive at best (Chapter 4). Moreover, eliminating sectoral exemptions generally provokes intense opposition from those affected (Ascher 1984: 465, Olson 1965).

NATIONALISM. Nationalist appeals are highly relevant for taxing extractive resources, since they are widely viewed as national patrimony and mining firms are often foreign-owned. Many developing countries have well-known histories of exploitation by foreign powers and/or companies engaged in resource extraction.[81] Mineral-resource nationalization in Latin America was extremely popular across wide ideological spectrums. The Chilean Congress, for example, unanimously approved copper nationalization in 1971. Evoking historical experiences of exploitation and national patrimony can mobilize nationalistic enthusiasm for taxing extractive resources. Proponents of such reforms need

---

[81] See for example Gamarra and Malloy 1995 on Bolivia.

only decry that foreign companies are stealing the wealth belonging to the nations' citizens.

Nationalist appeals are among the most effective legitimating appeals. Foreign firms may be more easily identifiable as a distinct group and more easily portrayed as exploitative than domestic elites.[82] Nationalist appeals can also be used to mobilize public support for taxing foreign firms operating in other economic sectors. However, histories of mineral exploitation and dependency help generate more intense support for taxing extractive resources, and in some cases widespread popular mobilization to that end.

Benefit-Side Strategies

Benefit-side strategies aim to shift attention away from tax increases. With a few exceptions, benefit-side strategies explicitly invoke or tacitly rely on the neoliberal imperative of fiscal discipline to draw connections between taxation and benefits. I classify these strategies according to who receives the benefits: popular sectors (linking to popular benefits), economic elites (compensation), or members of both groups (linking to universal benefits).

Linking to Popular Benefits
Welfare-state literature advocates linking to popular benefits as a way to minimize public opposition against broad-based taxes (Steinmo 1993, Wilensky 2002); I focus on this strategy's potential to mobilize public support for elite-targeted taxes.[83] The logic is similar to tax-side legitimacy appeals. Whereas the latter strategies emphasize a tax increase's inherent legitimacy, linking invokes legitimacy derived from the benefits the tax increase will finance. A prominent example is social spending, which often does not benefit economic elites in developing countries due to means testing and/or elite preferences for private services. Linking strategies allow governments to blame legislators who oppose reform for blocking popular benefits. Linking can also create political payoffs for legislators who support reform by letting them share credit for popular programs.[84]

Occasionally, linking to popular benefits can directly mitigate elite resistance. When redistributive demands are strong and/or popular sectors are highly mobilized, economic elites may agree to accept higher taxation to fund

---

[82] Moreover, to the extent that taxes on extractive resources affect primarily foreign or multinational companies, they may provoke less opposition from domestic business (Dunning 2008). However, the stronger the economic, organizational, or informal linkages between local elites and foreign firms in extractive sectors, the more the former will oppose these taxes (see Chapter 4 on copper taxation in Chile).

[83] In this context, linking to popular benefits does not entail a "fiscal contract" scenario, since benefits are not destined to elite taxpayers.

[84] See Boylan (1996) on Chile's 1990 reform.

social spending in order to promote social peace and preserve the political or economic status quo.[85] In such cases, linking to popular benefits becomes analogous to emphasizing stabilization (discussed below).

Linking can be achieved through discourse and/or reform design. Discourse alone is the weakest approach. Several techniques make links between taxation and benefits more evident and more credible. First, popular benefits and tax increases can be included within a single reform package so that they are debated simultaneously. Second, if the executive has exclusive initiative on fiscal policy, as in Chile, benefits can be made contingent on tax increases: a reform can be designed such that rejecting the tax increase automatically prevents spending measures from taking effect. Third, tax revenue can be formally earmarked.

Linking strategies can be more effective than tax-side legitimating appeals for pressuring legislators to approve tax increases. First, popular benefits like social spending will inherently draw greater attention and be perceived as more important by the public than elite-targeted tax reforms, which in and of themselves do not directly affect citizens at large.[86] For this reason, politicians often compete for votes by expanding social policy,[87] but partisan outbidding to tax elites is less common. Second, to exert electoral control over politicians, voters must perceive negative outcomes, associate them with policy decisions, and identify who is to blame (Arnold 1990, Hacker and Pierson 2005). Tight linking to spending through reform design helps voters make these connections by raising awareness of the negative consequences of failing to tax elites and helping voters associate those negative consequences with failed reform.

Linking to Universal Benefits: Emphasizing Stabilization

These strategies temper elite antagonism by emphasizing public goods that appeal to elites, such as national security or prestige,[88] sociopolitical stability, or economic stability. While these strategies may also generate public support for taxing elites, their role in tempering elite antagonism is particularly important. I focus on economic stabilization, which has been critical in developing countries and is now salient in many developed democracies as well.

Emphasizing stabilization aims to convince elites that impending economic crisis is more costly than higher taxes. The observation that economic

---

[85] See Chapters 3 and 9 on business acceptance of Chile's 1990 and 2011 tax increases. See Lieberman (2003) on South African elites' acceptance of taxation to resolve the "poor white problem" under apartheid.

[86] Hirschman (1973: 267, 217) draws similar conclusions regarding land taxes. Likewise, U.S. public opinion on taxes paid by the wealthy is described as "low intensity" (Graetz and Shapiro 2005: 254) or "remarkably superficial" (Bartels 2008: 176).

[87] E.g. Weyland (2006: 166–67), Garay (2014).

[88] Emphasizing national security helped South African governments secure elite cooperation to finance wars (Lieberman 2003: 140–48). In postcommunist countries, appealing to national prestige facilitated tax reforms required for EU membership (Appel 2011); a similar logic facilitated modest banking-secrecy reforms in Chile required for OECD membership (Chapter 6).

crisis – especially hyperinflation – disposes elites to tolerate costs associated with taxation or market reforms more generally is common in structural adjustment literature (Acuña 1994, Kingstone 1999, Weyland 2002).

Various conditions must hold for emphasizing stabilization to succeed. First, elites must perceive instability as imminent. A history of crises may increase receptiveness to warnings that economic instability will ensue if fiscal discipline is neglected. Second, elites must perceive instability as costly; fiscal indiscipline may threaten to undermine economic models or governments that economic elites support. If elites do not feel vulnerable, they have little reason to accept a tax increase. Elites may have options for minimizing the costs of instability, including moving assets offshore to protect their value; likewise, some sectors can endure inflation because of the nature of their assets. Third, elites must be convinced that fiscal discipline cannot be achieved without increasing taxes. Privatization, austerity, reducing state corruption, and international loans or aid must not be perceived as feasible short-term options.

In addition to reducing domestic elites' instrumental resistance to tax increases, emphasizing stabilization may circumvent concerns over their structural power. If tax increases build foreign investors' (creditors') confidence in government solvency and economic stability,[89] any negative reactions from domestic investors may be offset by additional foreign investment (loans).[90]

Compensation

These strategies provide benefits for economic elites ranging from subsidies to reforms they favor in other policy areas. Compensation is a central idea in fiscal-bargaining and market-reform literatures. Fiscal-bargaining research highlights "contracts" in which privileged groups accept tax obligations in exchange for "side payments," including services or participation in government (Levi 1988: 64, Bates and Lien 1985, Timmons 2005). Market-reform literature illustrates that compensation can effectively mitigate elite opposition to reforms in policy areas including trade liberalization and privatization (Corrales 1998, Schamis 1999, Shleifer and Treisman 2000, Etchemendy 2011).[91]

The type and scope of compensations needed to temper elite antagonism depend on their sources of power.[92] If economic elites are organized and cohesive, inclusive compensations may be necessary; if they are fragmented, compensating a few key groups may suffice. Generally, the stronger and more numerous the sources of instrumental power, the more significant compensations must be. Earmarking or contingency techniques can formalize the bargain and increase leverage for securing cooperation from politicians who have strong relationships with economic elites.

---

[89] See Mahon (2004: 26) on international bondholders' interest in strong tax systems.
[90] Argentina's transactions tax is an example (Chapter 6).
[91] See Pierson (1994) on compensation to facilitate welfare retrenchment.
[92] Levi (1988: 64) makes similar observations.

Compensation can also circumvent structural power. If a tax increase is accompanied by or linked to pro-growth measures, it is less likely to provoke disinvestment or capital flight. Taxes are one of many policies affecting profits, and favorable policies in other areas may offset the costs of higher taxation (Gelleny and McCoy 2001, Hacker and Pierson 2002).

2.5 POPULAR MOBILIZATION: COUNTERACTING (OR REINFORCING) ELITES' POWER

While economic elites are the central societal actors analyzed in the following chapters, popular-sectors – including labor unions, indigenous movements, student associations, and other organized social actors – can influence tax policy decisions when they are highly mobilized and capable of staging large-scale, sustained protest. Mobilized popular sectors may influence tax policy in various ways. First, their demands may create revenue needs, which can place tax increases on policymakers' agenda. For example, governments may be pressured to expand social spending programs or provide other benefits that existing resources cannot support.[93] Second, mobilized popular sectors may reject tax increases affecting their own members. Where popular sectors are highly mobilized, broad-based or regressive tax increases may be politically infeasible, just as elite-targeted tax increases may be infeasible where economic elites have strong sources of power. Third, on rare occasion, popular sectors may actively demand that elites be taxed more heavily, in accord with redistributive agendas.

Especially in the second two cases, popular mobilization may counterbalance the power of economic elites. Policymakers who would otherwise respond to business interests experience countervailing pressures to take popular demands into account for the sake of restoring order or even surviving in power. With regard to taxation, policymakers facing revenue needs may be compelled to rule out alternatives to direct tax increases when they might otherwise cater to business preferences for consumption tax increases. And economic elites may make strategic decisions to accept tax increases on their income and wealth to preserve social peace and preclude destabilizing confrontation with popular sectors that could much more seriously undermine their interests. Elites may also strategically acquiesce to tax increases if they anticipate that popular sectors will likely prevail in the ensuing battle of interests. Lieberman (2003) and Slater (2010), among other authors, note the importance of threats from below for compelling economic elites to consent to direct taxation.[94] Note that in my framework, popular mobilization does not reduce the power of economic elites; the latter's sources of power remain

---

[93] This dynamic arose in Chile in 2011 due to student protests (Chapter 9).
[94] See also Winters (2011: 227) on the populist movement and the creation of the U.S. income tax, Hacker and Pierson (2002: 298), and Schneider (2012: 69).

unaltered and may well be significant.[95] However, the countervailing effects of popular mobilization make it less likely that economic elites' sources of power will serve to secure their preferred policies.

Compared to electoral incentives operating during periods of normal democratic politics – which underpin the strategies for mobilizing public support discussed in the previous section – sustained popular mobilization to demand progressive taxation can have a much more substantial impact on policy decisions,[96] as demonstrated in Chapters 8 and 9. Yet this phenomenon is also rare, likely for similar reasons that taxing economic elites does not necessarily draw concerted attention or strong support from lower-income voters: clear links must be drawn between higher taxation of elites and concrete, visible benefits for lower-income groups and/or compelling norms of fairness. Natural resource taxation is more conducive to mobilization, given the emotive potential and nationalist sentiments at play.[97]

Instead of counterbalancing economic elites, however, it is also possible for mobilized popular sectors to act as circumstantial elite allies. By pursuing their own (perceived) interests, popular sectors may inadvertently advance elite interests as well. The empirical chapters include several such cases. In the first two cases, tax structures aligned the interests of lower-income sectors with economic elites. Labor unions demanded a reform that also benefitted elite taxpayers (Argentina's 2008 income tax reform, Chapter 5), and small farmers mobilized against a reform that also heavily taxed large, wealthy farmers (Argentina's 2008 export tax increase, Chapter 7). In the third case, popular sectors' misperceptions regarding tax incidence led them to oppose reform alongside economic elites (Bolivia's 2003 income tax proposal, Chapter 7).

2.6 CONCLUSION

The concepts of instrumental power and structural power are hardly new. Yet they have not been employed as complementary causal variables for explaining policy change in comparative cross-national research. Literature on business in comparative politics has instead tended to focus on interests, coalitions, and observable actions, without sufficient attention to when and why business preferences prevail in policy decisions. But before we can harness the significant explanatory leverage that instrumental power and structural power provide, these concepts must be theoretically refined and carefully operationalized so that they can be systematically assessed across different contexts.

The primary contributions of this chapter lie in these endeavors. First, drawing on insights from power resource theory, I identify observable sources of

---

[95] As Korpi (1985: 33) observes: "From the power resource perspective, power is not a zero-sum concept."

[96] Similar dynamics obtain with respect to social policy (Garay 2014).

[97] Examples beyond the Latin American cases considered here include strikes in Zambia demanding higher copper mining taxation (Manley 2012).

instrumental power that make deliberate political actions like lobbying more effective. I introduce the categories of relationships with policymakers (e.g., partisan linkages and recruitment into government) and resources (e.g., cohesion, technical expertise) to systematize these sources of instrumental power. Second, I operationalize structural power as a credible and economically significant threat that a policy will provoke reduced investment or other undesirable aggregate economic outcomes because of the market incentives it creates for profit-maximizing firms and investors. Recognizing the highly variable, context-specific nature of structural power is imperative for putting this concept to work. Third, I theorize two key ways in which instrumental and structural power can be not only complementary, in that they afford multiple channels of influence, but also mutually reinforcing. On the one hand, instrumental power can enhance structural power; lobbying and communication campaigns by economic elites with strong sources of instrumental power can persuade policymakers that the likelihood of disinvestment is higher than they might otherwise anticipate. On the other hand, structural power may augment instrumental power, by affording economic elites access and participation beyond what would be expected based on their sources of instrumental power alone, or by inducing policymakers to grant economic elites new sources of instrumental power (e.g., recruitment into government).

This chapter also clarifies that both instrumental power and structural power can operate at multiple stages of policymaking, including the critical agenda-formulation stage. Studying agenda setting requires attention to anticipated reactions, whether in the political arena (instrumental power) or in the economic arena (structural power). Distinguishing sources of instrumental power from political actions helps clarify that instrumental power can restrict the agenda, an important point that is often overlooked in literature on business power. Costly anticipated political battles can dissuade policymakers from attempting a reform, just as costly anticipated disinvestment may motivate policymakers to rule out other options. While it is not easy to assess from afar whether instrumental power or structural power is the key factor keeping a reform off the agenda, interviews with policymakers who made the key decisions provide a wealth of evidence to this end. Evaluating whether informants have motives to dissimulate (Bennett and Checkel 2014) and whether their retrospective views reflect considerations other than those that prevailed at the time (Hacker and Pierson 2002) is essential. Yet these problems are not insurmountable; triangulation among multiple informants and other sources of data helps protect against erroneous inferences.

The business power concepts as elaborated in this chapter help to both elucidate and systematize the casual complexity that arises when we seek to understand how and when economic elites succeed at influencing policy decisions in market democracies. Some authors have found that a single type of power or a single source of instrumental power provides adequate explanatory traction across their cases for the substantive issues they examine. But analyzing tax policy change in Latin America requires attention to multiple types and sources of power. Multiple causal pathways may contribute to an outcome in a given case, and different causal pathways may lead to similar outcomes across cases. Ascertaining which pathways operate – that is, distinguishing between structural and instrumental power and identifying the relevant sources of instrumental power – is critical to the explanatory enterprise. Economic elites have distinct power profiles in different contexts. The more types and sources of power they possess, the more often and more extensively their interests will prevail in policymaking.

While instrumental and structural power serve as the primary independent variables in this study, integrating business power into a broader theoretical framework that also examines government reform strategies and popular mobilization provides additional explanatory leverage across a broader range of cases. Governments can circumvent obstacles associated with business power by employing strategies that mobilize public support and/or temper elite antagonism, although the tax increases these strategies facilitate tend to be marginal when economic elites' instrumental and/or structural power is strong. Popular mobilization, when it arises on a significant scale, can improve prospects for reform by counterbalancing the power of economic elites and/or altering their strategic calculations, although on rare occasions popular mobilization may inadvertently advance elite interests.

The following two chapters apply this theoretical framework to analyze the challenge of increasing progressive direct taxes in Chile. Chapter 3 showcases the causal role of business power; business actors in Chile had multiple, highly institutionalized sources of instrumental power that greatly restricted center-left governments' tax policy agendas. Chapter 4 brings reform strategies into the analysis to explain how governments were able to enact incremental tax increases in this context of strong business power. Recourse to multiple reform strategies was necessary, yet revenue gains were marginal.

3

Organized Business and Direct Taxation in Chile

Restricting the Agenda

If you compare the tax structure of Chile with the U.S. or others, you will see that the proportion of indirect taxes – taxes on consumption – over the total tax burden is VERY high, and the proportion of direct taxes to ones that are more proportional to the level of wealth are very, very low. And that is because of a political problem.

— Former finance minister Eyzaguirre (interview, 2005)

In the extraordinary context of Chile's 1990 transition to democracy, the newly elected center-left Concertación coalition increased the very low corporate tax from 10 percent to 15 percent and made individual income tax brackets slightly more progressive. However, subsequent direct tax increases were marginal (Table 3.1). After twenty years of center-left rule, Chile's corporate tax rate remained one of the region's lowest at 17 percent (Table 3.2). Personal income tax brackets were later flattened, and reforms to close loopholes and fight evasion focused on indirect taxes rather than direct taxes. Consequently, direct tax collections held essentially constant at an average of 4.2 percent of GDP from 1993 to 2004 (Figure 3.1). Although widely cited research characterizes Chile as a progressive tax reform success story based on the 1990 reform (Weyland 1997), as of 2014 increasing direct taxation remained a pending goal of critical importance for building tax capacity and improving tax equity.[1]

The Lagos administration (2000–05) is a key period for analysis given the government's commitment to expanding social spending while maintaining fiscal discipline. Despite impressive poverty reduction in the 1990s, 20 percent of Chileans lived below the poverty line in 2000 (Cepal 2006: 74), and many of those who had risen above poverty remained in precarious economic conditions. And while poverty in Chile was low by Latin American standards, it

---

[1] Bachelet's April 2014 tax initiative was a major step in this direction (Chapter 9).

TABLE 3.1. *Expected Revenue Yield (% GDP), Direct Tax Reforms in Chile*

Aylwin	1990	CT and PIT increases	1.3
	1993	PIT cuts	−0.2
Frei	1998	Anti-evasion reform	0.1
Lagos	2001	Anti-evasion reform	0.04
	2001	CT increase / PIT cuts	0
	2001	Capital gains	−0.03
	2005	Eliminated tax benefit (57 bis)	0.02
Bachelet	2008	CT investment credit	−0.02
	2008	CT investment credit	−0.01

Source: Author's calculations using Finance Ministry estimates provided to Congress.

TABLE 3.2. *Corporate Tax Rates, Latin America*

	2000	2009
Maximum	37% (Brazil)	35% (Argentina)
Minimum	15% (Chile)	10% (Paraguay)
Chile	15%	17% (second lowest)
Regional Average	30%	28%

Note: Effective corporate tax rates are unavailable.

Source: KPMG's Corporate and Indirect Tax Survey 2009, www.kpmg.com/cn/en/issuesandinsights/articlespublications/pages/corporate-indirect-tax-survey-0-200910.aspx

remained high compared to developed countries (OECD 2012).[2] During the presidential campaign, Lagos outlined an ambitious social spending agenda to fight extreme poverty and improve access to education, health care, and other essential services. However, the government was not willing to increase spending without ensuring sustainable financing. The Concertación's ironclad commitment to fiscal discipline developed out of lessons taken from Allende's ill-fated economic policies and the ensuing coup and dictatorship. Prominent Concertación "technopols" blamed past economic crises and political turmoil on populist spending cycles and fiscal indiscipline.

Top leaders in the Lagos administration felt that general tax revenue and corporate taxation were too low. The former president and finance minister lamented that prevailing revenue levels could not support sufficient social spending: "There is a relation between a country's tax burden and the social benefits that country provides. And 18% [of GDP] for a country the size of Chile is very little….I think that there is going to have to be a serious debate

[2] OECD (2012) recommendations for Chile included more progressive taxes and higher transfers.

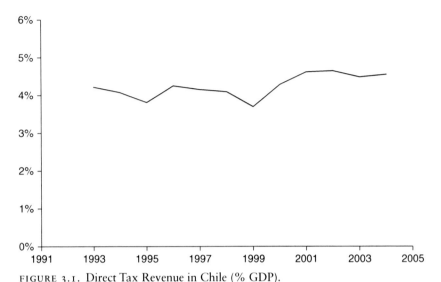

FIGURE 3.1. Direct Tax Revenue in Chile (% GDP).
Source: SII (2009); constructed with help from Michel Jorratt. Copper prices exogenously augmented tax revenue after 2004.

on the issue of taxation in Chile" (Lagos 2006, interview). Contrary to portrayals of Concertación Finance Ministry technocrats as inherently averse to tax increases and seeking above all to contain fiscal costs (Teichman 2009, Pribble 2013), Finance Minister Eyzaguirre (2007, interview) agreed with Lagos's assessment: "You will not find any country in the world with [similar] per capita income … with a lower tax burden. We are [in a] corner. It is *obvious* that we have to increase … public goods, including education, research and development, social protection." Eyzaguirre emphasized Chile's low direct tax revenue and asserted that corporate taxation should be much higher.[3] However, the government increased the corporate tax to only 17 percent, still short of the Concertación's modest original target of 20 percent for the 1990 reform, and progress on closing loopholes and curtailing direct tax exemptions was marginal. Why did the administration not pursue more significant direct tax increases to finance its social agenda?

---

[3] Similarly, twelve of the nineteen Lagos-era Concertación legislators I interviewed, including Foxley (2006), felt that corporate taxation was too low. An additional six legislators, including Boeninger (2005), were less concerned with the level of direct tax revenue but agreed that corporate taxation could be increased. Almost all felt the income tax system should be made more progressive by shifting the burden from wage earners and professionals to business and capital owners, although views differed on how to do so and to what extent. See also Lorenzini et al. (2006: 28). Some Concertación legislators held more conservative view on taxation; however, Eyzaguirre (interview 2007) recounted that there was consensus within the coalition on increasing the corporate tax at the outset of Lagos's term. Eyzaguirre (interview 2007) openly acknowledged that internal disagreements arose on other tax issues (Chapter 4).

This chapter argues that business's strong instrumental power kept all but marginal direct tax increases off the agenda in Chile. Section 3.1 explains why the integrated structure of Chile's income tax made increasing the corporate tax particularly relevant for improving tax capacity and equity. Section 3.2 argues that structural power cannot explain why significant corporate tax reform remained off the agenda throughout the Lagos administration; top policymakers did not believe that increasing the corporate tax would harm investment. Section 3.3 identifies the three main sources of business's strong and persistent instrumental power and explains the mechanisms through which these sources of power restricted the government's tax agenda. Partisan linkages helped block reforms in congress, and cohesion facilitated business mobilization against tax increases. Meanwhile, an informally institutionalized pattern of government-business concertation on economic policy created incentives for governments to avoid conflict with business on taxation. Section 3.4 illustrates these points by examining a case of marginal corporate tax reform in 2001, as well as episodes of corporate tax non-reform from 2000 to 2005.

Section 3.5 turns to the Bachelet administration (2006–10). Business's instrumental power and augmented structural power, along with record fiscal surpluses from skyrocketing copper prices, ensured that corporate tax reform would remain off the agenda. Finally, Section 3.6 revisits the 1990 reform, which I argue is best understood as an exceptional business-right concession in the extraordinary context of the democratic transition.

3.1 THE RATIONALE FOR INCREASING THE CORPORATE TAX

The Concertación inherited a unique integrated income-tax system from the Pinochet dictatorship. The corporate tax (CT) served as a withholding against (i.e., an advance payment on) personal income taxes (PIT) that business owners were required to pay upon receiving distributed profits. Profits reinvested in the firm paid only the low CT (17 percent from 2004 to 2010). But dividends entered the comprehensive PIT base, where they were subject to progressive marginal rates reaching 40 percent. To preclude "double taxation," corporate taxes already collected on profits at the firm level were credited against personal income taxes owed when those profits were distributed. Pinochet created this income tax system to encourage investment after the 1982 economic crisis. Because the gap between the CT and the PIT was so large, capital owners left the majority of their profits in the firm, where they paid the much lower tax rate. On average, firms retained 67 percent of their profits (Jorratt 2013: 81). By 2012, retained profits recorded in businesses' FUT (*Fondo de Utilidades Tributables*) ledgers, which keep track of owners' pending PIT tax credits, were equivalent to Chile's GDP.

However, the large gap between the CT and the PIT stimulated widespread tax avoidance. Capital owners found many ways to consume profits through the firm without formally withdrawing dividends and hence without paying the corresponding PIT. For example, goods destined for personal use could be registered to the firm or purchased on a company account. Moreover, many such purchases could be deducted from corporate taxes as costs necessary for production. Meanwhile, independent professionals avoided taxes by creating "investment companies," thereby transforming income that would otherwise pay the high PIT rates into corporate income taxed at only 17 percent. Essentially no regulations existed to prevent the formation of companies for the sole purpose of avoiding taxes. Accordingly, investment companies held more than 50 percent of Chile's retained profits (Jorratt 2009: 58).

Chile's income tax also created strong incentives for evasion; in 2005, only 35 percent of distributed profits were declared to the tax agency (Fairfield and Jorratt 2014). The tax agency was ill equipped to control this extensive evasion because the vast majority of businesses were organized as partnerships and close corporations rather than as publicly traded corporations. The small number of publicly traded corporations (0.05 percent of Chilean firms) are overseen by the *Superintendencia de Valores* (Securities Superintendency) and are subject to independent auditing, which minimizes possibilities for evasion. For partnerships and close corporations, the only way the tax agency could verify whether distributed profits were fully declared was to audit on a firm-by-firm basis. Moreover, the tax agency lacked automatic access to bank information on taxpayers' checking accounts, which would make it much easier to detect undeclared income on tax returns (see Chapter 6).

Capital owners and independent professionals, who have the opportunity to avoid or evade income taxes, tend to be much wealthier than dependent workers, whose taxes are automatically withheld from wages. In 2005, the ratio of profits to all other forms of income exceeded unity only for taxpayers in the top 1 percent. Accordingly, average effective income tax rates paid by the wealthiest Chileans were very low (Table 3.3).

Not only do wealthy Chileans pay low effective income taxes, but the tax base they control is large. The top 1 percent received 28 percent of all income reported to the tax agency in 2005 – fully 13 percent of GDP. But that top 1 percent paid an average effective income tax rate of just 15 percent; the top 0.1 percent received 6 percent of reported income but paid only a slightly higher rate (17 percent). By comparison, in the United States in 2004, the top 1 percent paid an average effective rate of 24 percent in federal income taxes alone; the top 0.1 percent paid 29 percent (Piketty and Saez 2006: 51).[4]

Various reforms could increase taxation of these highly concentrated income and profits. One possibility was closing loopholes that facilitated PIT

---

[4] Figures include corporate and individual income tax. For methodological notes on this comparison, see Fairfield and Jorratt (2014).

TABLE 3.3. *Reported Income[a] and Average Tax Rates, Chile 2005*

Cumulative Percentile[b]	Share of Total Reported Income (%)	Reported Income (% GDP)	Ratio of Profits to Other Income	Ratio of Profits + Independent Professional Income to Wage Income	Average Tax Rate[c] (%)
Top 10%	67	30	0.4	0.7	8.1
Top 5%	52	24	0.6	0.9	10
Top 1%	28	13	1.3	1.8	15
Top 0.1%	13	5.8	5.2	6.8	17
Top 0.01%	6.4	2.9	21	39	16

[a] Includes accrued profits imputed to business owners instead of distributed profits. See Fairfield and Jorratt (2014).
[b] Individuals over age 20.
[c] Taxes paid (corporate plus individual income taxes) divided by reported income with accrued profits.
Source: Author's calculations based on Fairfield and Jorratt (2014).

avoidance involving consumption through the firm.[5] Another option entailed imposing restrictions on the formation of investment companies. Increasing the corporate tax rate was a third option. Concertación governments considered all of these alternatives.

High-level policymakers in the Lagos administration and tax agency officials identified raising the corporate tax as the simplest and most effective way to increase taxation of under-tapped income and profits (interviews: Eyzaguirre 2007, Etcheberry 2005). In their view, as long as the gap between the corporate and personal income taxes remained large, taxpayers would have strong incentives to avoid or evade the personal income tax, and the tax agency would struggle to outwit private-sector tax consultants (Eyzaguirre 2007, interview).

3.2 BUSINESS'S WEAK STRUCTURAL POWER

Business's structural power with respect to corporate taxation was weak during Lagos's tenure: top policymakers did not anticipate that increasing corporate taxation would harm investment (interviews: Eyzaguirre 2007, Etcheberry 2005). According to the former finance minister, "The argument that you favor investment if the personal tax rate is way above the corporate tax rate is fallacious" (Eyzaguirre 2007, interview). In his analysis, instead of promoting investment in productive assets, the low corporate tax rate merely facilitated tax avoidance and evasion. "Set the corporate tax at the highest personal

[5] Prominent Socialist technocrat Marfán preferred this approach.

income tax rate," he advocated. "If not you are giving the choice of whether to pay 17 percent or 40 percent. Imagine what avenue they are going to choose." The finance minister viewed business's complaints that raising corporate taxation – by either increasing the tax rate or closing loopholes – would discourage investment as noncredible threats: "They were trying to argue that the economy was going to stop, that investment was going to stall, that ... small and medium enterprises were going to collapse.... My team was a very serious team, in terms of knowledge of sound economic theory – the arguments were nonsense." The finance minister did harbor concerns that increasing direct taxes could have had a negative economic impact during Lagos's first years in office, when the Chilean economy was suffering an East Asian crisis-related recession. But such concerns were not relevant in subsequent years; the economy soon recovered, and growth reached 6 percent in 2004.[6]

Record growth and investment following the 1990 corporate tax increase supported Finance Minister Eyzaguirre's position. President Aylwin's finance minister, Foxley (2006, interview), recounted: "[Business] threatened me that the day after the reform was approved, they would stop investing, period. The next year and the year after, there was record private investment." Although Chilean businesspeople clearly disliked paying taxes, their threats proved idle; investment behavior was not highly sensitive to tax rates. Some businesspeople even admitted that a corporate tax of 20 percent would have no impact on the economy (interviews: ABIF 2006, CChC-C 2005, Finance Ministry-B 2005). An influential business leader who had actively opposed tax increases even offered the following retrospective assessment of the two-point 2001 corporate tax increase: "It has been perfectly manageable ... in the end, it improved business productivity" (CPC-A 2005, interview).

Turning to foreign investors, international tax competition arguments are of limited relevance given the integrated income tax. The 35 percent withholding tax on repatriated profits (the analog of the 40 percent PIT for Chilean citizens), not the 17 percent corporate tax, was most relevant for foreign investors.[7] The low corporate tax on retained profits let investors partially defer payment of the withholding tax. While this tax deferral may have made Chile more desirable for foreign investors all else equal, increasing the corporate tax rate would not change their overall tax burden, aside from differences in the present and future value of tax payments. Further, Chile proved highly attractive in other dimensions including fiscal, monetary, and regulatory policy; Chile ranked within the top thirteen countries on

---

[6] Some Concertación economists did believe a corporate tax rate above 20% could deter investment (interviews: Marfán 2005, Foxley 2006). However, there was broad consensus within the coalition that a rate of 20 percent would have a negligible economic impact.

[7] Forbes uses Chile's 35 percent withholding tax in its "Capital Hospitability" rankings. *El Mercurio*, April 5, 2007.

the Heritage Foundation's Economic Freedom Index from 1997 to 2007. As Gelleny and McCoy (2001) argue, favorable policies in other areas offset the costs of higher taxation.

3.3 BUSINESS'S STRONG INSTRUMENTAL POWER

Although structural power was generally weak, business's strong instrumental power created major political obstacles to corporate tax reform. Instrumental power arose from three main sources: cohesion, partisan linkages, and government-business concertation. These multiple, highly institutionalized sources of power helped business influence not only the fate of reform proposals but also the scope of the government's reform agenda. Whereas earlier research emphasized business's ability to win modifications to the text of reform proposals (Silva 1996, 1998), I find that business's influence over the agenda was much more consequential. For the most part, business did not have to mobilize against corporate tax increases – the mere anticipation of business opposition deterred the Lagos administration from attempting anything but marginal reform.

Cross-Sectoral Cohesion

Business in Chile had remarkable capacity to unite and engage in collective action. Business tended to band together against tax increases, and dissenting opinions on tax issues were rarely voiced publically. Cohesion arose from strong organization as well as antistatist economic ideology.

Chile's encompassing associations are among the strongest in Latin America, thanks to a history of redistributive threats and state incentives for business to organize (Silva 1998; Schneider 2004a). The CPC (*Confederación de Producción y Comercio*), Chile's economy-wide business association, is the oldest in the region. Its directorate is composed of the presidents of Chile's six sectoral peak associations (industry, mining, construction, finance, agriculture, and commerce), which have substantial resources and membership. The CPC is highly respected within the business community. According to a former CPC president, "the CPC has a prestige that is almost unconditional, I would dare say, within the business sector" (CPC-A 2005, interview).

The CPC's strength derived from its ability to coordinate lobbying on issues of common concern and to forge consensus across sectors (Schneider 2004a: 171). The former CPC president recounted: "Businesspeople in Chile are absolutely united. We may dispute thousands of things, but when it comes to taking action in complex situations, business has a single voice. And it has been that way as long as the CPC has existed" (CPC-A 2005, interview). The CPC coordinated opposition to Frei Montalva's reformist government in the 1960s, which sought to implement land reform, and Allende's socialist government in the 1970s, which pursued radical redistribution and nationalization (Schneider

2004a: 162–63). Along with the industrial association, SOFOFA (*Sociedad de Fomento Fabril*), the CPC led business resistance to Allende and helped bring Pinochet to power (Silva 1996). Pinochet marginalized organized business while implementing radical economic restructuring, but the 1982 economic crisis and ensuing wave of protest compelled him to negotiate with business associations (Silva 1996). Thereafter, the CPC reassumed its role as the main interlocutor between executive-branch policymakers and business (Silva 1997).

Although the CPC's importance relative to the sectoral peak associations (especially SOFOFA) varied over time (Silva 1998: 220, Schneider 2004a), the CPC remained a key interlocutor between government and business following the democratic transition. The CPC had more immediate access to high-level government officials than the sectoral associations and was very active on tax issues (CChC-A 2005, interview). When asked about the relative importance of CPC efforts to defend business interests compared to the sectoral associations in the case of the 2001 Anti-Evasion Reform, the CPC's former general manager replied:

> I think it was very important, because we gathered opinions from all the sectors.... We represented a more consolidated opposition because we listened to and represented all [sectors]. If there were things that were specific to a sector, it was the respective association that took charge, but with the support of the CPC behind it. (CPC-B 2007, interview)

Sectoral-association informants agreed that the CPC played an important role in legitimating and coordinating opposition to tax increases (2005 interviews: SOFOFA-A, B, SNA-A, CChC-A, C, Mining-B).

In addition to strong organization, antistatist ideology helped unite business across sectors. Business championed the free-market, small-state, low-tax model implemented by Pinochet. The early influence of University of Chicago-trained economists who sought converts within Chile's private sector laid the groundwork for widespread adherence to these views (Valdés 1995). From 1975 to 1982, the "Chicago Boys" played a key role in formulating economic policy, which entailed radical market liberalization (Silva 1996). Pinochet replaced the original Chicago Boys with more pragmatic economists after the 1982 crisis, but the basic elements of the free-market, small-state economic model remained unchanged (Valdés 1995: 269–70, Silva 1996: 173–208). The dominant business groups of the 1990s and 2000s emerged as winners under this economic model and naturally supported the principles upon which it was based. As Silva (1998: 237) observes, "Business leaders were convinced that in democracy their associations must play a highly visible watchdog role in defense of the economic policies of that era. Thus, it was incumbent on the CPC to express unity of purpose where any policy of general interest was concerned."

Business leaders frequently expressed ideological commitments to low taxation. The former CPC president asserted: "Business's principle is that we do not

want the state to grow" (CPC-A 2005, interview). Likewise, a former SOFOFA president explained that business opposed tax increases "on the principle that the state should not increase its participation in the economy. Countries with lower tax burdens grow faster.... The state invests badly, spends badly, it's inefficient," (SOFOFA-C 2005, interview). Business even framed taxation as expropriation and defended tax benefits as "acquired property rights" (CChC-B 2005, interview; CPC 2000: 11). Because of these ideological views, even tax increases that exclusively affected a single sector could stimulate opposition from business as a whole. As a former CPC general manager explained, the association tended to take positions against sectoral tax increases "as a matter of principles" (CPC-B 2007, interview).

Partisan Linkages

Business enjoyed strong linkages to Chile's right parties, *Renovación Nacional* (RN), and especially the *Unión Democrática Independiente* (UDI), which together formed the *Alianza Por Chile* coalition. The core constituency relationship between business and the right is evidenced by programmatic convergence on economic policy. Both parties advocated neoliberal positions and opposed taxation, in accord with business preferences, although roll-call vote analysis shows that the UDI was the most consistent defender of business interests (Luna 2010). As an UDI deputy attested: "We are a party that has never been in favor of increasing taxes" (UDI-A 2005, interview). A former Socialist senator offered a more colorful assessment: "For the Chilean right, the tax system is like the Virgin Mary: you can't touch it. It's absurdly ideological. Every time we make any change, they threaten all hell – that capital will leave, that investment will decrease, that these are populist measures" (Bitar 2007, interview).

The UDI's defense of low taxation was rooted in its economically liberal, antistatist origins. The UDI was founded in 1983 by Chicago-trained economists and technocrats from the dictatorship, in conjunction with leaders of the corporatist *gremialista* movement, which emerged in the 1960s with the goal of eradicating Marxism (Pollack 1999, Garretón 2000). Although the *gremialistas* were originally conservatives rather than economic liberals, they ultimately embraced the free-market principles advocated by the Chicago Boys (Valdés 1995: 201), and the UDI came to represent "those most loyal to the military regime's economic and political model" (Pollack 1999: 89). Informal ties dating back to the dictatorship and shared class interests strengthened the relationship between the UDI and business. Pinochet government technocrats who became UDI members or sympathizers often served on the boards of business groups that benefited from Pinochet's privatizations (Silva 1997, Schamis 1999, Pollack 1999, Etchemendy 2011). Pribble (2013) provides evidence of continued overlap between UDI activists and the business community in the 2000s.

The RN also embraced the dictatorship's neoliberal economic model, although the party's origins were distinct from the UDI's. The RN developed from a heterogeneous amalgamation that included elements of Chile's traditional pre-Pinochet agrarian right and pro-military nationalists, as well as young professionals and businessmen who supported the dictatorship's economic policies but favored democratization (Boylan 1996: 25, Pollack 1999: 91–92, 111–12). Accordingly, the RN tended to be less ideological and less cohesive than the UDI. These characteristics, along with bitter power struggles with the UDI (Pollack 1999), occasionally facilitated limited RN support for Concertación tax proposals. However, tax increases and reforms to the economic model tended to elicit united Alianza opposition. As Garretón (2000: 66) observes: "The defense and preservation of the military regime's socioeconomic model is the strongest common element linking rightist sectors."

The right enjoyed consistent business support in the 1990s and early 2000s. CPC presidents publicly endorsed Alianza presidential candidates, including former Pinochet finance minister Büchi in 1989 and UDI politician Lavín in 1999. Outgoing CPC president Riesco and his successor Ariztía both openly proclaimed their identity as "right-wing businessmen" (and their loyalty to Pinochet) in 2000.[8] Former CPC president Guzmán served as a member of the Alianza's political committee in 2000 and maintained affiliations with UDI and RN think tanks;[9] likewise, former SOFOFA and CPC president Claro joined the UDI think tank's advisory board.[10] Furthermore, limited available evidence indicates that big business disproportionately funded the right and especially UDI (Luna 2010, Posner 2004: 73–74, Pollack 1999: 132). The Alianza's private donations exceeded the Concertación's by a factor of nearly four in 2005 (Luna 2010: 341). Private donations gave the Alianza a significant campaign-spending advantage; by one estimate, Lavín outspent Lagos in 2000 by U.S. $30 million (Angell and Pollack 2000: 364). Anecdotal evidence also suggests that business generously funded right-party think tanks, especially *Libertad y Desarrollo* (LyD) (interviews: CEP 2005, Finance Ministry-G 2007; Pribble 2013). One informant described LyD as the "gear" that "articulated the business world with the political world" (CEP 2005, interview).

As a core constituency, business exerted substantial influence over right-party policy positions. The right often took instruction on tax policy directly from organized business (interviews: Finance Ministry-G 2007, SII-A 2005, Eyzaguirre 2007). This dynamic was particularly apparent regarding tax initiatives affecting the private copper-mining sector. The former finance minister

---

[8] *La Tercera*, Dec. 11, 2000, *El Mercurio*, Dec. 18, 2000.
[9] *El Mercurio*, Nov. 19, 2000.
[10] Business associations often interacted closely with experts from these think tanks (interviews: CPC-C 2005, CPC-E 2012, LyD-B 2012), occasionally sharing technical advisors and recruiting staff from their ranks. The banking association appointed a former *Libertad y Desarrollo* director as its manager in 2012.

referenced these reforms to illustrate what he described as sometimes irrational dependency of the right wing parties on tor" (Eyzaguirre 2007, interview). In the 1990s, business hac vened in right party politics, frequently imposing its prefei (Pollack 1999; UDI-B 2005, interview). Thanks to this behav business association leaders came to be known as the "de f. ⌐ʋwers" (*poderes fácticos*) (Pollack 1999; UDI-B 2005, interview).

The right's strength in the Senate allowed it to effectively represent business interests. Electoral rules and malapportionment that favored the right (Siavelis 2000, 2005)[11] and authoritarian enclaves in the constitution gave the right veto power after the democratic transition and thereby augmented business power. Pinochet appointed nine "institutional" senators in 1990, and he himself assumed a seat for life. The right accordingly held a majority in the Senate from 1990 to 1997, even though the Concertación won the majority of elected seats.

The right's veto power eroded after 1998 when the terms of Pinochet's designated senators ended, and Pinochet's detention in London on charges of human rights violations terminated his Senate career. The constitution authorized the presiding Concertación government to select two new institutional senators to replace those appointed by Pinochet; the Supreme Court and Armed Forces named the rest. The two Supreme Court appointees and one of the Armed Forces appointees held more moderate views than their predecessors on economic issues, as the former Senate president (1998–2004) recalled:

The right always had success with the institutional senators on issues that were sensitive for the military – human rights, that type of thing, but those senators did not have a clear commitment to the right on economic issues. They were people of middle-class origins. There were two or three senators who were open to the Concertación government's position. (Zaldívar 2007, interview)

However, the right retained a strong presence in the senate from 1999 to 2005 (Table 3.4), and despite the three institutional senators' comparatively moderate views, winning their votes on sensitive issues like taxation was a challenge. Strong opposition from business and the right could not only sway these senators against reform but could also occasionally draw senators from the Concertación's more economically liberal wing, including former president Frei, who was himself a successful businessman, away from the government's fold.[12] However, on corporate taxation, executive-branch informants viewed maneuvering reforms past the right and institutional senators as the primary problem. Budget Director Marcel (2006 interview) maintained: "Basically, the reason why there have not been further tax increases since 1990 … more than

---

[11] See Zucco (2007) for a dissenting view on Chile's binomial system.
[12] Business had informal ties to some of the more conservative Concertación legislators, but partisan ties to the right were a more institutionalized and systematic source of power.

TABLE 3.4. *Balance of Power in the Chilean Senate*

Political Block	Senators (48 seats)	
	1998–2002	2002–2005
Center-Left: Concertación	24	23
Socialist Party (PS)	4	5
Party for Democracy (PPD)	2	3
Christian Democratic Party (PDC)[a]	15	12
Concertación-appointed institutional senators	3	3
Right: Alianza	17	18
Independent Democratic Union (UDI)	10[b]	11
National Renovation (RN)	7	7
Institutional Senators	6	6
Supreme Court & Armed Forces appointments		
Independents	1[c]	1

[a] Includes Frei, who occupied an unelected seat as former president beginning in 2000.
[b] Includes UDI-aligned independents and Prat, who resigned from RN in 1998 and officially joined UDI in 2000.
[c] Legal proceedings against right-aligned independent Errazuriz prevented him from participating in Senate votes after 1998.

the risk of affecting investment, is because the Concertación never had the votes to approve tax modifications alone; agreement from the opposition has always been required."

The Concertación's well-documented preference for negotiating broad-based accords rather than pushing reforms through congress by a narrow margin further augmented business power based on partisan linkages. Fishman's (2011: 236) concept of democratic practice, "the ways in which political actors … make use of the rights and possibilities for action provided by democracy and deal with others who are similarly engaged," applies well to this phenomenon. Democratic practice, which is shaped by historical trajectories of macro-political change, often transcends behavioral predictions based on formal institutional incentives. In line with this perspective, Concertación governments placed a premium on consensual politics following the democratic transition; key leaders including Foxley attributed the 1973 coup to the lack of national consensus on Allende's development model (Giraldo 1997), and they reasoned that reforms would secure greater legitimacy and stability if legislated with substantial opposition support (interview: Foxley 2006). Like government-business concertation (discussed in the following section), this practice of pursuing broader consensus than necessary for a minimum winning coalition persisted long past the period when it was arguably important for democratic consolidation.[13]

[13] The Concertación's tendency to underutilize the executive's extensive constitutional prerogatives (Siavelis 2002) is a related aspect of this democratic practice.

Government-Business Concertation

Concertation with business – regular government consultation with the CPC and sectoral associations – provided a third source of business power. While partisan linkages afforded instrumental power in Congress, concertation conferred instrumental power with respect to the executive branch. Other authors have observed that concertation helped business exert influence by providing easy access to top-level policymakers (Silva 1997, Teichman 2001). More importantly, I argue that this informally-institutionalized pattern of government-business relations created incentives for policymakers to avoid conflict with business over the latter's core interests.

During the democratic transition, Concertación governments cultivated business confidence by consulting with the CPC and its member associations on economic reforms, a practice established under Pinochet following the 1982 crisis (Silva 1996). Concertación leaders felt these measures were critical for ensuring investment and growth during a time of uncertainty, given that business openly supported Pinochet throughout the transition. Consultation helped quell business's fears, and investment surged during the 1990s (Silva 1997). Credible threats of disinvestment or a business-backed coup subsided after consolidation of neoliberalism and democracy by the late 1990s. However, consultation on all facets of economic policy and economic governance remained a defining characteristic of government-business relations, even in the absence of the conditions that originally led the coalition to embrace this model.

Concertación governments valued collaboration with business on a wide range of policy areas in part because of excellent macroeconomic outcomes associated with this model.[14] For example, business-government collaboration led to a series of reforms designed to promote growth that were championed by both President Lagos and his successor, Bachelet. The reforms were based on a SOFOFA proposal known as the Pro-Growth Agenda. The executive branch worked closely with SOFOFA while formulating the reforms; the Finance Ministry convened numerous working groups with business-association leaders and technical advisors.[15] Lagos expressed his enthusiasm regarding this collaboration when the joint proposals were announced in 2002: "We have here a joint effort from the public and private sector to improve the situation of Chileans, to create a more efficient country with clearer rules ... the Pro-Growth Agenda is a milestone."[16] More than twenty reforms were ultimately approved, including measures to promote small business, strengthen capital markets, promote venture capital, and modernize the state.[17]

---

[14] This interpretation builds on Schneider (2004a: 210).
[15] *El Diario*, Jan. 28, 2002.
[16] "Intervención de S.E. el Presidente de la República," Santiago, March 15, 2002 (www .sofofa.cl).
[17] SOFOFA, Memoria Annual, 2004–2005 (www.sofofa.cl). Business informants were less enthusiastic about the enacted reforms.

Further, business support on macroeconomic policy could be important for Concertación finance ministers, who generally adhered to orthodox economic principles. The coalition's left wing occasionally pressured finance ministers to deviate further from the neoliberal model than they felt prudent, as occurred during the 2000–01 recession. Collaboration with business allowed Finance Minister Eyzaguirre (interview, 2007) to counterbalance pressures from within the Concertación:

I did have a *lot* of opposition, because the ones that were saying that the model didn't work … and ask[ing] for more state involvement were very vocal.… The new generation of business leaders … saw that Lagos and I were macro-economically responsible, that [we] would defy the ones within our sector that wanted to be more Keynesian, and that at the end of the day when it comes to taxes we were sensible.… In economic policy in the end [there] was a big coalition of the center, … and the very ideological in both extremes were isolated. From the political point of view that was a very important step.[18]

This same dynamic whereby finance ministers sought business support on macroeconomic policies in the context of opposition from the Concertación's left wing continued under Bachelet (Section 3.5).

Given the value of collaboration with business, conflict over taxes could be costly for the government. Tax increases threatened business's core interests and ideological views. Furthermore, business correctly perceived taxation as a redistributive tool – one of the few available to a center-left government that embraced market economics. As Eyzaguirre (interview, 2007) explained: "The big entrepreneurs understand … that once we have agreed on a market economy, an open economy … taxation is the name of the war. Whatever points toward increasing the tax burden that in Chile is very low, would immediately unleash their total opposition." I therefore infer the following causal mechanism: concertation created incentives for the government to refrain from pursuing significant tax increases, because conflict over taxes had the potential to jeopardize support from business during critical periods or to disrupt productive government-business interactions on other issues.[19] Long time horizons and expectations of repeated interactions with business, fostered by Chile's stable institutional environment, may have contributed to this conflict aversion.[20]

---

[18] CPC support under Claro's leadership also bolstered the Lagos administration after the Public Works Ministry was implicated in the "MOP-GATE" corruption scandal (interviews: CChC-B 2006, CEP 2007).

[19] Although I do not directly observe this causal mechanism, I believe it is the best inference given the extensive body of data I collected (alternative arguments are noted where relevant). Whether conflict over taxes actually would have disrupted government-business collaboration is a separate question – what matters is how policymakers viewed the potential consequences and how much risk of disruption they were willing to tolerate.

[20] Flores-Macías (2012) invokes similar logic in arguing that strongly institutionalized party systems create incentives for negotiation and cooperation.

Concertation served as a valuable complement to partisan linkages. While partisan linkages were often the most important source of business power, the Alianza occasionally deviated from its core constituency's preferences to appeal to a broader electorate, as do all conservative parties (Gibson 1992). However, concertation reduced the likelihood that that the executive would propose significant tax increases when the right was most vulnerable to electoral pressure.

The Limited Role of Technical Expertise

Several authors suggest that technical expertise enhanced business influence in Chile (Silva 1997, Bull 2008). Technical expertise was certainly a prerequisite for government-business concertation; Finance Ministry officials, who were all highly trained economists, would have perceived few benefits to collaborating with business associations on economic policy had their representatives lacked technical expertise. However, technical expertise as a source of instrumental power in and of itself was secondary in importance to cohesion, partisan linkages, and government-business concertation in the realm of tax policy. Finance Ministry officials had sufficient expertise on taxation to independently assess business arguments, and they were attuned to the possibility that technical language aimed to legitimate business demands with little technical merit.[21] While policymakers sometimes agreed with technical points raised by business representatives, modifications to tax proposals resulting from government-business dialog were often purely political concessions.[22]

3.4 RESTRICTING THE AGENDA: THE DYNAMICS OF POLICY PROPOSALS UNDER LAGOS

Business's strong instrumental power restricted Concertación governments' tax policy agendas. Executive-branch authorities anticipated that tax increases would stimulate costly, coordinated opposition from business and the right, and when it appeared that sufficient votes could not be secured from among the institutional senators and/or the ranks of the right, reforms were dismissed as

[21] In contrast, Bull (2008) argues that business's technical expertise mattered for Asian trade treaty negotiations, since government officials knew little about that region.

[22] For example, although a construction association informant maintained that technical arguments convinced Finance Ministry officials not to eliminate a tax credit for the sector in 1998 (CChC-B 2005, interview), former finance minister Aninat (interview 2007) and former tax agency director Etcheberry (interview 2005) asserted that the exemption was unjustified; it was retained as part of the negotiated compromise with business and the right needed to pass the larger tax-reform package in the senate. Business's "technical" arguments against a 2008 proposal to restrict a construction-sector VAT benefit likewise failed to convince executive-branch policymakers, although these arguments helped business win concessions in Congress (Chapter 4).

infeasible. Meanwhile, informally institutionalized consultation with business associations created additional incentives to set aside sensitive tax issues in order to avoid conflict with the private sector. I illustrate these mechanisms by analyzing executive decision-making and legislative processes surrounding several tax reforms initiated by the Lagos administration and several cases of corporate tax nonreform.

The Anti-Evasion Reform

Anticipated opposition from business and the right kept corporate tax increases off the agenda in 2000 when the Lagos administration took office. These actors were especially recalcitrant, given business hostility toward the first socialist administration since the 1973 coup and the right's strong performance in the 1999 presidential election (Silva 2002). Consequently, although former finance minister Eyzaguirre (2007, interview) observed that "the big money is in direct taxes," the government proposed raising revenue for social spending by fighting *indirect* tax evasion, in order to minimize conflict with business and secure the votes needed in Congress. Reforms to redress problems created by the large gap between the corporate tax and top personal income tax rates were deemed infeasible:

> We didn't even try to pursue some other more important reforms that we discussed ... as we say, there was no water in the pool.... We were trying to make it more difficult for consultants or professionals to constitute societies [e.g. incorporate] in order to [avoid income taxes].... But we said we are not going to have political capital for that. (Eyzaguirre 2007, interview)

The politics surrounding the Anti-Evasion Reform illustrate the dynamics of the "tax war" phenomenon. Business and the right aggressively opposed the reform even though it focused on indirect taxes and contained only marginal tax increases associated with closing loopholes. All measures entailing increased taxation elicited cohesive business opposition coordinated by the CPC, even though several of the measures had sector-specific impacts. Cross-sectoral unity and partisan linkages helped business and the right consolidate into a single actor and strengthened their bargaining position. Former tax agency director Etcheberry (2005, interview), who helped negotiate the reform, recalled:

> The right and the business leaders ... it was the same thing.... I didn't know if I should negotiate with the senator leader of the opposition or with the president of the big enterprises. Sometimes I had to negotiate with both, because they work together.... Sometimes they were both in the same meetings saying the same things.... They coordinated among themselves, and it was public, it was not hidden.

Similarly, when asked if they had noticed any differences between business association and Alianza positions, Lagos (2006, interview) replied: "No, it was very monolithic," and Eyzaguirre (2007, interview) asserted: "At that time they were a block."

Although the administration ultimately secure
objectives, passing the reform required a major exp
ital (interviews: Etcheberry 2005, Lagos 2006, Eyza
languished in congress for almost a year while the e:
business and the right.[23] This "traumatic" (Eyzaguirr
couraged the administration from proposing more sign
subsequent years. As Lagos (2006, interview) explained:

When you are in government, what is important is to deliver.... ....ount your
chips, how many you have to fight. If I get involved in doing a ,...ofound tax reform, I
lose two, three years arguing about the tax system, and there is no AUGE [health care
reform], no education [reform] ... there is nothing.[24]

Other informants made similar comments regarding the political difficulty
of increasing taxes and the need to carefully choose which battles to pursue
(interviews: Executive Advisor-A 2005, Foxley 2006). Given strong business
power and the inherently conflictual nature of taxation, the government prioritized other issues.

The 2001 Corporate Tax Increase

The 2001 corporate tax increase further illustrates the mechanisms of business
influence in Chile. This small, 2-percentage-point increase left the corporate
tax far below the finance minister's preferred point and did not raise additional revenue (aside from marginal gains associated with reduced incentives
for avoidance and evasion), since it was combined with a personal income tax
cut. Nevertheless, the reform required complex negotiations and elicited ample
business-right opposition. This case not only evidences the significant extent to
which business's instrumental power restricted the government's agenda but
also demonstrates that influence after a reform was proposed tended to be
much less important by comparison.

Increasing the corporate tax was not on the Lagos administration's agenda in
2001 (interviews: Foxley 2006, Finance Ministry-B 2005). As described above,
significant political capital had been expended on the Anti-Evasion Reform,
and the administration did not wish to provoke additional conflict with business and the right. Instead, the corporate tax increase was spearheaded by
former finance minister Foxley, then-president of the senate finance committee. Foxley undertook the political challenge of negotiating with business, the
right, and Concertación parties to devise an acceptable reform, with the finance

---

[23] Dissent from some Christian Democrats also contributed to delays (Chapter 4).

[24] Regarding the corporate tax, Lagos (2006, interview) added: "When you ask me why didn't I
increase it [more], it's not that I did not want to increase it, it's that I did not want to take on
that battle, because I had other battles to fight.
– *It was about prioritizing?*
Clearly. And fighting a battle to deliver [win]."

ssurance that the executive, which holds exclusive initiative on tax-
cording to the Chilean constitution, would initiate the reform if broad
port could be secured.

The personal income tax cut was critical for making the corporate tax
increase politically feasible. "We wanted to increase the corporate tax," Lagos
(2006, interview) recalled, "but … it was necessary to include a candy" to placate business and the right. Accordingly, Foxley and his collaborators proposed
lowering the top marginal income tax rate from 45 percent to 35 percent in
exchange for increasing the corporate tax from 15 percent to 18 percent. Foxley
(2006, interview) sold the reform as a tax cut for the "middle class," on the basis
that wage earners were the only taxpayers unable to avoid or evade the high
personal income tax rates. Meanwhile, the corporate tax increase was justified
as imperative for financing the personal income tax cut. The Lagos administration made clear that it would not accept a reform that reduced net tax revenue,
arguing that neither social spending nor fiscal discipline could be sacrificed.

As anticipated, constructing an agreement with business and the right
proved difficult. Foxley (interview, 2006) described the process as "a political
mess" and asserted that the negotiations were "very complex, with a lot of conflict." While business and the right embraced the personal income tax cuts, they
opposed the corporate tax increase[25]; as Foxley recalled, "the corporate tax
was increased with big complaints from business and some of the right legislators."[26] Business and the right ultimately agreed to accept only a two-point corporate tax increase; to maintain revenue neutrality, the top personal income tax
rate was cut to 40 percent instead of 35 percent.[27] Nevertheless, UDI senators
ultimately voted en bloc against the corporate tax increase, despite approving
the overall reform initiative.

The 2001 corporate tax increase illustrates that business influence after a
proposal had been drafted tended to be insignificant compared to influence
over the government's reform agenda, an earlier and more critical stage of policymaking. The finance minister believed the corporate tax should be increased
"notoriously [*sic.*]:" presumably more than 20 percent (the Concertación's goal
for the 1990 reform) and closer to 30 percent (the Latin American average).
However, the proposed reform entailed increasing the rate to only 18 percent.

---

[25] Several business informants agreed that the gap between the corporate and top personal income
tax rates promoted evasion and avoidance, but their preferred solution was radically reducing
personal income tax rates; a few were willing to accept in exchange a corporate tax not exceeding 20 percent.

[26] See for example *El Mercurio*, March 12, 2001. Similarly, Zaldívar (interview, 2007) identified
the 2001 corporate tax increase as the tax reform that business and the right most opposed under Lagos.

[27] The Concertación's left wing, especially Socialists, opposed the personal income tax cut as regressive (interviews: Gazmuri 2006, Marcel 2006). Party discipline, loyalty to Lagos, and an
agreement to increase the minimum nontaxable income to benefit lower-bracket taxpayers ensured Socialist votes.

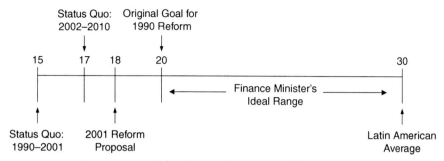

FIGURE 3.2. Corporate Tax Policy Space, Chile (Rates, %).
Source: Fairfield (2010); reprinted with permission from John Wiley & Sons publications.

The concession won by business and their right-party allies during negotiations before the bill entered Congress – reducing the proposed new rate from 18 percent to 17 percent – was trivial compared to business's ability to prevent much more significant reforms from even being discussed.[28]

The implicit threat of united business-right opposition thus shifted the range of tax rates under debate significantly toward business preferences (Figure 3.2),[29] removing important reforms from the agenda that government leaders may otherwise have sought to enact. This analysis agrees with Hacker and Pierson's (2002: 284) observation that "the most significant aspect of influence involves moving the decision-making agenda toward an actor's preferred end of the spectrum."

This finding regarding the importance of business's influence over the agenda contrasts with earlier research and illustrates that business in Chile was even more powerful than previously recognized. Silva (1997: 176–77) emphasizes business's ability to win modifications to drafted reform proposals based on easy access to executive-branch policymakers arising from government-business concertation:

Top policymakers set the agenda for incremental changes. After their technical commissions drew up draft legislation, it was circulated to the appropriate peak association.... Policymakers and business leaders then negotiated on the basis of those reports.... In virtually every interview, business leaders acknowledged that this system allowed them to alter proposed legislation in ways that favored their interests.

However, focusing on alterations to proposed legislation rather than agenda-formulation could lead one to conclude that business influence was less

---

[28] The finance minister did not advocate abruptly raising the corporate tax; yet a more substantial increase could have been phased in gradually, as was this two-point increase.
[29] Exclusive executive initiative on taxation precluded a better outcome for business and the right than the status quo.

significant than in fact was the case, as evidenced by the 2001 corporate tax reform. In fact, business was so powerful that it usually did not need to mobilize to defeat reforms it opposed; the mere threat of business-right mobilization sufficed to keep significant tax increases off the agenda.

Analyzing agenda formulation in Chile is imperative because the most critical political decisions are made before proposals are drafted. As others have observed (Luna 2014), reforms that are not deemed likely to pass in Congress are never initiated. A Finance Ministry (B 2005) informant explained this logic as follows:

> If we make an announcement, its because we have assessed that we have a real chance of moving forward ... in [the] Finance [Ministry], we do not make announcements if we have not thought carefully about political feasibility. There is a very large reputational cost for announcing a reform that later cannot be implemented in the legislature.

Analyzing open policy debates may not even be sufficient to assess the extent of business-right influence. Some reforms are known to be so controversial or politically problematic that the executive does not bother to test the waters; accordingly, actors not privy to inner circles within the executive branch may be unaware of leaders' true policy preferences. Interviews with top decision makers can be critical for ascertaining what reforms leaders wished to implement independently of perceived political constraints, which is in turn critical for assessing the full extent of business influence. In other words, as Hacker and Pierson (2002: 283) emphasize, we must distinguish between "induced" or "strategic" preferences and true preferences.

Corporate Tax Nonreform, 2003 and 2005

Business's strong instrumental power kept corporate tax increases off the agenda throughout the remainder of Lagos's term, even though the administration faced additional revenue needs in the aftermath of the Anti-Evasion Reform. In 2003, tariff reductions included in trade treaties signed with the United States and Europe made increasing other taxes imperative for financing social spending on health care and antipoverty programs without endangering fiscal discipline. The Finance Ministry proposed compensating the revenue lost to tariff reductions by increasing the VAT, despite objections from within the Concertación, rather than fighting with business and the right over direct taxes. Lagos (interview, 2006) explained this decision as follows:

> I had no option for increasing any other tax, because it would have been rejected.... The Concertación did not want to increase the VAT. They wanted the personal income tax, or the corporate tax. I told them: Why are you asking me for things that are impossible? This will not happen because the right will reject it in the Senate.[30]

---

[30] I judge this retrospective statement as a sincere representation of motives based on multiple, extensive interviews with Lagos over eight years as well as conversations with his colleagues

Business accepted the VAT increase with minimal complaints as the lesser evil, given that increasing the corporate tax was the obvious alternative (interviews: ABIF 2006, CEP 2007, Eyzaguirre 2007).

During the 2005 electoral campaign, the Lagos administration considered proposing a corporate tax increase, but the idea was ultimately discarded. In May 2005, the issue of inequality assumed a prominent role in the presidential campaign. Alianza candidate Lavín accused the Concertación of failing to reduce inequality during its fifteen years in power. The Lagos administration responded by proposing to eliminate a highly regressive income tax benefit inherited from the dictatorship that constituted a perpetual subsidy for wealthy stock owners. Although the UDI and RN had consistently defended the tax benefit since 1990, they voted in favor of the proposal to protect their candidate's credibility and electoral prospects, contrary to business's policy preferences (Chapter 4).

The right's unexpected support for equity-enhancing tax reform during the presidential campaign created a potential opportunity for further advances, and initiating a bill to increase the corporate tax was discussed informally – and privately – at the highest level. Top leaders in the administration recognized the opportune political conjuncture: "The opposition whenever elections are coming get very soft-hearted, that is precisely the moment where you can do these things" (Eyzaguirre 2007, interview). Meanwhile, Concertación legislators pressed the administration to seize the opportunity and propose additional redistributive reforms (interviews: Montes 2005, Bitar 2007). The former finance minister recalled, "At some points they [the right] were so incredibly hypocritical when they said we haven't done anything for income distribution, that we were tempted to send that bill."

However, the administration ultimately decided against a corporate tax initiative. Even in the extraordinary 2005 electoral context, government informants insisted a tax increase could not have been proposed without a concretely delineated revenue need to justify the initiative; linking tax increases to spending was perceived as imperative for circumventing business-right opposition, notwithstanding Lavín's professed interest in inequality. This aspect of the political calculus posed problems; informants asserted that the administration did not have sufficient time left in office to advance a major new social spending initiative and that doing so would undermine Bachelet's prerogative to define priorities at the outset of her term (interviews: Eyzaguirre 2007, Finance Ministry-B, C 2005, Executive Advisor-A, B 2005).[31]

---

and son. Eyzaguirre (2007, interview) explained the VAT increase similarly: "At the end of the day if you want to have some space, it is easier through the indirect taxes, with the right wing."

[31] While this argument may not sound satisfactory to an outside observer, the fact that multiple informants in different areas of government expressed the same view suggests the logic was compelling in the Chilean context.

Aversion to incurring additional conflict with business also dissuaded the administration from proposing a corporate tax increase. A mining tax legislated earlier that year involved a major battle with business (Chapter 4); eliminating the stock owner tax benefit antagonized business as well (interviews: Montes 2005, Lagos 2006).[32] Any additional tax initiative would have provoked extended debate and even greater conflict with business and the right,[33] and the administration did not wish to encumber Bachelet, the clear presidential front-runner, with a legacy of unresolved conflicts (interview: Finance Ministry-B 2005). My interviews with Lagos suggested that he viewed bequeathing good relations with business to Bachelet as an important achievement that would broaden the scope of what she could accomplish during her term.

This episode of corporate tax nonreform illustrates the importance of business's multiple sources of power. In this case, partisan linkages alone may not have sufficed to protect business interests. Given the salience of inequality in the presidential campaign, the right might conceivably have deviated from its core constituency's preferences for the sake of appealing to a broader electorate. However, government-business consultation bolstered business's instrumental power by creating incentives for the government to avoid additional conflict over taxes that could have jeopardized Bachelet's working relations with business associations. While no "smoking gun" evidence linking the conflict aversion described above to government-business concertation emerged, my accumulated body of interview data supports this inference (Eyzaguirre 2007, Lagos 2006, Finance Ministry-A, B 2005, Executive Advisor-A 2005, Montes 2005, Ffrench-Davis 2005).[34]

This case provides a remarkable illustration of business power, given that sending a corporate tax increase to Congress might have been electorally advantageous for the Concertación. Although opinions on this point differed within the coalition, with some asserting that it was best to forgo any discussion of taxes (interviews: Finance Ministry-B 2005, Velasco 2005), the former finance minister himself maintained that proposing a corporate tax increase would have put the right on the defensive (Eyzaguirre 2007, interview). Had the right prioritized its core constituency's interests by voting against a corporate tax increase, the Concertación could have demonstrated its opponents' resistance

---

[32] El Mercurio, May 28, 2005.
[33] Compared to the stockholder tax-benefit reform, government informants (interviews: Marcel 2007, Finance Ministry-B 2005, Lagos 2006) perceived that business and the right had greater leeway to frame any other tax initiative as deterring investment or harming the middle class, thereby justifying intransigent opposition. Some options, like restricting a regressive construction-sector VAT benefit, would also cause dissent within the Concertación (Chapter 4).
[34] Concertación technocrats' fear of inciting "populist" dynamics and societal demands that could run counter to technical principles they espoused (Pribble 2013) may also have contributed to the decision not to initiate further tax reforms in the electoral context. One informant noted: "Modifying tax laws on the basis of weekly dares would be irresponsible" (interview: Finance Ministry-C, 2006) although he did not explain why.

to redistributive reforms, undermining Lavín's credibility just months before the election. Sending popular proposals to Congress that the right opposed had proved an effective electoral strategy in the past; the right attributed Lavín's prior loss to Lagos partly to right legislators' votes against the Frei administration's proposed labor reform in 1999.[35] Nevertheless, the desire to contain conflict with business and the sense that another battle with business and the right over taxes would prove unmanageable prevailed.

3.5 CONTINUITY AND CHANGE: CORPORATE TAX NONREFORM UNDER BACHELET

At the outset of President Bachelet's term (2006–10), business's instrumental power appeared weakened. The right lost its senate majority, and business-right relations appeared more independent. These changes augured well for equity-enhancing tax reform; as Lagos (2006, interview) optimistically mused: "President Bachelet has more degrees of freedom than I had in that terrain." Nevertheless, corporate tax reform remained off the agenda. Business's instrumental power continued to deter direct tax increases. The Concertación's slim senate majority proved ephemeral, and despite shifts in the nature of business-right relations, partisan linkages remained strong. In addition, several factors that had not been relevant during Lagos's tenure contributed to nonreform. First, the new finance minister's perception of a significant trade-off between growth and direct taxation enhanced business's structural power. Second, a new economic context of record fiscal surpluses combined with slower growth lowered the priority of increasing taxation and created new political obstacles to reform.

Instrumental Power

In 2005, future finance minister Velasco (interview), then head of the committee designing Bachelet's program of government, pondered: "If I think as a politician a minute, ... I don't think I will be spending my political capital messing around with taxes.... In order to get a good chunk of [revenue] from direct taxes, you'd have to raise political hell." Regarding increasing the corporate tax, even by a few points, he asserted: "The business community will really agitate against it." These remarks suggest that business's instrumental power contributed to Velasco's subsequent disinterest in direct tax reform and would have helped keep such initiatives off the agenda even had the administration faced more pressing revenue needs.

Partisan linkages, along with cohesion and government-business concertation, remained a strong source of instrumental power for business, despite

[35] *El Mercurio*, May 3, 12, 2005.

changes in business-right relations discussed in the following section. Although the Concertación won its first senate majority in 2005, the right retained strong representation. Weakened internal discipline rendered the governing coalition's slim two-seat majority dysfunctional by early 2007,[36] and the balance of power reverted to parity between the left and right coalitions later that year when two Concertación senators became independents. Thereafter, as under Lagos, a few swing voters determined the fate of economic reforms in the senate (Finance Ministry-E 2008, interview).

Although the right retained its strength in Congress, at first glance, business's partisan linkages appeared less robust in the late 2000s. Business leaders refrained from overt participation in right-party politics, in contrast to their heavy-handed involvement in the 1990s; meanwhile, the right cultivated an image of greater independence from business to improve its electoral prospects, given repeated failures to win control of the executive branch. However, I argue that the fundamental core-constituency relationship remained intact. In practice, business continued to support the right, and the right continued to defend business interests, with occasional exceptions motivated by strategic considerations.

Business-Right Relations: The Distancing Trend

After 2003, a new generation of more moderate businessmen who eschewed open association with the right assumed leadership of the major peak associations.[37] A CPC (D 2008) informant explained: "We have a very clear policy in recent years of not allowing any criticism we make of the government to be interpreted as political. We criticize policies, but not with the goal of harming the government so that the opposition will win an election." From the Concertación's perspective, the change was "enormous" (Lagos 2006, interview). According to one informant: "Before, the business organizations were militantly right-wing. Today they probably are as well, but they involve themselves much less in political discussions" (interview, Marcel 2005). This change partly reflected the fact that the new business leaders were not as closely associated with the dictatorship as their predecessors. Pinochet's detention in London

---

[36] Multiple factors contributed to these problems. First, Bachelet's practice of distancing herself from Concertación party leaders (Boas 2009, Sehnbruch 2007) and Velasco's lack of membership in any Concertación party undermined executive-branch authority over coalition legislators. Second, Velasco's highly orthodox economic views provoked discontent among the Concertación's left wing. Third, the Christian Democrats' decline (Huneeus 2003, Navarrete 2005) exacerbated disciplinary problems. The PDC descended into disputes and power struggles after losing its prominent position within the Concertación – the PDC failed to secure the 2005 presidential candidacy, and its senatorial bloc fell from thirteen to six seats. PDC Senator Adolfo Zaldívar raised his political profile by criticizing the economic model and denouncing "collusion" between the political establishment and big business. He repeatedly broke ranks and left the Concertación in 2007.

[37] They included Claro, Lamarca, Bruno, and Somerville.

and the discovery of his tax evasion and embezzlement blemished the reputation of the older generation of business leaders who had remained fiercely loyal to the general (interview, UDI-B 2005), and may thus have facilitated the change of guard.

Under the new business leadership, overt coordination with the right parties and aggressive opposition to reforms that threatened private sector interests gave way to a new style of more cordial relations with the government. CPC president Claro demonstrated that a more respectful stance toward government could serve business interests. The move toward less confrontational business-government relations was facilitated by the fact that the reforms in Lagos's campaign platform that business most adamantly opposed, including the Anti-Evasion Reform as well as labor reforms, had already been legislated (interview CPC-A 2005). Claro's excellent personal rapport with top leaders in the Lagos administration (interviews Eyzaguirre, 2007) helped as well.

Simultaneously, the right intensified efforts to free its public image from close association with business. This strategic move, which began with Lavín's 1999 presidential campaign, was intended to improve the right's electoral prospects. An informant from the *Centro de Estudios Públicos* (CEP 2007), a think tank with close ties to business, explained:

One of the Alianza's weaknesses is that the population identifies it too much with business. And for some time, the Alianza has been trying to distance itself and show independence.... The Alianza feels that businesspeople do not contribute to its performance, rather, they are a burden.

Lavín avoided business involvement in his 1999 campaign (UDI-B 2005, interview); his effort during the 2005 campaign to embrace the issue of inequality, the traditional banner of the left, can be viewed as a continuation of this distancing strategy.

By the mid 2000s, many informants maintained that business-right relations had changed substantially. One observed: "Today there is much more distance between the political world of the right and the business world" (CEP 2007, interview). Another asserted: "On the one hand, a business community that is no longer monolithic, and on the other hand, political parties that are trying to assert independence, make it so that the *poderes fácticos* do not have as much influence" (UDI-B 2005, interview). Business leaders and UDI politicians continued to cultivate an image of mutual independence during the latter half of the decade. Business informants interviewed in 2011 consistently emphasized the apolitical character of the peak associations. Meanwhile, UDI politicians emphasized the party's mass base and the cross-class nature of its electoral coalition when asked about the party's relationships with business (2011 interviews: Silva, Coloma, Ulloa, Novoa). One UDI deputy endeavored to turn the tables, asserting that the Concertación, not the UDI, had most actively promoted business interests: "Business did very well under the left. The Chilean left worked for the rich. And we the UDI are working for those who have less. We are the popular right" (Ulloa 2011, interview).

Business as the Right's Less Overt Core Constituency

While the changes in business-right relations described above are noteworthy, in practice they did not significantly alter the core constituency relationship. The informant quoted in the previous section who asserted that business leaders no longer wielded as much influence in right-party politics was quick to point out that the comparison was relative:

They don't have as much influence. But they have influence. Let's not deceive ourselves. And they have a lot of influence, because they have the money. But it's not like the 1990s.
–The link with the right parties is weaker?
It's weaker than in the 1990s. I'm not saying it's weak. It's tight, it's tight. (UDI-B 2005, interview)

Other informants agreed that business-right ties remained strong, contrary to public appearances. According to a high-level Alianza advisor, despite the UDI's public, political discourse of being a popular party and its strong presence in poor communities, the UDI never abandoned business interests (Executive Advisor-C 2011, interview). Roll-call vote analysis from 2006 to 2008 confirms this assertion. Luna (2010: 340) finds that the UDI systematically opposed "legislative packages that could hurt business interests or potentially redistribute resources to lower social strata … the UDI seems to have fulfilled its promise to protect business elites."[38]

Continued electoral and financial support for the right from business further evidences the persistent core-constituency relationship. A key business informant who acknowledged that business had done extremely well during the Concertación's tenure in power asserted that nevertheless:

In general, businesspeople identify more with the UDI and the RN. The UDI has been the party that has most tried to defend liberal economic principles, and has been less inclined toward populist temptations, although there are some legislators in the UDI who are very seduced by the issue of votes. (ABIF 2011, interview)

Many business informants agreed that businesspeople tended to prefer the right parties, despite asserting that business associations were apolitical (2011 interviews: Mining-E, CChC-D, SNA-B), although several noted that partisan affiliations of all kinds existed within the business community (2011 interviews: CPC-E, CNCC). A survey of 330 business executives conducted during the 2009 presidential campaign confirmed strong business support for the

---

[38] Luna (2010) further demonstrates that cultivating a popular base is compatible with maintaining a core business constituency; UDI offered upper-income sectors programmatic representation and attracted lower-income sectors through charismatic appeals and small-scale clientelism.

right: 95 percent of respondents ranked Alianza candidate Piñera as the best for promoting economic growth, and 88 percent viewed him as the best candidate for promoting the interests of the respondent's firm or sector.[39]

Meanwhile, the limited campaign finance data available suggests that business continued to preferentially support the right, primarily the UDI. Chile's campaign donations law allows three types of private contributions: anonymous contributions, which cannot exceed U.S.$800, confidential contributions (*aportes reservados*), applicable for amounts over U.S.$800, and public (nonanonymous) contributions (Luna 2010). The identity of donors is not publicly available for anonymous or confidential contributions (Chile Transparente 2008). Following Luna (2010), however, one can reasonably assume that confidential contributions, which account for the vast majority of registered private contributions by value,[40] originate from businesses and wealthy individuals.[41] While businesses contributed to all major candidates, right-party candidates received a greater share of private resources. In the 2009 presidential campaign, Piñera received 56 percent of confidential donations, while Concertación candidate Frei received only 34 percent. In the 2009 congressional elections, the UDI received 53 percent of confidential donations made to lower-house candidates and 45 percent of those made to senatorial candidates. The RN placed second after the UDI with 20 percent of the confidential donations for lower-house candidates, while the PDC and the RN received respectively 17 percent and 16 percent of confidential donations for Senate races. Figure 3.3 shows the average value of confidential donations received per candidate for each major party; these data further illustrate the UDI's advantage. Together, right candidates (UDI and RN) received almost twice as much from confidential donations as Concertación candidates (PPD, PDC, PS, and PRSD) in the senatorial election; for the lower house, right candidates received four times as much as Concertación candidates.

In sum, business's partisan linkages to the right, particularly the UDI, remained intact during the late 2000s, despite the trend toward less overt mutual association. Business associations and the right were much less likely to openly coordinate opposition to reforms. Yet the right continued to defend business interests on economic policy, with occasional breaches driven by electoral imperatives or political necessity.

An Exception that Highlights the Rule
An instructive exception to the right's strong record of defending business interests occurred in 2007, when the Alianza voted against a corporate tax

---

[39] *El Mercurio*, Nov. 14, 2009.
[40] Confidential contributions accounted for more than 90 percent of private donations to congressional candidates in 2009.
[41] It is widely assumed that businesses make the majority of confidential donations. *El Mercurio*, Nov. 1, 2009.

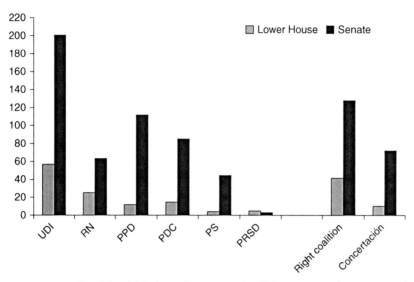

FIGURE 3.3. Confidential Private Donations in Chile, 2009 Parliamentary Elections (Millions of Pesos per Candidate).
Source: SERVEL (www.servel.cl).

benefit supported by business. The Finance Ministry proposed instantaneous depreciation for 50 percent of the cost of new fixed assets to promote growth and investment. Business championed the measure (CPC 2007), and the Alianza voted for the reform in the lower house as expected. However, the Concertación's left wing denounced the measure as a giveaway to big business that failed to address the needs of small and medium enterprises. These critics maintained that businesses standing to benefit had already planned investment projects and would initiate them with or without the tax break. Serious political problems ensued when a handful of Concertación senators refused to support the reform.

This situation created a multifaceted political opportunity for the right. By switching from supporting to opposing the reform, the Alianza could simultaneously exacerbate divisions within the Concertación, demonstrate independence from business, and claim to represent small and medium enterprises, a constituency the right and left had long vied to attract. The Alianza announced that it would reject the reform unless the government included tax cuts for small and medium businesses, appropriating arguments that the measure in question helped only big business.[42] The Finance Ministry responded by appealing directly to the business associations to convince the right to support

[42] *El Mercurio*, April 15, 2007.

the reform.[43] However, this move increased the Alianza's perceived returns to opposing the reform by making the breach between the right and big business even more manifest: "When the government asked business to intercede, the Alianza said no, we are independent from the business world. It was a precious opportunity that rarely arises in politics," (CEP 2007, interview). The reform was defeated in the Senate with negative votes from the Alianza and three dissident Conceratación senators.

The Alianza's opportunistic position succeeded in weakening the Concertación politically, although it did not necessarily establish the right's independence from business in the public eye (CEP 2007, interview). The Senate vote was interpreted as a major political defeat for the finance minister. Moreover, the Alianza's strategy deepened tensions within the Concertación, raised the political profile of dissident Concertación senators, and contributed to the permanent demise of the Concertación's Senate majority.

The Alianza's behavior is consistent with Gibson's (1992) expectation of periodic conflicts between right parties and their core constituencies resulting from attempts to attract a broader electorate. Yet the right soon returned to advocating pro-business policies. Alianza candidate Piñera included accelerated depreciation in his 2009 program of government,[44] notwithstanding his coalition's rejection of the measure in 2007.

New Factors Discouraging Direct Tax Reform

Although many perceived Bachelet as belonging to the Concertación's progressive wing, she appointed a finance minister with highly orthodox economic views who perceived little need for direct tax reform. In contrast to Lagos and Eyzaguirre, Finance Minister Velasco maintained that Chile's tax revenue was both adequate for the country's needs and appropriate for its development level. Whereas Eyzaguirre believed the corporate tax was too low, Velasco (2005, interview) felt it was "more or less where it should be."

The new finance minister's views on direct taxation augmented business's structural power. Whereas Eyzaguirre maintained that the low corporate tax simply promoted personal income tax evasion, Velasco (2005, interview) embraced the alternative view that the gap between the corporate and personal income tax rates stimulated investment.[45] Moreover, Velasco perceived a trade-off between growth and direct taxation, and he prioritized growth. Structural power, through Velasco's anticipation that corporate tax increases would in fact deter investment, helped ensure that reform would remain off the government's agenda. By his own account, Velasco dissuaded Bachelet, who did

[43] *El Mercurio*, April 14, 2007.
[44] *El Mercurio*, July 10, 2009.
[45] See Cerda and Larraín (2005).

TABLE 3.5. *Fiscal Surplus (Superávit Efectivo, % GDP), Chile 2005–2008*

	First Semester	End of Year
2005	2.8	4.7
2006	4.2	7.9
2007	5.3	8.7
2008	4.0	5.2

Sources: DIPRES 2009; Ministerio de Hacienda 2010.

not have economics expertise, from including tax increases (other than anti-evasion measures) in her 2005 program of government.[46]

A new economic context of abundance also helped remove direct tax increases from Bachelet's agenda. Soaring prices for Chile's leading primary-product export, copper, created record fiscal surpluses (Table 3.5, Figure 3.4). While windfall revenue from the state-owned copper company, CODELCO, was invested in a stabilization fund and hence could not be used to finance current expenditures, general tax revenues swelled thanks to high profits in the privately owned mining sector (Figure 3.5). Velasco maintained that prevailing tax revenue was sufficient to fund Bachelet's social spending initiatives, including a major pension reform.[47] In addition, the Finance Ministry reduced the fiscal surplus target established by the "structural surplus rule," implemented in 2000 as an anti-cyclic measure, from 1 percent to 0.5 percent of GDP in 2007. This adjustment freed an additional U.S.$650 million for investment in education.[48]

The context of fiscal surplus created new political obstacles to increasing taxation by weakening the government's ability to appeal to fiscal discipline. Opponents could make simple and compelling if technically questionable arguments that the government should spend the resources it already had. As the Socialist Party president explained:

The State has savings beyond what it has ever had in Chilean history, and that mass of money makes the discussion [of taxes] very difficult. I know that social spending must be financed with permanent income, that income from copper is transitory, but even

[46] Although Velasco's tax views were compatible with business preferences, business power did not influence his appointment as finance minister. Bachelet seriously considered Budget Director Marcel for the position (*Revista Cosas*, March 16, 2007). Marcel (2007, interview), like Eyzaguirre, felt income-tax reform was imperative. Considerations unrelated to economic policy favored Velasco, including Bachelet's interest in maintaining distance from the Concertación establishment and including new faces in her administration (Sehnbruch 2007); whereas Marcel was a PS militant, Velasco had no party affiliation. Further, Velasco and Bachelet developed a close friendship during the campaign.

[47] *El Mercurio*, Jan. 11, 2007.

[48] *El Mercurio*, May 22, 2007.

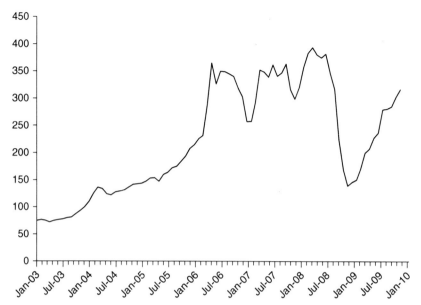

FIGURE 3.4. Copper Prices (LME Nominal Spot, U.S. ¢/Pound).
Source: Cochilco (www.cochilco.cl).

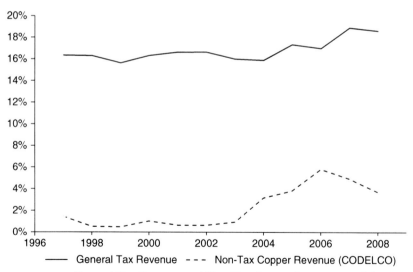

FIGURE 3.5. General Tax Revenue and Non-Tax Copper Revenue in Chile (% GDP).
Sources: DIPRES (2009), SII (2009).

TABLE 3.6. *Growth Rates (%),*
Chile 2004–2008

Year	Growth Rate
2004	6.0
2005	5.6
2006	4.6
2007	4.7
2008	3.2

Source: www.bcentral.cl: *Producto*
Interno Bruto Serie Anual.

so ... the political discussion is very difficult. It is practically impossible because immediately the facile argument is raised: if the state is so full of money, why does it need more? (Escalona 2007, interview)

This argument found adherents within the Concertación as well as the right. Even Concertación legislators who advocated increasing tax revenue agreed that the economic context made it extremely difficult to advance (Montes 2007, interview).

Meanwhile, slow growth motivated the executive to *reduce* taxes. While growth had reached 6 percent at the end of Lagos's term, it decelerated in the first years of Bachelet's term and dipped to 3.2 percent in 2008 (Table 3.6). Although growth rates were higher than during the four years following the East Asian Crisis, both the government and the private sector found them unsatisfactory. Given Velasco's perception of investor sensitivity to taxation, it is not surprising that the Finance Ministry proposed a battery of tax incentives between 2006 and 2008 intended to stimulate investment.

3.6 THE 1990 REFORM IN RETROSPECT

Based on the 1990 reform, Weyland (1997) characterizes Chile as a success story for progressive taxation. In accord with earlier research (Boylan 1996, Silva 1996), however, I argue that the 1990 reform entailed a modest though important advance that is consistent with expectations based on strong business power. This reform is best understood as a limited business-RN compromise during the unique conjuncture of the democratic transition.

Upon taking office, the Aylwin administration sought to increase the corporate tax from 10 percent to 20 percent and to change the base from distributed to accrued profits. These measures, along with personal income tax bracket adjustments and loophole eliminations, aimed to raise 3 percent of GDP to finance social spending. This proposal was nevertheless quite moderate. First, 20 percent remained a very low corporate tax rate by regional standards; the 1992 Latin American average excluding Chile was 35 percent (Sabaini 2005:

35). Moreover, the government publicly proposed that the corporate tax be increased to within the range of 15 percent to 20 percent signaling willingness to accept the lower target. Second, the reform merely reversed Pinochet's eleventh-hour giveaway to business – the dictatorship switched the base from accrued to distributed profits in 1989 (Marfán 1998), and corporate tax collections dropped to zero (Marcel 1997).

The moderate reform design and express willingness to compromise reflected the new government's recognition of business's strong instrumental power as well as structural power. As previously discussed, the right had veto power in the Senate, business was highly cohesive, and the Concertación wished to minimizing conflict with business given the uncertainty surrounding the transition. The Concertación further sought to demonstrate its commitment to neoliberalism, fearing that business might disinvest if policies appeared to revert to statist tendencies of the past (Foxley 2006, interview).

Business accepted the tax increase despite its capacity to resist for two reasons. First, key business leaders believed a moderate tax increase to fund social spending would help legitimize and consolidate neoliberalism, which was popularly viewed as benefitting only the rich (Bartell 1992, Boylan 1996, Weyland 1997). These leaders recognized that ignoring pent-up social spending demands "would threaten the long-term political and economic stability of the entire system" (Boylan 1996: 17). Second, the government emphasized that Pinochet's last-minute tax cuts jeopardized fiscal discipline and overheated the economy (Marcel 1997). The possibility of a fiscal deficit "played on [business's] greatest fear: resurgence of the populist economic policies pursued under the Allende Socialist government" (Boylan 1996: 16). In this context, the tax reform became "a symbol of the Concertación's economic responsibility, eliminating the specter of democratic chaos" (Marcel 1997: 68).

The RN's willingness to negotiate with the Concertación was also critical for the reform. Like business, the modernizing tendency that held leadership positions in the RN felt the reform would help legitimate and consolidate the neoliberal model. RN Senator Piñera recounted: "It was necessary to demonstrate that the model could serve everyone, since it was perceived as efficient but unjust" (interviewed by Marcel 1997: 61). Further, these RN leaders strategized that accepting the tax increase would enhance their electoral prospects by allowing the party to share credit for popular spending programs and building the RN's reputation as a centrist party (Boylan 1996, Pollack 1999). RN president Allamand wanted to moderate the party's platform to attract Christian Democratic voters (Pollack 1999). Although much of the RN resisted the tax increase (Marcel 1997), the modernizing tendency managed to deliver the party's votes in the senate. The UDI, in contrast, intransigently rejected the reform.

Before endorsing the reform, the CPC and RN secured concessions that eroded its progressivity and revenue-raising capacity. The corporate tax rate was set at 15 percent, not 20 percent; a two-point VAT increase was added to compensate, but the reform's anticipated yield fell by 1 percent of GDP. Further, the tax increases were made temporary; the corporate tax would revert to 10 percent in 1994, which necessitated renegotiating the reform in 1993. Finally, the government informally agreed not to pursue additional tax increases during the remainder of its term (Marcel 1997).

Moreover, the factors that compelled business to accept increased taxation were specific to the transition period. Business had little incentive to compromise on taxation by the mid-1990s, once the economic model appeared consolidated. Business accepted a permanent 15 percent corporate tax in 1993 to preserve fiscal discipline, but only in exchange for reducing top personal income tax rates, various tax benefits and investment incentives, and another Concertación promise not to increase direct taxes for the next four years (interviews: Marfán 2005, CPC-F 2005). Thereafter, business persistently lobbied for exempting reinvested profits from taxation (SOFOFA 2002, CPC 2007; interviews: Finance Ministry-B 2005, CPC-D 2008).

Meanwhile, changes in the balance of power within the Alianza led to more monolithic right opposition. First, the modernizing tendency lost ground within the RN. The reputations of Piñera and Matthei, leading modernizing tendency figures, were damaged by a 1992 scandal, and a more conservative politician replaced Allamand as RN's president in 1997 (Pollack 1999). Second, the hardline UDI gained seats in Congress at RN's expense in 1997 and 2001. Due to this realignment, the RN abandoned its strategy of negotiating accords with the Concertación. The government had to rely on business, which feared a fiscal deficit, to convince the party to accept the 1993 reform (Marcel 1997, interview: Marfán 2005).

Intransigent business-right opposition helped deter all but marginal tax increases under President Frei (1994–2000). Following the 1993 agreement with business and the right, income tax increases remained off the agenda, but for some attempts to close loopholes.[49] Although the Frei administration was not interested in increasing the corporate tax rate, which it viewed as adequate (Aninat 2007, interview), the right would have blocked any attempt to do so in the Senate.

3.7 CONCLUSION

Business's strong instrumental power, based on partisan linkages, cross-sectoral cohesion, and government-business concertation, kept significant corporate tax increases and direct tax increases more generally off the agenda from 1991 to 2010. Although President Lagos actively sought more revenue for social spending, and although his finance minister believed the corporate

---

[49] RN facilitated some loophole eliminations (Marfán 2005, interview), but business and the right defended many others as investment incentives.

tax was much too low, the government proposed only marginal initiatives to redress these problems. Business's instrumental power continued to constrain prospects for reform under President Bachelet, although unprecedented fiscal surpluses and the finance minister's concerns over business's structural power also contributed significantly to nonreform. Yet even a finance minister who felt direct tax reform was imperative for responsibly financing social policy expansion and perceived no credible threat of disinvestment[50] probably would have deemed reform politically infeasible given business's strong instrumental power. In light of this analysis, Chile's 1990 corporate tax reform is an exceptional case reflecting strategic calculations made by business and the right in the context of the democratic transition.

In contrast to earlier research (Silva 1998), I find that business influence over the reform agenda far exceeded business's more overt influence after the executive had proposed reform initiatives. This finding suggests that business was more powerful in Chile than previously understood. By and large, the mere anticipation of business-right resistance kept important reforms that the executive might otherwise have sought to enact off the agenda, without need for business to actively expend resources.

This chapter sheds further light on the Concertación's comparatively modest progress at expanding social spending (Garay 2014). Other authors have noted that Concertación technocrats' concern over fiscal discipline constrained progress on social spending, particularly given the absence of bottom-up pressure from within the Concertación (Pribble 2013) or from mobilized social sectors more broadly (Garay 2014). My analysis complements this research by identifying why Concertación leaders were so reluctant to push harder at building the tax capacity they viewed as imperative for responsible social spending. The crux of the problem during the Lagos administration was business power: Concertación leaders anticipated that initiatives to increase taxation would entail difficult and potentially unsuccessful or even detrimental political battles with business associations and the right.[51]

---

[50] Marcel, Velasco's contender for finance minister, fit this profile. He asserted: "The current tax burden is adequate for the policies that exist today, but for all that needs to be done in the future, the tax revenue is not there" (*El Mercurio*, March 17, 2007) and recommended "an important income-tax reform" (Marcel 2007, interview).

[51] Reluctance to initiate reforms lacking strong prospects for success left Concertación leaders vulnerable to politically damaging accusations that they were not committed to equity-enhancing reforms. Since business power acted at the agenda stage, written records provided limited evidence to the contrary. Accordingly, many maintain that blaming the right was merely an expedient justification for inaction (see Castiglioni 2005: 105–06). Although this view may hold some truth in other policy realms, evidence in this chapter along with the more extensive body of interviews with key policymakers that inform my analysis undermine this alternative hypothesis regarding Lagos administration tax politics.

4

Circumventing Business Power in Chile

Progress at the Margins

Strong business power not only kept corporate tax increases off the agenda as a revenue-raising tool in Chile but also precluded significant tax increases more generally. Business's instrumental power played a key role in restricting the reform agenda across tax policy areas, whether they affected cross-sectoral interests or particular sectors. Structural power occasionally limited the scope of reform as well. However, center-left Concertación governments developed a broad repertoire of reform strategies that facilitated incremental tax increases.

This chapter has two main goals. First, it provides additional empirical evidence of the mechanisms through which strong business power influenced tax policy, thereby strengthening the causal inferences behind the arguments introduced in Chapter 3 and generalizing beyond the case of the corporate tax rate. Second, it analyzes the strategic dynamics of tax policymaking in Chile, returning to key questions posed in Chapter 2: How and when can governments make economic elites pay higher taxes, and to what extent can they push the bounds of feasibility in contexts of strong business power? The approach Chilean policymakers adopted in addressing the first question entailed simultaneously employing multiple strategies for tempering elite antagonism and mobilizing public support, along with attention to opportune timing. However, outcomes across tax policy areas illustrate that the scope created for reform remained narrow, given business's strong and multiple sources of power. Expected revenue gains were modest, with most reforms less than 0.2 percent of GPD (Appendix 4.1).

The following sections analyze reforms in three key areas: controlling tax evasion, eliminating technically unjustified and regressive tax benefits, and strengthening mineral-resource taxation. The case studies encompass efforts to tax distinct economic sectors and illustrate a wide variety of reform strategies.

They include the most significant revenue-raising reforms since 1990 as well as the most emblematic equity-enhancing tax reforms.[1]

The chapter beings with an overview of the Concertación's reform strategy repertoire and salient features of the Chilean strategic context (Section 4.1). Section 4.2 examines the Lagos administration's 2001 Anti-Evasion Reform. Strategic design and associated equity appeals helped the government legislate the reform, which was a major revenue-raising success in the Chilean context. However, the government's framing strategy did not mitigate conflict with business and the right on many measures in the package, and significant concessions had to be negotiated. Section 4.3 turns to efforts to redress under-taxation of the privately owned mining sector, which culminated in a new mining tax legislated in 2005. After many frustrated initiatives, a mining tax avoidance scandal increased issue salience and mobilized public opinion in favor of reform, and proximity to the 2005 presidential election ultimately compelled business and the right to accept the modest initiative. However, contrary to theories that public opinion prevails over business interests on high-salience issues (Culpepper 2011, Smith 2000), the political space created for reform in this case remained narrow. Section 4.4 examines a second case in which high issue salience during the 2005 presidential campaign facilitated incremental reform. Equity appeals compelled the opposition to accept elimination of a regressive tax benefit for stock owners that business and the right had long defended; yet this reform was marginal in terms of revenue. Finally, Section 4.5 analyzes the Bachelet administration's 2008 reform to curtail a regressive construction-sector VAT exemption. Multiple strategies made the reform politically viable. Equity appeals as well as linking to both popular benefits and compensations for business helped forge a majority in Congress and contained conflict on what had previously been an extremely controversial issue. However, the measure passed only after the executive granted concessions that left the cost of the benefits included in the reform package uncompensated.

4.1 THE CONCERTACIÓN'S STRATEGY REPERTOIRE

Concertación governments drew on almost every strategy in the reform typology elaborated in Chapter 2. Attenuating impact to temper elite antagonism played a role in nearly every proposal, through phase-ins, temporary measures, and an overarching emphasis on incremental change. Likewise, Finance Ministry officials emphasized the need for fiscal discipline, a preemptive version of emphasizing stabilization to mitigate elite opposition, nearly every time

---

[1] Appendix 4.1 describes the case universe. I omit discussion of VAT increases, which elicited less business opposition, although the right often seized the opportunity to accuse Concertación governments of promoting regressive reforms inconsistent with their professed equity concerns.

a tax increase was proposed. This approach, coupled with elite compensation and/or linking to popular benefits, aimed to tap the Chilean consensus that spending required responsible financing – a lesson taken from Allende's policies and the economic and political turmoil that ensued. Linking to social spending was frequently employed to mobilize public support and legitimate tax increases. Although business and the right countered with arguments that revenue should be generated through reallocation and increased efficiency, informants from these sectors acknowledged that linking to social spending made it more difficult to oppose tax increases (interviews: UDI-A 2005, CPC-A 2005, CPC-B 2007). Likewise, Concertación informants asserted that tax increases were feasible only when the executive could argue that specific programs required funding (interviews: Finance Ministry-B 2005, Lagos 2006, Marfán 2005). However, tax-side equity appeals were as or more central for most of the cases discussed in this chapter.

Astute reform strategies not only aimed to circumvent business-right opposition, they were often also important for containing dissident within the governing coalition. When executives increased regressive taxes, as Lagos was compelled to do in 2003 given anticipated business-right rejection of other options (Chapter 3), linking to progressive social spending placated Socialists and other left-leaning Concertación legislators. Executives also faced internal dissent from the economically liberal wing of the coalition, whose members were more likely to agree with business and the right that tax increases would hurt growth and investment. Furthermore, Christian Democrats (PDC) were often susceptible to opposition arguments that tax increases would hurt middle-class sectors because their party was engaged in electoral competition with the right-wing UDI to attract middle-class voters. The PDC viewed the middle class as a "natural enclave of support" (Boeninger 2005: 25–26); yet the UDI made public its goal of attracting these voters away from the PDC (Huneeus 2003: 122). Competition intensified in the late 1990s and early 2000s as the UDI made significant electoral gains and surpassed the PDC as the party with the largest vote share in the 2001 parliamentary elections. Vertical equity appeals in conjunction with measures that narrowly targeted high-income taxpayers while leaving working professionals untouched could therefore be important for ensuring PDC support.

Yet notwithstanding governments' strategic acumen, tempering elite antagonism remained difficult, especially for direct tax increases. Efforts to mobilize public support did not necessarily drive the right to break ranks with business, particularly when elections were distant. And disciplinary breaches within the Concertación were not always precluded. The following analysis of Chile's 2001 Anti-Evasion Reform illustrates the potential and limitations of Concertación strategies in a nonelectoral context. While the reform was a revenue-raising success, it entailed a major political battle that discouraged the Lagos administration from subsequently addressing many important tax issues that remained pending (Chapter 3).

4.2 THE 2001 ANTI-EVASION REFORM

In August 2000, the newly elected Lagos administration sent an ambitious reform package to Congress designed to raise revenue for social spending by fighting tax evasion and avoidance. This approach was viewed as more feasible than increasing tax rates, given business's strong instrumental power and business-right antagonism toward the new Socialist administration (Chapter 3). Further, Concertación policymakers were concerned that major tax increases could discourage investment, given the economic recession.

The proposed anti-evasion measures included more funding and more auditors for the tax agency, stronger sanctions for breaking tax laws, and new powers to help the tax agency audit more effectively, including expanded access to bank information – the tax agency would be allowed to review bank information on loans and collateral. These and other anti-evasion measures accounted for 84 percent of the reforms' expected 2001–05 revenue yield.[2]

Measures to control tax avoidance accounted for the remaining 16 percent of expected revenue. These measures entailed closing loopholes and restricting income-tax benefits deemed technically unjustified. Examples included permanently eliminating a tax credit that allowed businesses to deduct property taxes from corporate tax obligations,[3] restricting accelerated depreciation, regulating the use of losses in mergers,[4] and lowering the gross-sales cutoff to qualify for presumed-income tax regimes in agriculture and transport. Given the center-left coalition's prior experience with similar initiatives, the administration anticipated that these tax base-broadening measures, which targeted large corporations and business owners,[5] would be highly controversial.

To manage opposition, the government employed both vertical and horizontal equity appeals. Regarding vertical equity, authorities regularly stressed that evasion favored the rich at the expense of the poor.[6] Lagos (interview, 2006) recalled: "I would say: when you go to buy a kilo of bread, you pay 18 percent VAT. You have no trick, no mechanism for paying less. The poor pay all their taxes. And it is just [fair] that the rich pay all their taxes." The finance minister made similar appeals: "Chileans must pay the taxes they owe, as do the immense majority, especially the most humble."[7] Regarding horizontal equity – the principle that taxpayers of similar means should bear similar tax burdens – the proposal text asserted: "Tax evasion entails great inequity

---

[2] Author's calculations based on Finance Ministry estimates provided to Congress.
[3] This benefit was temporarily suspended in 1998; governments regularly legislated "temporary" tax increases to temper business-right opposition.
[4] Businesses bought bankrupt firms – often simply accounting books of long-defunct companies – for the sole purpose of deducting losses from their tax obligations; Chile allowed infinite loss carry-forward and carry-back.
[5] SII 2000a, Proyecto 1486: Mensaje 178–342, Aug. 24, 2000, www.camara.cl
[6] *El Mercurio:* Sept. 10, 2000, March 14, 2001.
[7] *El Mercurio*, March 10, 2001.

between those who comply with their tax obligations and those who do not.…
From an ethical perspective, no one can oppose an initiative that pursues compliance with the law."[8]

The government extended these legitimating appeals to the income tax base-broadening measures. Horizontal equity appeals were directly applicable to several measures that curtailed sector-specific tax benefits. The finance minister explained: "The proposed changes tend to improve the allocation of resources by applying the same tax rates to [economic] agents of similar characteristics."[9]
More generally, the government equated tax avoidance with tax evasion in terms of impropriety, even though tax avoidance does not entail breaking the law. A private sector (interview, A 2005) informant described this strategy as follows: "[The government] deliberately mixed and confused tax avoidance, tax planning, evasion, and immorality.… There was a policy of confusing language in order to legitimate persecution of legal practices." Framing the income tax measures as curtailing morally unacceptable behavior rather than simply raising revenue aimed to delegitimate business-right opposition. Executive-branch officials consistently denied that the reform entailed tax increases. When a reporter asked why the government had proposed a tax reform, the finance minister replied: "I do not agree that this is a tax reform. Fundamentally what we have designed is a campaign against evasion."[10]

Concertación governments routinely linked tax increases to social spending, and the Anti-Evasion Reform was no exception. The proposal text explicitly listed the initiatives the revenue would fund, and the government emphasized that it could not move its social agenda forward until the Anti-Evasion Reform had been approved, lest fiscal discipline be jeopardized. However, linking to spending was secondary in this case. The Anti-Evasion Reform's inherent legitimacy, based on equity considerations, was so compelling that "the discussion was more about ethics than the purpose of the funds" (Lagos 2006, interview).

The reform design and equity appeals achieved some successes with business and the right. First, the government secured consensus on the goal of fighting evasion.[11] Business and the right supported some of the anti-evasion measures, including stricter rules and higher fines for fabricating fake VAT receipts. The former tax agency director recalled:

There are people who are really mafias who sell bills to augment [VAT] credits, so that the enterprise pays less VAT. That is a criminal activity, it's fraud. Well, in Congress it was rather easy to obtain more power to persecute and punish those people. Nobody

---

[8] Proyecto 1486: Mensaje 178–342, Aug. 24, 2000, www.camara.cl
[9] Ibid.
[10] *El Mercurio*, Oct. 8, 2000.
[11] The CPC (2000) professed "a strong position rejecting tax evasion, not only because this practice constitutes disloyal and illegitimate competition … but also because evasion constitutes a reprehensible ethical assault."

wants to protect somebody who is [engaging in] fraud in Chile. (Etcheberry 2005, interview)

Second, framing base-broadening measures as fighting morally reprehensible tax avoidance put business and the right on the defensive. Private-sector informants asserted that this strategy damaged business's public image (2005 interviews: Private Sector-A, Mining-B), and business and the right adamantly objected. However, to justify their opposition, business and the right were in the disadvantageous position of explaining the subtle difference between evasion and avoidance; the vast majority of citizens had no experience with these practices.

Available evidence suggests that reform design and equity appeals helped the government maneuver the package through Congress. Government informants attested that their strategy put significant pressure on the right and created space for modifications that otherwise would not have been possible. The former Senate president asserted that the right was in an "absolutely defensive position.... They were looking for any possible argument" against the reform (Zaldívar 2007, interview). Similarly, the former tax agency director, who participated in multiple negotiations on the bill, recalled:

I think we did it well politically. Lagos was in the press every day saying everybody must pay taxes. If he was at a rally with poor people, he asked: when you buy your bread you must pay your taxes, why don't other people want to pay their taxes? The right asked the government to stop that; they didn't want to be associated with illegal things and fraud.... It was a political battle that I think we won. (Etcheberry 2005, interview)

Other government informants made similar comments (2005 interviews: Executive Advisor-A, Boeninger).

More decisive evidence comes from statements by right politicians. The two right senators on the Finance Committee told the press that they abstained instead of voting against the reform because "otherwise, President Lagos would have said that the opposition is against combatting tax evasion."[12] One of these senators later explained: "The title [of the bill] ... evasion – it practically suggests going after criminals. It is very difficult to oppose someone who presents that framing" (Prat 2005, interview). Ultimately, the government secured approval of the reform package on the Senate floor from three institutional senators and abstentions – tacit acceptance – from seven right senators.

However, equity appeals and strategic reform design did not preclude intense opposition to many of the proposed measures. Business and the right adamantly rejected granting the tax agency more powers, particularly bank information access, which they argued violated privacy rights (CPC 2001). Business also complained about the government's plan to hire more auditors. The president of SOFOFA, the industry peak association, provocatively quipped that the administration had mused "I'm going to hire more inspectors and mess

---

[12] Senators Prat and Matthei quoted in *El Mercurio*, March 15, 2001.

with all the businessmen in Chile."[13] The right followed suit, arguing that the tax agency was already too powerful and that taxpayers did not have sufficient rights and protections. Direct appeals to business failed to build support on these issues. As the former tax agency director recounted, "I asked them: Why are you fighting this? You should be in favor. You don't evade taxes, it's your competitors who do…. Well, they want to have it both ways…. They don't want their competition to avoid taxes, but they want to have that possibility" (Etcheberry 2005, interview).

Meanwhile, although the government's framing strategy and equity appeals put business and the right on the defensive, the base-broadening measures remained highly controversial. Portraying the use of tax benefits as abusive and unfair antagonized business leaders, who resented the insinuation that they and their colleagues were engaging in illicit activities (Private Sector-A 2005, interview).[14] Business antagonism toward the government culminated in a famous speech delivered by the CPC president at a prestigious business conference, in which he provocatively turned to Lagos, who was present on stage, and declared: "Mr. President, please let us work in peace."[15]

Business and the right struck back against the base-broadening reforms in three ways. First, they countered that the bill did contain tax increases, government assertions notwithstanding. The CPC decried the reform as a "profound change to the rules of the game" that would increase the tax burden on those who already paid their fare share (CPC 2000), and the right denounced the proposal as a "hidden tax reform" and a "Trojan horse."[16] Second, business and the right asserted that the tax benefits promoted investment, not tax avoidance. Business association leaders even declared that eliminating these tax benefits would jeopardize economic recovery.[17] Third, business and the right countered the executive's vertical equity appeals by claiming the reform would hurt small and medium-sized businesses.[18] The latter two arguments were part of a broader strategy to strip the Concertación of small-business support and to draw conservative Christian Democrats away from the government's fold (Silva 2002).

These arguments did resonate with the conservative wing of the Christian Democratic Party (PDC) (Eyzaguirre 2007, interview). PDC dissent compelled the executive to remove several measures from early drafts of the reform, contributed to delays in the lower house of Congress, and even helped defeat one measure on the Senate floor. Restricting the presumed-income regimes

---

[13] *El Mercurio*, Oct. 6, 2000.
[14] *El Mercurio*, Nov. 9, 2000. Likewise, Senator Matthei (2006, interview) asserted that what the right opposed most about the reform was the government's introduction of the term "avoidance" and its moral condemnation of "perfectly legal" behavior.
[15] *El Mercurio*, Nov. 22, 2001.
[16] *El Mercurio*: Aug. 27, Oct 14, 2000.
[17] *La Tercera*, Jan. 20, 2001, *El Mercurio*, Oct. 17, 2000.
[18] CPC 2000; *El Mercurio*: Sept. 13, Dec. 13, 2000, April 15, 2001.

proved most problematic. Many Christian Democrats feared these measures would hurt small businesses already hard-hit by the recession, even though tax agency studies showed that ironically, presumed-income regimes primarily benefited large producers (SII 2000a). The executive accordingly left the presumed-income regime for agriculture untouched in the reform initiative, but Christian Democrats joined the right in voting against the measure that would restrict the transport sector's presumed-income regime. Further, key Christian Democrats were reluctant to grant the tax agency additional powers, which business and the right also claimed would hurt small businesses.[19] PDC opposition, along with business-right opposition, contributed to the executive's decision to exclude tax agency access to checking accounts from the reform proposal (Zaldívar 2007, interview); the measure granting the tax agency access to information on loans and collateral passed in the Senate amid significant controversy regarding the voting procedure and over strident objections from several Christian Democrats.[20]

If legitimating appeals failed to prevent disciplinary breaches within the Concertación, it is not surprising that efforts to mobilize public support did not induce the right to break ranks with business. The bill passed in the lower house thanks to the Concertación's majority; the right voted against the reform en bloc. And despite President Lagos's threats to make the reform an issue in the December 2001 parliamentary elections,[21] the right opposed the reform in the Senate, where the governing coalition was nearly tied with the opposition, until the executive negotiated concessions on the base-broadening measures that placated business. While business and the right did not embrace the final reform, informants agreed that it was far more acceptable than the original bill (interviews, 2005: CPC-A, CChC-B, SOFOFA-B, UDI-A; Matthei 2006; CPC-B 2007). Even so, the right voted en bloc against the two most lucrative income-tax base-broadening measures; these measures passed by a narrow margin during the "line-item" vote after the overall reform initiative was approved, thanks in part to support from one of the institutional swing-senators.

Why did efforts to mobilize public opinion have a limited influence on the right? One possibility, which cannot be directly assessed for lack of public opinion data, is that equity appeals did not generate strong public support. Yet the government did not include the issue in its own private polls given the expectation of overwhelming support for fighting tax evasion (interview: FDD 2012), and evidence presented above suggests that right legislators perceived public receptiveness to the government's framing strategy. Setting aside the

---

[19] *La Segunda*, Nov. 14, 2000.
[20] Diario de Sesiones del Senado, Legislatura 343, Extraordinaria, Sesión 46, May 16, 2001: 29–60. Not all Christian Democrats opposed these initiatives. Several asked the executive to reintroduce measures giving the tax agency much broader bank-information access that had been removed from the original reform drafts. *El Mercurio*, Aug. 27, 28, 2000.
[21] *El Mercurio*: March 10, 14, 2001.

question of how the public actually viewed the reform, there are many potential reasons why public opinion many not influence legislators' policy positions (Chapter 2). In this case, a likely explanation involves the nature of party-voter linkages in Chile. Luna (2010) argues that while upper-income voters support the right based on its programmatic positions, the UDI attracts low-income voters through small-scale, district-level clientelism and charismatic appeals. Therefore, the UDI could afford to ignore mass public opinion on tax equity without necessarily incurring electoral costs. In fact, one UDI deputy commented: "The immense majority of people never ask you about your position on tax issues. I have been a member of the Budget Committee for eight years. If you ask me if I think any of my actions in the Budget Committee has caused me to win or lose votes, I would have to say zero" (UDI-A 2005, interview).[22] Moreover, the parliamentary elections were many months away, giving voters ample time to forget the right's position on the Anti-Evasion Reform and granting the right plenty of time to draw attention to other issues. Despite these limitations, the case evidence along with the Concertación's prior difficulties legislating similar reforms suggest that without equity appeals, the right's bargaining position would have been stronger, and the government would have had to make even greater concessions.

The Anti-Evasion Reform proved a revenue-raising success; the legislation enacted was expected to raise approximately 1 percent of GDP, the largest increase since the 1990 tax reform. The reform's actual revenue yield exceeded this figure, possibly by as much as 50 percent (2005 interviews: Etcheberry, SII-A, Marcel). However, the scope that the government's framing strategy and equity appeals created for direct tax reform remained narrow. The income tax base-broadening measures entailed only about 0.1 percent of GDP. Moreover, the Finance Ministry left many important initiatives that the tax agency had proposed for controlling income-tax evasion and avoidance out of the reform, given anticipations of strong business-right opposition (SII 2000a, b; interviews: SII-A, B 2005, Jorratt 2005, Eyzaguirre 2007). As with the subsequent 2001 corporate tax increase (Chapter 3), business's capacity to restrict the reform agenda greatly overshadowed concessions won after the bill was drafted and sent to congress.

4.3 TAXING THE MINING SECTOR

In 2005, the Lagos administration legislated a new mining tax, which culminated a long series of largely frustrated efforts to resolve the problem of

---

[22] Another UDI informant explained: "There is no dramatic cost to voting against a tax increase" because "people on the right have a sensitivity against taxes.... Perhaps the marginal voter has some doubts, but on the whole we are talking to our constituencies" (Dittborn 2005, interview). The right's relevant constituency here is the programmatically oriented upper-income core, not the mass electoral base.

under-taxation in the privately owned mining sector. Business's instrumental power and institutional constraints inherited from the dictatorship thwarted progress during the 1990s. After 2002, increased issue salience improved prospects for reform. A high-profile case of tax avoidance mobilized public opinion against the mining companies and strengthened the executive's resolve. Lagos's 2004 royalty initiative was defeated in Congress despite strong public opinion in favor of reform, but a second proposal, which took the form of a "specific tax on mining," passed in 2005. Closer proximity to the 2005 presidential election placed greater pressure on the right to accept the second proposal; legislators faced higher political costs to voting against the extremely popular reform. Recognizing that pressure to tax the mining sector would only increase during the electoral campaign, business and the right made a strategic decision to accept the second reform, which they viewed as the lesser evil compared to its precursor.

Strong public support for reform in this pre–electoral context thereby counterbalanced business power. However, public opinion by no means overwhelmed business power. In contrast to theories that business interests lose to public opinion on high-salience issues, the political space created for reform was narrow. The 2005 mining tax was marginal in cross-national context and had a minimal impact on the mining sector's high profits.

Mining Sector Under-Taxation

Copper mining in Chile was nationalized in 1971 with widespread popular approval and unanimous congressional support. The market-oriented dictatorship did not privatize CODELCO, the state-owned copper company, but it laid the groundwork for private investment in the sector. International companies entered Chile in the 1980s to develop new copper fields, and private investment accelerated in the early 1990s. By 2002, CODELCO controlled only 33 percent of copper production (SII 2003: 31).

To encourage investment, the dictatorship rewrote the mining code on terms highly favorable to private companies. Mining concessions were treated as close to private property as possible given that the constitution asserted state ownership of subsoil copper (Finance Ministry-D 2005, interview). Further, mining investors could register their enterprises as partnerships, which enjoyed special accelerated depreciation privileges. Accelerated depreciation allows companies to defer taxes by applying future asset depreciation against current tax obligations. For corporations, accelerated depreciation applied only to the corporate tax, not to taxes on dividends. For partnerships, however, investors could also apply accelerated depreciation against taxes owed on distributed profits. Because mining companies' initial investments were so large, accelerated depreciation allowed them to register huge losses, thereby deferring corporate taxes for many years. Meanwhile, investors could withdraw financial profits without paying personal income taxes. This arrangement entailed "a credit at zero interest rate for the personal consumption of foreign investors," as Lagos's finance minister explained. "Normally you postpone the tax provided that the firm reinvests money. The way this [accelerated depreciation] law was written didn't require the firm to reinvest the money. It could be sent abroad to finance a yacht…. That was nonsense" (Eyzaguirre 2007, interview). Accelerated depreciation was one of many tax benefits that the dictatorship froze in place through Decree Law 600, which guaranteed mining companies tax invariability for twenty years.

Two avoidance mechanisms commonly used by multinationals helped mining companies further reduce their tax obligations. First, to avoid the 35 percent tax on dividends, they could distribute profits as interest payments on loans from related enterprises, taxed at only 4 percent. Accordingly, mining companies often maintained high debt-to-equity ratios. Second, companies could manipulate transfer prices, which involves contracting services or buying inputs from a related company abroad at above-market prices; these inflated expenses are deductible (in some percentage) from the Chilean subsidiary's income-tax base.

Thanks to these tax benefits and avoidance mechanisms, only two of the largest ten private mines[23] paid corporate income taxes between 1995 and 2003, and only three paid taxes on distributed profits. From 1991 to 2003, accelerated depreciation and sub-capitalization cost the state an estimated U.S.$443 million in potential tax revenue (SII 2003).

Instrumental Power and Institutional Constraints

Business's strong instrumental power, particularly cross-sectoral cohesion and partisan linkages, hindered efforts to redress mining sector under-taxation. Business cohesion extended to the mining sector, even though most of the largest mines were foreign-owned and belonged to a separate association, the Mining Council, which was not a CPC member. First, shared neoliberal, antitax ideology fostered domestic business solidarity with the mining sector. Second, indirect linkages counteracted the foreign-owned mines' formal organizational isolation from the domestic business associations (interviews, Mining-A 2006, Mining-B 2005). Some Chileans held shares in or owned mines belonging to both the Mining Council and SONAMI, which represented smaller, domestically owned private mines and did hold CPC membership. For example, Jean Paul Luksic, the president of Antofagasta Plc and an executive board member of the Mining Council, also held an individual membership in SONAMI.[24] In addition, the construction sector, an influential CPC member, had strong economic linkages to mining, which cultivated perceptions of common interest (interview, CChC-A 2005). The foreign companies also benefited from domestic

[23] These ten mines accounted for 59 percent of copper production.
[24] See www.consejominero.cl, www.sonami.cl

business's partisan linkages, even though their owners were not a relevant political constituency. The right parties opposed efforts to increase mining taxation in accord with their small-state, low-tax ideology and thanks to pressure from the CPC and its member associations to defend mining interests.

Initiatives to curtail mining-sector tax benefits therefore incurred opposition from the business associations and the right, especially UDI. Throughout the conflict that developed, these actors maintained that altering the mining sector's tax regime in any way would illegitimately alter the rules of the game and deter investment – notwithstanding Chile's comparative advantages that made copper mining highly profitable, as well as the low tax burden on mining compared to other countries.[25]

Institutional constraints inherited from the dictatorship further hindered reform. First, the Mining Concessions Law held constitutional status and could be altered only with a supermajority of four-sevenths. This constraint augmented business's instrumental power by making it easier for the right to block reform in Congress. Second, Decree Law (DL) 600 held treaty status and could not be violated without risking lawsuits in international tribunals, a prospect the executive branch found highly undesirable (interviews: Finance Ministry-C, D 2005). The DL 600 invariability clause strengthened the foreign mining companies' bargaining position; they would not have to pay tax increases unless they voluntarily chose to do so.

Successive Reform Attempts, 1998–2001

Business's instrumental power, and occasionally (perceived) structural power as well, repeatedly thwarted efforts to strengthen the mining tax regime. In the 1990s, the Finance Ministry advocated a technically appealing solution to the accelerated-depreciation problem: subjecting partnerships to the same tax rules applied to corporations. This approach simplified the tax code, promoted horizontal equity, and also curtailed tax avoidance beyond the mining sector. However, business and the right "viscerally opposed" the reform (interview, Finance Ministry-G 2007). Although it was included in a 1998 anti-evasion reform, the measure had to be removed during negotiations with the right in the Senate. Even if it had passed, it would have applied only to new investments in the mining sector, thanks to DL 600 (interview, LyD-A 2005).

The Frei administration also considered a copper royalty. Studies were completed in 1998, but the Finance Minister harbored concerns regarding

---

[25] According to a Colorado School of Mines study, copper mining profit margins in Chile were the highest among nineteen countries analyzed, while effective tax rates were the lowest (Otto 2000). The Fraser Institute's annual survey of mining companies placed Chile within the top three countries most favorable for investment and exploration from 2001 to 2003. A Mining Sector (I 2011) informant noted that the quality of Chile's resources and its political stability made the country "number one in copper production by far."

structural power once the East Asian crisis struck: "I would have had to be crazy – employment and growth were falling – to go for the tax" (interview, Aninat 2007). Further, the administration was too weak politically during its final years in office and had too little time left to take on a battle with business and the right over taxes (interview, Aninat 2007).

The Lagos administration tackled aspects of the mining tax problem in the 2001 Anti-Evasion Reform with limited success. Given failed prior attempts to equalize the status of partnerships and corporations, the administration tried a new approach to the accelerated-depreciation problem: restricting its use to the corporate tax only. The reform package also included a sub-capitalization rule; interest payments would be taxed as repatriated profits when debt to equity ratios exceeded 3 to 1. These measures were approved after some concessions to business and the right. However, DL 600 shielded existing investments from the new accelerated depreciation rules (interview, Finance Ministry-C 2006).

Building Momentum for Reform

A high-profile tax avoidance case in 2002 generated momentum for reform. Exxon's sale of the mine Disputada las Condes to Anglo American elicited popular outrage and government condemnation. Disputada had used all the available incentives and therefore paid no taxes in Chile during its twenty-four years of operation. Adding insult to injury, the multinationals conducted the U.S.$1.3 billion sale "offshore" by creating subsidiaries in the Cayman and Virgin Islands to avoid U.S.$300 million in capital gains taxes.[26] Lagos (interview, 2006) responded forcefully to the affront: "It was a tense moment.... I said to the companies: if you do this, you are going to have problems with me in Chile. Chile is a serious country." To force Exxon to pay Chilean taxes, the government legislated a special reform in July 2002. The multinational ultimately paid a modest sum of U.S.$39 million (Otto et al. 2006: 123).

The Disputada scandal mobilized public opinion against the mining companies and motivated the government to seriously consider a royalty. A high-level informant recalled: "The Disputada case made a very bad, very bad impression on public opinion. It was in the news every day" (interview, Finance Ministry-D 2005). The budget director identified this episode as a critical turning point: "The Finance Ministry historically had been reluctant to deal with the mining taxation issue, up until the sale of Disputada.... The behavior of the foreign investors was too opportunistic, and that reactivated the whole issue of why the mines paid so little tax. After that, the idea of the royalty advanced" (interview, Marcel 2005).[27]

---

[26] Special Mining Committee Report, Boletín S/672-12, May 17, 2004: 5.
[27] Another Finance Ministry (A 2005, interview) informant attributed this reluctance to structural power concerns.

Meanwhile, the Disputada episode gave momentum to Concertación royalty activists in Congress led by PDC Senator Lavandero. These legislators achieved a significant step forward in 2003 with the formation of a special senate committee to investigate mining-sector taxation. The committee's exhaustive hearings over the next year kept the royalty in the public eye, maintained pressure on the Finance Ministry to address the issue, and signaled to the mining sector that higher taxation was a concrete possibility (interview, Mining-F 2007).

From Avoiding Conflict to Initiating a Royalty

Given strong business power, the Finance Ministry did not pursue a royalty until late in Lagos's term. The idea was considered but ultimately discarded as an alternative to the 2003 VAT increase. The executive did not want another major tax battle after the Anti-Evasion Reform and the 2001 corporate tax increase that could disrupt relations with business again and anticipated that circumventing opposition in congress would be at best difficult (interviews: Eyzaguirre 2007, Finance Ministry-B, C 2005). A Finance Ministry (B 2005) informant recalled: "We were all worn out. At that point, proposing a royalty would have been crazy."

Instead, the executive pursued a "nonconfrontational approach" (interviews, Finance Ministry-C, D 2005) requesting that mines protected by DL 600 voluntarily renounce their tax privileges (especially accelerated depreciation). The Finance Ministry used pressure from Concertación royalty activists to strengthen its bargaining position. In exchange for renouncing tax invariability, the Finance Ministry assured the mines that it would not pursue a royalty.[28] If they did not accept this offer, the Finance Minister warned that the executive would be forced to send a much harsher tax bill to Congress; he told the Mining Council: "The Concertación guys are going to come for you, and it will be much more costly, believe me" (interview, Eyzaguirre 2007).

However, the mining companies did not agree to relinquish DL 600 protections. Finance Ministry informants attributed this decision to underestimation of both the executive's resolve to address the tax problem and support for a royalty among the public and legislators (interviews: Finance Ministry-C, D 2005, Eyzaguirre 2007). A mining sector informant, in contrast, attributed the decision to the perceived lack of credibility of the government's promise not to initiate a royalty, precisely because the mines recognized how much pressure was building for reform (interview, Mining-D 2005). When it became clear that the Mining Council would not accept the government's offer, the Finance Minister decided "to go for a royalty" (interview, Eyzaguirre 2007).

---

[28] *La Tercera*, Jan. 8, 10, 2004.

The 2004 Royalty Proposal

The 2004 royalty entailed a levy of 3 percent on annual copper sales, phased in gradually over three years. The Finance Ministry calculated that the royalty would only reduce mining profit margins from 20 percent to 19.5 percent (interview, Lagos 2006). This moderate design counteracted structural power arguments and undermined the Mining Council's campaign to bring international pressure to bear on the government.[29] When Australians complained about the proposed legislation, Lagos (interview, 2006) responded: "If you would like, I will withdraw this bill and propose instead the royalty you have in Australia – much higher!" The mining minister similarly dismissed concerns over investment, emphasizing the royalty's minimal impact on mining profits.[30]

More importantly, the reform design circumvented institutional constraints associated with DL 600. The invariability clause did not apply to the royalty, which technically was not a tax (Finance Ministry-D 2005, interview). If the proposal were approved, all mines would have to contribute more revenue to state coffers. Yet this advantage came at a cost: passing the reform required a four-sevenths supermajority, because it altered the Mining Concessions Law.

The royalty's remarkable popularity made winning enough opposition votes to pass the reform feasible. The royalty enjoyed strong inherent legitimacy, based on nationalistic sentiments that copper wealth belonged to Chileans and outrage that foreign companies were appropriating this wealth without fairly compensating the state. A survey conducted in April 2004 found that 67 percent of citizens favored a royalty, whereas only 15 percent disapproved. Support was not confined to Concertación loyalists; 60 percent of intended UDI voters and 80 percent of intended RN voters supported the measure (CERC 2004).

Yet the right's core constituency intensely opposed the reform. The mining sector rejected the royalty not only out of systematic opposition to higher taxation but also due to concerns over property rights. The problem stemmed from inconsistencies between the Mining Concessions Law, which treated concessions as tantamount to private property, and the constitution, which asserted state ownership of subsoil copper. The royalty bill sided with the constitution, emphasizing the state's "absolute, exclusive, inalienable, and imprescriptible ownership of the mines" and describing the royalty as a fee for extracting state-owned resources.[31] As a Finance Ministry (C 2005) informant recounted, the proposal's emphasis on state ownership "generated very strong uncertainty for the mining sector, regarding their right to concessions for the lifetime of the mine."[32] Similarly, a private sector informant asserted "The way the proposal

---

[29] *El Mercurio*, May 24, June 3, 2004.
[30] *El Mercurio*, June 23, 2004.
[31] Ibid.
[32] *El Mercurio*, April 20, 2004.

was formulated called into question mining property rights, and the companies were going to defend that to the death" (interview, Mining-D 2005). The domestic business community defended the mining sector's position. Although the Mining Council and SONAMI were the primary business actors involved, the CPC, and CPC president Claro in particular, actively participated in the opposition campaign (interviews: Eyzaguirre 2007, Finance Ministry-B 2005, Lagos 2006, Mining-B, C, D 2005, Mining-F 2007, CPC-B 2007, CPC-C 2005).[33] The CPC's former general manager recalled, "We were permanently coordinating with SONAMI to support it and defend its position" (interview, CPC-B 2007). Claro made regular press statements against the royalty and lobbied to ensure opposition from right-party legislators. In addition to principled solidarity and concern over changing the rules of the game for foreign investment, business associations feared the royalty could set a precedent for similar levies on other natural resource sectors like forestry or salmon farming (interviews: CPC-B 2007, CPC-D 2008). Horizontal equity considerations did resonate within the ranks of the domestic business community according to several informants (interviews: Finance Ministry-D 2005, Mining-E 2011, CEP 2005); one observed: "The business world was a bit uncomfortable with the fact that mining did not pay taxes" (interview, CEP 2005). In practice, however, horizontal equity considerations detracted from business cohesion only marginally. While the CPC was less active on the royalty compared to previous reforms with manifest cross-sectoral impact (interviews: CPC-B 2007, Mining-C 2005), its initiatives against the reform were nevertheless important from the mining sector's perspective (interviews: Mining-B, D 2005).

The right by and large voted in its core constituency's interest, despite the royalty's popularity. The UDI rejected the proposal en bloc. UDI arguments mirrored those advanced by the private sector; government informants commented on the extreme degree to which the party was willing to defend the mining sector (Finance Ministry-C 2005, D 2005, G 2007, Eyzaguirre 2007). Meanwhile, of fourteen RN legislators identified in preliminary consultations as potential royalty supporters,[34] only four voted for the proposal. Although the royalty won majorities in both houses, it fell short of the requisite supermajority.

Overwhelming public support for the royalty did give the right cause for concern. Municipal elections were approaching, and press coverage highlighted that opposition to the royalty by the right could improve the Concertación's electoral prospects.[35] The right worried that rejecting the royalty could prolong debate over mining taxation into the coming year, potentially affecting the 2005 presidential and parliamentary elections.[36] The Alianza endeavored to control political costs by proposing an alternative royalty bill (interview,

---

[33] *El Mercurio*, April 20, June 26, 2004.
[34] *El Mercurio*, June 22, April 20, 2004.
[35] *El Mercurio*, April 25, 2004.
[36] *El Mercurio*, April 23, 25, 2004.

UDI-A 2005), which ostensibly demonstrated the right's agreement that mining should be taxed more heavily.[37] A few Alianza legislators adjudicated between electoral pressures and business interests by abstaining from the vote, while others framed rejection of the royalty as a defense of the mining regions, which would not receive any direct share of royalty revenue.[38] Others were prepared to assume potential political costs. An RN deputy who voted against the royalty recalled: "It was difficult, but I vote according to what I think. I don't vote according to what the majority says. If we voted that way we would have Evo Morales here in Chile" (interview, Kuschel 2005).

The 2005 Mining Tax

In January 2005, the executive presented a second mining tax initiative. In the wake of the royalty's defeat, the Finance Ministry opted for a different design: a "specific tax" of 5 percent on mining profits. The tax base would be the same as the corporate tax base, but accumulated losses and accelerated depreciation, among other costs, would not be deductible.

Politically, the mining tax offered several advantages. Like any other tax, the initiative required only a simple majority in Congress. This proposal was also less threatening to the mining sector because it did not raise property-rights issues (interview, Finance Ministry-C 2005). However, companies with DL 600 protections could not be obliged to pay the new tax. To deal with this problem, the government included a new invariability clause as an enticement. Companies that relinquished the old invariability clause would pay a reduced specific-tax rate of 4 percent, and they would be exempt from future mining tax increases for fifteen years. The details of this incentive were negotiated directly with the Mining Council and representatives of the foreign companies to ensure that the companies would opt to pay the new tax (interviews, Mining-A 2006, Mining-E 2011).

In contrast to the royalty, the mining tax passed twenty-eight to five in the Senate; seven right senators voted for the reform. Business, meanwhile, implicitly accepted the reform. The Mining Council and the CPC denounced the mining tax – the domestic business community was even more concerned regarding the potential precedent for other sectoral taxes.[39] However, neither association lobbied actively against the bill (interviews: Finance Ministry-B,

---

[37] Eyzaguirre called the Alianza proposal a "joke." *El Mercurio*, Aug. 11, 2005.

[38] Diario de Sesiones, Cámara de Diputados, Legislatura 351a, Ordinaria, Sesión 19a, July 21, 2004: 32. The executive could have won more votes by earmarking royalty revenue to mining regions, but Lagos (interview, 2006) firmly believed that extraordinary copper revenue should be invested in research and development, following the Nordic approach.

[39] A CPC manager explained that the mining tax: "broke Chile's tax neutrality. They chose a productive activity, mining, because it had high profits, and we believed that was inappropriate. The same criterion could lead to specific taxes on other activities" (interview, CPC-D 2008).

C 2005, Eyzaguirre 2007, Marcel 2005, Mining-F 2007), and all of the large mines subsequently switched to the new invariability clause, upholding their end of the gentlemen's agreement reached with the executive branch (interview, Mining-A 2006).

Closer proximity to the national elections induced both the right and business to accept the popular reform. The mining tax went to the Senate floor in May; elections were scheduled for December. Consequently, the anticipated political cost of voting against the mining tax was significantly higher than in 2004. In addition, the right anticipated that the executive would initiate an even harsher proposal if the mining tax failed, given pressure from Concertación legislators and electoral calculations. The right would then be forced to either accept a proposal it opposed even more strongly, or reject a popular reform immediately before the presidential election and risk incurring the wrath of voters, who would have little time to forget the right's policy stance before entering the polling booths. Given these considerations, the UDI did not instruct its legislators to vote against the tax, breaking with its strategy of voting en bloc: "This is one of the few economic issues for which the UDI gave its legislators freedom in voting. We always try to formulate a single position on tax issues and economic reforms, because we know that one of the UDI's strengths is unity" (interview, UDI-A 2005). Another informant noted that opposing the reform was particularly difficult for legislators representing mining regions, where support for the tax was especially strong (interview, Dittborn 2005).

Business's stance of reluctant acceptance reflected similar strategic considerations. Furthermore, the mining sector viewed the specific tax as a lesser evil compared to the royalty, given that the Finance Ministry steered clear of property-rights issues. The following quotes illustrate this position:

With the first proposal, there was will to go against it very strongly. But with the second proposal, there was nothing left to do. The mining companies realized that they would not get anything by swimming against the current. It was useless. We had to try to close that chapter quickly. (Interview, Mining-D 2005)

The CPC took a pragmatic position. Neither the CPC nor the parties that traditionally supported the economic model defended the mining sector strongly, because the cause was politically unviable. (Interview, Mining-F 2007)

Finance Ministry informants made similar observations:

They understood that this was the last possibility for something reasonable. If the proposal had not been approved, the government would have had to initiate an extremely harsh reform, perhaps similar to what the Concertación legislators had proposed, and the opposition would have faced voting against it just before the elections. (Interview, Finance Ministry-C 2005)

In the end we convinced the mining sector that having that tax was better for them than raising the issue during the electoral campaign, because we did have some in the Concertación who wanted to go far beyond. So it was better for them to accept the moderate tax. (Interview, Eyzaguirre 2007)

Closer proximity to the national elections thus made the Finance Ministry's strategy of using the reform's immense popularity and pressure from the Concertación's left wing to threaten the mining sector more effective.[40]

The Important but Limited Impact of Public Opinion

High issue salience and strong public support were critical for pressuring business and the right to accept reform. However, the influence of public opinion was limited given the context of strong business power. The majority of Chileans likely would have supported a much more substantial levy, yet the mining tax had little impact on the sector's high profits, and the reform was marginal in cross-national context. That same year, Bolivia legislated a much more substantial levy on hydrocarbons, the country's main extractive resource (Chapter 8). The hydrocarbons tax applied a rate of 32 percent to the value of production, whereas Chile's 4 percent mining tax applied only to profits, a narrower tax base. In retrospect, the mining sector recognized that it had secured a very favorable deal (interviews, Mining-D 2005, Mining-F 2007). Likewise, government informants described the tax as "very small" or "very modest" (interviews, Finance Ministry-B 2005, Lagos 2006).

Business's instrumental power, enhanced by inherited institutional constraints, precluded more significant reform despite popular support. As Lagos (interview, 2006) recounted: "A higher rate would have been rejected. I preferred a lower rate so that the proposal would pass." Informants identified the royalty as one of the most difficult and controversial tax reforms attempted by the Lagos administration; the former president (Lagos 2006, interview) asserted that it was *the* tax reform that business and the right fought hardest against during his term.

4.4 ELIMINATING A REGRESSIVE INCOME TAX BENEFIT

High issue salience during the presidential campaign helped the Lagos administration legislate a second reform in 2005: eliminating a tax benefit for owners of new-issue stocks. Concertación technocrats had long condemned this benefit as regressive and technically unjustified, but while limitations were imposed in

---

[40] Pressure from public opinion and Concertación legislators likely would have grown even stronger had the debate extended into the following year, when copper prices more than doubled to reach a peak of U.S.$4/pound. A mining-sector informant observed: "Nobody ever thought that the price of copper would shoot up like it did.... Looking back, having closed the issue in that moment was very opportune. Very, very opportune" (Mining-F 2007). Similarly high prices following Chile's 2010 earthquake precluded government concerns over structural power (Finance Ministry-J 2011, interview) and contributed to the copper companies' strategic decision to accept royalty increases (Mining-I, J 2011), partly to avoid popular backlash and pressure for more radical reform. See Chapter 9 on other aspects of the 2010 tax reform that financed reconstruction.

the 1990s, eliminating the tax benefit remained off the agenda due to strong business-right opposition. However, an unexpected opportunity for reform arose in 2005 thanks to electoral competition initiated by the right on the issue of inequality. In this context, vertical equity appeals compelled the right to deviate from its core constituency's preferences.

Pinochet's Stock Owner Tax Benefit

Article "57 *bis*" of Chile's income tax code allowed owners of new-issue stocks to deduct 20 percent of the value of the original investment from their income tax base in perpetuity, as long as the stocks remained in the taxpayer's possession. Article 57 *bis* constituted a highly regressive and inefficient subsidy for wealthy investors. For a taxpayer in the top bracket who held roughly U.S.$31,000 of stocks for ten years, 57 *bis* guaranteed an average annual real rate of return, above and beyond market-based profitability, of 9 percent (Ministerio de Hacienda 2005: 93). The top centile of income taxpayers – a mere 0.5 percent of adults – received 72 percent of the fiscal benefit (SII 2005: 43). Article 57 *bis* was intended to stimulate capital-market investment after Chile's 1982 crisis, but Concertación economists agreed that no technical justifications remained by 1990. Instead, 57 *bis* reduced capital-market dynamism, since investors lost the lucrative tax benefit if they traded the stocks (Ministerio de Hacienda 2005: 94).

On average, 57 *bis* cost the state U.S.$41 million per year from 1990 to 1998, when the Frei administration managed to curtail the tax benefit, and U.S.$31 million per year thereafter.[41] While this fiscal cost was small in comparative terms, the accumulated loss was significant: U.S.$580 million from 1990 to 2005, which could have financed the first six years of *Chile Solidario*, the Lagos administration's flagship antipoverty program.[42]

Instrumental Power and Limited Prospects for Reform

Although Concertación administrations repeatedly assessed prospects for eliminating 57 *bis*, business's strong instrumental power kept the issue off the agenda for most of the 1990s. From 1990–97, governments avoided pressing for reform, given business and the right's adamant defense of the tax benefit as an "acquired property right" (Marfán 2005, interview). This association with property rights, a core business concern, made 57 *bis* a dangerous issue for the new democracy. Frei's sub-secretary of finance explained:

It is very important not to push the discussion to the point of undermining values that are important for bringing important social groups into the system.... The issue of

---

[41] Figures in 2005 dollars (Jorratt's database).
[42] Author's calculations, Informe 5863, Comisión de Hacienda, Cámara de Diputados, Jan. 21, 2003.

property rights in Chile generated enormous political ruptures in civil coexistence. The agrarian reform in the 70s, socialization of businesses during Allende's government, various rounds of arbitrary privatizations under Pinochet.... These are the issue that one does not want to reopen in the middle of a transition to democracy. (Marfán 2005, interview)

Motivations for avoiding conflict aside, the Concertación lacked sufficient votes for reform during this period, since the right and Pinochet's designated senators together held the majority of seats. Eliminating 57 *bis* was included in early drafts of the 1990 tax reform, but the above considerations, as well as low revenue yield, led the Alywin administration to drop the measure (2005 interviews: Marfán, Ffrench-Davis). The Frei administration declined several Concertación senators' request to include the issue in a 1995 bill to fund pension increases for similar reasons (interviews: Bitar 2007, Aninat 2007).

By sidestepping the issue of acquired property rights, however, the Concertación was able to restrict the use of 57 *bis* in a 1998 package to finance additional pension increases. The tax benefit was eliminated for new-issue stocks acquired after 1998, but investors who had purchased shares previously were not affected. Complaints invoking acquired property rights were therefore essentially absent from the congressional debate. Linking to social spending and compensations in the form of new investment incentives also mitigated business-right opposition (interview, Marfán 2005).[43]

Thereafter, the Lagos administration explored possibilities for definitively eliminating 57 *bis* on several occasions to no avail. The Finance Ministry decided against including the initiative in the Anti-Evasion Reform, anticipating avid business-right resistance (interview, Finance Ministry-H 2005). The issue was subsequently discussed on several occasions with the business associations, but their response was consistent, resolute rejection (Finance Ministry-B 2005, interview).

The 2005 Reform Opportunity

Electoral competition from the right on the issue of inequality gave the Lagos administration an unexpected opportunity to eliminate 57 *bis*. Given the unusually high salience of inequality during a presidential campaign, vertical equity appeals generated much stronger electoral incentives for the right to deviate from its core constituency's preferences than in 2001, when the government made similar appeals regarding the Anti-Evasion Reform.

In April 2005, Chile's bishops unanimously denounced the country's high and persistent inequality: "In our country, social differences – manifested in the quality of housing, consumption, health, education and salaries – reach

[43] *El Mercurio*, April 15, 2001.

scandalous levels."[44] This statement, which was stronger than the church's previous criticisms of inequality and received broad press coverage, created "quite a shock" (interview, Ffrench-Davis 2005). Moreover, the bishops called upon the presidential candidates to propose policies for reducing inequality.

During the following weeks, inequality became the central issue in the presidential campaign. UDI candidate Lavín perceived an opportunity to attack the Concertación on an issue central to its agenda. Lavín announced his support for the bishops and blamed the Concertación for Chile's persistent inequality and poverty.[45] The Lagos administration defended its record and denounced the right's history of blocking redistributive reforms.[46] The finance minister singled out the right's resistance to the Anti-Evasion Reform, which funded antipoverty programs.[47] Lavín persisted, blaming Lagos for failing to deliver his promise of "growth with equity:" "Inequality, Mr. President, continues.... There is a Chile that grows, but it is for the few, and the great majority have not yet benefited."[48] The exchange culminated in a carefully crafted challenge announced by Lagos: "The infamous Article 57 *bis* entails tremendous support for inequality.... Instead of just talking, why don't we agree to eliminate 57 *bis* in less than 24 hours?"[49]

This vertical-equity appeal proved highly successful.[50] In contrast to the Anti-Evasion Reform and the royalty, debate on 57 *bis* was minimal. Lavín accepted the government's challenge with enthusiasm: "Fantastic, we are all for equity. Let's do it."[51] The right legislators followed his lead, contrary to business's policy preferences. Although most of the right still maintained that the tax benefit was a constitutionally protected acquired property right (UDI-A 2005, interview), the proposal received unanimous approval in the lower house and only two negative votes in the Senate – both from nonelected institutional senators.[52] After fifteen years of business-right opposition, 57 *bis* was eliminated within a month.

Given the salience of inequality during the presidential campaign, the anticipated political cost to the right of defending business interests was much higher than in 2000–01. If the right had voted against the reform, the government would have enjoyed a double victory, demonstrating that the right was the main obstacle to enhancing equity in Chile, and that Lavín could not command authority over the oft-divided UDI-RN coalition. With only six months until the election, voters might well have remembered the coalition's policy

---

[44] "Hemos visto al Señor," April 22, 2005. http://documentos.iglesia.cl
[45] *La Nación*, April 27, 2005.
[46] *El Mercurio:* May 6, 11, 2005.
[47] *El Mercurio*, May 6, 2005.
[48] *El Mercurio*, May 7, 2005.
[49] *El Mercurio*, May 10, 2005.
[50] The government also linked the revenue to scholarships for low-income students.
[51] *El Mercurio*, May 11, 2005.
[52] Diario de Sesiones, Legislatura 353, Sesión 5, June 14, 2005: 69.

position and punished Lavín at the polls. Meanwhile, framing the reform as an investment disincentive or denouncing it as hurting the middle class were not viable options. A government informant explained: "57 *bis* clearly made no contribution to [economic] efficiency. It was a pure transfer of resources to rich people; there was no way to argue differently.... It was not possible for the right to oppose the reform after making that argument about inequality" (interview, Finance Ministry-B 2005).

Decisive evidence suggests that electoral concerns associated with Lagos's equity appeal and the timing of the reform motivated the right to accept eliminating 57 *bis*. UDI advisors attributed Lavín's narrow loss to Lagos in 1999 to the right's rejection of a popular labor-rights bill sent to Congress during the presidential campaign,[53] and they feared that rejecting the 2005 reform would impose similar costs. Comparing the two reforms, a Lavín advisor asserted: "The center-right is not willing to fall into the 1999 trap again."[54] Right informants confirmed that electoral calculations affected their vote on the 2005 reform. An UDI deputy candidly explained:

Our candidate made a commitment, and it was also a difficult moment for him. Therefore the political decision was made to support what the candidate said; we had to take maximum safeguards so that it would not be a disaster.... The opposition demonstrated that this time it would accept things that usually it was not disposed to accept so as not to harm the presidential option. (Interview, UDI-A 2005)

Likewise, a technical advisor from the UDI's think tank recounted that when he told legislators eliminating 57 *bis* was "a mistake," they responded: "No, we will lose votes if we don't approve it" (interview, LyD-A 2005). Meanwhile, former president Lagos (interview 2006) maintained that 57 *bis* never would have been eliminated had he not seized the opportunity to publicly challenge Lavín on the equity issue.

4.5 CURTAILING A REGRESSIVE VAT CREDIT

In 2008, the Bachelet administration restricted a regressive and costly VAT credit for constructing housing. Reform remained off the agenda during prior years given the construction sector's strong instrumental power and occasional structural power. However, activism by Concertación legislators paved the way for the executive to address the issue when an opportune moment arose. Multiple reform strategies made the VAT modification politically viable: vertical equity appeals and linking to benefits that appealed to voters, business, and the right helped forge a majority in Congress and contained conflict on what had been an extremely controversial issue. Yet this case again illustrates the narrow room for manoeuver that reform strategies create in contexts of strong

[53] *El Mercurio:* May 12, 13, 2005.
[54] *El Mercurio,* May 13, 2005.

business power. Despite the reform's highly strategic design, the VAT measure passed only after the executive made concessions that curtailed its revenue capacity, leaving the cost of the benefits in the reform package only partially compensated.

Business Power Deters Reform

When the dictatorship incorporated real estate into the VAT, a special tax deduction was created for construction firms with the goal of keeping consumer prices for homes from rising inordinately. However, this special VAT regime for construction was regressive and expensive. The tax agency estimated that 70 percent of the benefits accrued to consumers in the top 20 percent of the income distribution (SII 2005: 44), and many economists argued that the tax benefit directly inflated construction firms' profits (2005 interviews: Agostini, Finance Ministry-A). In 2004, the VAT benefit cost the state 0.3 percent of GPD; the accumulated cost from 1990 to 2008 reached almost U.S.$6 billion (Ministerio de Hacienda 2008). Concertación economists agreed that the tax benefit was technically unjustified and should be substantially restricted or eliminated (interviews: Marcel 2005, Finance Ministry-F 2007, E 2008, Foxley 2006, Aninat 2007, Ffrench-Davis 2005).

However, business power deterred reform. The construction sector enjoyed especially strong instrumental power in the congressional arena. Along with business's partisan linkages to the right, anecdotal evidence suggests that informal ties linked the construction sector to several Concertación legislators, including key Christian Democratic senators whose votes were critical for passing government initiatives (interviews: Montes 2008, Insunza 2007).[55] The construction sector's resource-based sources of instrumental power enhanced its lobbying capacity. The *Cámara Chilena de la Construcción* (CChC) was one of the largest and strongest of Chile's six sectoral peak associations, with 120–130 permanent staff members (interview, CChC-D 2011). The CChC was also the best-funded association, thanks to a unique financing mechanism. Rather than relying on member dues or donations, the CChC owned and operated multiple businesses that provided a substantial and stable source of revenue (interviews: CEP 2005, CChC-D 2011)[56]; anecdotal evidence suggests that construction made sizable campaign donations across party lines. The construction sector also had significant technical expertise; the CChC's studies department was reputedly one of the best, and it enjoyed association with prestigious economists including Felipe Morandé.[57] Although they did not share the CChC's technical assessment of the special VAT regime, Finance Ministry informants identified the CChC as

---

[55] http://ciperchile.cl, Oct. 3, 2008; Diario de Sesiones del Senado, Legislatura 356, Sesión 4a, March 19, 2008: 131; *Estratégia* March 20, 2008, *El Mostrador* April 22, 2010.
[56] Estimates of the CChC's patrimony reached a billion dollars (*La Nación* March 23, 2008).
[57] *La Nación*, March 24, 2008.

among Chile's most powerful business associations (interviews: Aninat 2007, Marcel 2007, Finance Ministry-F 2008).

The construction sector's influence on the VAT issue was enhanced by a strategic opportunity to exploit legislators' interest in protecting "middle class" constituencies. The UDI and PDC were openly vying to attract middle-class voters, and in a context of declining citizen identification with political parties (Luna and Altman 2011), electoral competition for unattached voters was particularly strong. In March 2008, 49 percent of respondents reported no partisan identity, compared to 28 percent in December 2001 (CEP 2008). Because housing was perceived as a critical issue for middle-class voters, the construction sector could make inroads among the governing coalition by arguing that eliminating the benefit would significantly increase home prices.

Given these considerations, the Lagos administration viewed VAT reform as politically unviable (interviews: Eyzaguirre 2007, Finance Ministry-A, B 2005, Foxley 2006, Montes 2005). Beyond conflict with business and the right, informants from both the Lagos and Bachelet administrations anticipated that maintaining discipline within the Concertación would be a challenge (interviews: Executive Advisor-A 2005, Bitar 2007, Finance Ministry-F 2007).

Structural power helped keep reform off the agenda while growth was slow. The construction sector, which accounted for almost 7 percent of GDP on average from 2003 to 2008, was viewed as critical for providing jobs and stimulating growth in recessionary periods. Former finance minister Aninat (interview, 2007) asserted that investment in construction and especially housing helped Chile emerge from the East Asian crisis, and Lagos (interview, 2006) felt the VAT reform should be timed carefully to avoid negative economic impacts. Similar concerns likely discouraged reform in 2006 and 2007, while growth proved disappointing (2008 interviews: Montes, Escalona). The Finance Ministry (F 2007, interview) also feared that Concertación legislators would succumb to CChC arguments that eliminating the tax benefit would hurt growth and employment. Therefore, even if the executive did not believe threats of reduced investment were credible, legislators' perceptions of the construction sector's structural power could have hindered VAT reform.[58]

Parliamentary Activism

As with the copper royalty, activism by Concertación legislators laid the groundwork for reform and pressured the executive to take action. Socialist Deputy Montes and colleagues took up the VAT issue in the early 2000s. When the Finance Ministry declined to initiate reform, they found a loophole to sidestep the problem of exclusive executive initiative on taxation: they proposed altering the definition of homes in the law such that the VAT benefit would apply

---

[58] The context of revenue surplus created further disincentives for reform (Chapter 3).

only to low-income housing.[59] Without active executive support, the proposal was destined for failure. The CChC lobbied intensively, and the initiative was defeated; thirteen Concertación deputies opposed the measure along with the right. However, the proposal initiated broader debate on the construction VAT regime. In 2005, the Finance Ministry publicly recommended eliminating the tax benefit (Ministerio de Hacienda 2005), and Bachelet incorporated the issue into her campaign platform.[60] Concertación activists continued pushing for reform after Bachelet's election. They initiated a second proposal with a higher limit on the value of homes eligible for the VAT benefit. Negotiations in the lower house raised the cutoff to roughly U.S.$84,000, and the Concertación majority approved the initiative.[61]

The activists' efforts paid off when the executive initiated a reform closely resembling their proposal. But while the Concertación legislators provided the groundwork for modifying the construction VAT regime, the Finance Ministry had been waiting for an opportune moment for reform. A Finance Ministry (F 2008) informant recalled: "We always knew it was going to be a difficult fight. The question was when, in what context, and in exchange for what."

Strategic Reform Design

In the context of slow growth, inflation, and rising energy costs, the Finance Ministry proposed a reactivation package including a two-year gas tax reduction and permanent stamp-tax (financial transactions tax) cuts. To compensate the revenue loss, the construction VAT benefit would be eliminated for high-valued homes. The reform design was highly strategic. The VAT measure was linked to benefits that appealed to business, the right, and legislators more broadly. The gas-tax reduction benefited middle and upper-income consumers – partially compensating the impact of restricting the VAT benefit – and firms, whose profit margins were squeezed by high energy prices (interview, CPC-D 2008). The tax cuts also appealed to business and the right's core programmatic preferences; they had previously advocated both tax reductions.[62] Embedding the VAT measure in a package dominated by tax reductions also counteracted arguments that would likely have been salient had the measure been presented independently: that the state did not need additional revenue, and that the VAT measure would harm growth and employment. Because it was designed to finance a permanent stamp-tax cut, the executive maintained that restricting the VAT benefit was essential for fiscal discipline. Further, the

---

[59] Boletín 3737-14, Dec. 14, 2004.
[60] Discurso de Michelle Bachelet, May 4, 2005. http://bacheletuc.blogspot.com/2005/08/sobre-la-desigualdad.html
[61] Cámara de Diputados, Legislatura 355, Sesión 126, Jan. 9, 2008.
[62] www.cpc.cl: "Discusión en Torno a la Depreciación Acelerada," June 24, 2007; *Segunda*, March 8, 2001, *El Mercurio*, March 4, 2008.

executive asserted that the positive impact of the tax cuts on job creation and growth would far outweigh any negative impact from restricting the VAT benefit (interviews: Finance Ministry-E, F 2008).

Moreover, the Finance Ministry made the tax cuts contingent on the VAT measure; the proposal wording ensured that the former could not be enacted if the later were rejected. Contingency, the strongest linking technique in Chile given that earmarking is unconstitutional, relies on exclusive executive initiative. While legislators can approve or reject measures in a tax bill, they cannot alter the text of an article. A Finance Ministry (F 2008) informant explained:

> We had to design the package so that those who would have voted against the VAT measure if presented alone would be willing to accept it.... Each of the tax cuts would take effect once the VAT modification became law. So if that measure were rejected, none of the others would take force. It was a strategy that made the reform viable. Otherwise, it would not have been possible. The interests defending the VAT benefit were very strong.

Finally, the VAT measure targeted upper-income consumers. The reform progressively scaled back the benefit for the top 5–15 percent of households and eliminated the benefit only for the top 5 percent.[63] The finance minister accordingly invoked vertical equity to counter the reform's detractors: "We are withdrawing this benefit for people ... who are among the richest 5 percent of Chileans. So please, don't try to tell us they are middle class."[64] Targeting the VAT measure also attenuated its economic impact and thereby further undermined structural power arguments. The proposal would affect only 10 percent of the housing market, and houses constituted only 30 percent of economic activity in the construction sector (interviews: Finance Ministry-E, F 2008).

Successes and Limitations

The reform design successfully neutralized concerns over the construction sector's structural power. A Finance Ministry (F 2008) informant recalled: "In that respect our arguments were very effective. I don't think anyone bought the argument that the reform was bad for the economy." Such arguments were much more prevalent during the discussion of the Concertación legislators' 2005 stand-alone initiative, which proposed a lower limit on the value of houses eligible for the VAT benefit. The CChC built its campaign against the 2005 proposal around claims that it would significantly reduce sales, discourage investment, and destroy more than 35,000 jobs (CChC 2005).[65] In 2008, in contrast,

---

[63] Proyecto 6133: Mensaje 1469–355, March 3, 2008, www.camara.cl; Ministerio de Hacienda (2008).
[64] *El Mercurio*, March 18, 2008.
[65] See also Informe de la Comisión de Hacienda, Cámara de Diputados, Boletín 3.737–14, July 12, 2005: 3.

the CChC and the right made only passing comments that restricting the VAT benefit would hurt the economy. The CChC made a single, much milder reference to growth and jobs during its extensive Senate presentation.[66]

Linking the VAT measure to tax cuts also precluded active business opposition beyond the construction sector – a concrete possibility given strong cross-sectoral cohesion. The CPC denounced the 2005 proposal, and business informants across sectors (2005 interviews: CPC-A, SOFOFA-A, C, CChC-A; ABIF 2006) anticipated active CPC resistance to any future proposal.[67] Yet CPC leaders limited their involvement to expressing support for the CChC when the press specifically asked about the measure (interview, CPC-D 2008). The CPC's public statements against the VAT modification were comparatively mild, and pronunciations of support for the tax reductions were more prominent in the press. The CPC did not send representatives to finance committee hearings, nor did it post statements against the VAT modification on its Web page, in contrast to most previous tax reform episodes, including the mining tax. The CPC's general manager recalled:

Since there were other initiatives in the package, and the package was a whole, in truth it was much more difficult to oppose. Perhaps if the measures could have been separated, which the government never wanted to do, as part of a very intelligent strategy ... we would have been able to prolong the discussion and argue against each of the problems. (Interview, CPC-D 2008)[68]

Notwithstanding these successes, the Senate Finance Committee rejected the VAT modification. Three Christian Democratic senators including former president Frei joined the right in opposing the measure, arguing that it affected households that could not be considered rich. Given the CChC's strong instrumental power and its astute strategy of exploiting concerns over "middle-class" voters, the proposal proved insufficiently elite-targeted. CChC representatives claimed the proposal would affect households in as low as the twenty-third percentile and that housing prices would increase by 8 percent rather than the government's projected 4 percent.[69] The Finance Ministry countered these arguments, pointing out that its own calculations used CChC data.[70] Nevertheless, the CChC's campaign tilted the balance in Congress against the reform. According to the former CChC president who coordinated the lobbying effort: "When we demonstrated that the measure affected people who were earning monthly incomes of a thousand dollars, that was when legislators from the government

---

[66] Informe de la Comisión de Hacienda, Senado, Boletín 5.752-05, March 25, 2008: 37.
[67] Two informants anticipated minimal CPC involvement (CChC-C, SNA-A 2005).
[68] Furthermore, the CChC felt well-positioned to wage the battle and did not request active CPC assistance (interview, CPC-D 2008). The VAT measure was also perceived as less threatening than the copper tax initiatives, given potential precedents for other sector-specific taxes (2008 interviews: CPC-D, CChC-D).
[69] Informe de la Comisión de Hacienda, Senado, Boletín 5.752-05, March 25, 2008: 35.
[70] Ministerio de Hacienda (2008).

itself decided to vote against it" (interview CChC-C 2008). The CChC's efforts also consolidated opposition from the right; several Alianza legislators had been open to restricting the VAT benefit,[71] but they firmly opposed the measure in light of the CChC's arguments (interview, Montes 2008).

Contingency of the popular tax cuts on the VAT modification failed to preclude pressure to preserve the tax benefit for a larger percent of households. The executive anticipated that the right and the PDC dissidents would vote against the measure on the senate floor (2008 interviews: Finance Ministry-E, F, Montes). Legislators may have been willing to do so for several reasons. First, from the right's perspective, the government would share blame for letting the tax cuts fall if the Finance Ministry refused to negotiate, especially since members of the governing coalition also opposed the VAT measure. Second, the executive could not credibly threaten to abandon the tax cuts if the VAT measure were rejected, given the Finance Ministry's clear conviction that they were important for stimulating the economy (interview, CChC-C 2008), as well as potential electoral benefits for the Concertación.[72] With municipal elections approaching, the government needed to preserve unity within the coalition; prolonging debate over the VAT measure could have exacerbated internal conflicts.

In this context, contingency was a double-edged sword, providing incentives for the executive, as well as the opposition, to compromise for the sake of the broader reform package. Congress approved the reform after the Finance Ministry targeted the VAT measure more narrowly at economic elites, such that only the richest 5–7 percent of households were affected (interviews: Finance Ministry-E, F 2008). The executive ultimately used contingency to compel the Concertación's left wing to accept this compromise negotiated with the right and PDC dissidents.[73]

Indirect evidence suggests that incentives to avoid conflict associated with government-business concertation further discouraged the executive from fighting harder to preserve the original version of the VAT modification. As a Finance Ministry (F 2008) informant explained: "A confrontation with the CChC is not good for the country. If we discredit the association, or if the association becomes the government's enemy, it's not good for the country either. We have to have an environment of healthy coexistence."[74]

Modest Progress in a Context of Strong Business Power

The 2008 reform's highly strategic design made curtailing the construction VAT regime feasible, despite strong opposition from the powerful construction

---

[71] *El Mercurio*, April 24, 2001.
[72] *La Segunda*, March 4, 2008; *El Mercurio*, March 4, 2008.
[73] *El Mercurio*, March 21, 2008; Diario de Sesión, Cámara de Diputados, Legislatura 356a, Sesión 9a, March 20, 2008: 18.
[74] Structural-power concerns could also be present here.

sector. Yet progress was modest. The negotiated modifications reduced the VAT measure's revenue yield by 29–40 percent. The reform package approved in Congress thereby entailed a permanent annual fiscal cost of U.S. $55–80 million. CChC informants were pleased with the final legislation, even though they maintained that restricting the benefit violated acquired property rights (interviews: CChC-C, D 2008). Given the constraints they faced, Finance Ministry informants believed the government had achieved the best deal possible (interviews: Finance Ministry-E, F 2008). Strong business power precluded more significant reform.

4.6 CONCLUSION

This chapter has illustrated how strong business power significantly constrained prospects for revenue-raising, equity-enhancing reforms across multiple tax policy areas in Chile. As with corporate tax rate politics (Chapter 3), anticipated reactions were a crucial element of policy processes more broadly. The Finance Ministry engaged in highly strategic behavior, assessing anticipated reactions in both the economic arena (structural power) and the political arena (instrumental power). Strong business power removed many issues from the agenda in addition to driving concessions at later stages of policymaking.

Center-left governments were able to make modest tax increases feasible by combining multiple strategies for tempering elite antagonism and mobilizing public support. The importance of the resulting reforms in the Chilean context should not be overlooked, yet these reforms did not accumulate into significant progress toward strengthening taxation of economic elites. By and large, reform strategies facilitated tax increases at the margins.

Despite Chile's limited success at taxing economic elites, tax "reform mongers" elsewhere in the world could advance their cause by drawing on insights from this chapter's analysis of Chilean reform strategies in action. For example, Chapter 8 examines a case of failed income tax reform in Bolivia that might have proven more successful had policymakers applied greater emphasis on vertical equity appeals in conjunction with a reform design that more narrowly targeted economic elites – a key lesson of Chile's 2008 VAT reform.[75]

Two broader findings of this chapter merit emphasis. First, the cases of mining taxes and the stock owner tax benefit further substantiate the point discussed in Chapter 3 that instrumental power based on partisan linkages tends to weaken during electoral periods. Conservative parties face the recurrent dilemma of managing their elite core constituency while simultaneously courting a mass base (Gibson 1992). When conservative parties face high-stakes elections, government strategies designed to mobilize public opinion have more potential to compel conservative politicians to deviate from business interests for the sake of drawing votes from broader constituencies. However, additional

---

[75] Similarly, Argentina's notorious 2008 soy export tax increase may have survived had the government's original reform linked proceeds to popular spending programs (Chapter 7).

sources of power beyond partisan linkages can mitigate the risk business faces of substantial policy change during electoral periods. Neither of the 2005 tax reforms examined in this chapter can be characterized as entailing other than incremental change.

Second, the cases examined in both Chapters 3 and 4 illustrate that structural power in Chile tended to correlate closely with economic cycles. Government policymakers and members of the center-left coalition in Congress displayed more concern over the possibility that tax increases would provoke reduced investment during periods of slow growth. However, slow growth to a certain extent was subjectively defined. What appeared to matter most was the state of the economy relative to policymakers' desired levels of growth, and/or the direction of change (acceleration or deceleration) compared to recent years. The Chilean case thus highlights the interplay between objective factors and policymakers' perceptions that combine to give business influence via structural power.

In contrast to the Chilean pattern, the following chapters on Argentina and Bolivia include examples in which the state of the economy – crisis in particular – had highly variable effects on structural power across tax policy areas and economic sectors. First, however, I return to the book's central cross-national comparison and illustrate how business's much weaker instrumental power in Argentina allowed governments to legislate much more significant tax increases than in Chile. In this context of weaker business power, government reform strategies were more effective at circumventing business opposition.

5

Weak Economic Elites and Direct Tax Policy Successes in Argentina

Direct tax increases following currency stabilization and VAT-broadening reforms in Argentina were more frequent and more significant than in post-transition Chile. Successive reforms increased Argentina's corporate tax rate from 20 percent to 35 percent, the highest in Latin America, while Chile's rate remained one of the region's lowest. Additional reforms in Argentina closed corporate tax loopholes, increased personal income tax rates, created and subsequently strengthened a modest national wealth tax, and granted the tax agency greater powers to fight income tax avoidance and evasion. The expected revenue yield of these reforms as a percent of GDP tended to be several times larger than those legislated in Chile (Appendix 5.1).[1] Tax legislation was certainly more volatile in Argentina than in Chile. Yet direct tax increases outstripped reform reversals by a large margin[2] and contributed to striking growth in direct tax revenue, interrupted only temporarily by the 2001 crisis (Figure 5.1).[3] In fact, Argentina experienced the greatest income tax revenue increase in Latin America from the early 1990s to the early 2000s (Sabaini 2005: 32). These facts challenge portrayals of

[1] Both countries enacted one major reform in the early 1990s with expected revenue exceeding 1 percent of GDP, but Argentina legislated more moderate reforms (seven) with expected revenue in the 0.1–1 percent of GDP range than Chile (one). Average expected revenue from tax increases, excluding the largest reform in each country, was 0.3 percent of GDP for Argentina versus 0.05 percent of GDP for Chile.

[2] The sum of Argentina's expected losses (−0.6 percent of GDP) exceeded Chile's (−0.3 percent of GDP). However, the net sum of Argentina's expected revenue changes reached 3.5 percent of GDP (1992–2009), whereas Chile's totaled only 1.2 percent of GDP (1990–2009) – essentially all of which came from the extraordinary 1990 reform.

[3] Administrative improvements (Eaton 2002) and privatization of enterprises which became profitable and paid taxes also contributed. Revenue dropped in 2002 due to economic crisis and multiple associated tax incentives (Gaggero and Sabaini 2002: 103–08) but recovered once these incentives were eliminated and growth resumed.

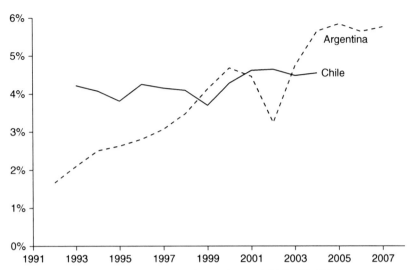

FIGURE 5.1. Direct Tax Revenue in Argentina and Chile (% GDP).
Note: Revenue collected by the central state, before transfers to subnational units.
Sources: SII 2009; DNIAF 2012.

Argentina as a weak tax state and arguments relating political instability and institutional weakness to reluctance or inability to increase tax revenue (Melo 2007, Sanchez 2011).

In this chapter, I argue that economic elites' much weaker instrumental power in combination with limited structural power gave governments greater leeway to increase direct taxes in Argentina compared to Chile. Structural power occasionally removed reform options from the agenda, but it did not deter policymakers from periodically proposing significant direct tax increases (Section 5.1). And the key sources of instrumental power that allowed Chile's economic elites to effectively resist direct tax increases were absent in Argentina (Section 5.2). Business lacked cohesion, and economic elites did not have partisan linkages to any major party in Congress. The nature and strength of business relationships with the executive branch varied across sectors, but given weak cohesion, sectors that did enjoy favorable relationships with executive-branch policymakers pursued their own particular interests rather than defending shared class interests. In this context, the executive could divide and conquer business opposition by offering sector-specific compensations and/or emphasizing horizontal equity. Meanwhile, vertical equity appeals consolidated support for reforms in Congress. Section 5.3 examines three corporate tax reforms that illustrate these dynamics and one exceptional case that highlights the general pattern of economic elites' weak influence over cross-sectoral direct taxes. Section 5.4 examines two key cases of direct tax reforms affecting upper-income individuals. Policymakers had significant leeway in this realm as well given economic elites' weak power. However, labor mobilization paradoxically drove a regressive income tax reform in 2008.

5.1 LIMITED STRUCTURAL POWER

Literature on globalization and taxation predicts a strong role for structural power in Argentina during the 1990s, given the context of economic liberalization and reduced controls on international capital flows, as well as the country's history of hyperinflationary episodes and capital flight. However, structural power exerted limited influence on corporate tax policy in accord with skeptics of the tax competition hypothesis (Gelleny and McCoy 2001, Garrett and Mitchell 2001). Taxes are one among many factors affecting investors' decisions, and Argentina's overall policy mix in the 1990s was highly attractive, given privatization at bargain prices and minimal regulation; Argentina ranked among the top 13 of more than 150 countries on the Heritage Foundation's "Economic Freedom Index" from 1996 to 1999. Given these considerations, technocrats from Menem's second administration (1996–99) were not concerned that income tax increases would discourage investment. Former economy minister Fernández (2005, interview) recounted: "We were completely friendly toward national and foreign capital.... At that time, everyone wanted to invest and take risks in Argentina. So we said to them: good, then pay income tax." Structural power surely placed upper limits on the extent to which policymakers were willing to increase direct taxes, but they nonetheless perceived leeway to legislate significant revenue-raising reforms.

While structural power did not preclude direct tax increases, it occasionally influenced the choice of tax instruments and reform design. For example in 1992, legislators' concerns over the macroeconomic consequences of a radical corporate tax reform contributed to the executive's decision to supplant the proposal with a more conventional corporate tax increase. In 1999 the De la Rua government (1999–2001) ruled out corporate tax increases for fear of negative economic consequences, given the recessionary context and pressures on domestic firms associated with the overvalued exchange rate[4] (former economy minister Machinea 2007, interview). Instead, the government proposed individual income tax increases and transfer price regulations to extract revenue from multinationals. After the 2001 crisis, governments refrained from increasing tax rates to promote investor confidence. Instead, they advanced reforms to close income tax loopholes, which they were confident would not create negative market signals (interviews: former economy ministers Lavagna 2006 and Miceli 2008). These alternative proposals were successfully legislated, thanks in large part to economic elites' weak instrumental power.

---

[4] The convertibility regime pegged the peso to the dollar and tied monetary expansion to growth in reserves.

5.2 WEAK INSTRUMENTAL POWER

Economic elites' instrumental power tended to be weak in Argentina. Business lacked cohesion at the aggregate level; sectoral divisions and organizational fragmentation made it difficult to stage collective action against tax increases. Relationships with legislators were weak – Argentina had no electorally relevant conservative party affording partisan linkages, and informal ties to legislators were rarely an effective means of influence given the institutional environment. Meanwhile, business-executive relationships conferred instrumental power at the sectoral level or lower. While certain sectors enjoyed recruitment into government or informal ties to executive-branch authorities during delimited time periods, they tended to pursue their own specific interests rather than defending common business interests.

Lack of Cohesion

Weak organization undermined business's capacity to engage in collective action. Whereas Chile's business associations are the strongest in Latin America, Argentina's are among the weakest and most fragmented (Schneider 2004a, Acuña 1998). Despite multiple attempts, big business failed to create an enduring encompassing association:

> The jumble of acronyms generated by mobilizations signified little more than transitory coordinating efforts.... By the 1980s coordinating groups had dropped the custom of creating new acronyms and referred to themselves simply by the number of associations involved: '*grupo de los 8*' or '*grupo de los 12*.' (Schneider 2004a: 174)

Sectoral associations also tended to be weak; multiple associations competed to represent a single sector, and organizations often lacked resources (Schneider 2004a). Weak capacity for interest intermediation and aggregation undermined sectoral cohesion and also hindered cross-sectoral alliances. Acuña (1998: 65) observes: "Intre-business contradictions and conflicts affected the *entire* spectrum of business organizations ... and generated a pattern of permanent tensions horizontally (between economic sectors ...) and vertically (... between forward and backward linked producers)."

Authors attribute business's organizational weakness to different factors. Schneider (2004a: 173) emphasizes interventions by political leaders, especially Peron, who sought to organize supporters and demobilize opponents within the private sector: "Over time these attempts exacerbated and reinforced existing economic cleavages, making encompassing collective action increasingly difficult." Parallel pro- and anti-peronist business associations, as well as politically salient divisions between transnational and domestic bourgeoisies, created an enduring legacy of fragmentation (O'Donnell 1978, Schneider 2004a). The absence of state incentives for business to invest in encompassing associations (e.g., privileged access to government officials) during subsequent decades perpetuated weak organization (Schneider 2004a). Acuña (1998: 57) in turn argues that instability of regimes, economic policy, and institutions dissuaded business from investing in encompassing associations: "Strategies based on common interests, which had to be anchored in mid- to long-term objectives, were inherently uncertain and risky."

Additional factors that can foster business cohesion, like shared ideology or a strong common identity, were also absent. While many business groups benefited from neoliberal reforms in Argentina, business informants did not express strong ideological views against taxation, in contrast to their Chilean counterparts. While business disliked tax increases, ideological opposition based on expansive views of property rights was a largely Chilean phenomenon rooted in the experience of class struggle under Allende's socialist experiment and the influence of Chicago-trained economists prior to and during Pinochet's dictatorship. Further, whereas class conflict and polarization in the 1930s, 1960s, and 1970s helped consolidate a strong common identity among Chilean capitalists,[5] episodes of conflict sparked by labor mobilization in Argentina did not forge lasting business solidarity given the strength and salience of internal divisions (Acuña 1995, Schneider 2004a). Moreover, redistributive policies pursued by labor-mobilizing governments in Argentina (e.g., Peron) did not threaten capitalists as severely as those advanced by Allende in Chile (Ascher 1984).

Business's lack of cohesion created ample opportunities for governments to divide and conquer. The executive could undermine collective action against tax increases by offering sectoral compensations with relatively low fiscal cost.[6]

Weak Relationships with Legislators

Argentina had no electorally relevant conservative party capable of providing economic elites with partisan linkages. Meanwhile, informal ties to legislators were a weak source of instrumental power given institutional incentives that encouraged discipline within the two major parties. Argentina's economic elites therefore lacked reliable allies in Congress.

Absence of Partisan Linkages

Gibson (1996) attributes Argentina's lack of a conservative party with economic elites as a core constituency to two factors. First, regional divisions created a legacy of organizational fragmentation among elites. Second, conservative politicians tended to abandon party-building endeavors when opportunities arose to participate directly in policymaking through connections to the executive branch, particularly during recurrent periods of military rule. In the

[5] E.g., Drake (1978) and Silva (1996).
[6] Etchemendy (2011) and Viguera (2000) describe similar strategies for market reforms in Argentina.

1980s, conservatives undertook more concerted party-building efforts, given that the military ceased to be a relevant political ally after the democratic transition (Gibson 1996: 101). The *Union del Centro Democrático* (UCD) emerged as an electorally viable conservative party capable of attracting middle-class voters away from the Radical Party (UCR), and it won a handful of seats in Congress. However, Menem's decision to implement liberalizing reforms advocated by the UCD and incorporation of key UCD leaders into his administration precipitated the party's "dramatic organizational and electoral collapse" in the early 1990s (Gibson 1996: 204). Once again, conservatives abandoned the party project when provided channels of access to state power. When conservatives were excluded from executive-branch policymaking during subsequent administrations, and when left tendencies within Peronism became dominant in the 2000s, economic elites had no viable party through which to seek representation. Various transient conservative parties formed following the UCD's demise, including Cavallo's Acción por la República (AR) in the late 1990s, López Murphy's RECREAR in the early 2000s, and Macri's PRO in the late 2000s (Ostiguy 2009), but they failed to gain consequential representation in Congress. Like the UCD, AR essentially dissolved after Cavallo's ill-fated incorporation into de la Rua's cabinet on the eve of the 2001 crisis.

Business, meanwhile, sought independence from political parties and provided no impetus to consolidate a conservative party (McGuire 1995, Gibson 1996, Acuña 1998, Schneider 2004a). Like conservative politicians, business preferred dealing directly with the executive branch, particularly during periods when party competition was restricted or prohibited. Business remained reluctant to rally behind the UCD in the 1980s, partly because the party's free-market ideology ran against pro-protectionist interests prevalent within the business community. Some businesspeople did support the UCD, but as Gibson (1996: 163) argues: "This support was dependent ... on the ideological commitment of individuals rather than on a shared sense in the business community of the importance of conservative party politics to the pursuit of protection of their class interests."

Of course, big business strongly supported Menem and his neoliberal program in the 1990s thanks to privatizations and other reforms that advanced their interests (Schamis 1999, Etchemendy 2011, Teichman 2001). However, business support for the Peronist Party (PJ) itself was more tepid (Ostiguy 1997: 24–25). This ideologically difficult-to-classify party had always contained tendencies spanning the full left-right spectrum. And sociocultural cleavages created distance between the PJ, which appealed to low-income constituencies based on distinctive mannerisms, language, and elements of identity associated with Peronism, and those businesspeople and economic elites who espoused a more refined, "high" culture, non-Peronist identity (Ostiguy 1997). Despite ideological affinity between big business and Menem on economic policy, the relationship between the PJ and business was certainly distinct from the institutionalized core-constituency UDI-business relationship in

Chile. When business influenced policy under Menem, that influence tended to flow not through PJ legislators or the party organization but rather through direct relationships with Menem and his cabinet, where policymaking authority resided (see below on business-executive branch relationships).[7] On occasions when the Menem administration did make policy decisions that diverged from business preferences (e.g., increasing direct taxes), the Peronist party was not a relevant source of business power for opposing reform. When Kirchner gained control of the party in the 2000s, Peronism moved decidedly to the left (Ostiguy 2009, Etchemendy and Garay 2010), severing the ideological affinity with big business that had developed under Menem.

Legislators from the PJ – even under Menem – and the centrist UCR, which together dominated Congress from 1992 to 2012, were relatively unsympathetic to big business and tended to agree that the tax system should be more progressive. Taxing big business and multinational corporations was especially popular with legislators, particularly as an alternative to increasing taxes on wage earners, a core Peronist constituency, and independent professionals, a core Radical constituency. Therefore, executives encountered little resistance in Congress when seeking to increase corporate taxation. Vertical-equity appeals helped consolidate support from legislators within these two party blocs. Likewise, tax increases that patently targeted wealthy individuals tended to enjoy cross-partisan support.

Limited Effectiveness of Informal Ties

Business occasionally enjoyed informal ties to legislators. A few business-association leaders were even elected to Congress; for example, PJ Deputy Sebastiani simultaneously served as president of the industrial association (UIA) from 1997 to 1998.[8] However, informal ties to the two main political parties or election to public office on their tickets usually did not constitute an effective source of instrumental power due to incentives created by Argentina's party-centered electoral institutions. Proportional representation via closed lists controlled by national and provincial party officials limited legislators' responsiveness to special interest groups (Eaton 2002). During Menem's first term, while he was both president of the nation and the most important authority within the governing party, Peronist legislators had particularly strong incentives to support the executive's reform proposals.[9] Breaches of discipline occurred primarily when reforms went against the interests of regional party authorities (often provincial governors), who also exerted significant influence over the career paths of legislators representing their provinces (Eaton 2002, Jones and Hwang 2005). Discipline within the governing party occasionally weakened,

---

[7] See Levitsky (2001: 47–48) on Menem's practice of ignoring the PJ party leadership and on PJ legislators joining the Menem bandwagon for fear of otherwise jeopardizing their careers.
[8] Former SRA president Alchouron also served in Congress (1999–2003) as an AR deputy.
[9] See also De Riz and Smulovitz 1991 and Jones 2002.

for example, during Menem's second term when his authority within Peronism and his control over legislators' career prospects declined (Eaton 2002). Under these conditions, business had better prospects for securing modifications to bills in Congress. However, as evidenced in the following case studies, lobbying in Congress tended to succeed primarily, and only to a limited extent, when a convincing case could be made that the proposed reform would negatively affect small and medium-sized businesses as opposed to big business or multinational firms.

Sector-Specific Relationships with the Executive Branch

Executive-business relationships in Argentina were highly variable and created instrumental power only at the sectoral or firm level, not at the cross-sectoral level as in Chile. Recruitment into government was common in Argentina from the postwar period through the 1990s (Schneider 2004a: 186). For example, Menem recruited financial-sector leaders and members of large business conglomerates into his cabinet. Some sectors enjoyed informal ties to executive-branch officials as well; agricultural producers established informal ties to the secretary of agriculture during the 1990s (Chapter 7). However, informal ties and recruitment into government were much less common under Kirchner (Schneider 2010).

Consultation with business associations was never institutionalized in Argentina. Instead, executives consulted with firms, groups, or subsectors of their choosing (Schneider 2004a). In the 1990s, Menem largely ignored business associations but often consulted with owners of the largest firms. During structural adjustment, conglomerates from the most economically important and concentrated industrial sectors were invited to the bargaining table in a process of "selective concertation" (Etchemendy 2011: 62–63). Business associations assumed a higher profile in the mid-2000s, when the Kirchner government negotiated periodic sectoral price agreements and directed tripartite wage bargaining (Etchemendy and Collier 2007, Richardson 2009). However, the government continued to divide and conquer business opposition to its economic policies through selective incentives, threats, and punishments. For the most part, these tactics allowed Kirchner to maintain the upper hand and formulate economic policy independently of business preferences (Bonvecchi 2011: 144).[10] This pattern of government-business interaction was very different from regularized consultation with cohesive peak associations in Chile, which created incentives to respect core cross-sectoral business interests.

Relationships with executive-branch policymakers afforded the privileged business actors substantial influence in the 1990s. Teichman (2001) maintains that networks, built around recruitment into government and informal ties,

---

[10] Consistent with this analysis, a business informant (UIA-B 2006) remarked: "An inopportune complaint [about government policies] could generate setbacks."

helped big businesses secure rents from privatization under Menem. Etchemendy (2011) argues that the privileged access, which allowed large firms and conglomerates to extensively shape economic liberalization, ultimately arose from these businesses' dominance within key industrial sectors.

In theory, firms and sectors that enjoyed privileged relationships with executive-branch policymakers could have used their instrumental power to influence cross-sectoral policies like corporate taxation. In practice, however, they defended only their own narrow interests. For example, the banking sector was very active when tax proposals specifically affected financial assets (Chapter 6), but it assumed a much lower profile on taxes with cross-sectoral impact (Section 5.3).[11] This behavior is unsurprising given weak business cohesion. Moreover, the large firms that shaped privatization processes did not use their instrumental power to block tax increases in the 1990s because Menem's broader economic policies in effect compensated them for the cost of higher taxes.

5.3 CORPORATE TAXES

Business exerted limited influence over the corporate tax agenda and the outcome of executive reform proposals, given weak instrumental power and limited structural power. Case studies from three presidential terms elucidate this pattern. The second Menem administration's 1998 tax reform illustrates the ease of dividing and conquering in a context of weak business cohesion and weak business relationships with legislators. The Kirchner administration's 2003 reform to control tax avoidance further illustrates the pattern of weak business influence; Argentina's most important grain export firms failed to win concessions from either the executive or Congress, despite strong opposition and concerted lobbying. The exceptional case of an unsuccessful, radical tax proposal in 1991 during Menem's first term highlights the rule of weak business influence on corporate taxation. Unusually intense business opposition, circumstantial allies, and a fortuitous convergence of interests with legislators together compensated for weak instrumental power. The alternative reform subsequently proposed in 1992, which raised a similar amount of revenue without drastically revising the tax code, was legislated without difficulty, conforming to the general pattern.

The 1998 Reform

The executive divided and conquered business opposition to corporate tax increases in 1998 by offering selective compensations. Given business's weak cohesion and lack of other sources of instrumental power, these concessions

---

[11] A Finance (D 2006) informant asserted: "The financial sector traditionally does not take positions on those [reforms] that do not directly affect the financial sector."

were of minimal cost compared to the revenue raised by the corporate tax increases. Meanwhile, equity appeals facilitated congressional approval at a time when the president's ability to maintain discipline within the Peronist party had declined.

Reform Design
The Economy Ministry's reform package contained two new corporate taxes – an assets tax and a tax on interest payments[12] – as well as a corporate income-tax rate increase from 33 percent to 35 percent. These measures, along with other tax increases in the package, would compensate a gradual reduction of employers' payroll taxes, which Menem's economic team viewed as important for stimulating recovery and job creation after the Tequilla crisis (Economy Ministry-A 2006, interview). The two new corporate taxes were designed to curtail evasion and avoidance. The former treasury secretary described the problem as follows: "17 companies were paying more or less two thirds of all corporate income tax revenue. It was ridiculous. Most companies never paid anything" (Economy Ministry-A 2006, interview).

In this context, the assets tax would serve two purposes. First, it would compel businesses that did not report profits to make a minimal contribution to state coffers. The assets tax would be credited against the income tax, such that it would not affect firms reporting taxable profits. Second, the assets tax would help reduce evasion of the individual wealth tax. Individuals frequently registered property and assets to corporations in order to avoid taxation (Economy Ministry-A 2006, interview). Adding a corporate assets tax would eliminate this source of revenue loss by restoring symmetry to the tax system. The tax on interest payments, meanwhile, would close a major income-tax loophole – non-taxation of interest earnings (Chapter 6). The new tax would curtail revenue loss from a commonly employed tax-evasion scheme known as a "back-to-back," whereby businesses deposited funds in a bank (often international), borrowed back from that same bank, and deducted the interest payments from their tax obligations (Economy Ministry-C 2006, interview).

Dividing and Conquering Business Opposition
The proposed corporate tax reforms stimulated business opposition across sectors. Industry vociferously complained that the tax on interest was unacceptable since businesses faced high interest rates after the East Asian crisis (Sidicaro 2002: 21, interview: Economy Ministry-A 2006). Agriculture, which was squeezed by the overvalued peso, unfavorable international prices, and high debt, objected that the government should reduce spending instead of increasing taxes. And business across sectors "hated the assets tax with all their guts" (Economy Ministry-C 2006, interview).

---

[12] *Impuesto sobre los Intereses Pagados y el Costo Financiero del Endeudamiento Empresarial*

Early on, the "Group of Eight," an informal group composed of presidents from each of the main sectoral peak associations that met sporadically during the 1990s, convened to coordinate united cross-sectoral lobbing.[13] The Group of Eight drafted a document harshly criticizing the reform, denouncing it as distortionary and recessionary, and calling for the government to reduce spending and improve tax administration instead.[14]

However, business's lack of cohesion allowed the government to divide and conquer by offering sector-specific compensations to the Group of Eight's member associations. The construction association withdrew its support for the joint declaration against the reform after the government announced it would halt an infrastructure project that the sector opposed.[15] The *Sociedad Rural Argentina* (SRA) also withdrew its support for the declaration after the government conceded to exempt grains from an agricultural VAT-rate reduction that the producers intensely rejected (Chapter 7).[16] Big businesses with large labor costs accepted the corporate tax increases in light of pending benefits from the eventual reduction of employers' payroll taxes. For example, the leading Argentine multinational Techint publicly announced its support for the goals of the tax reform package.[17] The financial sector, which also received compensations, responded to government pressure to refrain from publicly criticizing the reform.[18] That the financial sector greatly benefited from the economic model in the 1990s probably contributed to its decision to tacitly accept the tax increase; the Menem administration enacted many of the sector's recommendations in other policy areas.[19] A similar logic likely applied to Techint, a major beneficiary of Menem's privatizations (Etchemendy 2011).

These sector-specific benefits successfully deterred collective action, given the absence of a strong permanent encompassing association capable of enforcing a united front. The Group of Eight's document criticizing the tax reform was never made public, and it desisted from efforts at coordinating opposition by the end of June,[20] less than a month after the proposal had been announced and three months before Congress voted on the reform. The industrial association (UIA) deplored the banking and construction sectors' defections and continued to urge joint action against the reform, but to no avail.[21]

Uncoordinated lobbying by sectoral associations achieved little influence. Economy Ministry officials ignored complaints from the organizationally weak UIA; they dismissed the association's concerns as the interests of economically

---

[13] *Clarín*, May 29, 1998.
[14] *Clarín*, June 13, 1998.
[15] *Clarín*, March 7, June 21, 26, 1998.
[16] *La Nación*, June 26, 1998, *Clarín*, June 23, 1998.
[17] *Clarín*, June 5, 1998.
[18] *La Nación*, June 26, 1998, *Clarín*, June 13, 26, July 10, 1998.
[19] Additionally, the corporate tax increases had a minimal impact on the financial sector.
[20] *Clarín*, March 7, June 13, 21, 26, July 10, 1998.
[21] *Clarín*, June 21, 1998.

weak, noncompetitive, inward-oriented industries within the UIA (Economy Ministry-A 2006, interview).[22] The Economy Ministry also ignored the SRA and other agricultural associations, which continued complaining about the assets tax despite the VAT concession.[23] The Economy Ministry viewed these associations' demands as narrow sectoral interests that lacked legitimacy (Economy Ministry-A 2006, interview). Moreover, industry and agriculture were heavily involved in the types of avoidance and evasion that the new corporate taxes were designed to control (2006 interviews: Economy Ministry-A, B), which made it easy to delegitimize their opposition. For example, treasury secretary Guidotti remarked in the press: "When industry representatives say that taxes should only be reduced … because they discourage investment, it's a shameful argument.… All they are trying to do is perpetuate channels for evasion."[24] Legislators also paid little heed to the sectoral associations' uncoordinated lobbying (UIA-A 2006, interview). The two minor concessions granted responded to the perceived interests of small businesses: an increased exemption level for the assets tax and a cap on interest-tax payments.

Given weak business cohesion, the cost of dividing and conquering was low relative to the revenue gains from the tax reform. For example, concessions to agriculture on the VAT-rate reduction represented an annual revenue loss of 150–200 million pesos (0.05 percent of GDP).[25] By comparison, the assets tax and the tax on interest payments raised more than 1,400 million pesos (0.51 percent of GDP). The payroll tax cuts, meanwhile, were left to the executive's discretion; the reform delegated authority to the president on this policy. This compensation for labor-intensive businesses therefore entailed an uncertain future benefit that would be phased in only as current revenue levels permitted. The cost of the corporate tax concessions introduced in Congress was also minimal (2006 interviews: Economy Ministry-A, B).

Equity Appeals
While selective compensations helped the Economy Ministry manage business opposition, vertical-equity appeals forged support in Congress. The Economy Ministry's central task entailed aligning PJ legislators behind the reform. The PJ held a majority in Congress, but party discipline eroded during Menem's second term when he became a lame duck; Menem had much less control over legislators' career paths during his final years in office (Eaton 2002). Rebellion within the PJ compelled the Economy Ministry to remove excise tax increases from the 1998 reform, and breaches of discipline also occurred regarding proposed VAT-broadening measures (Eaton 2002: 165). However, equity appeals consolidated PJ support for the corporate taxes; the government framed the reform as taxing capital instead of labor:

[22] The UIA also included modern, competitive businesses (Etchemendy 2011).
[23] *La Nación*, July 18, Aug. 3, Nov. 7, 1998.
[24] *Clarín*, May 17, 1998.
[25] *La Nación*, Dec. 18, 1997, Feb. 15, 1998.

We had a couple of governors who traveled with us and explained the reform in political terms. Peron had a very old song "combatting capital," this idea that you are pro-worker ... they decided that this was consistent with a Peronist reform, that it was shifting the burden of taxation a little bit from labor to capital. (Economy Ministry-A 2006, interview)

Meanwhile, Economy Ministry officials emphasized that the new corporate taxes would target large businesses and tax evaders, groups that enjoyed little sympathy from legislators. Sub-secretary of tax policy Rodríguez-Usé explained to reporters that the corporate assets tax would "close sources of evasion and avoidance, because more than 50 percent of the large contributors declare no income tax."[26] PJ Deputy Lamberto made ample use of this argument during the debate on the bill:

I am tempted to read a list of the names of the largest businesses in the country that do not pay taxes. This is very similar to a feudal regime, ... where there are nobles and serfs: only the latter pay taxes. The nobles in Argentina on this list do not pay taxes. If all of the blocs accompany us with their votes, starting tomorrow we can make them pay.[27]

Lamberto's list of firms that had not paid income tax in 1997, which he subsequently read aloud, included well-known multinationals such as Mercedes Benz and Coca Cola, as well as Argentine firms like Petrolera Pérez Companc and Papelera del Plata. The list created an uproar in Congress and elicited a quick reaction in the press from the implicated firms.[28]

Equity appeals, along with minor modifications to ease the impact of the new taxes on small firms, mitigated opposition from the UCR as well. The corporate assets tax was relatively uncontroversial (2006 interviews: Economy Ministry-A, B), although the Radicals argued that small business would be affected along with large businesses. The PJ's agreement to increase the exemption level resolved the debate. The Radicals voiced stronger opposition to the tax on interest based on similar concerns. However, a cap on interest-tax payments to limit the burden on small firms alleviated tensions. Meanwhile, the Radicals and Frepaso, their left-leaning coalition partners, supported the other elements of the reform that targeted big business, including transfer price regulations and sub-capitalization rules.[29] The former treasury secretary recalled: "Everybody loved the chapter on transfer prices, because that was seen as revenue that would come at the expense of international companies. That was great, everybody loved it. Nobody came to complain" (Economy Ministry-A 2006,

---

[26] *Clarín*, May 14, 1998.

[27] Diario de Sesiones, Cámara de Diputados, 29a Reunión, Continuación de la 10a Sesión, Sept. 9–10, 1998: 183.

[28] *Clarín*, Sept. 11, 1998. The firms asserted they had not violated tax laws.

[29] Diario de Sesiones, Cámara de Diputados, 29ª Reunión, Continuación de la 10ª Sesión, Sept. 9–10, 1998: 37.

interview). Although the Radicals voted against the reform, they cooperated with the PJ to facilitate approval:

Since this was a proposal from the PJ, the Radicals could not support it explicitly. So they would choose an argument against it, but then they would provide ... the quorum for the proposal to be passed. We had meetings ... with Machinea, with Alfonsín, on this to obtain support from them. And in the end they provided the support – without voting for it. But if you want to really oppose something, you don't provide the quorum. You force the PJ to have to bring all of the votes themselves, not only of their party, but also some of the provincial parties.... So if the Radicals actually give you the quorum, things are much easier.... And many of the economists in the Radical party actually agreed with the reform.... Of course they wouldn't come out explicitly, but essentially they provided support to be able to pass it. (Economy Ministry-A 2006, interview)

Comparison with Chile

Whereas dividing and conquering through selective compensations proved highly effective in Argentina given business's weak instrumental power, cohesion and partisan linkages made that strategy less effective for managing business opposition in Chile. Consider the 2001 Anti-Evasion Reform (Chapter 4, Section 4.2). The executive ultimately negotiated many of the modifications to the proposed corporate tax base-broadening reforms with the affected sectors. However, each sector was in a stronger position to secure concessions given support from the strong economy-wide peak association and collaboration from right parties in Congress. Consequently, Chile's 2001 reform secured only marginal corporate tax increases, whereas Argentina's 1998 reform included more significant corporate tax increases. Similarly, the benefits required to secure the Chilean peak association's acquiescence to the 2008 reform that restricted the construction sector's special VAT benefit (Chapter 4, Section 4.5) were costly compared to the revenue saved – the proposed reform package was revenue neutral.

Thanks to business's partisan linkages, meanwhile, equity appeals in Chile tended to be less effective than in Argentina for maneuvering tax increases through Congress. The right parties defended the tax interests of business and upper-income individuals. Legitimating appeals could occasionally win right votes in the Senate, but primarily when the tax issue was salient in electoral politics (the stock-owner tax subsidy, Chapter 4, Section 4.4) and/or enjoyed strong popular support (the mining tax, Chapter 4, Section 4.3). In Argentina, with no electorally significant conservative party, equity appeals mobilized cross-partisan support for corporate tax increases.

The 2003 Transfer-Price Reform

The Kirchner administration's 2003 reform to control tax avoidance by export firms further evidences the Argentine pattern of weak business influence over corporate tax policy. In the absence of instrumental power or structural power, the major agroexport firms exerted no influence over agenda formulation and failed to win concessions after the reform was drafted, despite intensive lobbying directed at both the executive branch and Congress. The executive ignored the exporters' demands, and as in 1998, equity appeals delegitimated business opposition and mobilized cross-partisan support in Congress. The 2003 reform had a "tremendous" revenue impact (AFIP-F 2006, interview). Grain exporters' tax declarations nearly doubled, and the tax agency collected 2,700 million pesos of additional revenue from 2003 to 2005.[30]

Reform Design

Soon after taking office in 2003, Néstor Kirchner's administration announced a series of anti-evasion reforms. The first such reform aimed to control tax avoidance via "triangulation of exports," which involved manipulation of transfer prices by multinational corporations to reduce reported earnings in countries with relatively high taxes and to increase reported earnings in tax havens or countries with comparatively low taxes. The 2003 reform allowed the tax agency to make various presumptions regarding transactions between firms in Argentina and firms abroad and introduced other changes to transfer-price regulations that increased export companies' corporate tax liabilities. This reform represented a major step toward more effective tax agency regulation of transfer pricing and transactions involving tax havens that built on previous legislation passed in 1998 and 1999.

Article 2 of the 2003 reform addressed tax avoidance by agro-exporters, who often shipped grains through intermediaries that were actually members of the same corporation located in nearby low-tax jurisdictions (Panama and Uruguay). The other articles affected exporters across sectors, including autos, pharmaceuticals, tobacco, and petroleum.

Business exerted little influence at the agenda stage regarding the reform proposal's content. As with Chile's 2001 Anti-Evasion Reform, tax agency experts drafted measures to help them address problems they had identified. In response to my query, tax agency informants asserted that the executive branch did not leave any of the measures they proposed out of the bill that was sent to Congress, despite strong complaints from the affected business sectors (interviews: AFIP-D, E 2006).[31] This outcome contrasts starkly with the Chilean Finance Ministry's decision to include in the 2001 Anti-Evasion Bill only a small subset of the measures requested by the tax agency, on the grounds that strong business power made many of those measures politically infeasible.

---

[30] Acta, Comisión de Presupuesto y Hacienda, Cámara de Diputados (CPHCD), Oct. 4, 2006.
[31] Another AFIP (F 2006) informant noted that tax agency reform proposals generally received significant support from the executive branch and could not recall any proposal that the executive had turned down in recent years.

Chronicle of a Lobbying Failure Foretold

Given weak cohesion within the agricultural sector as well as among business more broadly, exporters were left to fight against the reform largely on their own. Agricultural-sector actors were organizationally fragmented and often had conflicting interests (Chapter 7). Agro-exporters did manage to mobilize some support from other members of the production chain despite these obstacles to collective action, but only after the reform had been approved in the Chamber of Deputies. Forty different agricultural-sector associations signed a public statement denouncing the reform that was released two weeks after the lower-house vote,[32] and producer-association representatives accompanied exporters to the Senate Budget and Finance Committee hearings.[33] However, this belated attempt at a united agricultural front bore no results. The Senate passed the reform after a brief debate on the floor that lasted barely over an hour.[34]

The broader business community, moreover, tended to support the government; concern over horizontal equity prevailed over business solidarity. For example, the *Asociación Empresaria Argentina* (AEA), an association representing some of Argentina's largest businesses, expressed support for the Kirchner administration's efforts to control evasion and tax avoidance, including the measures designed to control triangulation of exports (AEA 2006, interview). Even firms in other sectors affected by the 2003 reform did not publicly support the grain exporters.

The executive's equity appeals helped undermine the exporters' lobbying efforts. Economy Minister Lavagna and Tax Agency Director Abad regularly denounced the exporters' tax avoidance. Lavagna (2006, interview) asserted that this strategy was highly effective for managing opposition from the sector:

When they started pressuring, I announced the figures of how much those large businesses had exported, which was billions of dollars, and how much they had paid during the last five years. And that made them stop talking.... The taxes they had paid were minimal, it was so vulgar that they opted to be quiet.

The exporters did in fact continue to publicly oppose the reform and lobby for concessions. However, informants from the sector admitted that the government's approach placed them in a difficult position. One recalled: "It was a difficult political moment for the businesses in the sector" (Exporter-A 2006, interview).

Meanwhile, the exporters lacked informal ties to executive-branch officials that could be mobilized in favor of the sector's interests.[35] Not only

---

[32] *Clarín*, Aug. 27, 30, 2003
[33] *Clarín*, Sept. 13, 2003.
[34] *Clarín*, Oct. 2, 2003.
[35] See Chapter 7. The logic described regarding producers also holds for grain exporters.

did the Economy Ministry and the tax agency decline to take the exporters' complaints into account, but even the minister of agriculture, the exporters' most likely government ally, firmly supported the Economy Ministry's position (2006 interviews: AFIP-A, D, E). The minister of agriculture even repeated the Economy Ministry's accusations that export firms had engaged in massive tax avoidance at a celebration commemorating the Buenos Aires Grain Exchange's 149th anniversary.[36]

Without partisan linkages or informal ties to a major political party, the exporters were also in a weak position to win concessions in Congress. The associations representing the sector presented their position in both houses of Congress. However, like previous transfer-price reforms, the 2003 reform generated broad cross-partisan support. The PJ, UCR, and Socialists all voted in favor of the reform.[37] Congress ultimately passed the legislation with essentially no changes to the text sent by the executive branch (Capitanich 2006, interview). An export-sector informant summarized the resounding failure of the lobbying efforts as follows: "The government had a plan laid out and an objective to accomplish. The truth is that our presentations in the congressional Finance Committee and our informal conversations with the tax agency were not very productive. They didn't change a comma" (Exporter-A 2006, interview).

Unsuccessful Attempts to Invoke Structural Power
The exporters might have secured concessions despite weak instrumental power if they had managed to generate concern over the reform's macroeconomic consequences. To that end, the exporters asserted that the new regulations would destroy futures markets and reduce the value of exports.[38] Had such threats been perceived as credible, the exporters may have achieved significant concessions, given that grains were an important source of foreign exchange and a major source of tax revenue following the 2001 crisis (Chapter 7).

However, these arguments did not convince policymakers. Former economy minister Lavagna (2006, interview), former tax agency director Abad (2008, interview) and other members of the team that designed the reform (AFIP-A 2006, interview) asserted that they were confident it would have no negative effects. Their expectations proved correct; futures markets quickly adapted to the new regulations and continued to function normally after the reform was implemented (2006 interviews: Abad, AFIP-A, D, E).[39] Legislators

---

[36] *Clarín*, Sept. 27, 2003.
[37] Acta, CPHCD, Aug. 13, 2003; Diario de Sesiones, Reunión 13, 5a. Sesión Ordinaria, Aug. 13, 2003.
[38] Acta, CPHCD, July 2, 2003: 13, 14, *Clarín*, Aug. 25, 2003.
[39] Agricultural-sector informants also acknowledged that futures markets and producers prices had not been harmed (interviews: Bolsa Cereales 2006, Exporter-C 2008, SRA-A 2006).

were also largely immune to structural-power arguments. The executive branch maintained the upper hand in technical discussions throughout the debate in Congress.

Comparison with Chile

The 2003 reform highlights several differences between tax politics in Argentina and Chile. First, lack of cohesion created distinct dynamics in Argentina compared to Chile, where cohesion was strong. Argentina's grain exporters were left without business allies in 2003; horizontal-equity concerns prevailed over any incipient sense of business solidarity. In contrast, when multinationals faced similar reforms in Chile in 2001, the economy-wide business association came to their defense. Business solidarity in Chile prevailed over concerns regarding horizontal equity. In the worst-case scenario for reform-minded governments, the economy-wide peak association would actively defend any particular sector threatened by a tax increase, as in the case of the copper royalty. In the best-case scenario, broad compensations could dissuade the business community from actively mobilizing to support the sector affected, beyond the usual declarations of solidarity in the press. This situation prevailed in the case of the reform curtailing the construction sector's VAT credit, but only as a result of costly benefits for the broader business community included in the reform package.

Second, whereas it was often difficult for business to persuade legislators that reforms would hurt investment in Argentina, Chile's right parties shared and consistently responded to business concerns that tax increases would harm growth and investment. Moreover, the right parties' amplification of business's structural-power arguments at times motivated more conservative Concertación legislators to question aspects of executive-branch reform proposals.[40] In this manner, strong instrumental power had the potential to enhance structural power in Chile. In contrast, business's efforts to foment concerns regarding structural power from a position of weak instrumental power in Argentina did little to alter policymakers' perceptions.

The Unsuccessful 1991 Income Tax Overhaul

The first Menem administration's failure to legislate a major income-tax overhaul is an exception that highlights the pattern of weak business influence on corporate taxes. In this case, unusually broad and intense business opposition provoked by the radical nature of the proposal, circumstantial business allies in the form of respected academics and professional associations who anticipated that the new income tax system would cause a wide range

---

[40] A former Chilean Finance Ministry (I 2005) informant recounted: "If the right really raises a scandal, saying that this is going to cause loss of investment, there will be Concertación legislators who become concerned."

of economic problems, and a fortuitous convergence of interests with legislators who opposed the reform because the provinces would lose their share of national income-tax revenue together compensated for business's weak instrumental power.

Radical Reform Design

In late 1991, the Economy Ministry announced a radical tax reform. The income tax as well as employers' social security contributions would be replaced by two new taxes: a tax on distributed profits, and a tax on firms' primary surplus.[41] The latter would consist of an 18 percent tax on the value added by the firm, net of its labor costs. The primary surplus tax would be credited against a 30 percent tax on distributed profits.[42]

From the executive's perspective, the proposed reform solved multiple problems. First, it would broaden the tax base. Accumulated losses generated by inflationary adjustments and economic duress during previous years had severely eroded the corporate income tax base; replacing the corporate tax with the primary surplus tax automatically eliminated this problem. The primary surplus tax would also apply to interest earnings, which were exempt from the income tax. This loophole provided multiple opportunities for tax avoidance and created a bias in favor of debt financing rather than capitalization, which Menem's orthodox economic team viewed as distortionary. Second, the Economy Ministry believed the new taxes would be easier to administer and would thus curtail evasion. Third, the new tax system would equalize the tax burden paid by capital-intensive and labor-intensive firms. The Economy Ministry viewed high payroll taxes as a burden on labor and an employment disincentive, whereas capital-intensive firms benefited from various favorable tax treatments.[43]

The reform would yield an expected net revenue increase of 1.6 percent of GDP.[44] The primary surplus tax was the main revenue-raiser; it was expected to generate 5.7 percent of GDP per year, a major improvement compared to the income tax, which produced only 1.3 percent of GDP in 1991 (DNIAF 2012). Revenue from the primary surplus tax would compensate losses from eliminating employers' payroll taxes.

Despite its potential advantages, the proposal constituted a radical reform with far-reaching distributional consequences. Sub-Secretary of Public Revenue Tacchi, the reform's intellectual author, openly acknowledged that it would impose "a tremendous reorganization of business cost structures."[45] Moreover,

---

[41] The *Impuesto a las Ganancias Distribuidas, Dispuestas o Consumidas* and the *Impuesto sobre el Excedente Primario de las Empresas*.
[42] Acta, CPHCD, Dec. 25, 1991.
[43] Ibid.
[44] *Clarín*, Dec. 27, 1991.
[45] Acta, CPHCD, Dec. 25, 1991.

independent professionals anticipated major tax increases for capital-intensive firms, despite the administration's assertion that the reform would favor firms that pursued equity financing. A study by a well-known economist claimed that while taxes paid by labor-intensive businesses would decrease by 24 percent, those paid by capital-intensive firms would increase by 243 percent; other studies maintained that taxes paid by prominent firms traded on the stock market could increase six-fold.[46] Tax experts further noted the difficulty of anticipating the reform's actual impact, given the radical, complex nature of the changes and the lack of prior experience with similar taxes elsewhere in the world.

The radical design of the 1991 reform provoked multiple problems that did not arise in the cases previously analyzed. First, the significant yet uncertain impact of the reform elicited unusually broad and intense business opposition, consistent with Ascher's (1989: 464) observation that business tends to react negatively "not just to expected losses but also to the risk of incurring costs that cannot be anticipated." Given the radical nature of the reform, compensations in the package (reducing other taxes) did not mitigate opposition. Second, the reform elicited unanimous condemnation from professional associations and academics, whose technical expertise and prestige countered the Economy Ministry's authority. Intense opposition from business and independent experts, along with provincial authorities' concerns over revenue loss to the central government, engendered strong resistance in Congress. Had the executive pursued a more incremental, less complex reform, these problems could have been avoided.

Broad, Intense Business Opposition

All major business sectors intensely opposed the 1991 reform. UCR Deputy Baglini (2006, interview), a long-term Finance and Budget Committee member, recalled: "There are different ways one can complain, for example, 'I don't like the color of this shoe,' or, 'it's destroying my feet.' This was 'it's destroying my feet.'" Industry decried that the primary surplus tax would harm investment and production to unknown extents.[47] The financial sector opposed taxation of interest, asserting that "investors will redirect their money to countries that do not tax these funds ... there is a risk of entirely eliminating transactions that constitute billions of dollars for the country."[48] Exporters denounced the reform's "lamentable anti-export bias" and complained that the primary surplus tax imposed onerous, unrecoverable costs that would undermine international competitivity.[49] Agriculture, a capital-intensive, export-oriented sector,

[46] Acta, CPHCD, Feb. 5, 1992: 34/40.
[47] *Clarín*, Feb. 13, 1992.
[48] *Clarín*, March 11, 1992.
[49] *Clarín*, Feb. 28, 1992.

opposed the reform for similar reasons. Commerce, meanwhile, warned: "The tax burden inevitably will be passed on through prices."[50]

Opposition within industry and agriculture was unusually uniform, considering the multiple internal divisions afflicting these sectors. Large and small industries alike opposed the primary surplus tax. Representatives from large business groups including Techint expressed their concern by attending the Congressional Budget and Finance Committee hearings;[51] usually, only business-association representatives attended such meetings. Meanwhile, the *Consejo Argentino de la Industria*, which represented small industry, denounced the "primary surplus tax [as] discriminat[ing] in favor of labor-intensive business, which are the largest ones."[52] Likewise, large agro-export firms, along with all four of Argentina's agricultural producers associations, which together represented large producers, small producers, and cooperatives, aligned against the primary surplus tax. As Deputy Baglini (interview, 2006) recalled, the producer associations were "totally terrorized, all of them." On other occasions, the interests of the different constituencies within agricultural often conflicted.

Circumstantial Business Allies

Three professional associations[53] as well as academics from prominent universities joined business in denouncing the reform. These experts served as circumstantial allies who validated business objections.

Structural power was a prominent concern for these academics and professionals.[54] Contrary to the Economy Ministry's position, they maintained that reform would hurt investment and could even threaten macroeconomic stability. The Argentine Association of Fiscal Studies argued that the complexity of the new taxes and the difficulty of anticipating the ensuing tax burden would discourage foreign investment.[55] All three professional associations warned that countries with which Argentina had signed double-taxation treaties would not grant their nationals tax credits for the primary surplus tax, which could create additional disincentives for foreign investors. Concerns over structural power were also expressed through warnings that the reform would decimate exports, by imposing substantial additional costs in a context of trade liberalization, an unfavorable exchange rate, and low international commodity prices.

Given their prestige, technical expertise, and (at least nominal) independence from business and government, the academics' and professional associations' unequivocal presentations had a significant impact on legislators in the Budget

[50] *Clarín*, Feb. 27, 1992.
[51] *Clarín*, Feb. 13, 1992.
[52] *Clarín*, Feb. 27, 1992.
[53] The *Consejo Profesional de Ciencias Económicas, Colegio de Graduados en Ciencias Económicas*, and the *Asociación Argentina de Estudios Fiscales*.
[54] Actas, CPHCD, Feb. 5, 18, 1992.
[55] The CGCE described the reform as a "plunge into the unknown." Acta, CPHCD, Feb. 5 1992: 44.

and Finance Committee and fomented dissent against the reform. As Baglini (2006, interview) recalled: "Argentina's leading experts on the income tax came ... it was a massacre, just a massacre! I have never seen anything like it.... I can't remember a discussion of the same level – running a bill through a meat grinder." In light of the experts' presentations, the Radicals, who controlled about a third of the seats in the lower house, resolutely opposed the reform. The UCR delegation walked out of the Budget and Finance Committee hearing without signing the committee's report on the reform.[56] Only one deputy from the UCD, which tended to align with the PJ, openly supported the reform.[57] Many of the formal objection letters that opposition legislators submitted to the president of the lower house repeated concerns raised by the experts.[58]

Concessions Erode Revenue Capacity

The government granted multiple concessions in an effort to curtail business opposition and maneuver the reform through Congress. However, given the breadth and intensity of objections, accumulated concessions entailed severe revenue costs.

The Economy Ministry granted its first major concession, a nontaxable minimum for the primary surplus tax, the day after independent experts denounced the reform in the Budget and Finance Committee.[59] Shortly thereafter, Committee president Lamberto (PJ) announced additional deductions for agriculture and the possibility that industry would be allowed to deduct investments made after April 1990 from the primary surplus tax.[60]

Thereafter, the executive quickly lost control over the reform. PJ legislators added a host of additional concessions; for example, exporters were granted various deductions and exemptions, and previously issued corporate bonds were excluded from the primary surplus tax.[61] The bill advanced through the Budget and Finance Committee, but in a heavily altered form. The banking association, which remained unplacated, charged that "even Minister [Cavallo] is uncertain as to the current wording" of the bill.[62]

The extensive concessions eviscerated the bill's revenue-raising capacity. Revenue estimates for the primary surplus tax fell from U.S.$8,700 million to U.S.$765 million, only 0.5 percent of GDP.[63] Cavallo acknowledged that the reform would not raise revenue after the final committee hearing on the bill and announced a two-point VAT increase to make up the shortfall.

---

[56] *Clarín*, Feb. 27, 1992.
[57] *Clarín*, March 11, 1992.
[58] Diario de Sesiones, Cámara de Diputados, 1a Sesión Extraordinaria, March 11, 1992.
[59] *Clarín*, Feb. 20, 1992.
[60] *Clarín*, Feb. 21, 1992.
[61] *Clarín*, Feb. 27. 1992.
[62] *Clarín*, March 11, 1992.
[63] *Clarín*, Feb. 28, 1992.

With no net revenue at stake, the Economy Ministry had little incentive to fight for the reform. Cavallo still defended the package, maintaining that it would distribute the tax burden more equitably. However, the limited revenue capacity of the primary surplus tax contributed to his ultimate decision to withdraw the bill.[64]

Fortuitous Convergence of Interests with Legislators
Business mobilization against the 1991 reform benefited from one important additional factor: a fortuitous convergence of interests with governors and regional party authorities, who opposed the reform because it would replace a tax subject to automatic revenue sharing (the income tax) with a tax whose revenue would be retained by the central government (the primary surplus tax).[65] Legislators defended these provincial interests in Congress, since governors and provincial party bosses have significant control over their political careers.

Cavallo unsuccessfully attempted to court the governors by granting concessions relatively late in the game. A week before Congress was scheduled to vote on the bill, he announced that the provinces would receive 17 percent of the primary surplus tax revenue.[66] However, several PJ governors continued to resist, as did legislators from provincial parties, who had fewer incentives to support the executive.[67] Thanks to opposition from the Radicals and most of the UCD, the bill could not pass without support from provincial parties.[68]

The difficulty of aligning provincial legislators, along with the reform's compromised revenue capacity, compelled Cavallo to withdraw the bill shortly before it was to be debated on the floor of Congress.[69] Had Cavallo allowed the bill to come to a vote, the new taxes likely would have been defeated by an ample margin (Baglini 2006, interview); rumors circulated that the Radicals intended to withdraw from the chamber to prevent the PJ from securing the quorum needed to continue the session.[70]

Contrast with the 1998 Reform
The 1998 reform did not encounter the problems that undermined the 1991 income tax overhaul proposal, thanks to its more moderate design. Although the 1998 reform created two new taxes, their impact was neither as severe nor as unpredictable as the primary surplus tax, and the bill did not entail major revision of the tax system. Consequently, business opposition could be

---

[64] *Clarín*, March 11, 1992.
[65] The executive proposed a limited compensation scheme benefiting large provinces, but it left small provinces dissatisfied (Bonvecchi 2010: 86).
[66] *Clarín*, March 5, 1992.
[67] *Clarín*, March 11, 1992.
[68] *Clarín*, March 10, 1992.
[69] *Clarín*, March 11, 1992.
[70] *Clarín*, March 12, 1992.

managed at a much lower cost in terms of concessions. While opposition arose from multiple fronts, it was neither as broad nor as extreme. Within agriculture, producers and exporters were divided. Producers actively rejected the reform, but exporters had few complaints and remained aloof from the debate (Exporter-A 2006, interview). Within industry, small and medium-sized firms voiced the strongest objections (Economy Ministry-A 2006, interview).

Further, independent tax experts played a much less prominent role in the 1998 reform, and their assessments of the new corporate taxes were by no means as uniformly negative as their condemnation of the primary surplus tax; these differences can also be attributed to the less radical design of the reform. Academics did not participate in the debate, and only two professional associations made presentations during the committee hearings. While the first association opposed the corporate assets tax and the tax on interest,[71] the second observed that the assets tax could raise much-needed revenue and that the tax on interest legitimately addressed the problem of excessive corporate indebtedness.[72] The second association even suggested that the interest tax would benefit small businesses. Moreover, no major concerns regarding the reform's impact on investment or other macroeconomic indicators were voiced. By and large, independent experts did not legitimate business objections.

Accordingly, opposition in Congress was much less intense. While the Radicals objected to some elements of the 1998 reform, they collaborated with the PJ to allow the bill's approval, in contrast to their obstructionist behavior in 1992. Meanwhile, negotiations with governors over revenue-sharing issues decoupled from deliberations on the tax side of the proposal (Economy Ministry-A 2006, interview). The executive secured the central government's right to retain the additional revenue generated by the tax increases, but the provinces did not face a net reduction in revenue as they had with the income tax overhaul.[73]

A Successful Alternative: The 1992 Reform

After withdrawing the problematic income tax overhaul, the Economy Ministry proposed a less radical alternative: increasing the corporate tax rate from 20 percent to 30 percent and suspending the use of losses, as well as increasing the top personal income tax rate to 30 percent. Although the net revenue at stake was essentially the same,[74] this alternative avoided the problems created by the prior initiative.

Given that the new proposal entailed much more moderate changes, business opposition was minimal. The SRA lauded Cavallo's decision to withdraw

---

[71] Acta, CPHCD, May 27, 1992: 15, 18.
[72] Acta, CPHCD, April 22, 1992: 3, 20, 17–19, 31.
[73] The provinces also secured favorable overall revenue-sharing rules in 1998 (Eaton 2005).
[74] *Clarín*, Aug. 15, 1992.

the primary surplus tax as "a noble gesture that speaks of humility without limits," and while the UIA disliked the suspension of losses, it agreed to accept the cost with few complaints.[75] Because the income tax overhaul would have been much worse for many sectors, it made sense for business to support the government's decision by moderating their complaints about the alternative.

Further, the professional associations and academics condoned the new alternative. Experts had explicitly recommended that the government restrict the use of losses rather than replacing the income tax. Without independent experts legitimating their objections, business was in a weaker position to resist the reform.

Given business acceptance and expert approval of the alternative reform, as well as the absence of revenue-sharing problems – provinces retained a fixed percentage of income-tax revenue, and additional revenue-sharing agreements consolidated support in Congress (Bonvecchi 2010: 87) – the bill passed easily.[76] The Radicals voted against the proposal, but did not actively oppose it, and most of the UCD and the provincial parties voted in favor with the Peronists.[77]

5.4 INDIVIDUAL TAXES

The politics of taxing individual income and wealth in Argentina were similar to cross-sectoral corporate taxation, in that economic elites' weak instrumental power gave governments significant leeway for reform. In contrast to their Chilean counterparts, business associations usually did not lobby on individual taxes, and in the few cases where they did take positions, the concessions they secured were minor.[78] As in Chile, reforms viewed as affecting "middle-class" voters were not popular among legislators; however, tax increases targeting wealthy individuals tended to draw cross-sectoral support. For example, top personal income tax rate increases that accompanied corporate tax increases in the 1990s were generally uncontroversial. The case of the 1999 tax reform discussed below further illustrates these dynamics.

In the late 2000s, a new dynamic emerged: labor union mobilization to exempt members from income taxation in a context of negotiated wage increases and inflationary bracket creep. Concessions to labor that increased the income tax threshold had limited consequences for elite taxation until 2008, when a key component of the 1999 income tax reform was reversed. Although labor unions pursued their own economic interests, they served as

---

[75] *Clarín*, March 12, 1992.
[76] *Clarín*, March 20, 1992.
[77] *Clarín*, March 18, 19, 1992.
[78] Business opposed a wealth tax increase promoted by legislators in 1996 because some productive assets fell within the tax base, but the Group of Eight accepted increasing the income tax as an alternative.

circumstantial elite allies in demanding the 2008 reform, which alleviated the tax burden on top-bracket income taxpayers as well as wage earners.

The 1999 Reform

The De la Rua administration faced urgent revenue needs upon taking office in 1999, given a budget deficit of U.S.$7,000 million in a context of tightly restricted monetary policy (Gaggero and Sabaini 2002: 98). The tax reform legislated at the end of that year illustrates the typical political dynamics of individual direct tax increases: business association noninvolvement and cross-sectoral support for elite-targeted measures in congress.

Reform Design

The tax package included prominent measures to make individual direct taxes more progressive. These measures reflected the technical team's interest in redistributive fiscal policy and the assessment that Argentina's personal income tax did not raise sufficient revenue, along with concerns that additional corporate tax increases would be economically imprudent in the context of recession and competitivity pressures on Argentine firms related to the overvalued exchange rate, which could not be adjusted without abandoning the Convertibility regime (Machinea 2007, interview).

The most important component of the reform entailed making the individual income tax bracket structure more progressive by scaling back deductions for high-income earners. The percentage of the basic established deduction allowances that taxpayers could apply decreased gradually for higher income levels, reaching zero for those earning more than 221,000 pesos. This approach increased taxation of high-income earners without raising the top marginal tax rate, which the technical team felt should remain equal to the corporate tax rate. The proposal also modestly lowered Argentina's comparatively high exemption level to broaden the individual income tax base. Despite this adjustment, the income tax did not reach beyond members of the top income decile (Machinea 2007, interview).

The reform included two additional highly progressive measures. The first was an "emergency tax" on high incomes: a one-time additional levy of 20 percent on incomes exceeding 120,000 pesos, which exclusively affected taxpayers in the top 0.5 percent of the income distribution.[79] The second measure altered the wealth tax: a higher rate of 0.75 percent was established for assets exceeding 200,000 pesos, while the prior rate of 0.5 percent applied to lower valuations.

Business Noninvolvement and Cross-Partisan Support

While some elements of the 1999 reform were politically problematic, the progressive income- and wealth-tax measures proved largely uncontroversial.

---

[79] Author's calculation using Alvarado (2010).

Business associations for the most part were not relevant political actors. There were a few complaints that the income tax increases were recessionary and that the government should reduce spending instead.[80] But business did not undertake any substantial action to oppose the initiatives. The context of fiscal urgency surely contributed to business acquiescence. However, business simply was not a cohesive class actor in Argentina, in contrast to Chile, where organized business tended to defend the interests of upper-income individuals as well as firms and corporations.[81] Most of the business mobilization that did take place regarding Argentina's 1999 reform involved producers affected by excise tax increases on drinks and cigarettes: these narrow sectors did not face collective-action problems and simply defended their own particular interests.[82]

In the absence of a strong conservative party, there was cross-partisan cooperation in Congress on the tax measures targeting high-income earners. As former finance minister Machinea (2007 interview) recalled, "No one had problems with the emergency tax on high incomes; a few deputies even wanted to make it permanent. It hit very few people and was easy to sell." Likewise, the wealth tax increase elicited few complaints. The progressive elimination of income tax deductions was less popular among Radical legislators because it affected the party's constituency of independent professionals who were electorally important within the capital district. The media vociferously denounced this measure; renowned journalists were among those facing significant income tax increases. However, strong party discipline prevailed, and the Radicals solidly supported the reform in Congress.[83] The income tax modifications also elicited some complaints within the PJ, which naturally sought to differentiate its position from the UCR coalition government. PJ Deputy Lamberto voiced distaste for including statutory tax increases in the reform rather than focusing exclusively on fighting evasion, and another PJ deputy asserted that the income tax reform would hurt the middle class.[84] However, the excise tax increases, which activated regional interests in Congress, were far more controversial. Moreover, the PJ refrained from using its Senate majority to block the legislation. Although the Peronist senators introduced modifications, they deliberately approved them with a small enough number of votes that the Radicals could impose the original version of the reform in the lower house.[85] In fact,

---

[80] *Clarín*, Dec. 5, 21, 1999.

[81] Bolivia's business associations, which were stronger and more cohesive than Argentina's, also defended class interests. Even in contexts of fiscal distress similar to those Argentina encountered, Bolivian business associations actively opposed direct-tax increases affecting individuals (Chapter 8).

[82] *Clarín*, Dec. 23, 1999.

[83] All Radicals on the Budget and Finance Committee signed the reported bill. Reported bill signatures are often used to gauge party discipline (Eaton 2002).

[84] Acta, CPHCD, Dec. 15, 1999: 86; Diario de Sesiones, Cámara de Diputados, Dec. 15, 1999: 113.

[85] The governing coalition did not have enough seats in the lower house to override modifications approved by a two-thirds Senate majority (*Clarín*, Dec. 17, 1999).

several modifications made by the PJ, including raising the top personal income tax rate to 37 percent and eliminating the tax exemption for interest earnings, would have taxed the wealthy even more heavily.[86]

The 2008 Reform

The 1999 income tax reform remained intact for nearly a decade, despite the 2001 economic crisis and the Peronists' subsequent return to power. However, labor union mobilization in the late 2000s ultimately led to the demise of the progressive scaling back of deductions, known as "Machinea's Table." Ironically, in defending the economic interests of their own membership base, the unions advocated a regressive reform that also benefited Argentina's wealthiest taxpayers.

Labor unions in Argentina enjoyed a resurgence in the mid-2000s. Etchemendy and Collier (2007) attribute this phenomenon to tightening labor markets, the Kirchner government's interest in securing labor support to bolster its political coalition, and growth in sectors where unionization had traditionally been strong. The private formal-sector unions, amalgamated in the General Confederation of Workers (CGT), demonstrated strong mobilizational capacity and autonomy despite their alliance with the government. The number of strikes to demand wage improvements increased dramatically in 2005 and lent impetus to centralized tripartite wage bargaining between the government, unions, and business associations (Etchemendy and Collier 2007).

Income-tax grievances featured prominently among union demands by 2006. Negotiated wage increases in combination with inflationary bracket creep pushed significant numbers of workers into the income tax base. Whereas only 200,000 workers earned enough to pay income taxes in 2001, 800,000 workers were liable in 2007.[87] Governments had tacitly broadened the income tax base downward after 2001 by neglecting to adjust deductions and brackets for inflation. Beginning in 2006, however, union pressure drove repeated upward adjustments of the minimum taxable income and other deductions. Thanks to the 1999 reform, these adjustments primarily benefited lower-end income taxpayers and had only a limited impact on economic elites. According to Machinea's Table, taxpayers with annual incomes between 195,000 and 221,000 pesos could apply only 10 percent of the value of their deductions (including the minimum taxable income), whereas those with incomes in excess of 210,000 pesos were not allowed to apply any deductions (Table 5.1).

By 2007, unions were demanding not only periodic minimum taxable income increases, but also elimination of Machinea's Table to benefit workers

---

[86] The Radicals rejected the changes in the lower house because the Economy Ministry felt increasing the top personal income tax rate above the corporate tax rate was technically inappropriate, and eliminating the interest-earnings exemption elicited structural-power concerns (Chapter 6).

[87] *Clarín*, July 23, 2007.

TABLE 5.1. *Machinea's Table, Argentina's 1999 Reform*

Net Income (pesos)	Percent of Deductions (value) Applicable
0–39,000	100
39,000–65,000	90
65,000–91,000	70
91,000–130,000	50
130,000–195,000	30
195,000–221,000	10
>221,000	0

with higher salaries who could otherwise apply only a reduced percentage of deduction allowances. CGT leader Moyano reportedly asserted that the unions were unaware of Machinea's Table in 2003,[88] yet by the late 2000s, the deduction reductions affected a significant minority of formal-sector workers. Government technocrats were open to revising this aspect of the 1999 reform, given that the progressive deduction-reduction table created sharp tax increases across income brackets (interviews: Miceli 2008, Economy Ministry-E 2006). Taxpayers at the top of a bracket could face lower take-home income if they passed into the next higher bracket because the percent of deductions allowed decreased abruptly. The Labor Ministry also sympathized with the workers' complaints (Tomada 2006, interview). After a wave of strikes in mid-2007 led by highly paid oil-sector workers, the government eliminated deduction reductions for taxpayers earning less than 91,000 pesos but left the bottom four rows of Machinea's Table unaltered. This modification, along with further minimum taxable income increases, benefited approximately 600,000 workers.[89]

However, the CGT continued to push for full elimination of Machinea's Table. Due to additional wage increases and continued inflation, around 240,000 workers, particularly in the oil and trucking sectors, were subject to deduction reductions in 2008. Further, the 2007 reform exacerbated discontinuities for taxpayers on the cusp of the 91,000-peso threshold. Workers who passed from just below to just above the threshold saw their after-tax wages decrease by about 500 pesos per month.[90] The CGT rejected the government's initial proposal of revising the table to smooth out effective income tax rates. After several strikes, threats of additional mobilizations, and multiple negotiations, the government agreed to simply eliminate the remnants of Machinea's Table. The context of global economic crisis provided another justification for the reform; the government maintained that the tax cut would stimulate

[88] *La Nación*, Aug. 29, 2008.
[89] *Clarín*, July 28, 2008.
[90] *Clarín*, Aug. 31, 2008.

consumption and counteract recessionary trends.[91] The Chilean government pursued similar antirecessionary tax policies during this period.

While the unions had defended members of their working-class base, the 2008 reform constituted a regressive income tax cut. Workers who benefited from the reform belonged to roughly the top 2 percent of the income distribution,[92] by which criteria they themselves could be considered economic elites. Furthermore, the reform benefited economic elites much more broadly; taxpayers in the top brackets with nonwage income could now apply the full value of deduction allowances as well. Few observers besides former economy minister Machinea himself raised these points. The reform was unanimously approved in Congress, with just one legislator observing that it was not progressive. Most politicians applauded the reform as a benefit for the working class and a long-overdue revision of the income tax, which had not been effectively updated to the postcrisis economic situation.[93]

5.5 CONCLUSION

Economic elites' much weaker instrumental power, particularly at the cross-sectoral level, made it possible for governments to pass more substantial direct tax increases in Argentina than in Chile. Whereas business in Chile was highly cohesive thanks to strong organization and antitax ideology, business in Argentina lacked cohesion given weak organization as well as the absence of strong shared ideological views on taxation or any other sense of common identity. While business in Chile enjoyed partisan linkages to right parties with significant representation in Congress, no party in Argentina treated business as a core constituency. Meanwhile, informal business ties to legislators from Argentina's two main parties did not create significant instrumental power due to institutional incentives that encouraged strong party discipline and shielded legislators from lobbying. Finally, whereas concertation with peak associations in Chile created incentives for the executive to avoid conflict on taxation, executive-business relations in Argentina followed a sector-specific logic that did not confer instrumental power at the cross-sectoral level. Sectors that enjoyed recruitment into government or informal ties to the executive branch pursued their own particular interests instead of defending common business interests.

Given limited structural power with respect to corporate taxation as well as weak instrumental power, business tended to achieve little influence over direct tax policy. Thanks to weak business cohesion, the executive could divide and conquer opposition to cross-sectoral tax increases with sector-specific compensations at relatively low cost. When reforms sought to control evasion

---

[91] *Clarín*, Dec. 12, 2008.
[92] Author's estimates for adult population using AFIP 2008. The press reported estimates that fewer than 3 percent of workers would benefit (*La Nación*, Dec. 16, 2008; *Clarín*, Dec. 18, 2008).
[93] *Clarín*, Dec. 18, 19, 2008.

and avoidance, support for the executive based on horizontal-equity considerations trumped any sense of business-wide solidarity. Meanwhile, in the absence of partisan linkages, vertical-equity appeals consolidated support, or at least secured acquiescence, in Congress. Business achieved greater influence in the case of the 1991 income-tax reform largely because the radical proposal provoked opposition from other actors who served as circumstantial business allies. These dynamics contrast with corporate tax politics in Chile, where business tended to band together in defense of any sector threatened by tax increases, even if the reforms in question were designed to control tax avoidance, and vertical-equity appeals achieved limited success at winning right-party votes in Congress.

Whereas Chile's tax proposals were often intended to finance social spending, many of Argentina's tax increases aimed to secure macroeconomic stability. To the extent that business actors benefited from the economic model that fiscal discipline sustained and feared renewed hyperinflationary episodes, it could be argued that they were more willing to accept tax increases than in Chile. This logic often did contribute to Argentina's more substantial direct tax increases, especially in the 1990s. However, business actors often actively opposed tax increases, and weak business power meant that the concessions they secured were usually insignificant.

Economic elites' weak instrumental power also facilitated individual income tax increases in Argentina. No organized actors – whether business associations or political parties – defended the interests of wealthy individuals, with the exceptional case of the 2008 reform, in which labor unions inadvertently secured benefits for upper-income taxpayers by advancing the interests of their own (albeit highest-paid) members.

Despite Argentina's direct tax policy successes, much room for equity enhancing reform remains, particularly in the domain of individual income taxes (Cetrángolo and Sabaini 2009). Although elites lacked instrumental power, structural power contributed to limited progress toward increasing capital income taxation. Throughout Latin America, many forms of capital income are tax-exempt or enjoy special treatment compared to wage income. The next chapter, which examines financial-sector tax politics, includes the case of Argentina's interest-earnings tax exemption.

6

Sectoral Tax Politics in Argentina: Finance

The previous chapter established that Argentine governments were able to legislate significant direct tax increases given economic elites' weak power at the cross-sectoral level. However, some business sectors, including finance and agriculture, enjoyed instrumental and/or structural power during delimited time periods that helped block tax increases affecting their own sectoral interests. In contrast to the uniformity and stability that prevailed in Chile, business power in Argentina varied not only across sectors but also over time and across policy areas. This chapter explains when and why key tax initiatives affecting the financial sector succeeded, failed, or remained off the agenda by analyzing changes in the financial sector's power; the following chapter examines agricultural sector tax politics. The case studies in these two chapters illustrate how economic crisis, change in economic development models, turnover in the executive branch, and international pressures can alter business power, facilitating reforms that had been impossible during prior periods.

In the 1990s and 2000s, Argentine executives considered taxing interest earnings, expanding tax agency access to bank information, and taxing financial transactions. Section 6.1 examines the first two policy areas. Bank depositors' structural power, arising from a credible exit threat, along with the banks' instrumental power, based on recruitment into government and informal ties, kept initiatives in both policy areas largely off of the agenda in the 1990s. The banks' instrumental power declined after Argentina's 2001 crisis, as did depositors' structural power with respect to bank information access. In this new context, the tax agency obtained complete and automatic access to bank information. However, structural power remained strong with respect to interest-earnings taxation and helped keep reforms in this policy area off the agenda during the 2000s.

Section 6.2 presents a comparative analysis of tax agency access to bank information in Chile that highlights distinctive features of the Argentine case and the consequences of more consistent and generally stronger business power in Chile. As in Argentina, key initiatives in this policy area remained off the agenda during the 1990s and early 2000s. In the Chilean case, however, structural power was weak; business's instrumental power alone deterred reform. Strong international incentives in the form of conditionality for OECD membership created space for reform in 2009, but progress was marginal given strong business power. Compared to its Argentine counterpart, the Chilean tax agency's access to bank information at the end of the decade remained quite limited.

Section 6.3 analyzes Argentina's financial transactions tax, enacted in 2001 before the crisis. Whereas taxing interest earnings and expanding bank information access remained infeasible at this time, the transactions tax was implemented without difficulty. In this case, structural power was weak; the tax did not elicit an exit threat. The banks' instrumental power remained strong, but they did not actively oppose the tax given the minimal anticipated impact on deposits and the government's benefit-side reform strategies. After the crisis, governments maintained the transaction tax; the banks' instrumental power was weak during the subsequent decade, and they did not lobby actively against the tax.

6.1 BANK-INFORMATION ACCESS AND INTEREST EARNINGS

Before analyzing the politics of policy change in these areas, I briefly explain the importance of tax agency access to bank information and taxing interest earnings for raising revenue from economic elites. The first policy area posed challenges for both Argentina and Chile; the second is an Argentine problem: whereas Chile's income-tax base includes interest earnings, Argentina has a longstanding exemption for this income source.

Bank Information

Fighting tax evasion is critical for tapping Latin America's highly concentrated income and profits. Income tax evasion is a major problem throughout the region. Estimates range from 50 percent to 53 percent for Argentina and 42 percent to 64 percent for other Latin American countries (Alvaredo 2010, Jiménez et al. 2010). Personal income taxes in most of Latin America affect only the top 10 percent to 15 percent of adults. Within this elite, only the wealthiest can evade taxes. Income taxes are usually deducted automatically from workers' wages, whereas wealthier individuals with nonwage income must file tax returns and thus have opportunities to under-declare income and assets.

Tax agency access to bank information is crucial for fighting evasion (OECD 2000). Information access allows tax agencies to detect undeclared income and assets by cross-checking tax returns against bank records. Requiring banks to routinely provide information on customers' accounts and transactions is

TABLE 6.1. *Time Deposits in Private Banks in Argentina, 1995–2000*

	1995	1996	1997	1998	1999	2000	Average
Percent of Total Deposits (Checking accounts, savings accounts, time deposits, and other accounts)	65.2	63.5	65.9	67.5	69.7	71.7	67.3

Source: BCRA: *Informe de Entidades Financieras,* December values.

particularly useful for this purpose. Bank information access also deters evasion by increasing the perceived risk of being caught.

Laws vary worldwide regarding the types of information available to tax agencies and the conditions of access. In some countries, information is accessible only on a case-by-case basis; in others banks provide information en masse. In 2000, nineteen OECD countries required automatic reporting for at least some types of information, five maintained centralized databases accessible to the tax agency, and ten imposed no access limitations (OECD 2000: 36). While some countries retain strict banking-secrecy laws, the worldwide trend is toward expanded access (OECD 2007).

Argentina's tax agency obtained access to information on checking and saving accounts in 1992. This advance was made possible by a 1985 reform that exempted the tax agency from banking-secrecy constraints. After 1992, the tax agency sought access to time deposits, which grew quickly following stabilization and comprised more than 65 percent of all funds in private banks by the end of 1995 (Table 6.1). The tax agency suspected significant underreporting of assets in these instruments.

Interest Earnings

Interest earnings from financial assets are usually included in the personal income tax base. However, Argentina exempted interest earned from savings accounts, time deposits, and bonds due to economic instability and hyperinflation. Inflation rates exceeded interest rates such that earnings were purely nominal. Although convertibility in the 1990s eliminated inflation and financial investments became highly profitable, the interest-earnings tax exemption was periodically renewed.

Because businesses can deduct interest payments on loans and bonds from the corporate income tax, the interest-earnings exemption suppressed not only personal income tax revenue[1] but also corporate tax collections. First,

[1] Taxing bank-deposit interest earnings could have generated around 0.27 percent of GDP in 1999. Author's calculations ignoring behavioral effects, using BCRA data.

TABLE 6.2. *Cumulative Distribution of Individual-Owned Time Deposits in Argentina*

Size of Deposit (Threshold)	U.S.$, 1999		Pesos, 2005	
	Accounts (%)	Amount (%)	Accounts (%)	Amount (%)
10,000	50	88	50	90
30,000	13	56	NA	NA
50,000	6.0	42	9.6	51
75,000	NA	NA	5.0	39
100,000	1.9	29	NA	NA
250,000	0.40	18	0.6	15
750,000	0.10	12	0.1	6.7
1,000,000	0.08	11	0.06	5.3

Source: Author's calculations using BCRA: *Información Sobre Tramos de Depósitos*, *Información Diaria Sobre Depósitos y Obligaciones*.

businesses tended to distribute profits not as dividends, which were taxed, but as interest payments on corporate bonds, which were tax-free for the bondholder and tax deductible for the business. Second, the exemption stimulated evasion via "back-to-backs": businesses deposited funds in a bank and then withdrew those same funds as a loan, deducting the "interest payments" from the corporate tax base. Partly due to this widespread practice, 50 percent of the 1,600 businesses classified as large contributors declared no taxable profits in 1998.[2]

Taxing interest earnings would affect primarily economic elites. Because so few citizens earn enough to pay income taxes, exemptions inherently benefit upper-income individuals. Moreover, Central Bank statistics suggest that interest earnings are highly concentrated. Table 6.2 shows the distribution of time deposits held in U.S. dollars in 1999 and those held in Argentine pesos in 2005. These accounts generated roughly 71 percent (79 percent) of all interest earned by individuals in 1999 (2005). In 1999, 56 percent of these funds were concentrated in only 13 percent of accounts and were held in amounts totaling over U.S.$30,000. In 2005, 51 percent of funds were concentrated in only 9.6 percent of accounts and were held in amounts totaling over 50,000 pesos (roughly U.S.$17,000). Although the size of a given deposit need not be proportional to the owners' income, individuals with the largest deposits and hence the largest interest earnings likely fall within the top of the income distribution.[3] For comparison, the top 13 percent of time deposit accounts in 1999 comprised

---

[2] *Clarín*, May 17, 1998.
[3] High-income individuals may own multiple accounts, but low-income individuals likely do not; correcting for multiple ownership should make the distribution more concentrated.

at most 242,000 individuals; the top 1 percent of income earners comprised 233,000 individuals.

Structural and Instrumental Power Preclude Reform, 1990s

Broad consensus existed among Argentine economists, orthodox and heterodox, that interest earnings ideally should be taxed. Politicians across party lines also agreed that interest should be taxed; legislators often complained that the exemption unfairly favored the rich. Moreover, technocrats from both the Menem and De la Rua administrations discussed the possibility of taxing interest earnings. However, the executive branch never initiated a proposal to eliminate the exemption. Similarly, the tax agency was unable to obtain information on time deposits, despite active executive-branch interest in strengthening the tax agency, a cross-partisan consensus in support of anti-evasion measures, and repeated requests by the tax agency. Lack of progress in this policy area is remarkable given that access to time deposits did not require legislative approval. Thanks to the 1985 law that exempted the tax agency from banking-secrecy restrictions, the tax agency simply could have issued an administrative resolution requiring banks to provide this information.

Despite the otherwise favorable political context, the financial sector's structural and instrumental power kept eliminating the interest-earnings exemption and expanding bank information access off the agenda during the 1990s, but for a few largely unsuccessful initiatives. Strong structural power, based on a widespread perception that taxing interest earnings and/or granting the tax agency access to time deposits would cause investors to withdraw funds from the banks en masse, deterred reforms in both policy areas. Furthermore, the banks, which would have suffered directly from a loss of deposits, enjoyed significant instrumental power based on recruitment into government and informal ties to the executive branch.

Investors' Structural Power
The following quotation from a financial-sector informant (Finance-E 2006) encapsulates the structural-power problem:

> When convertibility reduced inflation, it no longer seemed necessary to exempt income from time deposits and savings accounts, because it was now real income, not nominal income. However, there is always the specter that taxing this type of income could lead to a run on the banks by depositors. It seems very inequitable that wage income is taxed but capital income is not. But the reason it has not been taxed since the exemption was established is to avoid a run on deposits.

As noted below, informants cited similar problems regarding bank information access. This section explains the logic of bank depositors' structural power in the 1990s.

High mobility and incentives to relocate savings in response to taxing interest earnings or expanding bank information access created a credible disinvestment threat. Financial assets tend to be highly mobile; funds can be transferred electronically worldwide. But in Argentina, savings were also physically mobile. Financial centers and tourist resorts in Uruguay are located just across the river from Buenos Aires, a ferry trip of only an hour, making it especially easy for wealthy Argentines to deposit savings abroad.

Moreover, policymakers were genuinely concerned that reforms in these policy areas would scare investors away from the banks. Public-sector and private-sector informants consistently asserted that memories of economic instability made Argentines highly sensitive to any changes in banking conditions. One financial sector informant explained that Argentina's history of hyperinflation, economic crises, and bank failures that destroyed savings, as well as state interventions that froze and effectively confiscated bank deposits, "generated a terrible sensation of uncertainty. And that sensation remains, that the banks are not so secure, and that you must be very attentive to banking news" (Finance-A 2008, interview). Similarly, former economy minister Miceli (2008, interview) spoke of a "generalized psychosis produced by collective memories" of financial crises.[4] Structural power thus had a cultural component: common national experiences created shared expectations about how investors would respond to reform.

Strict banking-secrecy rules in Uruguay created additional incentives to relocate savings in response to reforms in these policy areas. The Argentine tax agency could not obtain information about deposits and financial operations in Uruguay. Wealthy Argentines regularly evaded taxes by registering assets to corporations constituted in Uruguay, and tax agency informants commonly referred to Uruguay as a "tax haven" (interviews: AFIP-A, B 2006). One informant (AFIP-A 2006) summarized the rationale against bank information access as follows:

If you put in place this informational regime, the only thing you're doing is forcing transfers to Uruguay, and you don't know anything about deposits in Uruguay. So business gets done in Uruguay, and Argentina loses capitalization and investment, all because of the tax agency. That was the argument – that we were going to scare away deposits.

The head of the Peronist bloc in Congress expressed the argument against taxing interest earnings in similar terms: "Everywhere in the world interest earnings are taxed. But in Argentina, we have a tax haven on the other side of the Río de la Plata, and when we touch interest earnings the deposits flee – it has been almost impossible."[5]

---

[4] On how Argentina's history of economic instability affected macroeconomic policymaking, see Kaplan (2013).
[5] Deputy Lamberto, Diario de Sesiones, Cámara de Diputados, 29 Reunión, Continuación de la 10 Sesión, Sept. 9–10, 1998: 6.

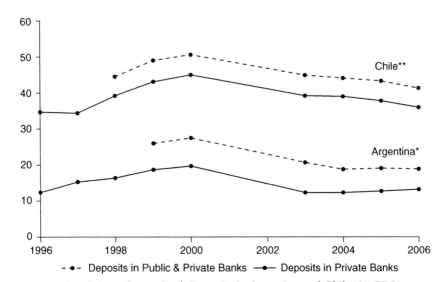

FIGURE 6.1. Private-Sector Bank Deposits in Argentina and Chile (% GDP).
Note: Corporate and individual accounts, December values.
*Sector privado no financiero y residentes en el Extranjero. **Sector privado.
Sources: BCRA: *Informe de Entidades Financieras*; SBIF: *Revista Información Financiera.*

Although it is difficult to objectively assess whether Argentine investors would actually withdraw deposits in response to reforms that might seem inconsequential to an outside observer, the "shallowness" of the banking sector (Finance-A 2006, interview) compared to countries of similar development levels provides evidence consistent with perceptions of significant risk, and/or the attractiveness of alternative investment options, that could dispose investors to relocate savings if the government eliminated the interest-earnings exemption or granted the tax agency access to time deposits. The value of deposits in private accounts as a percent of GDP in Chile was roughly twice as big as in Argentina (Figure 6.1).

The disinvestment threat created strong structural power because of the significant potential impact on the financial sector and the broader economy. Time deposits, which would be affected by both reforms, represented a large fraction of total deposits by value – an average of 70 percent from 1995 to 2000 – so massive withdrawals would have devastated the banks. And Central Bank studies following the 1995 Tequila Crisis illustrated that time deposits were the most volatile type of accounts (Finance-A 2008, interview).[6] Moreover, the

---

[6] One likely reason for the lower volatility of other accounts is that the ability to remove funds at any time provided a greater sense of security (Finance-A 2008, interview).

financial sector played a key role under convertibility, which stabilized the currency and spurred high growth rates. Large quantities of foreign capital in the form of portfolio and direct investment were critical for sustaining the economy. Much of the money entering the country was invested in the financial sector, which channeled funds to the productive sector as well as the public sector. Because of the financial sector's economic importance, large-scale time-deposit withdrawals could have had serious macroeconomic consequences.

The Banks' Instrumental Power

The perceived threat of reduced investment motivated the banks to oppose tax agency access to time deposits and taxing interest earnings. Unlike corporate taxation (Chapter 5), reforms in these policy areas threatened the banks' core interests – they feared they would lose depositors, which would have had a much greater impact on their profitability and viability than higher corporate taxes. The banks had significant instrumental power with which to influence policy decisions in these areas.

Instrumental power arose from recruitment into government and informal ties to executive-branch officials. Financial-sector leaders occupied important ministerial positions during the 1990s. For example, Maccarone, president of the Argentine bank association ADEBA from 1982 to 1993, served as Secretary of Finance during President Menem's first administration. In addition, orthodox economists from think tanks with ties to the financial sector such as CEMA were appointed to the Economy Ministry and Central Bank (Heredia 2004: 345).[7] President De la Rua's Secretary of Treasury, Vicens, also had close ties to the financial sector. Vicens developed a strong relationship with the banking sector while he served as Central Bank Director in the 1980s and later as a private consultant (Finance-A 2008, interview). In 2002 after leaving the government, he was elected president of the bank association ABA, formed from the merger of the international bank association and ADEBA in 1998.

Instrumental power based on recruitment into government and informal ties[8] helped the financial sector influence policy on multiple fronts, including social security reform, Central Bank reform, capital market reforms, and other aspects of financial sector reform. A long-time ADEBA official recalled: "In reality, we were very listened-to, not only on tax issues," (Finance-C 2006, interview). Similarly, Heredia (2003: 100) observes: "During the 1990s, the financial sector established itself as … one of the most powerful pressure groups."

In this case, economic importance enhanced the financial sector's instrumental power as well as its structural power. Since the economy's fate was closely

---

[7] *Pagina Doce*, May 19, 2002. Maccarone became head of the Central Bank in 2001.
[8] Technical expertise may also have contributed to the banks' instrumental power. ADEBA's conventions became important policy forums attended by government and international financial institution authorities; the Economy Ministry seriously reviewed ADEBA's policy papers (Heredia 2003: 97, Finance-C 2006, interview).

linked to the financial sector, it was natural for the executive branch to grant the banks privileged access. As the deficit grew in the late 1990s, the financial sector became even more important for sustaining the economy and convertibility. As a banking-association informant explained: "The government was placing a lot of debt, it needed the banks for that" (Finance-A 2008, interview). This reliance on the banks enhanced their instrumental power. The former secretary of treasury observed: "The banking association was a relatively important association since financing for the government and for enterprises was critical and the capital market was very complicated, so banks were a central voice" (Economy Ministry-A 2006, interview).

The financial sector's instrumental power helped keep access to time deposits and eliminating the income-tax exemption for interest earnings off the agenda in two ways. First, instrumental power enhanced structural power; recruitment into government gave the financial sector ample opportunity to reinforce concerns within the executive branch that these reforms would reduce investment in financial instruments. Second, on rare occasion when structural power failed to keep reform off the agenda, lobbying the executive branch served as an alternate means for blocking reform, as the following section illustrates.

The Aborted 1995 Bank Information Resolution

During the onset of the Tequila Crisis, the Economy Ministry detected a large number of undeclared bank deposits while investigating insolvent banks.[9] In the tax agency director's temporary absence, the acting head issued an administrative resolution demanding information on all bank deposits exceeding $12,000, including time deposits.[10]

The banks reacted quickly against the resolution. According to an ADEBA informant, the timing of the resolution exacerbated incentives for investors to withdraw their deposits:

> The sensation that a crisis was possible had not yet arrived ... until the tax agency announced that it would put in place an informational regime on time deposits – something they had been studying for a long time. They had the bad idea of communicating it in February of 1995, and this provoked fear and a small run on the banks.... When they announced this, the first reaction was that everyone wanted to take their time deposits out of the banks. (Finance-C 2006, interview)

Financial-sector lobbying exacted a quick reversal of the resolution. Bank-association representatives immediately contacted government officials, including (former ADEBA president) Secretary of Finance Maccarone (Finance-C 2006, interview).[11] A tax agency informant recounted: "There was pressure to backpedal, a very strong position on the part of the financial system that they

---

[9] *Clarín*, Feb. 15, 1995.
[10] *Clarín*, Feb. 15, 16, 1995; *Cronista*, Feb. 15, 1995.
[11] *Cronista*, Feb. 16, 1995, *Clarín*, Feb. 16, 1995.

were not going to comply with the norm," (AFIP-A 2006, interview). After meeting with Maccarone, Economy Minister Cavallo announced that the resolution would be retracted. Press reports suggest that he found the financial sector's arguments convincing: "In Economy, it was commented that the tax agency resolution had arrived at an unfortunate moment, with the public sensitized by the insolvency of several financial entities." [12]

Taxing Interest Earnings by Obfuscation

In 1998, the Economy Ministry proposed an alternative reform designed to tax interest earnings without eliminating the income tax exemption. The political process surrounding this short-lived reform and its aftermath illustrates the strong constraints created by financial-sector power as well as the advantages and drawbacks of the reform strategy employed: obfuscating incidence via burden shifting.

Although the perception that taxing interest earnings would provoke flight from the financial system was widespread, not all policymakers held this view. The treasury secretary and the sub-secretary of tax policy during Menem's second administration both felt that eliminating the interest-earnings exemption would have at most a limited effect on depositors' behavior (2006 interviews: Economy Ministry-A, B). However, perceived structural power in the congressional arena helped keep reform off the agenda. Governing-coalition legislators, including PJ Deputy Lamberto, president of the Finance and Budget Committee, opposed including interest earnings in the personal income tax, based on anticipations that investors would remove their money from the banks (Economy Ministry-B 2006, interview). [13] Opposition from these legislators helped dissuade the Economy Ministry from attempting to eliminate the exemption. [14]

Economy Ministry officials nonetheless believed interest should be taxed – to raise revenue, close loopholes, and eliminate what amounted to a state subsidy for corporate debt. To circumvent obstacles created by strong financial-sector power, they devised an alternative initiative: a 15 percent tax on corporate interest payments and corporate debt, [15] which would tax interest payments made by firms, rather than interest earned by individuals. This design obfuscated incidence via burden shifting. The Economy Ministry argued that the

---

[12] *Clarín*, Feb. 16, 1995.

[13] *Diario de Sesiones, Cámara de Diputados*, Sept. 9, 1998: 6.

[14] Structural power was the critical factor motivating legislators' opposition; the financial sector did not enjoy instrumental power in the congressional arena, and legislators viewed the banks unfavorably: "When they went to Congress, the banks had very little impact, because the banking sector was considered a very rich sector" (Economy Ministry-A 2006, interview). Legislators were more sympathetic to small businesses.

[15] The *Impuesto Sobre los Intereses Pagados y el Endeudamiento Empresarial*, modeled on the Comprehensive Business Tax proposed by Bush Senior advisors, was included in the 1998 reform (Chapter 5).

new tax would have the same incidence as including interest earnings in the personal income tax base, because the burden would be transferred from corporate debtors to individual creditors through interest rates. If interest were included in the personal income tax, banks would have to offer higher rates of return to depositors, which they would compensate by charging higher interest rates on loans to firms. Applying a tax on corporate interest payments would have the same outcome: higher effective interest rates on loans to firms. In practice, the impact of taxing interest, either with the new tax or by including interest in the income-tax base, would be distributed in some proportion between firms and depositors through changes in interest rates (Economy Ministry-A 2006, interview). The new tax was expressly intended to make taxation of interest earnings less visible to individual investors, and hence less likely to motivate flight from the banks and less likely to stimulate opposition from the banks and legislators.

Obfuscating incidence proved highly effective in these regards. Although the bank association did complain to Congress that the tax would raise the cost of credit and discourage investment,[16] the financial sector accepted the reform with minimal resistance (Economy Ministry-A 2006, interview). To win the sector's acquiescence, Economy Ministry officials explicitly presented the new tax as an alternative to eliminating the interest-earnings exemption: "We said, 'Look, we came up with this tax on debt because what we thought about doing before was eliminating the exemption,' and of course they told us 'Yes, that would be much worse than the tax on debt'" (interview: Economy Ministry-B 2006). Financial-sector informants confirmed that assessment (Finance-C, D 2006). The tax on corporate debt also precluded resistance from governing-coalition legislators. References to any potential negative impact on bank deposits were essentially absent from discussion of the tax in the press and in Congress. In fact, few legislators understood that the tax burden would be transferred to interest earnings, despite repeated explanations from government technocrats.[17] An opposition legislator recalled: "It was like learning Aramaic or some other extinct ancient language; no one understood what it was about" (Baglini: 2006, interview). Congress approved the new tax in 1999.

Despite the legislative success, the obfuscation strategy had a major drawback that led to the reform's untimely demise: the attempt to exploit burden shifting created uncertainty about the actual incidence of the new tax. Opposition-coalition economists did not believe the perfect-market assumptions needed to make taxing corporate interest payments equivalent to taxing individuals' interest earnings actually held (interviews: Machinea 2007, Sabaini 2006). They felt the new tax imposed an undue burden on small businesses,

---

[16] The tone of the complaint was mild, however, and the discussion was brief (Acta, CPHCD, May 20, 1998).

[17] Economy Ministry technocrats cultivated PJ support by framing the new tax as a tax on capital (Chapter 5).

which already faced much higher interest rates than big firms. Accordingly, the De la Rua administration gradually phased out the tax after winning power in 1999.

Yet like their predecessors, De la Rua's economic team firmly believed that interest earnings should be taxed (interviews: Machinea 2007, Sabaini 2006), and they discussed eliminating the income-tax exemption as part of the 1999 tax reform, which raised revenue to control the growing deficit and sustain convertibility. Sub-secretary of tax policy Gómez-Sabaini made at least one public statement expressing his interest in eliminating the exemption.

However, concerns within the administration over structural power, along with financial-sector opposition, ultimately deterred reform. Gómez-Sabaini's statement aroused immediate opposition from Treasury Secretary (and future ABA president) Vicens, whose opinion coincided with the banking sector's. Moreover, the president himself feared that eliminating the tax exemption would motivate depositors to remove their money from the banks. Finance Minister Machinea (interview, 2007) ultimately agreed that incorporating interest earnings into the income tax was infeasible due to structural power:

> We depended very much on the financial markets, because we had to obtain $20,000 million to finance the debt payments. That was the problem, our Sword of Damocles all of the time.... With any strong noise in the markets, we were very weak, because we needed a lot of resources to finance the debt.... When we took office, we had only 45 days of money to pay the debt.... So this tax on [interest from] deposits, which was quite reasonable – we had discussed it internally, we thought that at some point it would have to be done – in this context of such weakness, such vulnerability, no. It was not reasonable.

Although the executive decided against eliminating the interest-earnings exemption, the Peronist opposition introduced this measure in the senate to replace other tax increases in the 1999 reform that they rejected. Whereas Peronist legislators had opposed this measure during the Menem administration, they now extolled its virtues. PJ Senator Gioja declared: "This is the time ... to undo the regressive character of our tax system.... If wage income pays, how can interest income not pay?"[18] However, Radical legislators, who had themselves advocated taxing interest earnings on previous occasions, rejected the modification in the lower house, in accord with the executive's structural power concerns. As longtime Radical legislator Baglini (interview, 2006) observed, perhaps unsurprisingly, governing-coalition legislators took structural power more seriously than opposition legislators:

> When one is in the opposition, one says: "What are we waiting for to tax the time deposits of those millionaires!" The ones who are on the other side, in the government, their hands shake when they think: "Look, tomorrow we could have a run on the banks, and we will have to use up the reserves."

---

[18] Diario de Sesiones, Senado, Dec. 28, 1999.

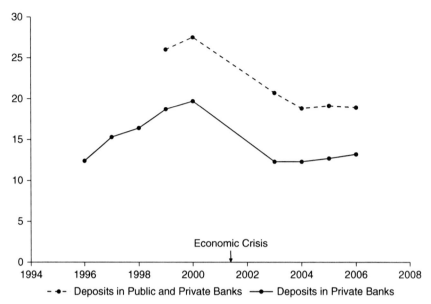

FIGURE 6.2. Private-Sector Bank Deposits in Argentina (% GDP).
Notes: Includes checking accounts, savings accounts, time deposits, and other accounts. December values.
Source: BRCA: *Informe De Entidades Financieras.*

Bank information Access Post-2001: Weakened Financial-Sector Power

The financial sectors' structural and instrumental power declined significantly after 2001 because of Argentina's economic crisis and increasing oversight of the financial system in response to international pressures. In the absence of business-power constraints, the tax agency finally obtained access to time deposits.

The 2001 crisis undermined structural power by reducing the vulnerability of the economy and the financial sector to any potential disinvestment that the reform might have provoked. From a macroeconomic perspective, the financial sector played a much less important role in the economy after the crisis and the ensuing demise of convertibility. The massive run on the banks leading up to the crisis and the freezing and subsequent devaluation of deposits that remained in the banks drastically reduced the relative size of the sector. Deposits in public and private banks as a percent of GDP fell from 28 percent in 2000 to an average of only 19 percent from 2003 to 2006; deposits in private banks decreased from 20 percent to 13 percent of GDP (Figure 6.2). While governments sought to strengthen the financial sector, maintaining a high value of deposits was much less critical for stability in the post-convertibility era. From the financial sector's perspective, furthermore, time deposits were less important. After the

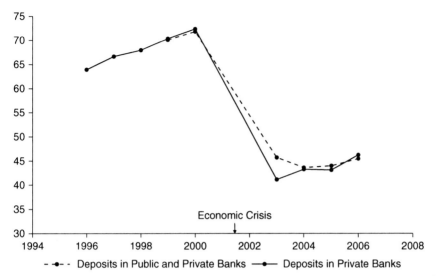

FIGURE 6.3. Time Deposits in Argentina (% Total Private-Sector Deposits, December Values).
Source: BCRA: *Informe de Entidades Financieras.*

crisis, the value of funds in time deposits relative to other accounts declined significantly, partly because much lower interest rates made time deposits less attractive investment instruments, and partly because customers preferred ordinary savings accounts with unrestricted access, given their loss of confidence in the banking system. Time deposits as a percent of the total value of deposits in private banks dropped from an average of 68 percent from 1996 to 2000 to only 42 percent from 2003 to 2006 (Figure 6.3). Additional time-deposit disinvestment would thus have had a much smaller impact not only on the economy as a whole but also on the banks, compared to the precrisis era.

In addition, widespread adoption of anti–money-laundering measures, in response to international pressure following the terrorist attacks in the United States, reduced the disinvestment threat associated with tax agency access to time deposits. The banks perceived that their customers would be much less likely to react negatively if the tax agency obtained time-deposit information in this new context. An ADEBA informant (Finance-C 2006) explained:

Today it is not the same as in 1995. People were more sensitive during the Tequila crisis.... Now it is completely different. Everyone knows that AFIP [the tax agency] controls bank operations, as do the banks, because of money laundering.... People are more and more aware that if they are going to do a transaction in a bank, it will be monitored.

Accordingly, investors who did not want the tax agency to have information about their assets would not have deposited large sums of money in the financial system after 2001. The banks' clientele was thus less likely to include people who would withdraw deposits in response to expanded information access. Further, the new context of international concern over money laundering legitimated tax agency access to bank information, making investors less likely to interpret tax agency requests for time deposit information as a sign that their savings might be insecure. Tax agency access to time deposits therefore created weaker incentives to relocate savings after 2001. International pressures in this case therefore had an indirect influence on prospects for reform, by helping to reduce investors' structural power.

The banks' instrumental power also declined after the 2001 crisis. Recruitment into government ended with convertibility and the change of economic model. During the Kirchner administration, there were far fewer connections and much less ideological affinity between the financial sector and cabinet members. This new state of affairs was not surprising given the reduced economic importance of the financial sector as well as popular outrage against the banks for not ensuring their savings in the aftermath of the crisis.

Weakened structural and instrumental power allowed the tax agency to obtain full access to time deposits in 2006 without difficulty. Once the threat of disinvestment and its anticipated impact declined, structural power no longer hindered reform.[19] Not only were the banks less opposed to giving the tax agency time-deposit information, they were also in a much weaker position to resist had they wished to, given their reduced instrumental power and lingering public antagonism toward the financial sector (interview, AFIP-A 2006).[20] The decline in structural power, however, was the critical factor that made reform possible; even if the financial sector's instrumental power had remained strong, the banks probably would not have resisted. The tax agency's involvement in other initiatives, including several major anti-evasion reform packages, explains why it did not pursue the issue of time-deposit information until 2006.[21]

Interest Earnings Post-2001: Persistent Structural Power

Despite advances on bank information access, no reforms were initiated to tax interest earnings after 2001, since structural power with respect to this policy area remained strong. First, policymakers continued to perceive that eliminating the tax exemption would create strong incentives for investors to withdraw their remaining savings from the banks. A government informant explained:

[19] Funds in time deposits grew from December 2006 through May 2007, suggesting that the reform did not have a significant impact on investor behavior.

[20] The financial sector was reluctant to make demands on the Kirchner administration for fear of further degrading its public image. The banks maintained a low profile during Fernandez de Kirchner's presidency, fearing that otherwise the public would demand and/or the government would embrace policies impinging on their renewed profitability (Finance-B 2008, interview).

[21] In the post-2001 context of greatly weakened business power, the tax agency also obtained access to financial transfers into and out of the country, which proved impossible during the 1990s (BCRA: Comunicación A 3840, Dec. 19, 2002 (www.bcra.gov.ar); AFIP-A 2006, interview).

Today, the population is still very sensitive because the debacle [2001 crisis] was not so long ago, and people totally lost confidence in the banks. Deposits are only just now starting to return to the banks. If you suddenly tax [interest] income, people will take their money out in fright, and once more the banks will be left without money. It could produce a run on the banks. (Interview, Economy Ministry-G 2006)

Former finance minister Miceli (interview, 2008) argued against reform following a similar logic:

You have to be very sure that if you tax interest earnings, deposits will not flee from the banks. At least another ten years will have to pass before enacting this tax. Argentina has a history of financial crises every ten years. In 1980 during the military dictatorship, ten banks went broke in a financial crash … people withdrew their deposits en masse. In 1989–90, Plan Bonex was implemented. Everyone who had deposits in the banks was told they couldn't touch their money. The government gave them a ten-year bond. Terrible. No one believed anything anymore. Then came Cavallo's Convertibility, confidence returned, people went back to the financial system, then came the 2001 crisis. Everyone withdrew their deposits. There was the *corralito*.… If we reach the year 2010 or 2012 without anyone robbing the people's deposits, then we can talk about [taxing] interest earnings.

The 2001 crisis therefore enhanced perceptions of investor sensitivity to taxing interest earnings by renewing memories of economic instability.[22] In contrast to bank information access, no other factors counteracted incentives to relocate savings. Whereas the salience of fighting money laundering made investors less likely to interpret tax agency access to time deposits as a sign that their savings were insecure, taxing interest earnings could still be perceived as a red flag. Moreover, taxing interest earnings reduces the profitability of bank deposits, whereas tax agency access to bank information has no direct impact on profits. All else equal, taxing interest earnings should inherently create stronger incentives to relocate funds than granting the tax agency information on time deposits.

Second, the potential impact on the financial sector of disinvestment provoked by taxing interest earnings remained consequential, even though the broader economy would have been much less affected than in the 1990s. Interest-earning accounts, which included both time deposits and savings accounts, still contained the majority of funds in the banks after the crisis (Figure 6.4). Whereas time deposits – the only accounts affected by the 2006

[22] As the above interviews indicate, bank depositors at large were expected to withdraw their funds if the government tried to include interest earnings in the progressive income tax – either because they perceived (correctly or incorrectly) that they would legally owe taxes on their interest, or because of the Argentine hypersensitivity to banking conditions. However, structural power still arguably resided primarily with economic elites: both before and after the crisis, roughly 1 percent of the adult population owned approximately 50 percent of the funds deposited in interest-earning accounts (author's calculations, BCRA data). Middle- and lower-income depositors' contribution to structural power in this case worked to benefit economic elites, given that only upper-income individuals would be required to pay consequential taxes on interest earnings.

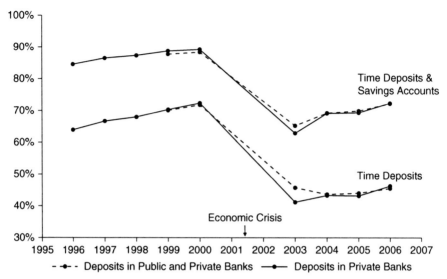

FIGURE 6.4. Interest-Earning Accounts in Argentina (% Total Private-Sector Deposits, December Values).
Source: BRCA: *Informe De Entidades Financieras.*

bank information access reform – contained only 44 percent of funds at the end of 2005, time deposits and saving accounts – which would both be affected if interest earnings were taxed – contained 70 percent of funds.[23] Changes in the structure of deposits brought about by the 2001 crisis therefore did not reduce the financial sector's vulnerability to potential disinvestment provoked by taxing interest earnings as much as they reduced vulnerability to potential disinvestment provoked by expanded bank information access (Figure 6.5). Furthermore, policymakers were concerned that taxing interest earnings would hinder the financial system's recovery by discouraging clients from returning to the banks. As former economy minister Lavagna (2006, interview) explained, "We had to prioritize *la bancarizción* [use of the banking system]."

The reduced revenue-raising capacity of interest-earnings taxation also discouraged reform (interview: Lavagna 2006). Not only did the value of private funds deposited in interest-earning accounts decline after the crisis, but interest rates fell as well, to roughly half their value during the 1990s.[24] A rough estimate using 2005 data yields a potential revenue gain of only 0.08 percent of GDP for taxing interest earned on bank accounts, compared to a more substantial figure of about 0.3 percent of GDP in 1999.[25] Competing priorities

---

[23] Private-sector deposits in private and public banks. Author's calculations using BCRA, *Informe De Entidades Financieras.*
[24] BCRA, *Tasas de Interés por Depósitos.*
[25] Author's estimates using BCRA: *Información Diaria Sobre Depósitos y Obligaciones; Información sobre Tramos de Depósitos; Tasas de Interés por Depósitos; Balances Consolidados del Sistema Financiero.* Further, tax evasion via back-to-backs, a problem linked to the interest-

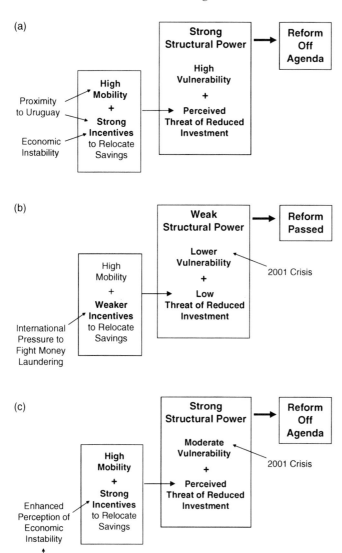

FIGURE 6.5. Financial-Sector Tax Politics in Argentina.
a. Expanding bank information access and taxing interest earnings, 1990s; b. Expanding bank-information access, post-2001; c. Taxing interest earnings post-2001.

also helped keep reform off the agenda, despite interest within the Economy Ministry in revising the exemption toward the end of Kirchner's term (interviews: Economy Ministry-D, E 2006). The administration was particularly

earnings exemption, was less prevalent after 2001, thanks to stricter regulations, better oversight, and improved information systems (AFIP-A 2006, interview).

concerned with keeping interest rates low after 2005; taxing interest earnings could have driven interest rates up (interviews: Economy Ministry-D, E 2006, Finance-A 2008). These additional concerns aside, however, interviews suggest that structural power would have sufficed to keep the reform off the agenda.[26]

6.2 COMPARATIVE PERSPECTIVE: BANK-INFORMATION ACCESS IN CHILE

Like its Argentine counterpart, the Chilean tax agency had sought increased bank information access since the early 1990s to control evasion. Income-tax evasion in Chile (47.4 percent) was nearly as high as in Argentina (49.7 percent) (Jiménez et al. 2010: 58). Whereas the Argentine tax agency needed access to time deposits, the Chilean tax agency sought access to checking accounts. The Chilean tax agency won access to information on interest earnings from bank deposits in 1995 and bonds in 2001. However, access to checking accounts was a much more powerful tool for detecting undeclared income, given the country's structure of deposits and dominant forms of evasion, just as time-deposit information was most critical for controlling evasion in Argentina (interviews: Jorratt 2007, AFIP-A 2006).

Access to checking accounts remained off the agenda in Chile through 2008. Whereas by 2006, bank information access in Argentina was more extensive than in many European countries (2006 interviews: AFIP-A, D, E), Chile appeared on a list of eight financial centers that still had not implemented OECD standards (OECD 2009). The Chilean tax agency could obtain checking-account information only with judicial authorization and only in cases where fraud had already been detected. Deposit information therefore could not be used to screen tax returns for undeclared assets. In Argentina, in contrast, banks routinely provided all information on deposits and transactions that the tax agency deemed relevant for controlling evasion (AFIP-F 2006, interview). In 2009, Chile finally passed a reform that loosened banking-secrecy rules for checking accounts; however, the scope of the reform was quite limited.

Chile's lack of progress on checking-account access before 2009 is remarkable given similar international pressures to loosen banking secrecy in the post-9/11 era as those Argentina experienced. Moreover, failure to reform prevented Chile from signing double-taxation treaties with the United States and other developed countries that required bank information access as part of these agreements; Chilean governments had actively pursued double-tax agreements since 1990 (interviews: Etcheberry 2005, SII-C 2007).

---

[26] Structural power also deterred a related reform: taxing capital gains on stocks and real estate, which would have been more lucrative than taxing interest earnings after 2001. Lavagna (2006, interview) decided against taxing capital gains to promote capital- and real-estate market recovery.

As in Argentina, business power is crucial for understanding the timing and extent of reform in Chile. In contrast to Argentina, however, structural power did not hinder reform in Chile; tax agency access to checking deposits elicited no credible threat of disinvestment (Etcheberry 2005, interview). First, checking accounts are much less mobile than savings accounts. Because checking accounts are regularly accessed, it is much more difficult to move them offshore. Second, Chile's banking system, currency, and economy had been remarkably stable since the late 1980s; the conditions that created incentives for Argentine depositors to remove funds from the banks in response to changes in tax agency oversight were absent in Chile. Moreover, prior experience suggested that Chilean depositors would not alter their behavior in response to greater tax agency oversight. When the tax agency obtained access to bank records on interest earnings in 1995, the only observed response was an increase in interest earnings declared on tax returns (Etcheberry 2005, interview).

Instead, business's strong instrumental power and cross-sectoral opposition to reform explain the tax agency's limited access to bank information. In contrast to Argentina, where business leaders outside the financial sector expressed little concern over the issue, the broader business community in Chile opposed loosening banking secrecy (CPC 2000: 6, interviews: CPC-A 2005, CChC-B 2005, Etcheberry 2005, Aninat 2007).[27] According to tax agency informants, this opposition arose from reluctance to empower the tax agency to effectively audit individual income taxes. Large firms are closely monitored and rarely evade taxes, so granting the tax agency access to checking accounts would have little impact on their tax burden. However, business associations in Chile represented not just the interests of firms and corporations but also the interests of capital owners and upper-income individuals. A high-level tax agency informant explained:

Big business owners do not want the tax agency to look over their personal checking accounts – not the *business's* checking account, but the *personal* account. The business associations say they have nothing to hide: our accounts are open for review. But in a more concealed manner, they lobby against reforms to open checking accounts. (SII-C 2007, interview)

Simply put, in the words of the former tax agency director, "In Chile people don't want the tax agency to have the information. They realize that they will have more trouble evading taxes" (Etcheberry 2005, interview). Opportunities for evasion aside, resistance to banking-secrecy reform was congruent with business preferences for a small, minimally regulatory state.

---

[27] A former CPC (A 2005) president asserted: "I defend the tax agency because it is super-efficient, modern, a source of pride for Chile. What I protest and oppose – this does not mean that it should have easy access to our checking accounts. We can't be besieged by the tax agency, with inspections and examinations."

Instrumental power arising from cohesion, partisan linkages, and government-business concertation (Chapter 3) deterred reform. The tax agency requested access to checking accounts while the 2001 Anti-Evasion Reform was being designed, but the Finance Ministry dismissed the idea as infeasible. A tax agency informant (SII-C) interviewed in 2007 remained pessimistic regarding prospects for reform in the foreseeable future; a Finance Ministry informant (F 2007) expressed enthusiasm for granting the tax agency checking-account access but reported that the government had not discussed the issue.

In 2009, however, a context of growing international consensus in favor of lifting banking secrecy, in conjunction with international pressure of a qualitatively different type – OECD membership conditionality – placed access to checking accounts squarely on Chile's agenda. In the aftermath of the 2008 global financial crisis, OECD countries redoubled their efforts to promote banking-secrecy reform in order to better regulate the financial sector and control global tax avoidance, and the tide began to turn in favor of greater transparency when Switzerland announced it would loosen its banking-secrecy rules in March 2009. During the final stages of Chile's application process, the OECD made loosening banking secrecy an explicit membership requirement.

The Bachelet administration proposed reform in April 2009 amid significant controversy; among four reforms required for OECD membership, loosening checking-account banking secrecy was expected to be the most difficult, given resistance within the right coalition.[28] However, whereas prior pressure for reform from the United States and other international actors had little effect, the national prestige and benefits associated with OECD membership created political space for reform. References to the OECD membership requirement were pervasive in news coverage,[29] and the government regularly emphasized this imperative. Overt enthusiasm for joining the OECD on the part of more moderate Alianza politicians and business statements in favor of this prospect[30]

---

[28] *El Mercurio*, July 11, 2009. Various opposition legislators announced they would vote against the reform, and the UDI's think tank, which had strong ties to business, rejected the reform (*Nación*, July 7, 2009).

[29] Out of forty-five *El Mercurio* articles on the banking-secrecy proposal during its design and deliberation in Congress, thirty-five noted OECD membership conditionality, and thirty prominently featured the issue. Only three articles mentioned Chile's appearance on the OECD grey list. International relations literature on the related issue of anti–money laundering policies emphasizes the minimal benefits to small developing countries of adopting international standards and the grave economic consequences of being blacklisted (Sharman 2008). The Chilean case differs in that potential economic problems associated with gray-listing were accompanied by strong positive incentives for conforming to international standards: OECD membership as well as enhanced domestic tax capacity. Rather than standards being forced on a country that otherwise had no interest in adopting them, international pressure in this case enhanced the government's ability to enact reforms it viewed as desirable but may not otherwise have been able to legislate. Literature on structural adjustment provides similar examples of governments using international pressures to strengthen their hand (Mahon 2004: 24).

[30] *El Mercurio*, Aug. 7, 2009; CPC communiqués: March 14, 2008, June 2, 2009.

support the inference that OECD conditionality tempered opposition to the reform – particularly considering business and the right's prior resistance to tax agency access to checking accounts. In response to repeated Concertación calls for Alianza presidential candidate Piñera to clarify the opposition's position on the reform, Piñera announced: "I am absolutely in favor of Chile's full incorporation into the international community and the OECD. For that reason, we must collaborate on fighting drug trafficking, money laundering, terrorism – so we will have to open banking secrecy."[31] The CPC's general manager expressed similar reasoning:

We were entering the OECD, and one of the OECD's demands was [banking secrecy reform]. So we understood that and we were in favor of it.

–So entering the OECD was more important than banking secrecy?

Correct, and we understood that well.

–Is OECD membership good for attracting investment?

Clearly, without doubt. It means more prestige, being in a privileged position to attract investment. (Interview, CPC-E 2011)

Finance Minister Velasco emphasized similar points to counter opposition from a few intransigent UDI senators.[32]

As expected, given business's strong instrumental power, however, the reform proposal was extremely limited in scope. The tax agency would be able to request checking account information in cases where evasion or fraud had not yet been detected. However, the tax agency would be required to obtain express consent from the account owner authorizing the bank to release information; otherwise the case would be sent to the courts, and the tax agency would not be able to obtain the information without judicial authorization,[33] just as before the reform. Access remained restricted to a case-by-case basis; checking account information could not be used for general auditing purposes.[34] These substantial restrictions prompted former tax agency director Etcheberry to publicly criticize the proposal: "I see no reason why the tax agency should not have broad access to bank information. The proposal is very limited."[35] While the reform complied with the minimal OECD requirements, it gave the tax agency very little additional capacity to cross-check tax

---

[31] *El Mercurio*, July 8, 2009.

[32] Diario de Sesiones del Senado, Legislatura 357a, Sesión 58, Extraordinaria, Oct. 14, 2009: 107.

[33] Proyecto 6871: Mensaje 204–357, April 29, 2009 (www.camara.cl); *El Mercurio*, Aug. 6, 2009. Negotiations with the right introduced this requirement for explicit consent, yet the only change from the original bill was to interpret no response from the account holder as lack of consent. The need for judicial review if the account holder declined access was always present. This case again illustrates the much greater importance of business influence over the reform agenda and design compared to later stages of policymaking (Chapters 3, 4).

[34] *El Mercurio*, June 25, 2009.

[35] *El Mercurio*, July 14, 2009.

declarations against bank records in order to detect evasion. In practice, tax agency sources viewed the reform as having had essentially no impact.[36] The contrast with Argentina, where tax agency access to bank information is automatic, essentially unrestricted, and can be used to screen declarations at large for evasion, remains stark.

6.3 TAXING FINANCIAL TRANSACTIONS

In March 2001, Economy Minister Cavallo legislated a financial transactions tax as an emergency measure to control Argentina's growing deficit. The 0.25 percent tax, later increased to 0.6 percent, affected checking-account debits and credits. This tax proved attractive for two reasons: it was difficult to evade, since banks automatically withheld the tax, and it provided the Treasury with an immediate – and daily – source of revenue. The transactions tax was anticipated to generate 2 percent of GPD annually[37]; it raised 1 percent of GDP in 2001 after only nine months (DNIAF 2012). As in many other Latin American countries where similar taxes were implemented in times of fiscal distress, the transactions tax became a permanent feature of Argentina's tax system.

2001 Reform: Weak Structural Power and Government Reform Strategies

One might suppose that a financial transactions tax would have been infeasible under convertibility – like taxing interest earnings, taxing transactions imposes costs on bank customers that could create incentives for them to avoid the financial system, which played an essential role in the economy. However, whereas taxing interest earnings and granting the tax agency access to time deposits remained off the agenda until after the economic crisis, the transactions tax was implemented without difficulty in early 2001. Weak structural power largely explains this outcome. In contrast to the other two policy areas, taxing financial transactions did not elicit an exit threat. The banks therefore accepted the transactions tax and did not use their instrumental power, which remained strong in 2001 prior to the crisis, to oppose the measure.

Structural power was weak because the proposed tax affected only checking accounts, which are much less mobile than savings accounts. Because checking accounts are regularly accessed, it is much more difficult to place these accounts offshore, especially for businesses. Opening a checking account in Uruguay would not be feasible because of increased transaction costs arising from interactions with foreign banks and different financial regulations (Finance-A 2008, interview). Further, whereas individuals could decide to withdraw funds from checking accounts and guard cash at home, businesses – particularly large

---

[36] Personal communication, Jorratt, Jan. 27, 2013.
[37] *Clarín*, March 24, 2001.

corporations, which must operate in the formal sector – did not have that option. In 2001, 82 percent of the funds in checking accounts belonged to businesses rather than individuals,[38] making any potential exit threat minimal. In addition, checking accounts were empirically less sensitive to changes in banking conditions than time deposits (Finance-A 2008, interview).

Given depositors' weak structural power, the banks did not strongly resist the transactions tax. Compared to taxing interest earnings, the banks viewed the transactions tax as a lesser evil. When asked if the sector was concerned about the transactions tax when the measure was announced, an ABA informant replied: "At first, yes. But it was going to affect checking accounts. It would have been different if it affected time deposits, which are more volatile" (Finance-A 2008, interview). Similarly, an ADEBA informant asserted that in contrast to the transactions tax, "taxing interest earnings attacks the heart of the banking business" (Finance-C 2008, interview). Because the transactions tax did not elicit a credible exit threat, it would have little impact on the financial sector, aside from administrative costs. Businesses with checking accounts, rather than the banks, would bear the actual burden of the tax.

Government reform strategies further minimized financial sector opposition. The administration compensated the banks by packaging the transactions tax with another measure that counteracted possible disincentives for using checking accounts: lowering the legally allowed maximum for cash payments from 10,000 to 1,000 pesos.[39] The law required payments of more than 1,000 pesos to be made with either checks or bank cards.

The government also emphasized stabilization in the context of serious concerns regarding the future of the economy and convertibility. Although the crisis did not culminate until December 2001, references to fiscal emergency and a possible default on the burgeoning debt, which reached 52.8 percent of GDP by the end of 2000 (Lagos 2002: 18), were frequent after Economy Minister Machinea's resignation in March and the resignation of his successor, Lopez-Murphy, two weeks later.[40] Argentina's risk ratings had more than doubled since 1999 and continued to increase (Lagos 2002: 18); their upward progress was regularly reported in the news and became a matter of public concern (2008 interviews: Finance-B, C).[41] Accordingly, access to international credit was becoming more restricted. The economy minister emphasized that the transactions tax would help remedy these growing signs of economic instability, and the bill destined the transaction-tax revenue to a "Public Emergency Fund" to protect public credit and economic competitivity.[42] Even orthodox economists who viewed the tax as distortionary agreed it was necessary to bolster state coffers, reduce the deficit, and thereby protect Argentina's

[38] BCRA, *Informe de Entidades Financieras*, July 2001.
[39] *Clarín*, March 23, 2001.
[40] *Clarín*, March 26, 27, 2001.
[41] *Clarín*, March 24, 2001, *La Nación*, March 29, 2001.
[42] *Clarín*, March 22, 2001.

international reputation as a good place to do business.[43] In effect, by raising revenue quickly, the transactions tax could reduce the risk of international capital flight, which threatened the entire economy and convertibility.[44] The transactions tax did have a positive short-term effect on investor expectations; after the Senate approved the reform, the stock market experienced a small rebound.[45]

Compensation and emphasizing stabilization proved effective. Bank leaders expressed support for lowering the cash payment maximum and publicly recognized the importance of increasing tax revenue. Regarding the first point, a Banco Ciudad representative observed that tighter restrictions on cash payments "will increase people's need for bank accounts and bring us new clients."[46] On the second point, ABA's president asserted when asked about the transactions tax: "If we don't close the fiscal gap, we will have to borrow money at such high rates that the damage to the economy would be worse."[47] Some complaints over administrative costs were voiced; the banks were given only four days to establish the new informational systems necessary to withhold the tax from their clients (ABA 2001a). And some bankers did express concerns regarding the tax's impact on their customers and the banking system.[48] However, ABA released a formal communiqué urging Congress to approve Cavallo's economic plan, transactions tax included.[49]

Compensation and emphasizing stabilization also encouraged the private sector more broadly – including those who would actually bear the burden of the transaction tax – to accept the reform. As part of the same package – the "Competitivity Law" – Cavallo proposed multiple stimulus measures including new tax benefits for business that would offset the cost of the transactions tax.[50] The private sector reacted positively to the announcement. The UIA and SRA, among other associations, openly supported Cavallo's package.[51]

The Impact on Checking Accounts

In retrospect, the transaction tax's impact on checking accounts appears to have been minimal. Checking accounts did begin to decline after Cavallo announced the initiative on March 22; by April 4 when the tax was implemented, the

---

[43] *Clarín*, March 26, 2001.
[44] The financial sector and policymakers defended the currency regime until the bitter end (Woodruff 2005).
[45] *Clarín*, March 27, 2001.
[46] *Clarín*, March 23, 2001.
[47] *Clarín*, April 4, 2001. Although banking sector informants interviewed in 2008 (Finance-A, B, C) did not remember the transactions tax being perceived as a measure that would improve risk ratings, they agreed that the banks accepted the tax largely because of pressing state revenue needs.
[48] *Clarín*, March 23, 2001.
[49] Ibid.
[50] *Clarín*, March 22, 2001.
[51] *Clarín*, March 23, 2001

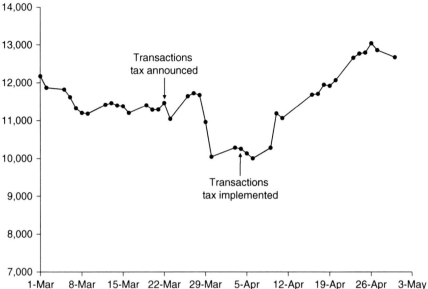

FIGURE 6.6. Checking Accounts in Argentina, March–April 2001 (Millions of Pesos).
Source: BCRA: *Información Diaria Sobre Depósitos y Obligaciones.*

value of checking-account funds had fallen by 11 percent. However, the government quickly enacted additional measures that curtailed the problem. Most importantly, the Central Bank decreed that businesses could not open savings accounts, which ended one obvious way to avoid the tax.[52] Thanks to these measures, checking accounts recovered by mid-April (Figure 6.6).

Further, the banks felt the transactions tax played a minor if any role in the broader process of declining deposits that culminated in the December 2001 crisis. An ABA report written in December 2002 pinpointed the beginning of the run on the banks to March 2001, but the report identified events including the resignation of two economy ministers, the issuing of emergency public bonds, and the removal of the head of the Central Bank in April as the instigators of this process; the transactions tax was not mentioned (Lagos 2002: 17). ABA's 2001(b) *Memoria* (Chapter 2: 1) briefly mentioned the transactions tax as a factor that exacerbated negative expectations in March, but the tax was not discussed elsewhere in the eighty-seven-page document.

Post-2001: Weak Instrumental Power and Financial Sector Indifference

Postcrisis governments maintained the transactions tax because of its revenue-raising capacity.[53] From 2004 to 2007, the tax raised an average of 1.8 percent

---

[52] *Clarín*, March 31, 2008, 2001, ABA 2001b.
[53] Economy Minister Lavagna reduced the rate, however.

of GDP per year (DNIAF 2012). The Kirchner administration also lauded the transactions tax as progressive, based on the assertion that primarily the middle and upper classes maintain bank accounts (Economy Ministry-D 2006, interview).[54] Neither President Kirchner nor his successor Fernández de Kirchner encountered real resistance from the financial sector or from the private sector more broadly, despite regular complaints that the tax was distortionary and discouraged use of the financial system. Given business's weak instrumental power and the absence of serious opposition, retaining the tax was politically unproblematic.

The banks did not mount any concerted campaign against the transactions tax after the crisis (interviews: Finance-B, C 2008) for two reasons. First, consensus on the impact of eliminating the tax appeared lacking. Some financial-sector informants asserted that the tax encouraged clients to minimize transactions and discouraged broader use of the banking system (interviews: Finance-A, C 2008). But not all those who held this view believed eliminating the tax would have a positive short-term behavioral impact (Finance-A 2008, interview). Other informants believed the tax did not create significant disincentives for using the banking system; businesses lacked feasible alternatives to operating with checking accounts, and the Internet made banking more convenient than in the 1990s (Finance-B 2008, interview).

Second, the banks viewed the transactions tax as a problem that should be handled by the businesses that paid the direct cost of the tax. Political action followed a sectoral logic in Argentina, given business's lack of cross-sectoral cohesion (Chapter 5). Instead of defending common business interests, each sector focused on the issues that most directly affected its own particular interests. Accordingly, an ADEBA informant explained the banks' low level of activity on the transactions tax as follows:

It's not something that we are talking about constantly, because it's not an issue only for the bank.... It's not exclusive to the sector. We are looking at other issues. For example, some provinces want to apply a tax on net capital-raising. If we collect funds in a province and we don't lend them within that province but somewhere else, we have to pay a tax on the amount that is not loaned within the province of origin. That *is* something for the [financial] sector to say: listen, no. (Finance-C 2008, interview)

Transactions-tax politics in the post-2001 era therefore resembled cross-sectoral corporate tax politics more closely than the sector-specific politics of taxing interest earnings.

Even if the banks had actively opposed the transactions tax, they probably would not have been able to exert influence given their weak instrumental power in the postcrisis era. Likewise, the business sector more broadly was in a weak position to influence tax policy. Achieving influence in this case would have

---

[54] This statement is probably partially correct, but it is difficult to evaluate incidence because the tax is paid primarily by businesses, which may pass the burden to other economic factors.

required significant instrumental power and concerted collective action, given the importance the Kirchner administrations placed on the transactions tax.

6.4 CONCLUSION

Table 6.3 summarizes how structural power, instrumental power, and reform outcomes varied across the three policy areas discussed in this chapter. Factors other than business power also contributed to the outcomes. Low revenue-raising capacity helped remove taxing interest earnings from the agenda in Argentina after 2001, executive reform strategies facilitated enactment of Argentina's transactions tax, and OECD conditionality facilitated limited tax agency access to checking accounts in Chile. However, business power accounts for most of the variation in outcomes across policy areas, over time, and across countries.

Strong business power, whether structural, instrumental, or both, tended to remove reform from the executive's agenda. In Argentina, structural power in combination with instrumental power made reform infeasible in the cases of taxing interest earnings and granting the tax agency access to time deposits in the 1990s. When one means of influence failed, the other blocked progress in these policy areas. But strong structural power alone prevented reform even when instrumental power was weak. The perception of an exit threat kept taxing interest earnings off the agenda after 2001, notwithstanding the fact that the financial sector's instrumental power declined dramatically after the economic crisis. Conversely, instrumental power alone precluded broad tax agency access to bank information in Chile. Similarly, counterfactual analysis suggests that strong instrumental power could have allowed Argentina's financial sector to block the transactions tax in 2001, had the banks opposed the measure, even though structural power was weak in this policy area. Only when both structural power and instrumental power were weak – or when the financial sector was not averse to reform – did significant progress occur, as in the Argentine cases of bank information access after 2001 and the financial transactions tax.

Regarding structural power, the cases illustrate the importance of both mobility and incentives to relocate investment for creating a credible exit threat. When bank accounts were mobile and policymakers anticipated that reform would create incentives for investors to relocate their deposits, a credible exit threat helped remove reform from the agenda, as in the Argentine cases of expanding bank information access in the 1990s and taxing interest earnings during both decades. When accounts were not mobile, structural power was weak, even if reform imposed costs that might otherwise create incentives for depositors to move their funds elsewhere, as in the case of Argentina's transactions tax on checking accounts and tax agency access to checking accounts in Chile. And when accounts were mobile, but policymakers did not perceive that reform would create incentives to relocate funds,

TABLE 6.3. *Overview: Financial-Sector Power and Tax Policy Outcomes in Argentina and Chile*

	TAXING INTEREST EARNINGS		BANK INFORMATION ACCESS			FINANCIAL TRANSACTIONS TAX	
	Argentina		Argentina		Chile	Argentina	
	1990s	Post-2001	1990s	Post-2001	1990–2000s	2001	Post-2001
Structural Power	Strong High mobility + strong incentives	Strong High mobility + strong incentives	Strong High mobility + strong incentives	Weak Weak incentives	Weak Weak incentives	Weak Low mobility	Weak Low mobility
Instrumental Power	Strong	Weak	Strong	Weak	Strong (business broadly)	Strong but not exercised (indifferent)	Weak
Outcome	Off Agenda	Off Agenda	Off Agenda	Significant Reform	Off Agenda/ Limited Reform	Enacted	Retained

structural power was also weak, as with tax agency access to time deposits post-2001 in Argentina.

The cases in this chapter also evidence the specificity of structural power to particular country contexts, classes of asset owners, international environments, and policy areas. Argentina's history of periodic economic instability and capital flight, which contrasts with Chile's post-transition stability, contributed to the Argentine financial sector's structural power in key cases. Another factor unique to Argentina contributed as well: the capital's proximity to a country with strict banking secrecy rules. Yet the financial sector's structural power was hardly uniform over time or across policy areas. The factors that explain the variation in the financial sector's structural power are again highly context-specific. Structural power therefore should not be treated as a trait of a given sector. Instead, it must be evaluated on a case-by-case basis, taking into account the incentives that the policy of interest creates in a particular situation and whether potential threats of reduced investment or capital flight are actually credible.

7

Sectoral Tax Politics in Argentina: Agriculture

Like financial-sector power, agricultural-sector power in Argentina fluctuated over time. The tax initiatives examined in this chapter further elucidate how economic crisis, changes in economic models, and alteration in the executive branch drive changes in business power, altering prospects for reform. However, while the financial sector enjoyed a period of strong instrumental and structural power in the 1990s, the agricultural sector was comparatively much weaker throughout most of the studied period, giving policymakers greater leeway to impose tax increases on producers. Yet initiatives occasionally failed in contexts of relatively weak agricultural-sector power due to contingent factors or strategic errors.

Argentine executives endeavored to raise revenue from the agricultural sector by (paradoxically) reducing the VAT on grains and by taxing agricultural exports following the 2001 crisis. Section 7.1 examines the first policy area, which provoked strong opposition from agricultural producers. Whereas a 1998 initiative failed, reform was enacted in 2002 during the height of the crisis. While the producers' instrumental power was comparatively weak throughout this period, informal ties to the secretary of agriculture helped prevent reform in 1998. Contingent factors bolstered the producers' position and helped their interests prevail. However, changes associated with the economic crisis further weakened the producers' power. Their informal ties became less effective given the secretary of agriculture's reduced authority within the cabinet during a time of urgent fiscal needs. Meanwhile, export firms' strong structural power and support for reducing the grains VAT rate in 2002 counteracted producers' opposition and contributed to reform.

Section 7.2 examines agricultural export taxes, which were imposed at significant rates in 2002. Subsequent administrations periodically increased export tax rates, disregarding producers' objections until 2008. This case illustrates the importance of assessing sources of power before assuming that taxation depends on the consent of societal actors. The Argentine producers were unable to exert influence on export taxes given their lack of any relevant source of power, instrumental or structural. However, in a context of accumulated grievances, a particularly provocative export tax reform catalyzed collective action in 2008, despite the producers' previously weak cohesion. Sustained collective action ultimately contributed to the reform's demise. While this episode might appear to confirm expectations in the taxation and democracy literature that taxation stimulates demands for greater voice, accountability, and state benefits,[1] collective action lending force to those demands was hardly a foregone conclusion. The novel design of the reform, which sparked massive protests, constituted a major government strategic error that could have been avoided.

7.1 VAT POLITICS

VAT evasion in the countryside was a major problem in the 1990s. When agriculture was included in the VAT in 1989, the tax agency faced the daunting challenge of controlling approximately 200,000 new taxpayers (AFIP-A 2006, interview). Producers were widely dispersed throughout Argentina's interior provinces, making them especially difficult to monitor.

VAT evasion in agricultural was a far more serious problem than in other sectors. Argentina is a major agro-exporter: 80 percent to 85 percent of grains, soy, oil seeds, and their derivatives were shipped to external markets. Because international agreements mandate that domestic taxes cannot be passed on to foreign consumers, the state reimbursed exporters for their VAT payments. Export firms purchased grains and meat from intermediaries. Intermediaries in turn often offered to purchase goods from producers with cash at above-market rates if producers did not apply the VAT to the sale. Intermediaries then forged VAT receipts so that their documents appeared to be in order when they resold to exporters. The intermediaries thus made significant profits through tax evasion, while the state reimbursed exporters for VAT payments that had never entered state coffers. The critical point is that the state did not simply forgo potential revenue due to evasion; rather, the state lost actual revenue from general tax collections by reimbursing exporters for VAT payments that the treasury never received. Grains-sector evasion estimates ranged from U.S.$300 to $800 million annually; meat-sector evasion cost the state an additional U.S.$700–800 million.[2]

The Unsuccessful 1998 Initiative

In 1998, the tax agency proposed cutting the VAT on grains and meat from 21 percent to 10.5 percent. This measure would reduce incentives for evasion

---

[1] See Ross (2004), Moore (2004), and Gervasoni (2010) for reviews.
[2] *La Nación*, Dec. 18, 1997, June 27, Feb. 15, 1998.

in the commercialization chain and would automatically cut reimbursements owed to exporters by a factor of two. Counterintuitively, lowering the VAT rate would increase tax revenue by curtailing the outflow of resources that enriched intermediaries at the state's expense.

Although one might expect producers would welcome the VAT reduction, they rejected the initiative. Led by the *Sociedad Rural Argentina* (SRA), producers asserted that they would incur unrecoverable VAT credits, since inputs like agrochemicals would remain taxed at 21 percent. Concern regarding unrecoverable VAT credits had motivated the SRA to advocate including agriculture in the VAT in 1989; unless the VAT applied to sales as well as inputs, producers could not transfer their costs forward to consumers. Producers particularly opposed reducing the VAT on grains, because cultivation was undergoing a technical revolution that entailed substantial long-term investment and significant input costs (interviews: SRA-B 2006, SRA-C, D 2008). An SRA (B 2006) informant explained that reducing the VAT on grain sales but not inputs "could have caused a setback of eight to ten years.... If revenue collection had won, technological modernization would have lost." Producers also disliked the timing of the reform. The executive sought to implement the VAT reductions before the 1998 harvest; producers had already made production decisions under the uniform 21 percent VAT regime.[3]

The producers ultimately obtained two major concessions: the VAT reduction was postponed until after the harvest, and grains were excluded from the reform. This success was not inevitable. The producers' structural power was weak, and their instrumental power, based on informal ties to a single line ministry, was tenuous.

Producers' Weak Structural Power

Despite producers' complaints that the VAT reduction would harm investment and production, their structural power was weak. The government's economic team anticipated no negative economic consequences, because they did not believe that producers would accumulate unrecoverable VAT credits. A tax-agency technocrat who participated in negotiations with producers recounted:

We did dozens of studies that proved that 10.5 percent [VAT rate] was more than enough to absorb their credits, unless the seller evaded.... We did dozens of cost-structure models; the secretariat of agriculture's models were very close to ours.... Publications in specialist journals coincided closely with our models. Even so, the sector resisted.... They brought up extreme cases to reject generalizations. (AFIP-A 2006: interview)

Another informant likewise found the producers' arguments inconsistent and "very amusing" (AFIP-C 2006, interview). Throughout the policy process, the Economy Ministry and Tax Agency maintained that reducing the VAT would not hurt producers.

---

[3] *La Nación*, May 12, 1998.

Producers' Tenuous Instrumental Power

The producer's instrumental power was also relatively weak. Informal ties to Secretary of Agriculture Solá constituted their primary source of power. Solá, an agricultural engineer, held the position from 1989 through 1998 except for a brief interlude (1991–92). During his long tenure, Solá developed close working relations with producer associations, especially the SRA and *Confederaciones Rurales Argentina* (CRA) (interviews: SRA-C, D 2008). Solá also developed personal connections with leading producers, including a strong friendship with the president of CARBAP, an important CRA member federation.[4]

However, informal ties tend to afford highly contingent influence, and the producers lacked strong ties to executive-branch authorities in charge of tax policy. Economy Minister Fernández was an academic from CEMA, which had ties to the financial sector, and Tax Agency Director Silvani was an IMF professional. The producers' instrumental weakness with respect to the executive branch contrasts with earlier periods (1955–83), when SRA members were frequently granted important government appointments (Schneider 2004a).

The producers lacked other sources of power that might have bolstered their position. They did not enjoy strong relationships with legislators. No electorally significant party treated producers as a core constituency. Argentina's two main parties prioritized other groups; the UCR's core constituency was the urban middle class (Gibson 1996), and the PJ, which drew its strength from labor in urban centers and clientelistic networks in poor peripheral provinces (Gibson and Calvo 2000, Auyero 2000, Levitsky 2003), was historically antagonistic toward agricultural producers, although relations improved under Menem.[5] Large producers had long been isolated from party politics (McGuire 1995: 202), and party preferences varied widely among both large and small producers (Heredia 2003, FAA 2008: interview). Meanwhile, as explained in Chapter 5, informal ties to legislators from the main political parties usually did not constitute an effective source of instrumental power because of strong party discipline and incentives created by Argentina's electoral institutions (Eaton 2002).

Turning to resources, one producer association, the SRA, had significant technical expertise, including a permanent team of economic advisors, but as in Chile, Tax Agency and Economy Ministry officials were highly trained technocrats capable of independently evaluating private-sector arguments. As discussed above, these officials found the producers' arguments against the VAT reform self-serving and ill founded.[6]

Moreover, the producers patently lacked cohesion, given organizational fragmentation, geographical dispersion, and heterogeneity. The SRA, the oldest and most prestigious of the four organizations, represented the largest producers and

[4] *Clarín*, May 22, 1998.
[5] Menem appointed the head of agro-export giant Bunge & Borne as his first economy minister.
[6] Although SRA informants asserted that they won concessions because of their technical arguments (SRA-C 2008, interview), interviews with government officials indicated otherwise.

was historically associated with the landed rural elite. CRA represented large producers as well, although its members tended to own fewer hectares than SRA members. The *Confederación Intercooperativa Agropecuaria* (CONINAGRO) represented agricultural cooperatives, which agglomerated smaller producers. The *Federación Agraria Argentina* (FAA) represented the smallest producers. Given their different constituencies, conflicts of interest among the associations were common. For example, the FAA favored state regulations and policies to prevent land concentration, whereas the SRA advocated free-market policies (2006 interviews: CONINAGRO, SRA-E).[7] Meanwhile, CONINAGRO had stronger incentives to support anti-evasion measures than the other associations because cooperatives operated in the formal sector and were hurt by evasion elsewhere in the agricultural sector (2006 interviews: CONINAGRO, Lamberto). Although the four associations did lobby the executive jointly on issues of common concern, without an encompassing organization or other factors that could promote cohesion, coordination was loose and short-lived.

Chronicle of a Lobbying Success Un-foretold
The producers' tenuous instrumental power did not provide a strong basis for defeating the 1998 initiative. Their position was strengthened by a fortuitous convergence of interests with the secretary of agriculture, and the concessions ultimately depended on a contingent decision by President Menem.

Lack of cohesion made the producers slow to coordinate responses to the initiative. CRA and CONINAGRO initially expressed support, while the SRA opposed the measure.[8] These contradictory responses partly reflected the complexity of the VAT issue; it was difficult for ordinary producers to understand the reform's impact (SRA-B 2006, interview). The SRA worked to align the producer associations against the reform, and a month later, the four associations issued joint statements denouncing the problem of unusable VAT credits.[9] However, common positions and loosely coordinated lobbying were not enough to win concessions; the secretary of agriculture deferred to the Economy Ministry and Tax Agency's pro-reform position, and the executive sought congressional authorization to reduce the VAT by decree.

Lobbying Congress also proved unsuccessful, given the producers' weak instrumental power in that arena and the cross-partisan consensus in favor of anti-evasion measures (Chapter 5). The proposal was quickly approved; the Radicals and the progressive party Frepaso endorsed the reform as a component of their own political platforms and voted with the PJ majority.[10]

During the subsequent stage of policymaking, the producers managed to secure the secretary of agriculture's assistance, not only on the basis of informal

[7] *Perfil*, May 25, 2008, *La Nación*, Oct. 4, 2007.
[8] *La Nación*, Jan. 8, 1998.
[9] *La Nación*, Jan. 29, 1998.
[10] *La Nación*, March, 12, 2009.

ties, but also thanks to Solá's personal interests: he planned to run for governor of Buenos Aires.[11] Solá reportedly felt the Economy Ministry and Tax Agency's failure to consult with him as they pushed the VAT reduction forward over the producers' objections undermined his authority.[12] This weakness, and failure to deliver benefits for producers – his natural constituency – could have damaged his electoral prospects. Accordingly, he became a strong advocate for the producers (SRA-B 2006, interview), arranging meetings for them with the tax agency director and economy minister.

Solá's position in favor of the producers ultimately prevailed. Solá pushed hard to postpone the VAT decree until after the harvest – a key objective for the producers that would temper the reform's impact. Solá took advantage of a trip to Santa Fe with President Menem to discuss the issue and arranged meetings between Menem and local producers.[13] The day before the decree was scheduled to take effect, after another meeting between cabinet members and producers had ended without concessions, Solá finally convinced Menem to postpone the reform. Rumors circulated that Solá threatened to resign if the decree were enacted.[14] Menem's interest in avoiding conflict with the producers before the SRA's Rural Exposition inauguration, where he would deliver the keynote address, reportedly contributed to his decision to side with Solá.[15] After postponing the decree, Menem instructed the cabinet to devise a compromise with the producers,[16] which ultimately entailed exempting grains from the VAT reduction.

The producers' success was not a foregone conclusion. One could imagine a plausible counterfactual in which Menem did not concede to Solá's entreaties. Had the timing of events evolved differently, the Economy Ministry and Tax Agency's position may have prevailed. Informal ties to the secretary of agriculture, a cabinet member who was not directly involved in tax policy formulation – even in combination with Solá's personal interest in advancing the producers' demands – were a weak basis for influence.

The Successful 2002 Initiative

Argentina's 2001 economic crisis altered agricultural tax politics by weakening the producers' power and bringing a new actor with strong structural power onto the stage: agroexport firms. In the crisis context, exporters strongly supported reform, and the producer associations were unable to prevent reduction of the grains VAT rate.

---

[11] *La Nación*, Jan. 15, 1998.
[12] *La Nación*, May 21, 1998.
[13] *La Nación*, May 20, 23, 1998.
[14] *La Nación*, May 23, 1998.
[15] *La Nación*, June 27, 1998.
[16] *La Nación*, May 20, 1998.

Producers' Weakened Power

The producers' structural power, which was already weak in 1998, declined after the crisis. The end of convertibility and devaluation of the peso created windfall profits for export crops. International grain prices were increasing, and production was expected to reach new records.[17] Producers' profits grew steadily; by one estimate, profits per hectare in 2002 were more than nine times the 1998–2000 average (Rodríguez and Arceo 2006). In this context, tax increases were unlikely to alter producers' incentives; claims that higher taxation would hinder investment and kill the goose that laid the golden egg[18] were not credible. Moreover, if executive-branch technocrats did not believe the producers would have unrecoverable VAT credits in 1998, they found that argument patently fallacious in 2002. As the former tax agency director recalled: "Reducing the rate really hurt no one…. Everyone was making important profits, because their prices were multiplied by three, and their costs were still in pesos. It was a propitious moment for the modification" (Abad 2008, interview). An SRA informant recognized the producers' disadvantageous position in retrospect: "Our technical arguments were weakened because the relation between prices and inputs had changed" (SRA-C 2008, interview).[19]

Meanwhile, informal ties to the secretary of agriculture were an even weaker basis for influencing tax policy in the crisis context. Given the priority of fiscal stabilization, the economy minister held unchallenged authority within the cabinet and was unlikely to respond favorably to line ministers' efforts to promote sectoral interests that ran counter to the state's urgent revenue needs. As a grains-sector informant observed, when the economy was weak, the secretary of agriculture "had no clout"; following the crisis, "everything was subordinated to what the Economy Ministry said" (Bolsa Cereales 2006, interview). Accordingly, although the producers had informal ties to several individuals who served as Secretary of Agriculture during 2002, those ties were a less effective source of instrumental power than in 1998.

Exporters' Structural Power Promotes Reform

Grain-export firms emerged as important actors in 2002. The grains VAT reduction benefited exporters because the state regularly fell into arrears on VAT reimbursements, which imposed significant financing costs on the firms. In 1998, exporters opted not to actively support the VAT reduction in order to maintain good relations with producers (interviews: Exporter-A, B 2006, AFIP-A 2006, Fernández 2006).[20] However, exporters adamantly supported the

---

[17] *La Nación*, Feb. 6, March 30, Aug. 3, Dec. 12, 2002.

[18] *La Nación*, Sept. 7, 2002.

[19] Producers nevertheless opposed the VAT reduction as strongly as in 1998 (interviews: SRA-C, D 2008). Despite their improved economic situation, they maintained that some subsectors would be hurt, and they opposed the reform on principle.

[20] Exporters made a few public statements supporting VAT reduction, but they were published after the producers obtained concessions. *La Nación*, June 27, Aug. 8, 1998.

measure in 2002 because of the crisis. Following devaluation and dollarization of debt, the state owed exporters an onerous U.S.$800 million.[21] Exporters found VAT reimbursement arrears of this magnitude intolerable in the context of numerous other impediments, including the *corralito* and associated restrictions on financial transactions, price instability, and uncertainty regarding economic policy. Although exporters maintained a low public profile, avoiding open confrontation with producers (interviews: Exporter-B 2006, Exporter-C 2008), tax agency informants perceived that "The export sector was clearly on our side.... The exporters separated themselves from the presumed coalition they had formed with the rest of the production chain [in 1998] and supported the measure" (AFIP-A 2006, interview). The former economy minister, tax-agency director, and treasury secretary all identified exporters as government allies on the 2002 reform (interviews: Lavagna 2006, Abad 2008, Lamberto 2006).

Export firms were consequential actors given their strong structural power after the financial sector's collapse. In the context of default and massive capital flight, the state depended on grain exports for foreign currency. In early 2002, grain exports accounted for 60 percent of Argentina's foreign exchange.[22] Exporters periodically suspended their operations during the first quarter of 2002 due to uncertainties and market problems associated with the crisis,[23] and they frequently linked their actions to the VAT arrears problem.[24] The exporters' structural power thus took the form of credible and occasionally realized, largely market-coordinated withholding threats that jeopardized state solvency and macroeconomic stabilization.[25] The government could not afford for exporters to halt their operations, nor could it afford to reimburse exporters for VAT payments that had never entered state coffers. VAT reduction therefore became urgent during the height of the economic crisis.

The Producers' Failed Attempts to Block Reform

The exporters' structural power helped place VAT reform squarely on the agenda early in 2002. Suspension of grain purchasing in January compelled the government to promise exporters U.S.$590 million of accumulated VAT reimbursements in nineteen installments. In exchange, exporters agreed to sell

---

[21] *La Nación*, Feb. 2, 1998.
[22] *La Nación*, Aug. 3, 2002. Dependence on exporters for foreign exchange was a recurrent theme in Argentine history (Viguera 2000: 34, O'Donnell 1978).
[23] *La Nación*, Jan. 15, 17, 26, 29, 30, Feb. 2, 11, March 12, April 18, 2002.
[24] *La Nación*, Jan. 29, 30, Feb. 2, 2002.
[25] Withdrawal from grains markets may also have involved an element of political coordination (instrumental power). On one occasion, export firms discussed deliberately suspending grain purchases to bolster their demands (*La Nación*, Jan. 29, 2002). However, debate on a commercialization strike ended with agreement that each firm would make its own purchasing decisions while CIARA attempted to negotiate with the government (*La Nación*, Jan. 30, 2002).

at least U.S.$100 million on the currency market during the following month.[26] Exporters threatened to withdraw from the market again if the government did not make good on its promise.[27] In this context the government initiated a proposal to lower the grains VAT rate. Continued pressure from exporters to resolve the arrears problem during the following months overshadowed producers' objections to the reform. In May, exporters complained that the state's VAT arrears had increased by U.S.$500 million, despite payments on previously incurred debt. The *Cámara de la Industria Aceitera de la República Argentina* (CIARA) announced that its members had no alternative but to suspend commercialization: "It is not a threat, it is simply reality: the firms cannot continue financing the state."[28]

During this period, producers also failed to win concessions on a barrage of other policies that imposed higher costs on agriculture. Secretary of Agriculture Paulón advocated for converting producers' debt into pesos and lowering the rate of newly introduced export taxes, but the Economy Ministry held firm on both issues.[29] Paulón resigned after the administration doubled export taxes on grains.[30]

Later that year, with the VAT bill pending final approval in Congress, the producers' prospects for winning concessions improved. The worst of the economic crisis had passed, export taxes were replenishing state coffers, and export-firm market withdrawal was less likely. In addition, the producers had informal ties to new secretary of agriculture Lebed. Lebed had family connections to farmers and grain intermediaries and developed close relationships with producers in Buenos Aires during his tenure as minister of agriculture in the provincial government.[31] Both Lebed and the minister of planning asked the economy minister to withdraw the VAT reduction.[32] Lebed even lobbied Congress on the producers' behalf.[33] His efforts to oppose the measure from within the cabinet prolonged the debate and helped the producers make some inroads in Congress.[34]

However, the secretary of agriculture remained in a weak position to win concessions, given the administration's continued prioritization of revenue concerns and sustained pressure from exporters for timely VAT reimbursements.[35] President Duhalde sided with the economy minister, and the producers lost ground in Congress. Duhalde enjoyed strong support in Congress – legislators

---

[26] *La Nación*, Feb. 9, 2002.
[27] *La Nación*, Jan. 23, 2002.
[28] *La Nación*, May 22, 2002.
[29] *La Nación*, March 23, 2002.
[30] *La Nación*, April 9, 2002.
[31] *La Nación*, Sept. 23, 2002, *Clarín*, Aug. 10, 17, 2002.
[32] *La Nación*, Oct. 4, 2002.
[33] *La Nación*, Sept. 23, Oct. 2, 2002.
[34] *La Nación*, Dec. 14, 2002.
[35] *La Nación*, Dec. 10, 12, 2002.

had appointed him to the presidency after Rodríguez Saá's resignation – and the executive was able to align deputies behind the proposal without difficulty (Lamberto 2006, interview). Lobbying against the grains VAT reduction would have been difficult even if the producers had enjoyed stronger relationships with legislators. The reform enjoyed broad support because it was perceived as benefiting consumers. In addition, given the technical complexity of the issue, producers found it difficult to counter perceptions that the VAT initiative also benefited producers (SRA-D 2008, interview).[36] Congress approved the reform in December.

7.2 EXPORT TAXES

In 2002, after the collapse of convertibility and devaluation of the peso, President Duhalde imposed taxes of 10 percent on the sales value of major agro-export crops. The taxes were collected from export firms, which passed the burden to producers through depressed purchasing prices. Rates on most agroexports were soon increased to 20 percent. President Kirchner maintained the export taxes throughout his term and increased rates several times. The tax on soy, the most profitable agroexport, reached 27.5 percent in January 2007 and 35 percent in November 2007. President Fernández de Kirchner increased the rate to 44 percent shortly after taking office in 2008.

Export taxes served multiple purposes. First, they extracted substantial revenue from the highly profitable agricultural sector, and unlike most other taxes in Argentina, export taxes were not subject to revenue sharing with provincial governments. Export tax revenue, much of which derived from soy, helped the central government reestablish fiscal solvency after the 2001 crisis and subsequently sustained the fiscal surplus, which was regarded as critical for preserving stability. Second, export taxes were a key component of industrial policy; they equalized the profitability of primary and processed products, thereby stimulating agro-industry, which generated substantial employment (Economy Ministry-F 2006, interview). Third, export taxes suppressed prices for basic consumer goods. Argentina is a major exporter of wheat and meat, which are also key wage goods, so when exports become more profitable, domestic prices also rise.[37] The taxes therefore helped control inflation and poverty following the 2001 crisis (Di Gresia 2004). Fourth, the taxes were arguably progressive; the bulk of the burden probably fell on large landowners (interviews: Artana 2006, Sabaini 2006). Some economists even argued that export taxes should be classified as direct taxes on agricultural income (Cetrángolo and Sabaini

---

[36] Nevertheless, substantial debate occurred in the lower house; various legislators voiced the producers' arguments against reform (Diario de Sesión, Cámara de Diputados, March 13, Dec. 18, 2002).
[37] This logic did not apply to soy, which was primarily exported (Richardson 2009).

2009). However, export taxes did not target economic elites; large and small producers alike were affected.

The producers resented the fundamentally redistributive nature of the export taxes, which harnessed resources from agriculture to benefit the government's urban constituencies, and they strongly opposed the periodic rate increases. However, the producers' complaints went unheeded from 2002 through early 2008. Yet in response to the March 2008 export tax increase, the producers staged a series of massive protests that paralyzed Argentina. These unanticipated protests led to the demise the reform – a major political defeat for the Fernández de Kirchner administration.

The producers were unable to influence export tax policy through early 2008 because both their structural power and their instrumental power were weak. This weakness facilitated imposition of many other policies contrary to their interests. However, in a context of accumulated grievances, the novel design of the 2008 export tax reform resolved the producers' longstanding collective-action problems by intensifying shared grievances and convincing all subsectors that massive protest was the only way to achieve influence. The sustained protests in turn contributed to reversing the 2008 reform by imposing heavy political costs on the government. Public opinion turned against the executive, and divisions emerged within the governing coalition that provided new political opportunities for the producers.

Producers' Weak Structural Power

The producers' structural power was weak from 2002 through early 2008 because policymakers did not believe that export tax increases would create disincentives for investment or production. Despite high export taxes, which depressed producers' prices, production remained very profitable due to the devalued peso and high international prices. Average profits per hectare between 2002 and 2004 were more than twice the average from 1991 to 2001 (EIU 2004: 31). Increasing land prices were another indication of high profitability despite taxation (Miceli 2008, interview). Soy profits were particularly high (Figure 7.1); although they declined at the end of 2004 due to a dip in international prices (Figure 7.2), they increased again after 2005. The 7.5 percentage point November 2007 tax increase did not alter the upward course of profits over the following months. And although the 9 percentage-point March 2008 tax increase depressed profits, they nonetheless remained above their November 2007 values.

Despite the producers' complaints about export taxes, they benefited greatly from the undervalued peso, which would not have been sustainable without export taxes (Economy Ministry-F 2006, interview). Rodriguez and Arceo (2006) estimate that producers' profits would have been on average 55 percent lower in 2003 and 2004 if the exchange rate had remained one to one as under convertibility in the 1990s. Inflationary pressures after 2004 eroded the

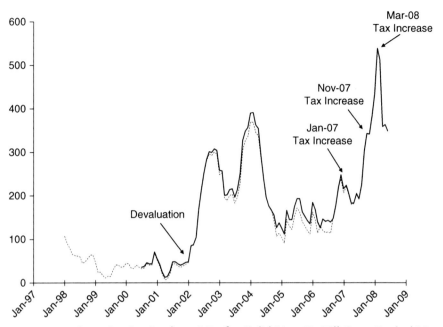

FIGURE 7.1. Argentine Soy Producers' Profits (Solid Line: No Till Crop, Dashed Line: First Harvest; Pesos/Ton).
Source: Ciappa (2005: 23–24). Reproduced with kind permission from Springer Science+Business Media B.V.; *Studies in Comparative International Development*, 46, 2011, p. 432, "Business Power and Protest: Argentina's Agricultural Producers Protest in Comparative Context," Tasha Fairfield, Fig. 1, © Springer Science+Business Media, LLC 2011.

contribution of exchange rate policy to producers' profits (Ciappa 2005); however, rising international prices after 2006 compensated that effect.

Under these circumstances, producers faced market incentives to continue investing, and policymakers anticipated that production would grow despite export tax increases. A high-level Economy Ministry (D 2006, interview) official, for example, asserted that export taxes did not alter investment behavior, whereas he did describe the financial transactions tax, another important revenue-raising instrument, as distortionary. In the case of soy, policymakers' perceptions were correct: production increased from 30.0 to 47.5 million tons from 2002 to 2007 (Figure 7.3).

Producers' Weak Instrumental Power

The producers also lacked instrumental power. Relationships with the executive branch, which had authority to alter export taxes by decree, remained weak after 2002. Representatives from the sector were not recruited into government, nor

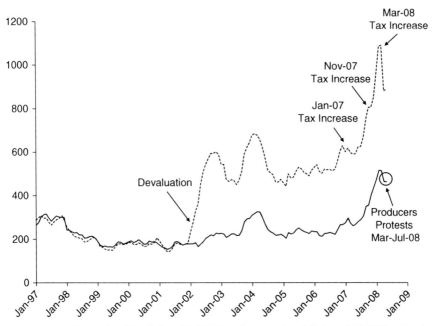

FIGURE 7.2. Argentine Soy Prices (Solid Line: International Prices, U.S.$/Ton; Dashed Line: Producers' Prices, Pesos/Ton).
Source: Onofri: Precios FAS (dataset shared with author); CIARA: Precios FOB (www. ciara.com). Reproduced with kind permission from Springer Science+Business Media B.V.; *Studies in Comparative International Development,* 46, 2011, p. 433, "Business Power and Protest: Argentina's Agricultural Producers Protest in Comparative Context," Tasha Fairfield, Fig. 2, © Springer Science+Business Media, LLC 2011.

did they have strong informal ties to officials with significant authority in the executive branch. Professional economists without connections to agriculture headed the Economy Ministry. Lavagna's (2002–05) private sector experience was in industry; Miceli (2005–07) had been a board member of the Bank of the Province of Buenos Aires; Lousteau (January–April 2008) had been chairman of that same institution. Secretary of Internal Commerce Moreno (2005–present), an important figure in Kirchner and Fernández de Kirchner's cabinets, also lacked ties to agriculture. Secretary of Agriculture Campos (2003–07) and his successor Urquiza (2007–08) were agronomists with private-sector experience, but there is no evidence to suggest strong ties to the producer associations. Moreover, any informal ties they may have had were either superseded by loyalty to Kirchner (in the case of Urquiza, who had worked closely with the future president while both were politicians in the province of Santa Cruz),[38] or inconsequential, given the secretary of agriculture's inferior status within the

---

[38] *Clarín,* Jan. 18, 2006.

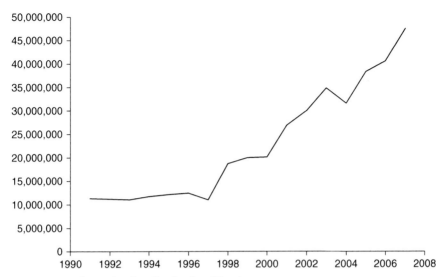

FIGURE 7.3. Argentine Soy Production (Tons).
Source: CIARA (www.ciara.com). Reproduced with kind permission from Springer Science+Business Media B.V.; *Studies in Comparative International Development*, 46, 2011, p. 434, "Business Power and Protest: Argentina's Agricultural Producers Protest in Comparative Context," Tasha Fairfield, Fig. 3, © Springer Science+Business Media, LLC 2011.

authority structure of the executive branch. The secretary of agriculture was subordinate to the economy minister and (in practice) to the secretary of internal commerce. Furthermore, Kirchner maintained tight control over his cabinet and played a central role in formulating economic policy.

Nor did the executive branch engage in institutionalized consultation with producer associations. Producers could obtain meetings with executive-branch officials at the latter's discretion, but there was no expectation that consultation would precede policy decisions affecting agriculture. The ad hoc nature of executive-producer consultations is highlighted by fact that the producers' interlocutor within the government frequently changed; the secretary of agriculture was not always the relevant official.

Other authors have emphasized that exclusive executive authority on export taxes hindered the producers' ability to defend their interests (Richardson 2009: 244). Yet a crucial overlooked point is that producers lacked relationship-based sources of power with respect to the executive branch. Had they enjoyed informal ties or recruitment into government, like the financial sector in the 1990s, they might have made headway in staving off tax increases.

Further, the producers would have been ill positioned to influence policy even if export tax increases had required congressional approval, given that their relationships with legislators remained weak. Producers did have informal ties to legislators; Santa Fe Senator Reutemann (2003–present), an import figure in the Peronist party, was himself a producer. However, party-centered electoral institutions (Eaton 2002) and strong party discipline within the governing coalition, which held an absolute majority in the senate after 2005, continued to temper this potential source of power. Kirchner consolidated top-down, uncontested leadership within the Peronist party after the 2005 congressional elections (Etchemendy and Garay 2010), making Peronist governors and legislators unlikely to challenge the president on key components of economic policy.

Failure to Coordinate Protest, 2002–2007

Given their weak structural power and ineffective lobbying due to weak instrumental power, producers periodically considered economic protest to defend their interests. However, without a strong encompassing organization or other sources of cohesion, the producers could not forge and maintain consensus on priorities or strategies. The small-scale, uncoordinated commercialization strikes that did take place against export taxes and other policies the producers opposed were largely inconsequential.

The four producer associations were divided in their views about strikes and the terms of their opposition to export taxes. The CRA and FAA frequently advocated strikes, whereas SRA and CONINAGRO preferred dialog with the government whenever possible. Informants from these associations asserted that strikes imposed high costs on producers, were difficult to coordinate and sustain, and accomplished little beyond antagonizing the government (2006 interviews: SRA-A, E, CONINAGRO). In contrast, CRA's decentralized, bottom-up structure made its leaders very responsive to its membership base, which tended to advocate confrontation when lobbying failed (2006 interviews: CRA-A, SRA-A).[39] Further, although all producers opposed the export taxes, the FAA was open to accepting the taxes if the revenue funded benefits for small producers, whereas the large producer associations rejected the taxes on principle (2006 interviews: SRA-A, CONINAGRO).

Given the producers' lack of cohesion, governments could easily divide and conquer; agricultural-sector tax politics mirrored cross-sectoral corporate tax politics in this regard (Chapter 5). The government could offer benefits to small producers to preclude formation of a united opposition front (Miceli 2008, interview). Selective and/or general punishments such as exclusion from meetings with the government or suspension of measures that producers favored raised the cost of protest. As long as the government held out the possibility of negotiating compromises, the SRA and CONINAGRO were unlikely to protest, given their view of strikes as an ineffectual last resort. At worst, the government could expect the CRA and/or FAA to initiate short strikes that could be largely ignored.

---

[39] See also Sidicaro (2002: 189).

A few examples illustrate these dynamics. The Duhalde administration's decision to increase export taxes from 10 percent to 20 percent in April 2002 provoked strong producer opposition, despite gains associated with currency devaluation.[40] The CRA and FAA proposed a strike when it became clear that lobbying would not yield results. However, the SRA and CONINAGRO declined to participate, given their aversion to confrontation.[41] Further, despite its strong objections to export taxes, the SRA advocated accepting the measure given the dire need for revenue to stabilize the economy following the 2001 crisis (SRA-C 2008, interview); the government also delegitimized resistance from wealthy producers by informally linking export tax revenue to antipoverty programs for citizens hard-hit by the collapse.[42] President Duhalde then split the FAA and CRA by simply promising to announce measures addressing their broader demands the following month.[43] The FAA accordingly withdrew its support for protest. The CRA proceeded with a commercialization strike, but the four-day protest had at most a symbolic impact.[44] Duhalde's failure to make good on his promise had few repercussions. The FAA mounted its own strike in response, but this action also had little impact, since the other associations did not participate.[45]

The four associations similarly failed to stage coordinated protest against multiple state interventions in agricultural markets during the last years of President Kirchner's term (Fairfield 2011: 437). These policies instead provoked small, predictably inconsequential strikes and government reprisals that reinforced views of protest as counterproductive (2006 interviews: SRA-A, CONINAGRO, CRA-A).

The partial exception to the rule of uncoordinated protest was a nine-day commercialization strike in December 2006. The SRA's directorate narrowly voted to join the FAA and CRA in a strike against beef export quotas.[46] The SRA's participation gave the strike potential to inflict greater economic impact, given that its members were the largest producers, and the government recognized the strike as the largest in two decades.[47] However, like its predecessors, it was too short to cause adverse economic consequences; it was clear to all actors that the availability and price of meat would not be affected.[48] The government held firm, accusing the producers of disregarding the needs of Argentine consumers. After the strike ended, the government announced subsidies for wheat

---

[40] *La Nación*, April 6, 2002.
[41] *La Nación*, April 5, 11, 13, 25, 2002.
[42] *Clarín*, April 4, 2003, April 5, 2002.
[43] *La Nación*, April 28, May 25, 2002.
[44] *La Nación*, April 28, 2002.
[45] *La Nación*, May 27, 2002.
[46] *Clarín*, Dec. 2, 8, 2006. Quotas were intended to increase domestic supply and reduce consumer prices.
[47] *Clarín*, Dec. 5, 2006.
[48] Ibid. *La Nación*, Jan. 17, 2007.

and corn, but to the producers' dismay, these compensations were financed by increasing the soy export tax from 23.5 percent to 27.5 percent in January 2007. In the SRA's analysis, the protest had merely "worsened relations with the government and produced new reprisals."[49] Accordingly, the SRA resumed its approach of seeking dialog.

The cycle of ineffective lobbying punctuated by minor protests continued throughout 2007. The 2007 export tax increases were largely unchallenged, despite universal producer condemnation. The FAA and CRA initially clamored for protest when Kirchner announced an additional 7.5 percentage point soy export tax increase in November 2007; however, they ultimately agreed with SRA and CONINAGRO that strikes against the outgoing administration would be pointless. The associations pinned their hopes on president-elect Fernández de Kirchner's apparent openness to working more closely with the producers.[50]

Emergence of Large-Scale Protest, 2008

Export tax politics changed dramatically in March 2008 when the newly inaugurated Fernández de Kirchner administration increased the soy export tax from 35 percent to 44 percent. Given the producers' manifestly weak structural and instrumental power, the government did not anticipate negative economic outcomes or consequential political resistance. However, the reform catalyzed unprecedented protest and cohesion among the four associations.

How were the producers able to break the cycle of ineffective lobbying punctuated by small-scale, uncoordinated protest? Literature on contentious politics posits that changes in the political opportunity structure encourage collective action (Tarrow 1994: 86). Accordingly, one might hypothesize that massive, sustained protest erupted in 2008 because the new government was weaker than its predecessor, leading the producers to perceive that protest would be more effective. However, electoral results and opinion polls indicate that the government was strong in early 2008. Fernández de Kirchner won the October 2007 election in the first round with 45 percent of the vote; the governing coalition made major gains in the gubernatorial races and won majorities Congress. Fernández de Kirchner enjoyed approval ratings of 57 percent in February and March prior to the 2008 reform (Ipsos-Mora). One might also hypothesize that the producers thought the economy would be more vulnerable to a strike in 2008; however this scenario does not fit either. The current account showed a surplus, the balance of trade was healthy, and unemployment had been declining in the months preceding the strike.[51] Inflation was a growing concern, but the government could blame

[49] *La Nación*, Jan. 18, 2007.
[50] *La Nación*, Nov. 3, 7, 2007.
[51] Radar Macroeconómico. www.bcra.gov.ar

a strike for raising prices. Moreover, producer association informants did not mention any strategic calculations related to perceived vulnerability of the government or the economy when asked about the origins of the 2008 protests.

Instead, I advance a policy-centered explanation (Pierson 1993, 1994, Skocpol 1992, Garay 2007) for this unusual episode of business collective action. The design of the 2008 reform, which was perceived as extraordinarily objectionable, played a key role in resolving the producers' collective-action problem by intensifying common grievances and convincing all four associations that sustained protest was both feasible and imperative. Two key features of the reform provoked ire. First, the magnitude of the tax increase was large: 9 percentage points. While profits estimates suggest that, on average, producers were well positioned to absorb the tax increase given rising international prices (Figure 7.1), the FAA's assertions that small producers on marginal or remote land were hard-hit (interview: FAA 2008) may well have been accurate.[52] However, magnitude alone cannot explain the producers' reaction; the 2007 tax increase was also large.

Second and more importantly, the 2008 reform established a new system of variable export tax rates that frustrated the producers' expectations of future gains from increasing international prices. Henceforth, export tax rates would increase or decrease automatically as international prices fluctuated. Effective export tax rates would be calculated using a table of marginal tax rates corresponding to different international price levels. The table included a top marginal rate of 95 percent applicable if soy surpassed a very high U.S.$600 per ton.[53] Although the effective export tax rate would never reach 95 percent, this extremely high top marginal rate ensured that producers' prices would rise much more slowly than international prices after the threshold. In addition, producers feared that rising input costs would outpace increases in producers' prices and erode their profits (2008 interviews: SRA-D, CRA-B). The variable rate scheme and the 95 percent top marginal rate in particular outraged the producers. They felt they should rightfully reap increasing profits as international prices rose and denounced the reform as confiscatory. In the words of one informant: "Because the tax rates became mobile, the producers would not receive anything from an increase in international prices. The state would take everything," (FAA 2008, interview). According to another informant, "They imposed a maximum price, because above U.S $600/ton, if prices went up 100 dollars, the government took 95 dollars, and the producer kept 5. That was what we fought against. They took away the expectation that your product [price] could increase" (SRA-D 2008, interview). These sentiments, and especially assertions that the new rate scheme in practice imposed maximum prices,

---

[52] Personal communication, César Marcelo Ciappa, 2008.
[53] MECON, Resolución 125/2008: Art. 4

were repeated regularly in the press.[54] That tax rates would automatically decrease if international prices fell did not quell the producers' outrage; they focused instead on the immediate effect of the tax increase and the 95 percent top marginal rate, which acted as a red flag.

In a context of accumulated grievances in other policy areas, the 2008 reform pushed the producers past a threshold of frustration and resolved their collective-action problem.[55] When asked how the producers managed to finally forge a united front, an SRA informant responded: "Because of the horror of the measure, because it was very confiscatory. And when you are attacked very strongly, you unite" (SRA-D 2008, interview). The 2008 reform was "the drop that overflowed the glass" (CRA president),[56] and "the limit that made the whole sector scream in unison" (SRA-A 2008, interview). An FAA (2008) informant expressed a similar assessment:

The export tax increase itself was a problem, but in addition it detonated the discontent that already existed within the sector, due to very bad policies in livestock, dairy, and various regional products, very poor functioning of the grains markets.... A set of reasons motivated the four-month conflict. But clearly the detonator was the tax increase.

The 2008 reform convinced all the producer associations that large-scale protest was both necessary and feasible. On the one hand, the reform dashed hopes that the new administration would be more accommodating than its predecessor. On the other hand, because producers were so outraged, a massive strike would be easier to initiate and sustain. This context alleviated the SRA's concerns over the difficulty of launching massive protest. In fact, the producer associations experienced strong pressure from below to initiate and prolong the strike. The four associations called a two-day strike after the export tax increase was announced[57] but decided to extend the protest indefinitely once they saw the "massive reaction from the producers" (FAA 2008, interview). Over the next three months, the strikes were fueled and sustained by enthusiasm from producers on the ground, many of whom did not belong to any of the associations (2008 interviews: FAA, CRA-B). At various points during the conflict, belligerence among the bases, along with strong demands for the associations to maintain a united front, pushed SRA and CONINAGRO leaders to endorse prolonged protest when they might otherwise have preferred cooling-off periods (2008 interviews: CRA-B, FAA, Zavalía).[58]

---

[54] *Clarín*, March 27, 2008. Producers also asserted the reform would destroy futures markets, but such accusations were probably overstated. The 2003 anti-evasion reform provoked similar accusations, but futures markets quickly adapted (Chapter 5).

[55] This interpretation agrees with Richardson (2009: 251–52), who sketches a "tipping point" explanation.

[56] *La Nación*, March 16, 2008.

[57] *Clarín*, March 13, 2008.

[58] *La Nación*, March 22, 2008.

While outrage among the bases against the 2008 reform spurred massive participation, increasing interactions among the four associations in previous years provided a basis for enhanced coordination among the leadership. By 2006, presidents and staff of the SRA, CRA, and CONINAGRO were meeting monthly to evaluate policy developments (CONINAGRO 2006, interview). While these associations' staff members had long maintained good working relationships (interviews: SRA-A, E 2006), cooperation improved during 2006 (CRA-A 2006, interview). Moreover, the December 2006 strike laid the groundwork for future coordination between the SRA, CRA, and the FAA.[59] Until then, interactions between the two large producer associations and the FAA had been infrequent, given their historic differences of interest (interviews: SRA-A 2008, CONINAGRO 2006). Early in the 2008 conflict, the four associations took a historic step toward organizational integration by creating an Enlace Committee to facilitate joint decision making. The Enlace Committee helped the associations achieve a degree of coordination that differed qualitatively from the informal collaboration of previous years (SRA-A 2008, interview).

Throughout the extended conflict, intense opposition to the 2008 reform overshadowed differences on other issues and helped sustain cohesion, despite recurrent tensions among the associations. Whereas the government had divided and conquered in previous years by providing selective benefits for small producers, this tactic failed to break the FAA away from the other associations in 2008. Modifications to the new tax rate scheme and increasingly generous and inclusive compensations offered as the conflict advanced were consistently rejected. Small and large producers alike fixated on overturning the 2008 reform, to the detriment of their material interests. Ironically, Argentina's soy export tax rate at the end of the conflict would have been lower had the variable tax rate scheme remained in place, due to falling international prices.

Antigovernment sentiments and moral values contributed to intransigence. As an SRA (A 2008) informant recalled: "It was no longer only a struggle against the variable export taxes, it became a matter of principles: saying 'enough' to an authoritarian government." In this regard, the producer coalition resembled the broad-based estate-tax repeal coalition in the United States (Graetz and Shapiro 2005). Just as Argentina's small producers would have been better off accepting compensations rather than remaining in the antireform coalition with large farmers, American family farmers and small businesspeople would have been better off accepting exemptions offered by Democrats who favored maintaining the estate tax, compared to the terms of the repeal secured, with its long phase-in and abrupt sunset clause. Yet they declined these offers, privileging morality and principle above purely material

[59] *Clarín*, Dec. 13, 2006.

interests – the estate tax was framed as an immoral "death tax" (Graetz and Shapiro 2005: 148).[60]

Components of Business Protest

Economic protest through commercialization strikes was a central feature of the conflict. These strikes halted sales and delivery of agricultural products to domestic and export markets with the goal of forcing the government to revoke the 2008 reform. Especially for soy, these actions were not coordinated by market signals, since production and commercialization remained profitable for most producers despite the tax increase. Instead, sustaining these measures required collective action. Like all business strikes, participants incurred non-trivial short-term costs (Chapter 2). Halfway through the first major strike (March 11–April 2), the producers had forfeited an estimated U.S.$95.5 million in potential revenue.[61] Although grains were stored for sale at a later date, producers paid significant opportunity costs by passing up the high prices that prevailed during the strikes (CRA-B 2008, interview); soy reached a record U.S.$547 per ton in July.

During subsequent strikes, producer associations sought to target export markets to avoid antagonizing the public; food shortages in Buenos Aires incurred widespread public repudiation.[62] Commercialization strikes did not deplete the national treasury or foreign-exchange reserves. Export tax revenue registered increases every month compared to the previous year's values, thanks to high international prices and exports of previously purchased stock.[63] Export companies continued selling dollars; the value of accumulated foreign exchange sales by June 2008 was 1.7 times the equivalent figure for 2007.[64] However, grains noncommercialization significantly depressed export activity and contributed to the broader costs of the protracted conflict. By mid-June, the total cost was estimated at U.S.$3,400 million, an anticipated 1 percent of GDP.[65] This economic damage created multiple political pressures on the government to resolve the crisis.

In addition to economic protest, the producers employed tactics often used by nonbusiness actors, including roadblocks, demonstrations, and rallies. Estimated participation in some mobilizations reached 200,000 individuals.[66] These events

---

[60] Ironically, Argentina's large producers also would have been better off materially had they not adamantly rejected the variable export tax rates. Due to decreasing international prices, the soy tax rate in fall 2008 would have been approximately 30 percent had the 2008 reform remained on the books, whereas the rate reverted to 35 percent after the March decree's demise.

[61] *Clarín*, March 23, 2008.

[62] *Pagina 12*, April 8, 2008. *La Nación*, May 27, 2008.

[63] DNIAF 2007, 2008: Recursos Tributarios, www.mecon.gov.ar, *Clarín*, May 6, 29, June 5, 2008.

[64] Liquidación de Divisas, www.ciara.com

[65] *Clarín*, June 16, 2008.

[66] *La Nación*, May 26, July 16, 2008.

counterbalanced similar shows of strength organized by government supporters as both sides vied to gain the upper hand. Massive rallies and demonstrations also gave the producers an edge over the government in framing battles. By showcasing massive participation from small and medium-sized producers alongside large producers, these events counteracted efforts to portray the protestors as privileged elites.

Reversal of the 2008 Reform

While the outcome of the protests was not inevitable, the producers ultimately secured their goal of overturning the 2008 reform. Sustained protests imposed heavy political costs on the Fernández de Kirchner administration in the form of negative public opinion, discontent among the business community, mobilization of urban anti-Peronist sectors, and divisions within the governing coalition. These costs eventually compelled the executive to grant significant concessions. Protest and coordinated lobbying, facilitated by stronger organization and cohesion, helped tip the balance in favor of the producers in Congress, where the reform's fate was ultimately decided.

The administration initially saw little need to negotiate. Structural-power arguments that the reform would provoke reduced investment still lacked credibility. The new export tax rate set producer prices back to their late-2007 values; the secretary of economic policy asserted: "If it was profitable to produce soy two months ago, it will hardly stop being profitable now. Soy [prices] increased 70 percent in six months."[67] Given the producers' history of collective-action problems, authorities likely expected that strikes would be short-lived.

The executive tried to manage opposition with vertical-equity appeals, describing the export taxes as a progressive tool that redistributed wealth from agrarian elites to the urban poor; this strategy helped delegitimate producers' complaints in previous years (CRA-A 2006, interview). On March 25, Fernández de Kirchner denounced the producers' protests as "the strikes of the most profitable sectors" and asserted "export taxes are a profound means of redistributing income."[68] However, the producers' united front undermined this strategy; small producer participation challenged assertions that the protests reflected elite interests. A CRA (B 2008) informant candidly observed: "If [the government] had confronted a sector representing only the right, it would have been very easy to discredit. Since the groups had united, from the right [SRA] to the left [FAA] ... it was very complicated [for the government]." Opinion polls suggest that the government's framing strategy was unsuccessful in this new context; 59 percent to 60 percent of respondents reacted negatively

---

[67] *La Nación*, March 13, 2008.
[68] *Clarín*, March 26, 2008.

to the president's speech.[69] The producers, meanwhile, sought to reframe their struggle as a battle between provinces and central government: "The path we have undertaken is not just for ourselves. It is for all Argentines who want a federation without centralist and unitary practices."[70] This framing capitalized on discontent among governors over the executive's discretionary allocation of export tax revenue to provinces, rather than automatic revenue-sharing.[71]

While opinion polls reported widely ranging levels of support for the producers during the conflict, the evidence suggests that a substantial proportion of citizens viewed the producers' demands as legitimate.[72] Ipsos-Mora found that the percent of respondents who felt producers contributed "some" or "a lot" to the country increased from an average of 85 percent from 2002 to 2007 to 92 percent in May. Moreover, the sustained protests generated public frustration with the government. Negative ratings rose steadily from 36 percent prior to the March strike, to 70 percent in May when producers staged their second major strike (Figure 7.4).

Discontent also grew among business actors beyond agriculture, who had not opposed export taxes previously; many business leaders recognized that eliminating the taxes would hurt the fiscal surplus, which helped ensure macroeconomic stability. The industrial association (UIA) and the *Asociación Empresaria Argentina*, a large business-owners association, had publicly affirmed the necessity of export taxes.[73] However, this support gave way to growing concern over the generalized economic costs of the protests and measured statements of solidarity with the producers. For example, the UIA warned it would not sign a cross-sectoral government-business development accord if the producer associations did not participate.[74]

Meanwhile, frustration with the lengthy conflict and the government's confrontational rhetoric provoked anti-Peronist mobilization in upper-income neighborhoods of the capital and urban centers of soy-producing provinces. The first such demonstration took place after the president's March 25 speech, in which she strongly defended the export tax increase. Subsequent demonstrations erupted during the second and fourth producers' strikes.[75]

As protest continued, old power struggles within Peronism were reactivated, and the Kirchners' coalition showed signs of strain. Rival Peronist leaders like Duhalde and Rodríguez Saá perceived an opportunity to contest the Kirchners' authority. Other high-profile dissident Peronists who opposed the 2008 reform

[69] *La Nación*, April 6, 2008; *Pagina 12*, April 8, 2008.
[70] *Clarín*, May 10, 2008.
[71] E.g. *La Nación*, April 3, 2008.
[72] Segundo Encuesta Nacional Sobre Imagen de Gestión, May 20, 2008, datamatic.com.ar; *La Nación*, May 27, 2008.
[73] *La Nación*, Aug. 13, 2005; March 18, 2008.
[74] *La Nación*, March 27, 2008, *Clarín*, April 27, 2008.
[75] June demonstrations drew 900–1,000 people. *Clarín*, June 17, 2008.

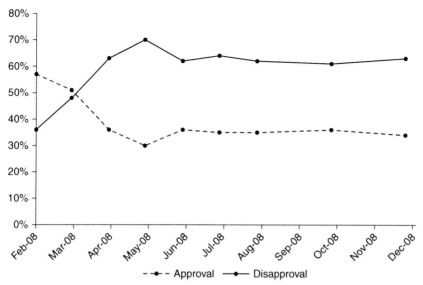

FIGURE 7.4. Monthly Government Approval Ratings, Argentina, February–August 2008.
Source: Ipsos-Mora (data shared with author, 2011). Reproduced with kind permission from Springer Science+Business Media B.V.; *Studies in Comparative International Development*, 46, 2011, p. 446, "Business Power and Protest: Argentina's Agricultural Producers Protest in Comparative Context," Tasha Fairfield, Fig. 4, © Springer Science+Business Media, LLC 2011.

included Senators Reutemann and Menem. Cracks developed within the ranks of the Kirchners' supporters as well. Later in the conflict, Vice President Cobos openly criticized the government and advocated for Congress to decide the fate of the reform. Tensions also developed with Kirchner-coalition governors and legislators from conflict-ridden soy-producing provinces.

Facing intransigence from producers and growing economic and political costs, the government ultimately submitted the reform to Congress. This decision, which followed a wave of renewed antigovernment protests, constituted a notable abdication of authority; export tax policy in Argentina had long fallen under the purview of the executive branch without legal challenge. This move granted the producers' demand that all tax reforms require congressional approval.[76]

The producers' protests, along with coordinated lobbying, contributed to the reform's narrow rejection in the Senate. There were enough defections among the government's ranks to force a tie. Vice President Cobos cast the deciding

[76] "Proclama de Gualeguaychú" April 2, 2008, www.ruralarg.org.ar

vote against the reform, to the government's consternation. Fears of continued strikes helped tip the vote against the reform.[77] According to producer-association informants, legislators recognized that approving the reform would merely prolong the crisis: "The legislators realized that it was not just agriculture's problem, but that the economy in the interior of the country would be paralyzed" (SRA-C 2008, interview). Political pressure from producers within their districts also weighed heavily on many legislators. The producers, previously diffuse and fragmented, were emerging as a potentially coherent electoral constituency, and they staged confrontational demonstrations in front of legislators' personal residences.[78] Meanwhile, with the help of the Enlace Committee, producers mounted an intensive, coordinated lobbying campaign (SRA-A 2008, interview). An SRA (D 2008) informant attested to the importance of both coordinated lobbying and protest for defeating the reform:

It was hard work. We went door to door visiting all the deputies and all the senators. We were explaining in all the commissions.... And apart from that, the social pressure from all the producers, I think that was very important. Investment stopped with the protest, everyone saw the impact of reduced investment, the economic collapse.... It was the sum of everything.

While the producers' resolve to sustain protest was critical to the reform's demise, government strategic errors contributed as well. Chief among these errors was the provocative reform design and its very high, very visible top marginal tax rate. Had the government chosen a less extreme top rate or simply waited to impose additional tax increases until international prices increased further, instead of establishing a fixed table of tax rates, protest might have been averted. In retrospect, the government's confrontational rhetoric, which spurred the producers' enthusiasm for protest and alienated public opinion, was also an error. Offering more substantial compensations for small producers earlier on might have dissipated conflict. And earmarking the tax increase to popular spending programs from day one might have bolstered public support and undermined the producers' opposition; the bill sent to Congress dedicated the revenue to health care, housing, and roads, but it was too late by then to save the reform.

7.3 CONCLUSION: ARGENTINA'S SECTORAL TAX POLITICS

Chapters 6 and 7 have described sectoral tax-policy successes and failures that are important not only within the Argentine context but also remarkable in a broader comparative context. Argentina achieved major accomplishments in tax policy areas affecting both finance and agriculture. Limited bank information access in the 1990s hindered the tax agency's ability to control income

---

[77] *La Nación*, June 4, 2008.
[78] *Clarín*, July 7, 12, 15 2008.

tax evasion; however, the tax agency obtained full and automatic access to all relevant types of bank information after 2001. Argentina's tax agency accordingly became one of the world's most powerful in terms of information access, significantly surpassing the much-lauded Chilean tax agency.

Likewise, agricultural VAT evasion was a problem of extraordinary dimensions in the 1990s because products destined primarily for export were included in the tax base. Given the obligation to reimburse exporters' VAT payments, evasion within the agricultural sector cost the state revenue from general tax collections. By 2008, tax agency, exporter, and producer informants agreed that this problem was resolved (interviews: AFIP-A, C 2006, Abad 2008, Exporter-A, B 2006, FAA 2008), thanks to the VAT reduction on grains, along with improved withholding regimes and other administrative advances. The former tax agency director asserted that these reforms contributed significantly to reducing VAT evasion from 35 percent in 2002 to 20 percent in 2007 (AFIP 2008: 6, Abad 2008, interview), among the lowest in Latin America (Sabaini et al. 2012: 35).[79] Improved VAT control freed the tax agency to focus on reducing income-tax evasion in agriculture (AFIP-C 2006, interview).

Further, export taxes extracted significant resources from agriculture after 2002, helping to sustain a macroeconomic model that proved highly successful for growth and poverty reduction.[80] Critics asserted that export taxes reinforced the Kirchners' authoritarian tendencies by enhancing the president's capacity to control provincial leaders through discretionary transfers, and some authors argue that reliance on taxes requiring minimal bureaucratic effort or engagement with citizens foster antidemocratic tendencies (Moore 2004, Toye and Moore 1998). However, Argentina's democratic institutions remained strong (Levitsky and Murillo 2008). Moreover, export taxes had a democratic and redistributive aspect in that they helped fund social spending that poor urban sectors demanded,[81] by extracting revenue from the wealthy countryside. And by increasing the central government's share of tax revenue, export taxes helped sustain fiscal discipline and economic stability; the provinces' ability to secure highly favorable revenue-sharing rules for domestic taxes posed recurrent problems in the 1990s (Eaton 2002, 2005). Other critics charged that export taxation discouraged development of domestic tax capacity, as many authors argue occurs with resource rents and/or aid (Karl 1997, Dunning 2008, Morrison 2009). But while abundant export tax revenue may have contributed to removing some reforms from the agenda, this politically and administratively "easy" revenue source did

---

[79] Argentina's tax agency even provided technical assistance on VAT control to European tax agencies (AFIP-A 2006, interview).

[80] At least through 2007, when inflation and signs of other economic troubles commenced. See Richardson (2009), Etchemendy and Garay (2010), Calvo and Murillo (2012).

[81] See Garay (2007, 2014) on expansion of benefits for informal-sector workers in response to collective action.

not discourage efforts to improve domestic tax collection, as evidenced by expanded tax-agency access to bank information and a series of other anti-evasion initiatives.

Yet failures also occurred in financial- and agricultural-sector tax policy. Argentina's interest-earnings tax exemption undermined revenue capacity during the 1990s and remains a source of inequity in the tax system. And the 2008 export tax reform failed spectacularly, causing a loss of significant potential revenue gains given surging soy prices.

Analyzing sectoral business power is critical for explaining Argentina's tax policy successes and failures. Whereas business achieved little influence on cross-sectoral taxes, finance and agriculture enjoyed instrumental and/or structural power during specific periods that helped them influence policies of special concern for their sectors. However, tax initiatives occasionally failed in contexts of relatively weak sectoral power due to contingencies or government strategic errors.

Variation in Instrumental Power

In contrast to Chile, where business power was strong, stable, and homogeneous, the sources and the strength of instrumental power in Argentina varied substantially across sectors and over time. Sources of instrumental power during the 1990s included recruitment into government and informal ties to executive-branch authorities for the financial sector, and informal ties to the secretary of agriculture for producers. The financial sector enjoyed stronger instrumental power thanks to more pervasive executive-branch connections; producers had weaker connections to a single line minister with less authority over tax policy. These sectors' instrumental power helped block tax-agency access to bank information, taxation of interest earnings, and reduction of the VAT rate on grains during the 1990s. However, contingent factors contributed to the latter outcome, given the producers' relatively weak instrumental power.

The financial sector and agricultural producers both lost instrumental power after 2001, partly because of the economic crisis and its aftermath, and partly due to turnover in the executive branch. The change of economic model provoked by the crisis decreased the financial sectors' economic importance and generated widespread public outrage against the banks; subsequent administrations did not include individuals with ties to the financial sector. The context of economic crisis also contributed to a shift in authority within the executive branch in 2002, rendering producers' informal ties to their sectoral ministry a less effective source of power. Thereafter, Presidents Kirchner and Fernández de Kirchner did not appoint cabinet members with strong ties to producers. Meanwhile, other sources of instrumental power remained absent. In this context, post-crisis administrations expanded tax-agency access to bank information, reduced the VAT on grains, and imposed and increased export taxes.

However, despite weak producer power, the ill-designed 2008 export-tax increase provoked widespread outrage and resolved the sector's long-standing collective-action problem. Sustained commercialization strikes and coordinated lobbying, facilitated by greater organizational integration, contributed to the reform's demise.

Variation in Structural Power

Structural power also varied significantly, not only across sectors and over time, but also across policy areas. The cases examined in Chapter 6 illustrate that structural power is not simply a sector-level characteristic but depends on the policy in question. The financial sector's structural power hindered tax-agency access to bank information during the 1990s and made taxing interest earnings infeasible throughout the studied period. Structural power in both cases took the form of a credible exit threat. However, structural power was weak in another financial-sector tax policy area: taxing bank transactions. Whereas the former two policy areas affected highly mobile and volatile interest-earning accounts, the latter affected much less mobile checking accounts.

Turning to agriculture, the producers' structural power was weak with respect to VAT reduction and export taxes throughout the periods considered. Reforms in these policy areas did not elicit credible disinvestment threats. Policymakers anticipated no negative economic consequences to reform, nor did market-coordinated withholding occur in the aftermath of these reforms. Overturning the 2008 export tax increase required collective action because commercializing grains remained rational from an individual profit-maximizing perspective. The export tax case illustrates once again that mobility alone is not sufficient to create structural power; producers could have shifted from soy to other crops in response to export tax increases, yet because soy remained so profitable, tax increases did not create incentives for them to do so.

Economic crisis in some cases enhanced and in others reduced structural power. The 2001 crisis increased the financial sector's structural power with respect to interest-earnings taxation by making depositors even more sensitive to the risks and opportunity costs of investing in interest-earning accounts. The crisis also temporarily enhanced agro-exporters' structural power by increasing the state's reliance on these firms for foreign exchange; withholding threats provided extra impetus for the 2002 grains VAT reduction. In contrast, the crisis weakened the financial sector's structural power with respect to bank-information access by reducing the share of funds in time deposits and the size of the banking sector itself, thereby reducing the economy's vulnerability to any disinvestment the reform might have provoked. The change of economic model precipitated by the crisis also reduced the producers' (already weak) structural power, but for very a different reason: agriculture received windfall profits from currency devaluation, which belied producers' arguments that taxation would deter investment.

Economic Crisis and Reform

This analysis advances research on how crises affect prospects for economic reform by highlighting the diversity of mechanisms that may come into play. The above observations are consistent with Brooks and Kurtz's (2007) contingent view of the relationship between crisis and market reform; crisis may either hinder or facilitate reforms in different areas. Brooks and Kurtz demonstrate that different kinds of crises can have distinct effects on prospects for reform in a given policy area, and they emphasize that crisis differentially shapes societal interests surrounding distinct policy areas. The cases examined in this and the previous chapter show that, in addition, a single crisis can have varying effects on prospects for reform across different policy areas, and that crisis may have differential effects on business power – that is, business actors' ability to defend their interests.

Regarding the effects of crisis on political decision-making structures and prospects for reform, several cases in these chapters corroborate findings from early literature on structural adjustment. Authors argued that economic crisis tends to centralize decision-making authority "to presidents and their inner circles" and sideline attention to societal interests (Heredia and Schneider 2003: 16).[82] Similarly, Argentina's 2001–02 crisis stimulated concentration of authority within the top echelons of the executive branch, reducing producers' prospects for influencing tax policy by relegating their sectoral minister to a secondary role within the cabinet. Yet as other authors have also illustrated,[83] the more general argument that crisis makes governments less responsive to interest groups does not always hold. The interests of business actors were taken into account during crisis periods when they retained structural power or strong sources of instrumental power. Argentina's agro-exporters, whose structural power was strong in 2002, are an example.[84]

Finally, the cases examined in these two chapters illustrate mechanisms linking crisis and reform that are distinct from those highlighted in Weyland's (2002) innovative research. Drawing on prospect theory, Weyland (2002) argues that countries are more likely to adopt reforms during severe economic

---

[82] Nelson (1990), Haggard and Kaufman (1992), Conaghan and Malloy (1994), Acuña and Smith (1994).

[83] E.g., Schneider (2004b), Etchemendy (2011).

[84] Likewise, business groups with close ties to government officials greatly benefited from Pinochet's reforms during and after Chile's 1982 crisis (Schamis 1999), and large firms with easy access to the executive and substantial material and technical resources were courted by Argentine reformers in the early 1990s (Etchemendy 2011).

crisis because when policymakers are in the "domain of losses," they become more inclined to accept risks associated with major policy changes that might reverse crisis but could potentially make things worse. Yet with regard to tax policy, Argentine policymakers did not display risk-acceptance during times of crisis; they consistently avoided reforms that carried substantial risk of reduced investment, whether before, during, or after crisis. Instead, crisis facilitated tax reform either by reducing associated risks of negative economic outcomes (bank-information access), or by increasing risks of negative outcomes if reforms were not enacted (grains VAT reduction).

8

Bolivia's Tax Policy Tightrope
Powerful Elites and Mobilized Masses

The previous chapters on Chile and Argentina have demonstrated the causal leverage that business power provides for explaining tax policy change both in contexts of remarkable stability – Chile – and in contexts where economic conditions were much more variable, alteration in government was frequent, and institutions were more fluid – Argentina. The present chapter applies the instrumental and structural power framework to a radically different context characterized by extraordinary social upheaval and profound institutional decomposition – Bolivia during the early 2000s, where popular mobilization enters as a critical casual variable alongside business power. In analyzing Bolivian tax politics, I demonstrate the significant traveling potential of the theory developed in Chapter 2.

In Bolivia, the power of economic elites and popular mobilization interacted to produce divergent outcomes across different tax policy areas between 2003 and 2006, the period when governments faced pressing revenue needs, prior to Evo Morales's presidency and the natural-resource boom. During this period of extreme social unrest, the threat of mass protest against policies perceived as regressive removed broad-based tax increases from the agenda and compelled governments to propose tax increases that targeted economic elites. However, economic elites' significant instrumental power helped them block tax increases during later stages of policymaking, unless popular sectors mobilized in favor of reform. Tax politics became a high-stakes balancing act as governments tried to walk the line between antagonizing powerful elites and antagonizing mobilized masses.

The chapter begins by assessing the instrumental power of economic elites at the outset of the studied period (Section 8.1). Business enjoyed much greater instrumental power than in Argentina, but the sources of power were not as strong and institutionalized as in Chile. I then describe the nature and extent of popular mobilization in Bolivia (Section 8.2), which reached far more massive levels and was more consequential for tax politics than in Chile and Argentina. The chapter then analyzes the political dynamics surrounding three attempted reform episodes.

Section 8.3 examines the Sánchez de Lozada administration's (2002–03) proposed tax on high-income earners. Given weak structural power, as well as weaker instrumental power than in Chile – where governments were reluctant to attempt significant tax increases due to anticipation of costly political battles with business – Bolivian business actors failed to deter the executive from initiating the income tax proposal. Business prepared to mount a concerted campaign to block the tax in Congress, but unanticipated popular protest forced the executive to withdraw the initiative. Popular mobilization in this case unintentionally advanced the interests of economic elites; civil society organizations incorrectly perceived the tax as a threat to their own members. The government's strategic errors contributed to these perceptions.

Section 8.4 examines the Mesa administration's (2004–05) attempts to raise tax revenue. The income tax protest and subsequent episodes of mass upheaval that had forced Sánchez de Lozada to resign profoundly shaped Mesa's tax agenda. In 2004, the executive proposed a wealth tax designed to preclude popular protest by more obviously and more narrowly targeting economic elites. As a consequence, however, the initiative provoked even stronger elite opposition, and business used its substantial instrumental power, which had increased in the congressional arena, to block the initiative. In contrast, business accepted a financial transactions tax that was viewed as a lesser evil; emphasizing fiscal stabilization helped the government secure business acquiescence.

Section 8.5 examines the 2005 hydrocarbon reform. The hydrocarbon sector's (perceived) structural power gave policymakers cause for caution when considering changes to the royalty regime, and the multinationals received support from a significant portion of the Bolivian business community and hence benefitted from the latter's instrumental power. However, popular demands to extract revenue from this natural-resource sector forced the issue onto the national agenda and overwhelmed business power. The threat of social upheaval if popular demands were not met pressured policymakers to impose increasingly harsher terms on the hydrocarbons companies, despite the sector's substantial power.

8.1 BUSINESS'S INSTRUMENTAL POWER

During Sánchez de Lozada's second term, economic elites enjoyed instrumental power based on cohesion and, to a lesser extent, informal ties to policymakers. In comparative context, business's instrumental power was of intermediate strength: much stronger than in Argentina, although weaker than in Chile.

Cohesion

As in Chile, organization formed the backbone of cohesion. Bolivia has a strong, prestigious economy-wide business association, the *Confederación de Empresarios Privados de Bolivia* (CEPB). Founded in 1962, its member organizations include departmental business federations and sectoral business associations throughout the country. The CEPB had long been an important actor in national politics; it played a key role in pressing for democratization in the early 1980s and subsequently mobilized business opposition against the leftist Siles administration, including capital strikes in 1984 (Conaghan and Malloy 1994: 95–97, 121–24). The CEPB was a key interlocutor between government and business in the two decades following the democratic transition. As Eaton (2007: 88) observes: "In contrast to many other Latin American countries, the comprehensive nature of the CEPB and its overlapping sectoral and geographic organization have consistently given business a unified voice in the national government."

Business organization was also strong at the regional level, particularly in the economically dynamic department of Santa Cruz, which generated 30 percent of the country's GDP and 37 percent of its tax revenue from 2002 to 2004.[1] The *Federación de Empresarios Privados de Bolivia-Santa Cruz* (FEPB-SC) and the *Cámara de Industria y Comercio* (CAINCO) aggregated business interests across sectors. An Export Chamber informant (CADEX 2007) explained: "Normally we coordinate business positions – it's not that exporters agree with a decision but forestry disagrees. We have the FEPB-SC – it includes 90 percent of Santa Cruz's business associations, and that's where positions are coordinated." The growing threat to property rights posed by MAS's ascent in national politics encouraged Santa Cruz's diverse business interests to close ranks behind the leadership of these departmental peak associations (particularly CAINCO) (Eaton 2007).

A strong common identity constructed in contraposition to the large informal sector also contributed to cohesion. Organized business regularly emphasized that the small "formal sector" it represents bears the full burden of taxation, whereas firms and entrepreneurs in the informal economy – 70 percent of the private sector according to CEPB estimates (CEPB 2006, interview) – do not pay taxes and thereby create unfair competition.[2] This "formal sector" identity is largely an upper-class identity; the informal sector comprises primarily subsistence activities and small venders. However, the division between organized business and the informal sector does not coincide strictly with class; business informants were quick to point out that the informal sector includes large entrepreneurs who should bear a sizable tax burden. In fact, La Paz is home

[1] INE (www.ine.gov.bo), SIN (www.impuestos.gov.bo).
[2] "Formal sector" here need not directly correspond to those who pay taxes as opposed to those who evade. Businesses belonging to the self-identified "formal sector" may evade as well.

to a small but prosperous indigenous elite that has made fortunes by trading in contraband, particularly electronics (interview: Finance Ministry-B 2006, Salman and Sologuren 2011). Further, many medium-sized businesses "hide" in simplified tax regimes designed for small contributors in agriculture, transport, and commerce. A racial dimension reinforces the "formal sector" identity: organized business is largely of Hispanic descent, whereas the informal sector is largely indigenous. Organized business, not only in Santa Cruz (Eaton 2007: 89) but also in La Paz, tended to view indigenous elites with "suspicion and derision." For example, the CEPB president (interview 2006) derogatorily referred to President Morales as "*ese indio.*" Shared antagonism toward the informal sector played a similar role to neoliberal ideology in Chile by uniting organized business against tax increases.[3] In the CEPB president's (2006, interview) words: "As long as the problem of informality remains unresolved, we disagree with the creation of any tax whatsoever – whether it's Banzer, Quiroga, Sánchez de Lozada, Mesa, or now Morales. Work on resolving the problem of informality first."[4]

However, national-level cohesion was weaker than in Chile (though still much stronger than in Argentina) due to strong regional identities. Bolivia has a long history of regional conflicts and rivalries between elites in the western Andean departments, including La Paz – the political capital, and elites in the lowland departments, including Santa Cruz – the economic capital (Dunkerley 1984, Roca 1999, Eaton 2007). Santa Cruz and Tarija, two of the four lowland departments known collectively as the *media luna* given the crescent-shaped area they cover, occasionally even threatened to secede (Faguet 2012: 22). Perceived differences in orientation toward the state contributed to regional business identities. Despite massive subsidies from the La Paz-based national government in the 1970s, Santa Cruz elites viewed their success as the fruit of individual entrepreneurship and free markets, whereas they perceived that their counterparts in La Paz depended heavily on state resources (2007 interviews: Ortiz, CADEX, CAINCO-C, FEPB-SC-B; Eaton 2007). Regional identities were exacerbated by Bolivia's overlapping economic and ethnic cleavages; the highland departments contain the country's largest indigenous populations and highest poverty levels.[5]

---

[3] Although business in Chile and Argentina also advocated fighting evasion rather than increasing taxes, a "formal sector" identity of this sort was absent. In Chile, other factors promoted business cohesion. In Argentina, where the informal sector is also large, there is no racial dimension to consolidate a distinct "formal sector" business identity given so many other divisions that undermine cohesion.

[4] Other business informants made similar statements (2007 interviews: ASOBAN-A, B, CADEX, CNCB, CAINCO-B, Hydrocarbons-A, FEPB-SC-A, FEPB-SC-C 2007). See also CAINCO 2003a, 2004b.

[5] Gamarra and Malloy (1995: 210) note that historically, Bolivia's lowland-highland regional conflict "was essentially racist."

Tempered Informal Ties to Parties

Economic elites also enjoyed pervasive informal ties to Bolivia's traditional political parties: MNR, MIR, and ADN. Despite very different origins, these parties converged in supporting the neoliberal economic model by the mid-1980s, prompting the CEPB president (interview 2006) to describe them all as right parties receptive to business positions. However, the traditional parties were largely nonprogrammatic patronage machines (Gamarra and Malloy 1995), and ADN, which came closest to connecting with business through partisan linkages, had essentially collapsed by 2002. Furthermore, Bolivia's party-centered electoral system tempered business's informal ties to parties, making this source of power less effective during Sánchez de Lozada's presidency.

ADN (*Acción Democrática y Nacionalista*), founded by former dictator Banzer, approximates Gibson's (1992) definition of a conservative party; business and economic elites, particularly in Santa Cruz, formed the core constituency. ADN's ranks included "notable businessmen who had served in Banzer cabinets" (Conaghan and Malloy 1994: 126).[6] Although peronalistic ties to Banzer held the party together, he also pushed "to develop the party as the principal voice for the Bolivian right" (Conaghan and Malloy 1994: 126). Banzer himself had close relationships with Santa Cruz economic elites, particularly in agriculture and industry (Eaton 2007). During his rule from 1971 to 1978, he channeled cheap credit to Santa Cruz through the state agricultural bank, to the immense benefit of agrobusiness; much of the debt was never collected (Conaghan and Malloy 1994). Policies during Banzer's subsequent presidential term (1997–2001), including property tax cuts, also favored Santa Cruz's agrarian elites.[7] ADN essentially disappeared after the moribund Banzer resigned in 2001; it held only one Senate seat and 4 out of 130 seats in the lower house from 2002 to 2005.

MNR (*Movimiento Nacionalista Revolucionario*) and MIR (*Movimiento de Izquierda Revolucionaria*), which formed the core of Sánchez de Lozada's coalition and together held a narrow majority in Congress from 2003 to 2006, developed informal ties with business in the 1990s. MNR originated in the 1950s as a populist, mass-based party promoting state-led development; however, party founder Paz Estenssoro (1985–1989) supported neoliberal reforms after the democratic transition.[8] The MNR included prominent businesspeople within its ranks, most importantly, Sánchez de Lozada, author of the neoliberal adjustment plan implemented with business support under Paz Estenssoro.[9]

---

[6] See also Gamarra and Malloy (1995: 417).

[7] Banzer implemented a proposal drafted by the Santa Cruz agricultural association that exempted the value of investments like irrigation from the property-tax base (CAO-A, interview 2007). Sánchez de Lozada reversed the reform.

[8] Coppedge (2007) subsequently classifies MNR as a center-right party.

[9] The MNR's old guard and traditional patronage networks persisted alongside the more technocratic, neoliberal wing, but the former was marginalized from economic policymaking (Gamarra and Malloy 1995).

Sánchez de Lozada was one of the country's wealthiest businessmen and had ties to the CEPB (Conaghan and Malloy 1994). MIR, ostensibly a social-democratic party, also developed ties to business in the 1990s (Gamarra and Malloy 1995: 414); for example, MIR Senator Vaca Diez, who served as senate president in 2004, was a self-described agricultural businessman from Santa Cruz.[10] Both MNR and MIR had ties to economic elites in the prosperous *media luna* departments, especially agrarian elites (interview: Mesa 2006; Eaton 2011), although ADN had been most closely associated with that constituency. MNR and MIR shared political representation of this region after ADN's collapse. Of the *media luna*'s twelve senators from 2002 to 2005, seven belonged to MNR, four to MIR, and one to ADN.

However, as in Argentina, party leaders' control over legislators' career paths thanks to party-oriented electoral rules (Eaton 2002, Carey and Shugart 1995) tempered business's informal ties to Bolivia's traditional parties. Legislators were elected through a closed-list system; citizens cast a single vote for their party preference, and party leaders determined who occupied the seats won. A 1993 reform mandated that half of the lower house would be elected via single-member districts, but this system still left significant power in the hands of party leaders (Gamarra 1997, Mayorga 2005, Barr 2005). This system encouraged discipline in Congress on major executive policy initiatives, particularly when the president of the nation was also the president of his party, as was the case from 2002 to 2003. Sánchez de Lozada had secured authority over other factions within MNR following Paz Estenssoro's retirement (Conaghan and Malloy 1994: 416, Mayorga 2004: 38); internal elections in 2001 reinforced Sánchez de Lozada's status as the party's "undisputed caudillo."[11]

Sánchez de Lozada also maintained control in Congress and curtailed business influence by distributing patronage to the governing coalition parties. This tactic was imperative in Bolivia; presidents from 1985 through 2005 all had to form pacts with at least one other party to secure a majority in Congress, and patronage employment was the glue that held them together (Gamarra and Malloy 1995).

Tempered Informal Ties to the Executive

Economic elites also had informal ties to the executive branch during Sánchez de Lozada's term. The president himself was a prominent businessman, and several of his ministers, including Sustainable Development Minister Justiniano, had close connections to Santa Cruz agricultural elites. However, informal ties are a highly contingent source of power that depends on characteristics of the policymakers involved. Sánchez de Lozada prioritized technical criteria

---

[10] *La Razón*, March 6, 2004.
[11] However, the MNR remained divided between the old political guard and the president's technocratic wing (Mayorga 2004).

over business interests in the realm of economic policy, and key ministers were committed to the president's reform agenda and shared his long-term vision for the country. In addition, Sánchez de Lozada staffed the Finance Ministry with professionals and protected them from the pressures of patronage politics (interview, Finance Ministry-B 2006). Therefore, while informal ties facilitated business access to executive policymakers, they provided only a limited basis for influence. For example, in 2003 the administration reversed a property tax reform implemented during Banzer's presidency that had amounted to a give-away to Santa Cruz's landed elite. Landowners adamantly rejected the change but were unable to block it despite informal ties to cabinet members. My inter-view with Justiniano (2007), who played a key role in mediating tensions with Santa Cruz landowners in this case, indicated that he shared the president's conviction regarding the importance of reversing Banzer's reform despite his own friendships with members of the affected class.

8.2 POPULAR MOBILIZATION

Business and economic elites were not the only societal actors to be reckoned with in Bolivia; popular sectors mattered as well. From 2000 to 2006, Bolivia experienced a "virtually continuous cycle of protest" (Barr 2005: 70) against the political system and the exclusionary socioeconomic status quo. In a con-text of growing dissatisfaction with Bolivia's traditional political parties and the neoliberal economic model, a wide range of sectors took to the streets.[12] Coca-growers led by Morales demanded an end to eradication campaigns, Aymara leader Quispe sought to overturn white political and cultural domi-nation, citizens opposed privatizations they feared would lead to higher prices for basic services, and the Bolivian Workers Confederation (COB) demanded higher wages.

Protests created crises for national governments. Demonstrations initiated by a particular sector with specific demands often sparked much broader mobilization, culminating in paralysis of urban centers. Cochabamba's April 2000 "water wars" are one example; protest spread to the capital, La Paz, and to other departments, halting transit and compelling the government to declare a state of emergency (Mayorga 2005, Arce and Rice 2009, Silva 2009). Coca-growers strikes later that year, joined by informal-sector workers, university students, and transport workers, paralyzed Cochabamba again for almost a month (Barr 2005). Roadblocks created far-reaching disruption, particularly after 2000 when stone and tree-trunk blockades were supplanted by massive

---

[12] Weyland (2009) links the rise of protest and radical left challengers to the discovery of gas reserves, which undermined tolerance for neoliberalism's emphasis on austerity and fiscal disci-pline. Silva (2009) emphasizes the role of coca-eradication campaigns that stimulated peasant mobilization, which became to hub of broader protest movements.

physical occupation, making it more difficult for authorities to restore order (Arce and Rice 2009: 92).

Against this backdrop of mobilization, Morales's indigenous-left party MAS (*Movimiento al Socialismo*) made significant gains in Congress, challenging the traditional party system. Morales won a seat in the lower house in 1997, and MAS won significant minorities in both houses in the 2002 congressional elections at the traditional parties' expense.[13] From 2003 to 2006, MAS held eight of the senate's twenty-seven seats; the traditional parties fell from twenty-one seats during the prior term to sixteen seats. Although few political actors anticipated that Morales would become president in 2006, MAS's strong showing in the 2002 elections posed a clear and serious threat to the status quo. By early 2003, observers were wondering whether the weakened traditional party system would survive (Gamarra 2003).

8.3 SÁNCHEZ DE LOZADA'S ILL-FATED 2003 INCOME TAX

The failed 2003 income tax is a remarkable case in which popular sectors served as circumstantial business allies. Business power was not strong enough to keep this issue off the executive's agenda, but popular protest forced the government to withdraw the initiative before business could mount a concerted lobbying campaign against it in Congress.

The Modest Proposal

Bolivia enjoys a dubious distinction as Latin America's only country with no individual income tax. In 1986, the Paz Estenssoro administration eliminated this tax in the context of stabilization and structural adjustment, given technocrats' assessment that the tax agency would be hard-pressed to administer the newly established VAT, let alone enforce a progressive income tax. In its place, the reform created the "RC-IVA" – a flat "income tax" that allowed taxpayers to deduct the value of goods and services consumed if they presented valid VAT receipts with their tax returns. The RC-IVA was intended not to tax individual income, but to control VAT evasion by encouraging consumers to demand valid receipts.

By the early 2000s, technocrats agreed that Bolivia needed to reestablish a personal income tax. The RC-IVA had failed to control evasion; instead of promoting VAT compliance, it stimulated a large market for false VAT receipts (interview: Finance Ministry-D 2007; Coelho et al. 2004, Cossio 2006). Moreover, the absence of a personal income tax constituted a massive loophole in the tax system that undermined revenue capacity and equity. Among the more serious associated problems, businesses could simultaneously avoid the

---

[13] On MAS's emergence as a political party, see Van Cott 2005. On MAS as a social movement, see Yashar 2005.

corporate tax and transfer income and profits to their owners and executives tax-free by paying inflated salaries, which were deductible from the corporate tax base (interviews: Finance Ministry-B 2006, Cuevas 2007). Income accruing to high-income professionals and business owners was a substantial, untapped tax base. Meanwhile, tax agency capacity improved greatly during the 1990s, undermining administrative arguments against the income tax. A former vice minister of tax policy and international consultant (Finance Ministry-D 2007, interview) asserted that Bolivia's tax agency had become one of the best in Latin America.[14]

Sánchez de Lozada, who had overseen the 1986 tax reform as Paz Estenssoro's finance minister, sought to reestablish the income tax at the outset of his second presidency. In addition to long-standing technical considerations, the administration faced a deficit of almost 9 percent that made tax reform imperative (interviews: Finance Ministry-A 2007, Justiniano 2007). The administration accordingly designed a moderate income tax that would raise 1 percent to 1.5 percent of GDP. The tax would have a flat rate of 12.5 percent with a single threshold, such that the effective tax rates paid would be progressive, rising from 3 percent to 11 percent (interview: Finance Ministry-B 2006). The technical team recommended a threshold of four to six times the minimum wage; the tax accordingly would have affected about 2.4 percent of the economically active population. However, Sánchez de Lozada sent the proposal to Congress with a threshold equivalent to twice the minimum wage to leave room for bargaining with legislators (interviews: Finance Ministry-A 2007, B 2006, Justiniano 2007). Given the tiny size of the formal sector, the proposed tax would still affect fewer than 6 percent of Bolivians.[15]

Business Opposition

Business reacted strongly against the proposed tax. The CEPB and the Santa Cruz business associations alike claimed the tax would penalize the formal sector, deepen Bolivia's recession, create pressure for higher wages, and even force businesses to close due to contraction of demand (2006 interviews: CEPB, Finance Ministry-B; 2007 interviews: Justiniano, FEPB-LP, CAINCO-B, C).[16] Organized business assumed a class-defensive position as in Chile, protecting the interests of upper-income individuals as well firms and corporations. When asked about business opposition to the income tax, the former president replied: "The most sensitive part of the businessman or league [association] is their pocket" (interview, Sánchez de Lozada 2010).

---

[14] "The IMF recognizes it; the IADB recognizes it. The levels of administrative efficiency, the yield in terms of the ratio of auditors to taxpayers – it is an excellent tax agency" (Finance Ministry-D 2007, interview).
[15] Author's calculations using Cossio (2005: 21) and INE data (www.ine.gov.bo).
[16] *La Razón*, Feb. 4, 11, 2003, *El Deber*, Feb. 1, 2003.

However, business was not able to keep the income tax off the government's agenda. Structural power was weak; the finance minister pointed out that the individual income tax was far less distortionary, more growth-friendly, and would have a smaller impact on businesses than other revenue-raising options, such as increasing fuel taxes or Bolivia's distortionary turnover tax (interview, Finance Ministry-A 2007). Furthermore, business's arguments that any tax increase would contract economic activity and prolong recession were of little import to the executive given the urgency of closing the fiscal gap. The planning minister recalled: "The president said: 'It's this [income tax] or a *gasolinazo*' – a very big gas tax hike – 'there is no other way, or the state will have to stop paying salaries and there will be chaos'" (interview, Justiniano 2007).

Meanwhile, business's instrumental power was not strong enough to deter the executive from initiating the reform. Although cohesion was much stronger than in Argentina, business lacked the institutionalized relationships with policymakers that formed a basis for predictable influence and thereby restricted the agenda in Chile. Despite fervent business opposition – as the former president recalled, "they were just up in arms and screaming and yelling about it" – Sánchez de Lozada (interview 2010) anticipated that he would be able to maneuver the reform through Congress. Economic elites' informal ties to legislators notwithstanding, he asserted: "On the big policy issues, the people [legislators] would hold to discipline.... You can usually come to a deal with Congress, because basically they are interested in patronage" (interview, Sánchez de Lozada 2010). Nevertheless, business began to mobilize a united front against the income tax and prepared to lobby in Congress as soon as the proposal was announced.[17]

Popular Protest

Ironically, however, protest by popular sectors that the executive never intended to tax forced the government to withdraw the proposal before business opposition gained momentum. Police, teachers unions, and university students clashed with the military for two days in the capital, while indigenous organizations, the COB, and Morales condemned the tax and planned additional demonstrations.[18] Remarkably, most of the protesters did not earn enough to pay the tax

---

[17] Passing legislation was not easy when business lobbied intensely, as occurred regarding a major 2003 tax code reform. A finance ministry informant recalled: "All of the senators had these papers on their desks – opposition, government senators, everyone. And these were the business organizations' reasons why not to approve the tax code. The *Empresarios Privados* [CEPB] and CAINCO. *Empresarios Privados de Bolivia*, with the seal and everything.... The senators and the congressmen were using this as the guideline to oppose the law" (Finance Ministry-B 2006, interview). However, the government managed to impose discipline on its coalition; the informant estimated that the law included 80 percent of the changes the government sought to enact.

[18] *La Razón*, Feb. 1, 10, 2003.

(interviews: Finance Ministry-A 2007, B 2006). Twenty-nine people were shot in the fray between the military and the police (Gamarra 2008). Civil society blamed the government for the deaths. Sánchez de Lozada responded by rescinding the tax bill.

Multiple factors contributed to the income tax's demise via popular protest. The broader political context was highly unfavorable for the government. Equally important were the government's own strategic errors in reform design and framing.

Inopportune Context

Sánchez de Lozada's government quickly became the focal point for popular opposition to Bolivia's economic model and political system, and widespread antigovernment sentiments predisposed civil society to react against the income tax. Sánchez de Lozada won only 22.5 percent of the vote in 2002, partly because of his association with neoliberal reforms that were perceived as exacerbating poverty and inequality,[19] and he was extremely unpopular by early 2003. As his former vice president explained, "The country had come to the conclusion, due to the systematic campaign against Sánchez de Lozada, that he was a *vendepatria* – that he had given away the natural resources and that he was anti-Bolivian" (interview, Mesa 2006). Conflicts with striking coca growers in January further augmented antipathy toward the government: "People felt the government had repressed the demonstrations. The government's image was very damaged," (interview, Mesa 2006).

In this context, the income tax created an opportunity for MAS and other sectors to attack the government, voice their grievances, and advance their own political agendas. Morales demanded higher taxation and outright nationalization of multinational hydrocarbons companies, in line with MAS's nationalistic, statist ideology. Although the income tax proposal was actually congruent with MAS's redistributive demands, Morales's priority was winning power, rather than supporting incremental reforms proposed by his chief political adversary.[20] The police, meanwhile, took to the streets largely because the national budget, sent to Congress with the income tax bill, did not include salary increases (interviews: Finance Ministry-B 2006, C 2007). The police added the income tax to their list of grievances during the first day of the protest,[21] at which point other sectors opportunistically joined the demonstrations under the banner of protesting the tax.

---

[19] Ironically, Sánchez de Lozada's reforms surpassed a narrow neoliberal agenda to include innovative welfare-enhancing and democratizing reforms, like basic health care and decentralization (Weyland 2009, Faguet 2012).

[20] A member of Sánchez de Lozada's technical team (interview, 2006) recalled that after he explained the tax, a MAS representative argued with his compatriots that the party should support the tax because it would benefit poor people.

[21] *La Razón*, Feb. 12, 2003.

Association with the much-maligned neoliberal model and IMF also contributed to popular rejection of the income tax. Sánchez de Lozada and his technical team believed the income tax was necessary and intended to implement it independently of IMF recommendations; however, the proposal was announced while negotiations with the IMF were underway. As the former finance minister recalled: "It was implicitly linked to an IMF agreement; it looked like an imposition by the IMF" (interview, Finance Ministry-A 2007). Many organizations that opposed the tax made explicit reference to the IMF's supposed involvement.[22]

Strategic Errors

Beyond the above factors, government strategic errors played a critical role in the income tax bill's untimely demise. The reform design was technically appealing given its simplicity, but it undermined the inherent legitimacy the income tax should have enjoyed based on vertical equity. Because the proposed tax had a flat rate instead of a progressive bracket structure, it was incorrectly perceived as regressive and unfair. And the threshold of only twice the minimum wage suggested that the tax was broad-based, even though the vast majority of Bolivians earned far less than that cutoff.

Media coverage reinforced these misperceptions. A prominent newspaper headline read: "Everyone alike will pay 12.5% of their salary,"[23] and articles consistently referred to the income tax as a "tax on wages," rather than a tax on all income sources including rents and interest, which would affect the richest Bolivians.[24] Civil society leaders reiterated these misperceptions, whether in response to media coverage and genuine confusion[25] or simply on the pretext of opposing the government. A COB leader asserted: "The tax on wages will deepen poverty" while another lamented: "once again the burden of economic responsibility is placed on the shoulders of the workers"; Morales made similar statements.[26] Quispe even decried that *campesinos* would ultimately bear the cost of the tax.[27]

The government did not adequately counter these misperceptions by emphasizing that the reform targeted economic elites. Although Sánchez de Lozada

---

[22] *La Razón*, Feb. 10, 2003.

[23] *La Razón*, Feb. 11, 2003.

[24] Government informants accused the media of manipulating coverage to foment opposition to the tax (interview, Finance Ministry-A 2007); the former president emphasized economic elites' control over the media and public opinion (interview, Sánchez de Lozada 2010). With the exception of the two important examples above, however, newspaper coverage was not grossly inaccurate; TV coverage could not be obtained for analysis. Moreover, it is difficult to evaluate whether media control was a consequential source of business power, given the absence of opinion polls on the reform.

[25] A COB (2007, interview) leader conveyed remarkable lack of understanding about this issue.

[26] *El Deber*, Feb. 6, 2003, *La Razón*, Feb. 10, 2003.

[27] *La Razón*, Feb. 11, 2003.

initially explained that the tax would affect the rich rather than the poor,[28] some of the president's statements portrayed the tax as broad-based. In the context of what the government described as a pending fiscal crisis, Sánchez de Lozada announced: "We have asked the middle class to assume this sacrifice."[29] This "middle class" in reality comprised a tiny, privileged group of highly paid wage earners and independent professionals.[30]

A visibly progressive tax targeted more narrowly at elites, combined with stronger and more consistent equity appeals, may well have precluded protest.[31] In retrospect, government informants recognized these strategic errors. One asserted: "If we had sent it [the bill] with [a deduction of] six [minimum wages], a lot of arguments [against the tax] would have fallen apart automatically," (interview: Finance Ministry-B 2006).[32] Others lamented the government's insufficient efforts to explain the tax to the public (2007 interviews: Finance Ministry-A, C, Cuevas).

Circumstantial Popular Sector-Business Alliance

By opposing the income tax, popular sectors served as circumstantial business allies. In pursuing their own perceived interests, they inadvertently defended the material interests of Bolivia's tiny economic elite. This example is similar to the cases of Argentina's labor unions, which advocated income tax cuts in 2008 that also benefitted top-income earners (Chapter 5), and Argentina's small farmers, who protested against export tax increases alongside large producers in 2008 (Chapter 7). However, whereas tax structures aligned union members' and small farmers' economic interests with economic elites in the Argentine cases, popular sectors in Bolivia thoroughly misperceived tax incidence. Yet their opposition to the income tax also advanced the agenda of destabilizing the government, which would eventually undermine economic elites' interests.

Remarkably, Bolivia's business associations sought to cultivate this circumstantial alliance with the government's leftist opposition in 2003. Notwithstanding the broader threat MAS posed to economic elites, CEPB president Calvo met with Morales to discuss joint opposition to the measure;

---

[28] The president asserted: "The tax will affect those with the most income, those who earn interest or rents.... The basic criteria ... is to not harm the poor." *La Razón*, Feb. 10, 2003.

[29] *La Razón*, Feb. 11, 2003.

[30] In retrospect, Sánchez de Lozada (interview, 2010) rationalized this statement as follows: "The people who are walking around indignant saying Obama is going to raise taxes on people who make 250,000 a year – those people don't have a lot of free cash, they are not the ones who are running the hedge funds. Those are the ones you worry about from a voting perspective, and that may be why I put that spin on it – because everyone thinks they are middle class." However, this approach backfired by failing to differentiate the few who would pay from the majority who would not.

[31] Some speculated that the reform would still have provided an excuse to oppose the government. One informant noted that by that time "the objective was political, to bring the government down" (interview, Justiniano 2007).

[32] The former planning minister made similar comments (Justiniano 2007, interview).

CAINCO president Matkovic agreed that business should join forces with MAS against the tax.[33] Meanwhile, the Santa Cruz business associations met with the COB's departmental branch to discuss opposing the tax. Government informants attributed business's willingness to coordinate with MAS to short-sightedness (interviews: Sánchez de Lozada 2010, Finance Ministry-B 2006); economic elites' medium-term interests would have been much better served by supporting Sánchez de Lozada rather than siding with the forces that ultimately brought about his downfall and ushered in a government openly antagonistic to their interests.

The Proposal's Legacy

The protests sparked by the 2003 income tax proposal had a lasting impact on Bolivian policymakers. Technocrats in the Mesa administration and the Morales administration agreed that Bolivia should have a personal income tax, but all felt that pursuing this objective entailed major risks of renewed popular protest, even though a tiny fraction of the population would be affected (interviews: Cuevas 2007, Finance Ministry-E 2006, 2007). Remarkably, an article hidden from the public eye in a reform passed by the Sánchez de Lozada administration later in 2003 granted the executive decree power to reduce the percentage of receipts deductible from the RC-IVA tax base. This measure allows the executive to transform the RC-IVA into a crudely designed income tax with no need for congressional approval or public deliberation, simply by reducing the fraction of deductible receipts to zero (Cossio 2006: 90). Yet memories of the 2003 protest are so strong that no subsequent administration has yet dared to use this authority. The income tax lacks legitimacy due to its association with neoliberalism and Sánchez de Lozada – popularly viewed as "public enemy number one" (interview, Mesa 2006) and convicted in absentia for alleged crimes against humanity in relation to deaths during the October 2003 uprising. The former planning minister explained of the income tax: "It's a very delicate issue, and its Goni's issue" (interview, Justiniano 2007). No government wished to introduce a tax that in any way resembled Sánchez de Lozada's failed initiative.

8.4 MESA'S 2004 TAX REFORM

When Mesa assumed the presidency after Sánchez de Lozada's resignation, he inherited a 9 percent budget deficit and high levels of sociopolitical instability. The executive proposed two new taxes: a wealth tax and a financial transactions tax. Whereas popular sectors acted as circumstantial elite allies in 2003, their influence was distinct in 2004: the proposed taxes were designed to overtly target economic elites in order to preclude popular protest. However,

---

[33] *La Razón*, Feb. 12, 2003, *El Deber*, Feb. 12, 2003.

the wealth tax stimulated broad, intense business opposition, a drawback of the targeting strategy. While business and economic elites could not keep the wealth tax off the agenda, their substantial instrumental power contributed to the tax's subsequent demise. Lack of active support from MAS and popular sectors sealed the wealth tax's fate. Business also opposed the transactions tax but ultimately accepted it as the lesser of two evils. The government's strategy of emphasizing stabilization secured tacit business acceptance and acquiescence from the traditional parties in Congress.

Reform Design

President Mesa's primary objective in designing the 2004 tax proposal was to preclude renewed popular protest in the aftermath of the February 2003 protest and the October 2003 uprising that forced Sánchez de Lozada from office. Mesa quickly ruled out a suggestion from his technical team to reduce gas subsidies (interview, Nogales 2007), given that a reform with broad-based impact would stimulate widespread popular rejection. Like their predecessors, Mesa and his finance minister believed Bolivia needed a personal income tax, but reintroducing a similar proposal was not feasible. As Mesa (2006, interview) recounted, "Goni's tax, which was very moderate, demonstrated in a brutal manner that this was not a possibility. We did not want to risk a measure that had been rejected so dramatically." Revenue-raising tools would have to more narrowly and more visibly target economic elites.

The proposed taxes satisfied these criteria. The wealth tax had a very high exemption level of U.S.$50,000.[34] There was little room for confusion over tax incidence; the vast majority of the population was patently excluded from the tax base. According to one of the reform's authors, the wealth tax would affect only 3 percent of the population (interview, Finance Ministry-D 2007), half as many people as the failed income tax. Furthermore, it was impossible to misconstrue the wealth tax as a burden solely on wage earners. The wealth tax would apply to land, homes, vehicles, and other visible manifestations of accumulation (along with less visible assets like stocks). Similarly, the transactions tax appeared to affect only the tiny minority of Bolivians with bank accounts (although as an indirect tax, its actual incidence is difficult to assess). According to Finance Ministry calculations, 5 percent of all account holders owned 80 percent of the funds in bank deposits (interview, Cuevas 2007).

Ample vertical equity appeals in conjunction with reform design successfully precluded popular protest. Mesa emphasized that only the rich would pay and explicitly noted that other alternatives would affect many more citizens:

---

[34] *La Razón*, Feb. 12, 2004.

The taxes affect those with the most income and the informal sector that has not paid taxes in the past – but not the señora who sells in the street.[35]

My moral objective with both taxes is to not hit the weakest and poorest, to avoid a *gasolinazo*, and to avoid a *garrafazo*.[36]

The latter option entailed increasing the price of household fuel canisters, a highly regressive, broad-based revenue-raising alternative. The minister of sustainable development made similar equity appeals to legislators.[37] Government informants felt that thanks to these efforts, the general public accepted the taxes (interviews: Mesa 2006, Finance Ministry-D 2007).

Concern over dire fiscal need and popular mobilization predominated consideration of business power during the agenda formulation stage. Structural power was potentially strong with respect to the transactions tax, which created disincentives for using the banking system. The tax would affect transactions involving not only checking accounts, but also more mobile savings accounts. Announcement of the proposal in fact provoked a small reduction in bank deposits.[38] However, the economic team feared far worse outcomes if the taxes were not enacted: spiraling inflation or even hyperinflation if the government had to cover its budget obligations by borrowing from the central bank (interview, Cuevas 2007). Business's instrumental power would pose major problems later in the policymaking process, especially for the wealth tax. But this possibility was not anticipated, given the primary imperative of precluding popular protest. A member of the technical team reflected on the wealth tax: "We thought it was politically feasible. What happened is that we looked at it more from the angle of those who would not reject it. But it turned out that those who rejected it rejected it very forcefully – probably beyond what we expected" (interview, Finance Ministry-D 2007).

Business Opposition to the Wealth Tax

The strategy of visibly targeting economic elites precluded popular protest at the cost of antagonizing elites by directly threatening their common class interests (Chapter 2). The wealth tax elicited intense business opposition. The CEPB and the Santa Cruz peak associations alike denounced the proposal. Opposition was strongest from Santa Cruz landowners, whose material

[35] *El Deber*, Feb. 9, 2004.
[36] *La Razón*, March 12, 2004.
[37] *La Razón*, Feb. 20, 2004.
[38] U.S. $60 million – approximately 2 percent of deposits – were withdrawn in late January; Mesa's finance minister asserted that this response would be temporary (*El Deber*, Feb. 20, 2004). Sánchez de Lozada's finance minister considered and dismissed a financial transactions tax in 2003 for fear of provoking massive withdrawals, given that the banking system was "very fragile." However, he recognized that the 2004 tax did not provoke any lasting problems (interview, Finance Ministry-A 2007).

interests were most threatened, but business opposition was cross-regional and cross-sectoral. Former minister Justiniano (interview, 2007) recalled: "It was violently rejected, much more than the personal income tax.... Everyone agreed to disagree with the proposal: industrialists, commerce, agriculture, et cetera." The growing redistributive threat posed by mobilized popular sectors and the rise of MAS likely intensified organized business's class-defensive response to the wealth tax, a case of the type that motivated Ascher (1984: 228) to observe: "Clarity, when it mobilizes a powerful opposition, is counterproductive" for redistributive reforms.

Business opposition is striking given that the wealth tax, like the income tax, would exclusively affect individuals. Once again, Bolivian business associations defended the interests of not only companies but also their owners and economic elites more broadly. Several informants explained the associations' opposition to the wealth tax by noting that businesspeople themselves owned property (interviews: CAINCO-A 2007, Ortiz 2007). The blurring of lines between business interests and individuals' interests is also evidenced by business associations' repeated assertions that the wealth tax would include business assets, which blatantly contradicted the text of the proposal. Although the government repeatedly clarified that the tax would apply exclusively to individuals (interview, Cuevas 2007),[39] business leaders consistently claimed or implied that it would also apply to businesses (interviews: CEPB 2006, Ortiz 2007, FEPB-SC-C 2007, CAINCO-B, C 2007, FEPB-SC-A 2007).[40] This misrepresentation helped business associations argue that the wealth tax would harm investment and threaten jobs, a strategy that legitimated their opposition and helped recruit legislators to their cause.[41]

Horizontal equity appeals failed to win business support, given the direct threat the tax posed to elite interests. The government argued that the wealth tax would capture the "big fish" in the informal sector, given the comparative ease of identifying physical assets. The sustainable development minister announced: "For the first time we are imposing a tax on those who have accumulated wealth informally."[42] But business insisted that the tax agency would not be able to effectively collect the tax and argued that instead of creating new taxes, the simplified regimes for small taxpayers should be eliminated to curtail evasion by larger firms illegally registered under these regimes.[43] Business

---

[39] *La Razón*, Feb. 18, 2004, *El Deber*, Feb. 18, 2004.
[40] *El Deber*, March 6, 2004.
[41] These efforts to instrumentally enhance structural power bore some success in the context of informal ties to the traditional parties and business cohesion. Former MIR Deputy Soruco (2007, interview) recounted: "I supported the Santa Cruz business position because of their strong and solid argument: it's important to preserve jobs, and this type of tax restricts investment capacity" (Soruco 2007, interview). Former MIR Senator Vaca Diez (interview 2007) likewise explained that his party opposed the tax because it would hurt investment.
[42] *La Razón*, Feb. 3 2004.
[43] E.g., CAINCO (2004a: 5–6).

essentially argued that the informal sector alone should bear the burden of any revenue-increasing measures. While Finance Minister Cuevas (2007, interview) perceived that horizontal equity appeals contributed to less intense rejection from business in La Paz compared to Santa Cruz, peak associations from both departments actively opposed the tax.

Business's Instrumental Power

During Mesa's presidency, instrumental power remained of intermediate strength compared to Chile and Argentina; however, business was in a stronger position to block tax increases compared to 2003. Business lost its informal ties to the executive branch – Mesa appointed a cabinet of independents that excluded the Santa Cruz agricultural elite for the first time since the transition to democracy (Eaton 2007) – and cohesion declined slightly. However, instrumental power with respect to Congress increased.

Bolivia's regional business cleavage became more salient and acquired an organizational dimension in February 2004, when the FEPB-SC withdrew from the CEPB. Differences of opinion regarding how best to defend business interests provoked the rupture. While the CEPB was willing to support Mesa's general plan of government – if not the wealth tax – in the aftermath of the protests that forced Sánchez de Lozada's resignation, business associations in Santa Cruz assumed a more intransigent position and charged that the CEPB was not adequately defending business interests.[44] An exit strategy unavailable to La Paz elites contributed to business intransigence in Santa Cruz. Given the department's dynamic economy and geographic separation from the capital, Santa Cruz elites began to demand a radical version of regional autonomy that would shield them from the growing redistributive threat posed by the rise of MAS (Eaton 2007, 2011). Cohesion in Bolivia during Mesa's presidency was therefore strong but "bifurcated." Two business blocks – one coordinated by the CEPB and the other by the Santa Cruz peak associations – mobilized independently to defend their interests, occasionally voicing different demands and employing different strategies. However, these two fronts were strong and internally cohesive, affording business much greater influence than uncoordinated opposition in Argentina.

The modest decline in business cohesion was more than offset by another change: informal ties to parties became a much more effective source of instrumental power after 2003. The institutional context had not changed. But Mesa was a political outsider. A professional journalist with no political affiliation, he was Bolivia's first president who did not lead a major political party. Accordingly, Mesa had no control over legislators' career paths. Legislators from the traditional parties therefore had fewer incentives to align behind the executive, and they were free to be much more responsive to business interests.

[44] *La Razón*, Feb. 27, 2004, *El Deber*, Feb. 28, 2004.

Mesa's decision to appoint independents to his cabinet further undermined his relationship with Congress, which by his own account was very difficult (interview, 2006). In this context, business lobbying in Congress, particularly with respect to the MNR and MIR, which together held fifteen of twenty-seven Senate seats, could be highly effective.

Coordinated Opposition Defeats the Wealth Tax

Bifurcated cohesion and untempered informal ties to parties helped business defeat the wealth tax by facilitating coordinated business lobbying and coordinated business-traditional party opposition, similar to the dynamic observed in Chile's 2001 Anti-Evasion Reform (Chapter 3). Given the regional division, the CEPB and the Santa Cruz peak associations worked independently; the FEPB-SC announced after withdrawing from the CEPB that it would negotiate separately with the government.[45] However, the respective lobbying efforts mounted by the two business blocks were highly coordinated. The CEPB was the primary interlocutor with the government for business beyond the *media luna*. It engaged in regular dialog with the administration in pursuit of concessions,[46] and the CEPB's directorate met frequently to define consensus positions as the government's tax proposal evolved through various stages.[47] Meanwhile, CAINCO and the FEPB-SC sustained constant pressure against the wealth tax. Statements by the leaders of these associations were often nearly identical in content, suggesting a high level of consensus and coordination among organized business in Santa Cruz.

The traditional political parties meanwhile defended economic elites' interests in congress. Former president Mesa (2006, interview) asserted: "Those who lobbied to block this tax were the richest sectors of the country, through their congressional representatives." Other government informants made similar comments regarding the business-traditional party nexus (interviews: Nogales 2007, Cuevas 2007). Business informants likewise acknowledged the importance of their lobbying efforts with MNR, MIR, and the remnants of ADN (2007 interviews: CAINCO-C, CNI).

Business in Santa Cruz achieved a particularly noteworthy level of coordination with the traditional parties. The former head of the Santa Cruz parliamentary bloc, MIR Deputy Soruco (interview, 2007), described the legislators' collaboration with the peak associations as: "very, very close. This [wealth tax] was one of the issues we worked on most closely with the team of people from CAINCO and the FEPB-SC – Marinkovic. We worked with him on this issue and many others."[48] As the struggle against the wealth tax progressed, overt business-party coordination extended throughout the *media luna*. In early

---

[45] *La Razón*, Feb. 27, 2004.
[46] *La Razón*, March 3, 2004.
[47] *La Razón*, March 9, 2004.
[48] See also *El Deber*, Jan. 3, 2004.

March, legislators and business leaders from Santa Cruz, Tarija, Pando, Beni and Chuquisaca held a five-hour meeting and issued a joint statement rejecting the wealth tax.[49] Of the traditional parties' sixteen Senate seats, twelve were elected from these five departments. As Mesa remarked: "The business lobby, particularly from Santa Cruz, was very strong among the parties that held the majority – MNR and MIR were going to block the measure." Likewise, a member of his technical team recalled: "Legislators were very attentive to what the private sector wanted. The people from the business federation came from Santa Cruz to work directly with the legislators, and they killed the proposal" (interview, Nogales 2007).

Facing broad business opposition and lacking governing-coalition votes, the administration was compelled to negotiate concessions directly with business. In early March, the government met with the CEPB and agreed to revise the wealth tax. The CEPB "made clear its total disagreement"[50] with the tax and demanded modifications that would restrict its base, including exemptions for stocks and savings accounts.[51] CAINCO and the FEPB-SC declined to recognize the CEPB-government agreement and continued demanding the withdrawal of the wealth tax. Facing continued opposition in Congress, particularly from legislators representing the *media luna*, the administration granted a major concession to landowners: the wealth tax was redesigned as a tax on urban property, entirely exempting agricultural land.[52] This measure met with applause from the Eastern Agricultural Chamber (CAO), but the Santa Cruz peak associations nevertheless opposed the alternative property tax (CAINCO 2004a, interviews: FEPB-SC-B 2007, CAINCO-A 2007).

These concessions not only failed to appease the Santa Cruz peak associations but also incurred popular censure given the erosion of vertical equity. The modified property tax, like the original wealth tax, would leave most of the population untouched, but it also exempted those perceived as the wealthiest Bolivians. A member of Mesa's technical team recalled: "Public opinion was very critical.... They thought it was favoring the landed oligarchy from the east. The discourse was: 'The landed hacienda-owning oligarchy is winning more and more'" (interview, Finance Ministry-D 2007). Given continued business opposition and popular rejection, legislators voted down the property tax in Congress.

Absence of Popular Support

Lack of support from MAS and organized popular sectors sealed the wealth tax's demise. Like the income tax, the wealth tax was ostensibly congruent

---

[49] *El Deber*, March 9, 2004.
[50] *El Deber*, March 2, 2004.
[51] *El Deber*, March 3, 2004.
[52] *La Razón*, March 6, 2004.

with MAS's redistributive agenda; however, the party remained largely silent on the issue while Mesa struggled to mollify business and align the traditional parties. While MAS supported Mesa on some issues, Morales's priority was to differentiate himself from the administration and win power. When the government exempted rural land from the tax, MAS seized the opportunity to criticize Mesa for ceding to the landed oligarchy,[53] implicitly supporting the original version of the wealth tax but only after the fact (interview, Cuevas 2007). Like the traditional parties, MAS opposed the revised property tax in Congress, as well as the financial transactions tax, arguing again that the government should instead tax the hydrocarbon sector,[54] a demand that garnered enthusiastic popular support.

Likewise, the wealth tax inspired no active civil society support. Mesa's vertical-equity appeals precluded popular mobilization against the tax, but despite his strong public approval ratings, as Mesa (2006, interview) recounted, citizens "were not going to go out in the streets to defend my measures." Like MAS, popular sector leaders remained silent until the government had lost the battle:

When it had been discarded and only the transactions tax was approved, then many people who had been silent before appreciated the proposed wealth tax as the fairest option ... and they criticized the government for not holding firm.... The problem was that when this government they criticized was fighting for the tax, no one supported it. (Finance Ministry-D 2007, interview)

Business Acquiescence to the Transaction Tax

In contrast to the wealth tax, business ultimately accepted the financial transactions tax, which was viewed as the lesser of two evils (2007 interviews: CAINCO-B, C, FEPB-SC-A, Ortiz, ASOBAN-C, FEPB-LP, CNI). The lower visibility of this tax and its less certain incidence compared to the wealth tax may have contributed to less intense business rejection, even though both taxes would raise comparable amounts of revenue. The transactions tax did not single elites out as a class to the same degree as the wealth tax, and businesses would likely be able to pass some of the burden of the transactions tax to labor or consumers, whereas the wealth tax would directly affect owners' pocketbooks.[55]

---

[53] *La Razón*, March 6, 15, 2004.
[54] Senado, 87 Sesión Ordinaria, March 11, 2004.
[55] Regarding horizontal equity, some believed the informal sector did not use the financial system and hence the transactions tax would affect only the formal sector (CAINCO 2004a, interviews: Cuevas 2007, CADEX 2007). Others asserted it would affect both formal and informal sectors (interview, CEPB 2006). If informal-sector entrepreneurs did deposit funds in banks, the transactions tax would be automatically withheld, whereas the wealth tax could potentially be evaded.

As with Argentina's transactions tax (Chapter 6), the government's emphasis on fiscal stabilization convinced business that some compromise was imperative. The administration regularly called attention to the gaping budget deficit and the potentially devastating consequences of failing to raise tax revenue; feasible spending cuts and austerity alone could not make up the shortfall. The government's appeals grew increasingly urgent as Congress debated the tax proposals. A major newspaper reported:

The Government warned of the General Treasury's imminent illiquidity if Congress does not approve the proposal by the end of the month.... Executive-branch authorities warned of a new inflationary spiral in the country, like that experienced between 1982 and 1985, when the national currency became devalued by 25,000 percent.[56]

In a country that had experienced hyperinflation in the recent past, business could not completely ignore the government's revenue needs. The former CAINCO president explained business's position: "If we were knocking down the wealth tax, in the end we had to negotiate something," (interview, CAINCO-C 2007). The financial sector, which had the most to lose from inflation, was particularly responsive to the government's appeals. Despite concerns that the transactions tax could discourage use of the financial system, the sector accepted the measure as necessary (interview, Cuevas 2007).[57] The general manager of the banking association's Santa Cruz branch explained: "At that time we were running a deficit of more than 5 percent.... And well, in a way we of course oppose it, but ... since it was absolutely necessity to reduce the level of the deficit, we finally negotiated what we could in order to get clear terms for the transactions tax when it was applied" (interview, ASOBAN-A 2007). The CEPB and the Santa Cruz peak associations also accepted the transactions tax, after securing various modifications. Informants from these associations also identified the deficit as the primary motivation (interviews: CEPB 2006, CAINCO-B 2007).

8.5 THE 2005 HYDROCARBON REFORM

In 2005, the Bolivian Congress legislated a new hydrocarbons law that dramatically increased taxation of this extractive sector. A 1996 hydrocarbons law reform had reduced royalties from 50 percent to 18 percent to encourage investment and exploration. Along with far-reaching changes that expanded the state's regulatory role and obliged companies to renegotiate their contracts with the state, the 2005 reform created a new "direct tax" of 32 percent of the value of production. Hydrocarbons companies subsequently paid total effective tax rates of approximately 56 percent, including VAT, other indirect taxes, and corporate taxes (interview, Finance Ministry-E 2006), whereas their effective

---

[56] *La Razón*, March 10, 2004.
[57] See also *La Razón*, Feb. 3, 21, 2004.

tax burdens had previously ranged from 28 percent to 35 percent (interview, Mesa 2006). A contrast with Chile's copper tax highlights the impressive magnitude of Bolivia's hydrocarbon tax increase. Chile's "specific tax on mining," also legislated in 2005, levied a mere 4 percent not on the value of production, but on profits, a narrower tax base (Chapter 4).[58] And in contrast to the Bolivian reform, the Chilean reform carefully sidestepped property-rights issues.

Popular mobilization in Bolivia played a critical and direct role in producing this remarkable tax increase. In a context of social and political upheaval and Morales's growing importance in national politics, mass mobilization to demand not only higher taxation, but even outright nationalization, overwhelmed substantial business power. Popular mobilization and sustained pressure from MAS forced the issue of hydrocarbon taxation onto the agenda and subsequently motivated Congress to legislate a much harsher law than the executive initially proposed.

Business Power and the Hydrocarbons Sector

At first glance, Bolivia's hydrocarbon reform appears to support the common-sense view that taxing foreign companies is easier than taxing domestic businesses. However, as evidenced by the case of copper in Chile (Chapter 4), foreign-owned natural resource sectors can have substantial power. Even if foreign firms have large sunken costs, they may have structural power stemming from policymakers' concerns over future investment, which could be diverted to other jurisdictions. And linkages to domestic business allow multinational companies to benefit from the former's instrumental power. Along these lines, I argue that Bolivia's hydrocarbons sector enjoyed strong (perceived) structural power. And instrumentally, while it was hardly as well-positioned as Chile's copper sector, the Bolivian hydrocarbons sector cannot be characterized as weak.

In contrast to the income and wealth taxes, structural power was strong with respect to the hydrocarbons reform. Executive-branch authorities, along with a sizable block of representatives in Congress, perceived a credible threat that the radical royalty increases and substantially greater state role in the hydrocarbons sector demanded by popular sectors and MAS would hurt investment (interviews: Mesa 2006, Jemio 2006, Nogales 2007). President Mesa and his ministers recognized that despite its problems, Sánchez de Lozada's 1996 hydrocarbons law had been tremendously successful in attracting foreign investment (interviews: Nogales 2007, Mesa 2006); reserves multiplied dramatically during the following years (Pacheco 2004, Figure 8.1).

---

[58] Both countries' extractive-resource taxes were legislated while commodity prices were rising but prior to dramatic subsequent increases.

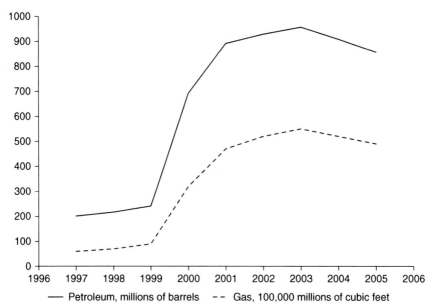

FIGURE 8.1. Proven and Probable Hydrocarbons Reserves in Bolivia.
Source: www.INE.gov.bo.

Significant revisions to the 1996 hydrocarbon regime could have had the reverse effect on investment, thereby jeopardizing Bolivia's plans for hydrocarbons-led development. Attracting additional foreign investment was critical because Bolivia lacked the capital, technology, and expertise to develop its very deep natural gas reserves on its own.[59] Bringing these reserves into production for export to Argentina and Brazil was seen as crucial for correcting troubling macroeconomic imbalances and driving longer-term growth and development.[60] Since hydrocarbons accounted for the majority of Bolivia's exports – an average of 55 percent from 2002 to 2004 (INE) – declining investment in the sector could have exacerbated Bolivia's economic problems. Moreover, the executive worried that increasing royalties and changing the "rules of the game" would damage the country's reputation and cause it to lose foreign investment not only in the hydrocarbons sector, but throughout the economy (Jemio 2006, interview). Some MNR and MIR legislators, especially those representing Santa Cruz, even worried that reform could pro-

---

[59] The Hydrocarbons Chamber estimated that Bolivia needed U.S.$1.8 billion to develop its gas reserves (*El Deber*, July 24, 2004). On government concern that radical reform would preclude such investment, see *El Deber* Oct. 23, 2004.

[60] Mesa's 2005 referendum included a question carefully worded to elicit support for exporting gas.

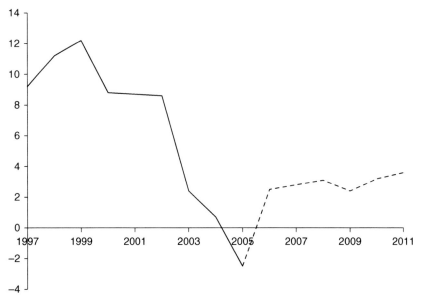

FIGURE 8.2. FDI Net Inflows, Bolivia (Solid Line: Prereform Tend; Dashed Line: Postreform Trend; % GDP).
Source: WDI Online.

voke the multinationals already operating in Bolivia to leave the country (interviews: J. Torres 2007, Jemio 2006).[61]

The context of declining FDI during this period (Figures 8.2, 8.3) likely exacerbated these concerns. The hydrocarbons companies warned at many points during the reform process that the changes under consideration would lead to continued stagnation and decline or even exit[62]; the investment slow-down made these threats credible.

The possibility that companies would initiate international arbitration if the terms of their contracts were altered was a related concern. Such actions, which the companies explicitly threatened[63] and, according to a Hydrocarbons Chamber informant (A 2007), seriously considered,[64] could have further damaged Bolivia's reputation and its potential for attracting investment. Former

[61] Former president Jaime Paz (MIR) warned that reform could cause serious investment problems (*El Deber*, Oct. 5, 2004).
[62] On these efforts to instrumentally enhance structural power, see *El Deber*: Feb. 7, May 25, July 24, Sept. 10, Oct. 23, 2004; March 24, 2005.
[63] E.g., *El Deber*, Feb. 7, 2004.
[64] "*Was it an option that was seriously considered …*
    – Yes, yes, yes.
    – *or was it just part of a strategy for…*
    – No, no, no, it was serious."

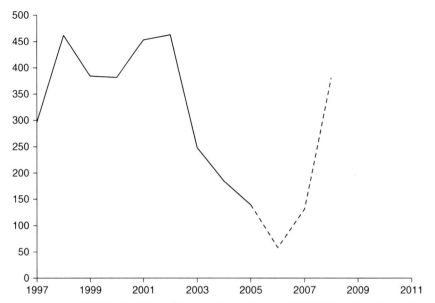

FIGURE 8.3. FDI in Bolivian Hydrocarbons Sector (Solid Line: Prereform Trend; Dashed Line: Postreform Trend; Millions of U.S.$).

Note: Exploration and exploitation of crude petroleum and natural gas.

Source: www.INE.gob.bo.

finance minister Jemio (2006, interview) recalled: "The government and the conservative legislators always considered that the companies could go to arbitration or stop investing in the country." After Congress approved the 2005 reform, almost all of the companies did issue trigger letters opening the possibility of arbitration after a mandatory cooling-off period (2007 interviews: Hydrocarbons-A, C).

It may seem surprising that policymakers perceived the hydrocarbons sector's structural power as strong in a context of rising commodity prices (Figure 8.4). As argued in Chapter 7, high international prices were a key factor leading to the Argentine soy producers' weak structural power; policymakers anticipated that investment and production would continue despite higher taxation. Likewise, one could argue that hydrocarbons companies in Bolivia had more to gain by accepting higher taxes and continuing their profitable operations, rather than scaling back investment or initiating arbitration and thereby risking popular backlash and pressure for even more radical policies. In fact, as of 2007, none of the companies had pursued arbitration.[65] And according to government figures, investment in the hydrocarbons sector recovered to pre-2003

---

[65] Panamerican subsequently pursued arbitration over nationalizations in 2009 and losses related to the 2005 reform.

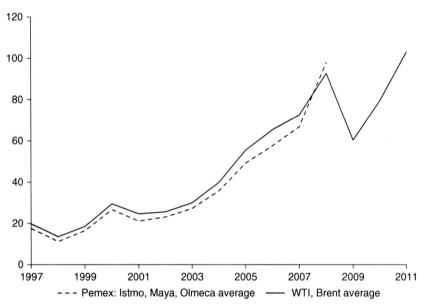

FIGURE 8.4. Hydrocarbons Prices (U.S.$/Barrel).
Source: www.INE.gob.bo.

values in 2008 (Figure 8.3), despite additional hydrocarbons reforms enacted by Morales in 2006. In retrospect, Mesa (interview 2006) reflected:

> Today I recognize that we were operating with too much caution, with a very conservative interpretation of the power Bolivia had and the great business the hydrocarbons companies were running here.... At the time I believed the [2005] reform could put Bolivia's relationship with the world of foreign investors at risk.... I was mistaken – in the poker game, the hydrocarbons companies were bluffing. They did not even have a full hand.[66]

This case therefore offers an illustration of the disjunctures that can arise between policymakers' perceptions regarding anticipated reactions and the actual consequences of reform (Chapter 2: Table 2.2, quadrant b).[67] Given the uncertainty that prevailed during this period of profound social, institutional, and economic instability, it is perhaps unsurprising that the Mesa administration failed to correctly calculate how the hydrocarbons companies would actually respond. The unprecedented and unforeseen surge in hydrocarbon prices that continued past 2005 surely contributed to the investment recovery.

---

[66] Some policymakers interviewed in 2006–07 disagreed with Mesa's retrospective views on the impact of the 2005 reform and Morales's additional reforms. Former Minister Jemio (2006, interview) felt these measures did suppress international investment. Hydrocarbons sector informants (A, B 2007) (unsurprisingly) concurred.

[67] Manley (2012: 27) identifies similar instances of effective structural power threats that were "probably not credible in hindsight" regarding mining taxation in Zambia.

Beyond structural power, the hydrocarbons sector also benefitted from domestic business's instrumental power, even though the sector was dominated by foreign companies and lacked organizational ties to domestic business associations. The Santa Cruz peak associations played an active role in defending the hydrocarbons companies, whose operations were located exclusively in the eastern lowland departments (interviews: Jemio 2006, CAINCO-C 2007, CAO-B 2007). Although taxing the hydrocarbons sector elicited less opposition than the wealth tax (2007 interviews: Nogales, FEPB-SC-C), which would have directly affected Bolivian elites, the *media luna's* domestic business community was keen to ensure respect for the hydrocarbon companies' contracts. Business feared that contract violations would lead to reduced investment in the eastern departments, and the agricultural sector in particular feared that contract violations would portend broader property-rights violations, in a context of growing conflict over land tenure (2007 interviews: Hydrocarbons-A, CAO-A; Eaton 2007). In addition, economic linkages to the hydrocarbons sector were strong; domestic businesses in the eastern departments that provided services to hydrocarbons companies shared common economic interests (interview, G. Torres 2006, Eaton 2007).

However, the hydrocarbons companies largely failed to secure support from business beyond the hydrocarbon-producing departments; this tax issue primed the business community's regional cleavage. Whereas the CEPB actively opposed the wealth tax, it did little to discourage the hydrocarbons reform, aside from issuing statements regarding the need to respect contracts and the rules of the game for foreign investment[68] (interviews: Jemio 2006, Cuevas 2007, Hydrocarbons-A 2007, CAINCO-C 2007, CAO-B 2007).[69] In fact, some La Paz business leaders were open to the possibility of taxing the hydrocarbons sector more heavily (interview, Zaratti 2006). First, additional revenue from multinational hydrocarbon companies made tax increases affecting their own operations less likely. The Hydrocarbons Chamber president recalled: "Several business groups said oh, what a great thing for them to pay more. That will ensure that the government won't want to increase the VAT or the corporate tax"; this view predominated in La Paz and the highland departments where hydrocarbons were not produced (interview, Hydrocarbons-A 2007).[70] Second, the CEPB recognized that the hydrocarbon sector's privileged tax status was a time bomb for business more broadly given increasing popular mobilization: "The CEPB president back then made a declaration that they should pay more – it was very little – and recommended that they voluntarily increase their taxes before there was a popular backlash – as there has been!" (interview,

---

[68] See for example *El Deber*, March 8, 2005.
[69] However, some La Paz business informants reported strong concern over these issues and minimized regional differences (2007 interviews: ASOBAN-B, CNCB).
[70] Two informants felt this logic also operated among business in eastern provinces (Nogales 2007, Cuevas 2007).

CEPB 2006). The CEPB's position provoked the Hydrocarbons Chamber to withdraw from the national confederation in early 2004, adding an organizational dimension to the cleavage.

Compared to commodity-export sectors in the other countries studied, Bolivia's hydrocarbon sector was in a position of intermediate strength for defending its interests. Its structural power as perceived by policymakers at the time was substantial, and it had strong allies in the Santa Cruz business associations and could therefore also benefit from domestic business's informal ties to the traditional parties. In contrast, Argentina's producers had essentially no sources of power to resist large export tax increases on their agricultural commodities (Chapter 7). However, hydrocarbons companies in Bolivia were weaker in instrumental terms than their copper counterparts in Chile. In the Chilean case, the foreign copper companies' informal ties to the domestically owned extractive sector, in conjunction with domestic business's stronger cohesion and partisan linkages, provided a stronger basis for deterring tax increases (Chapter 4).

If popular mobilization had not come into play in the Bolivian case, one might surmise that the hydrocarbons sector would have experienced more significant tax increases than Chile's copper sector but more modest tax increases than Argentina's soy producers. However, popular mobilization became the decisive causal factor, overwhelming business power and driving more radical reform than would otherwise have been expected.

Popular Mobilization Overwhelms Business Power

Nationalization or at least much higher taxation of hydrocarbons was an integral component of popular demands by 2003. The state hydrocarbons company had been capitalized in 1996 on terms popularly perceived as extremely favorable to multinationals (Zaratti 2004). Although the reforms contributed to tremendous growth in the sector and discovery of vast new reserves, foreign ownership and under-taxation of the hydrocarbons sector came to embody all the perceived evils inherent in Bolivia's neoliberal model: foreign companies reaped massive profits by exploiting the country's natural resources, the state received a pittance in remuneration, and the majority of Bolivians suffered poverty and socioeconomic exclusion. Lazarte (2005: 447) observes: "In a situation of poverty, growing inequalities, and economic crisis, gas appeared to many sectors of the population as the last opportunity to deal with the country's problems." Nationalist sentiments enhanced the mobilizational potential of the hydrocarbons issue (Chapter 2); Arce and Rice (2009: 96) note the "deep-seated rejection of neoliberalism as a form of neocolonialism" with which the hydrocarbons regime was associated.[71]

---

[71] See also MAS 2005.

The wave of mobilizations known as the "gas war" that culminated in the October 2003 uprising forced the hydrocarbons issue onto the national agenda. In addition to calling for a constituent assembly, MAS, the COB, Quispe's indigenous movement, and other popular-sector organizations demanded hydrocarbons-law reform and a referendum on exporting natural gas. President Sánchez de Lozada, author of the 1996 reform, had no intention of overhauling the hydrocarbons law, although several clarifications and modifications were planned that would have helped resolve the problem of hydrocarbon under-taxation.[72] Sánchez de Lozada declined to address popular demands until the conflict had escalated beyond control (Lazarte 2005). In the wake of the massive demonstrations that forced Sánchez de Lozada to resign, Mesa embraced the core elements of the so-called "October agenda," including a hydrocarbon-policy referendum and revision of the 1996 law. Given that protests over these issues had forced the country to the brink of chaos, it was clear that significantly increasing hydrocarbon-sector taxation – if not more fundamental reforms – was a prerequisite for social peace. While pressure from business in Santa Cruz and their allies in Congress to avoid substantial changes was strong, the government's fear of popular uprising took precedence. Former hydrocarbons minister Torres (2006, interview) recalled:

There were two extreme positions. There was the far left, which wanted nationalization – they wanted us to take everything.... The other extreme did not want us to change anything. We were in an intermediate position of saying: if we do nothing given the social problem, if we don't change anything, the problem will continue. And if these changes are delayed, the social problems will grow, and there will be a blood bath. What we wanted as a transition government was to avoid that blood bath. We didn't want deaths. There had already been sixty deaths under the previous government.... We had to look for solutions.

Throughout the next year, pressure from MAS and popular sectors drove first the executive branch and then Congress to accept reforms imposing increasingly harsher terms on the hydrocarbons companies. The executive's first reform proposal, drafted in April 2004, was a compromise that it hoped would satisfy MAS and civil society without causing investment to plummet or violating contracts, which the administration feared would provoke the hydrocarbons companies to seek international arbitration (interviews: Mesa

[72] The 1996 reform included a surtax on windfall profits, to take effect after companies recovered their investments, when production and international prices were high. However, the details were never formally codified. Sánchez de Lozada's technical team intended to implement the surtax, but disagreements within the administration, along with broader political and social problems, delayed progress. The administration did not advertise its plans for the surtax to placate popular sectors, probably in part because the technically complicated tax would have been difficult to explain. Ironically, the surtax could have produced as much revenue as the 2005 reform in combination with Morales's subsequent alterations to hydrocarbon companies' contracts (interview, Finance Ministry-B 2006).

2006, Jemio 2006, Nogales 2007). Accordingly, the government negotiated the terms of the proposal directly with the hydrocarbons companies. On the one hand, the proposal included substantial tax increases for the most profitable hydrocarbons fields, which the companies reluctantly accepted given the events of October 2003. Former hydrocarbons minister Nogales (2007, interview) recounted that he told the companies: "The people want blood, as much blood as I can take, but I will not kill you." On the other hand, the proposal maintained incentives for exploration and investment, tax increases would be phased in gradually, and lower tax rates would apply to smaller, less profitable operations. The hydrocarbons companies viewed this compromise favorably (interview, Hydrocarbons-A 2007).

However, MAS's growing political strength, predicated on mobilizational capacity, compelled Mesa to include more radical measures in the July 2004 gas referendum. To secure Morales's endorsement of the referendum (interview, Nogales 2007), Mesa included as question 2: "Do you agree with recovering State ownership of all hydrocarbons at the wellhead?"[73] This question, which implied nationalization, helped ensure that MAS would not boycott the referendum, a move that would have undermined Mesa's legitimacy and his ability to maintain order. The other referendum questions were ambiguously worded in an effort to obtain the highest possible support (Nogales 2007, interview). Question 5, which included the issue of taxation, was patently multibarreled as well as ambiguous:

Do you agree that Bolivia should export gas in the framework of a national policy that: meets the gas consumption needs of Bolivians, stimulates industrialization of gas in Bolivia, charges taxes and/or royalties on the hydrocarbons companies reaching 50% of the value of production of gas and petroleum, and allocates the resources from export and industrialization of gas primarily to education, health, roads, and jobs?[74]

All the referendum questions were approved with strong support (72 percent of valid votes in favor for question 2 and 62 percent for question 5).[75] But while the referendum strengthened Mesa in the short term, the design of the questions created political opportunities later on for MAS and those who favored more radical hydrocarbons-law changes (Lazarte 2005: 587). Question 2 set a precedent for altering the companies' contracts much more fundamentally than Hydrocarbons Minister Nogales (2007, interview) thought appropriate; this question provoked his resignation.[76] Further, MAS maintained that question 5 mandated a uniform 50 percent royalty on hydrocarbons production,

[73] Decreto Supremo 27507.
[74] Ibid.
[75] However, 23 percent to 29 percent of ballots were blank or null for these questions (www.cne. org.bo).
[76] Nogales (2007, interview) objected that the state had never owned rights to oil once it left the ground.

whereas the executive intended that the sum total of taxes on the sector would reach in some cases but never exceed 50 percent (G. Torres 2006, interview). As the Hydrocarbons Chamber president recalled, the referendum was a key turning point in the policymaking process that led to an outcome far less favorable for the companies than the April draft proposal (Hydrocarbons-A 2007, interview).

Thereafter, the executive quickly lost control over the reform, given Mesa's weak relationship with Congress, and pressure from MAS coupled with fear of popular protest led legislators to endorse the more radical measures suggested in the referendum questions. MAS's influence on the reform design outweighed the size of its relatively small congressional bloc, thanks to its mobilizational capacity. The former president of the House of Deputies Finance Committee recalled:

> MAS had an enormous capacity to participate in the debates … above all they had a great capacity to coordinate pressure on congress with the social organizations, outside in the streets. Big marches and demonstrations … obviously Congress was used to ceding to these pressures – they were very strong. (J. Torres 2007, interview)

In this context, the executive's proposal, which increased taxes gradually according to specified production criteria and other technical considerations, was not politically viable: "President Mesa's proposal complied with the referendum because taxes reached 50 percent, but only in the very long term – maybe in the year 3000 – and with very high production levels. In that sense, it was a deceitful proposal," (J. Torres 2007, interview). Popular mobilization helped forge consensus in favor of a flat, up-front rate of 50 percent. MAS Deputy Torrico (interview, 2007) explained: "The people in the streets were obliging us to do that. There were no big problems [in Congress] – the people were rising up." Even the traditional parties felt compelled to endorse a 50 percent tax rate as well as obligatory contract renegotiation. Former senate president Vaca Diez (interview, 2007) recalled: "The MNR ultimately assumed a political position of saying OK: the referendum said 50 percent, so it will be 50 percent; that property rights be recovered, so we'll recover property rights at the wellhead. All the strength of those who governed with Sánchez de Lozada was lost when Sánchez de Lozada fell."

Given the threat of popular mobilization, the Hydrocarbons Chamber and the Santa Cruz business associations achieved little influence in Congress. Informal ties to legislators were insufficient to defend their interests. The reform ultimately passed with traditional-party votes; MAS opposed the final legislation for strategic reasons. Remarkably, MNR and MIR representatives from Santa Cruz did not close ranks with business against the reform, in contrast to their open coordination against the wealth tax. Former MIR deputy Soruco (2007, interview), who had worked closely with the Santa Cruz peak associations against the wealth tax, lauded the hydrocarbons reform as major accomplishment: "In my farewell speech as president of the House of Deputies, I thanked MAS for its stubbornness and obstinacy in insisting. Thanks to that stubbornness, we achieved something very important for Bolivia." Ironically, senate president Vaca Diez, an agricultural businessman from Santa Cruz who might have opposed the reform under other circumstances, was charged with enacting the new hydrocarbons law in the midst of strident objections from the Santa Cruz peak associations,[77] given President Mesa's decision to neither promulgate nor veto the legislation.[78]

Revenue-sharing measures in the reform, along with strong popular approval from *media luna* residents, helps explain the breach between traditional-party legislators and business. Four percentage points of the new tax were earmarked for each hydrocarbon-producing department, which entailed a massive revenue influx. And although the threat of popular mobilization was stronger in western departments, higher taxation of hydrocarbons was tremendously popular among Santa Cruz voters – 88 percent of valid referendum votes in Santa Cruz supported question 2 on state ownership of hydrocarbons at the wellhead, compared to a slightly higher 93 percent in La Paz.[79]

Comparison with Copper Taxation in Chile

Weaker business power made the Bolivian hydrocarbons sector vulnerable to more substantial tax increases than Chile's copper sector. Yet popular mobilization played a critical role in driving Bolivia's radical reform, which imposed much larger costs on extractive companies than would otherwise be expected considering that the hydrocarbon sector did have substantial power. Taxing foreign-owned extractive companies was quite popular in both countries. But in Chile, citizens were not mobilized and hence played a very limited role in the policy process. Popular opinion had little effect on reform design; business power was the predominant consideration for policymakers. Voters could retrospectively punish politicians at the polls, but the prevailing conditions of normal democratic politics gave politicians who opposed taxing the copper sector leeway to avoid that fate. Moreover, policymakers faced no threat of social disruption if they rejected popular proposals. In contrast, popular sectors in Bolivia were central political actors thanks to their extraordinary mobilizational capacity, and they advanced radical demands – not just higher taxation of hydrocarbons, but also nationalization. Faced with a potential social uprising that could overturn the political order, Bolivian politicians conceded

---

[77] *El Deber*, May 6, 2005.
[78] Mesa feared the legislation would provoke disinvestment and international lawsuits, but a veto would have provoked massive protests.
[79] www.cne.org.bo

to many of the popular sectors' demands, including a major tax increase on hydrocarbons companies. Had popular sectors played a similar role in Chile, the copper tax legislated may not have been so marginal, notwithstanding strong business power. The following chapter substantiates this counterfactual by analyzing the effect of sustained student protests on corporate taxation under the Piñera administration.

8.6 CONCLUSION

Tax politics in Bolivia during the early 2000s entailed high-stakes political battles involving powerful elites and mobilized masses. Economic elites had substantial instrumental power (Table 8.1), arising from bifurcated cohesion and informal ties to Bolivia's traditional parties, which placed them in a stronger position to influence tax policy than their Argentine counterparts. Bolivian elites were much more cohesive than Argentina's sectorally fragmented elites, and during Mesa's government, informal ties to parties – otherwise tempered by party-centered electoral institutions as in Argentina – became a much more effective source of power given the outsider president's weak authority over the traditional parties. However, business's instrumental power was weaker than in Chile, where cohesion was not marred by regional divisions and relationships with parties were based on partisan linkages to programmatic right parties. Bolivia's conservative right party (ADN) had all but vanished from Congress; business relationships with the declining MNR and MIR were based largely on informal ties, which afford more contingent influence than partisan linkages. Furthermore, popular mobilization counterbalanced business power in Bolivia – with the exception of the 2003 income tax, where popular sectors acted as circumstantial elite allies. Weaker business power compared to Chile, along with the threat of massive popular mobilization against policies perceived as regressive, meant that business in Bolivia could not keep initiatives to tax income and wealth off the agenda. But stronger business power compared to Argentina made it possible for business to defeat initiatives later in the policy process, as in the case of the 2004 wealth tax. However, popular sectors could overwhelm business power if they mobilized in favor of reform, as occurred with the 2005 hydrocarbons reform.

Bolivia during the early 2000s provides an interesting and challenging context for assessing the reach of the business power framework. During this period of profound change, with a party system in flux and political engagement far outstripping institutional bounds, business power was not the only factor contributing to tax policy outcomes. Several of the reform cases analyzed in this chapter were arguably overdetermined. For example, the wealth tax conceivably could have failed even if business had not marshaled its sources of instrumental power against the reform, given Mesa's lack of control over the governing coalition and ensuing congressional-executive branch

TABLE 8.1. *Overview: Business's Instrumental Power in Cross-National Context*

	CHILE (1990–2009)	BOLIVIA		ARGENTINA (1992–2008)
		Sánchez de L. (2002–03)	Mesa (2003–04)	
INSTRUMENTAL POWER	STRONG	INTERMEDIATE		WEAK
Cohesion	Strong Economy-wide organization, neoliberal ideology	Intermediate-Strong Economy-wide organization, formal-sector identity; latent regional division	Intermediate Regionally-bifurcated economy-wide organization	Weak Organizational fragmentation
Relationships with Legislators	Strong Partisan linkages	Weak-Intermediate Tempered recruitment and informal ties: executive control	Intermediate Untempered recruitment and informal ties: weak outsider president	Weak Ineffectual recruitment and informal ties: strong executive control
Relationships with Executive	Strong Informally-institutionalized concertation	Weak-Intermediate Tempered recruitment and informal ties: president prioritized technical criteria	Weak Exclusion from cabinet	Weak Recruitment and informal ties relevant at sectoral level only

rivalries, as well as Morales's prioritization of strategic considerations over redistributive concerns in his bid to win national power. Yet when analyzed in conjunction with popular mobilization, business power still provides substantial leverage for explaining when and to what extent economic elites were able to defend their interests. Indeed, a comprehensive explanation of agenda formulation and the fate of tax initiatives requires attention to business power.

9

Tax Developments under Left Rule in Bolivia and Right Rule in Chile

This chapter briefly analyzes counterintuitive tax policy developments following the primary periods examined in previous chapters: progressive tax nonreform under the left in Bolivia and progressive tax reform under the right in Chile. One might expect a left government with a heterodox development program to promote progressive taxation as a redistributive tool, yet taxes on income and wealth were not part of President Morales's (2006–) agenda in Bolivia. Meanwhile, the ascent of Chile's right coalition to the presidency created expectations of continued direct tax nonreform, yet President Piñera (2010–13) legislated Chile's largest corporate tax increase since 1990.

Whereas strong business power played a central role in dissuading the Chilean left from pursuing significant direct tax increases, the legacy of Bolivia's failed 2003 income tax proposal, MAS's prioritization of a more radical transformative agenda, and of course the economic and political importance of natural-resource revenue play a much greater role than business power in explaining the low salience of progressive direct taxation on the left's agenda in Bolivia. Piñera's tax increase is the more surprising outcome in light of the analysis in previous chapters. I argue that an unusual conjuncture involving unanticipated revenue needs and strong concerns over public opinion motivated the right-coalition government to legislate a temporary corporate tax increase in 2010. While business power remained strong, the Piñera administration did not face the same opposition to tax increases that Concertación governments confronted, given the unique circumstances that prevailed. A new development in Chilean politics – sustained popular mobilization demanding both expanded social spending and progressive taxation to finance it, in a context of broader antibusiness sentiment – drove the administration to make the increase permanent in 2012. Chilean tax politics accordingly acquired features that had characterized Bolivian tax politics six years earlier: popular mobilization forced tax increases onto the agenda, counterbalanced business power, and altered business's strategic calculations. The chapter concludes with some reflections on partisanship and tax policymaking.

9.1 MORALES'S TAX AGENDA

Although technocrats in the Morales administration believed that Bolivia needed an individual income tax, this and analogous progressive tax issues remained off of the government's agenda. An obvious hypothesis following previous chapters is that domestic economic elites' instrumental power contributed to this outcome. Although instrumental power with respect to the executive branch declined with Morales's election to the presidency, parties with close ties to business remained strong in Congress from 2006 to 2009. PODEMOS, an incipient right coalition constructed on ADN's remains, secured almost half of the Senate seats. Like ADN, PODEMOS enjoyed its strongest support in Bolivia's prosperous lowland departments. Several *media luna* business leaders became prominent PODEMOS politicians, including Senator Ortiz, former general manager of CAINCO, and Deputy Franco, former vice president of the Santa Cruz livestock federation. Moreover, business cohesion fostered significant capacity for collective action outside formal policymaking arenas, as illustrated by massive Santa Cruz autonomy protests beginning in 2004, which business associations helped to orchestrate (Eaton 2007, 2011).

However, interview evidence suggests that business power played at most a secondary role in removing income tax reform from the government's agenda. None of the six MAS informants I interviewed mentioned concerns regarding business-PODEMOS reactions when I asked about prospects for proposing an income tax. When I then inquired directly about potential resistance from these actors, two informants responded that it would indeed be difficult to secure approval in the Senate, given the opposition's ties to wealthy Bolivians and strong business organization in the *media luna* departments (2007: Torrico, Carrazana). Two informants downplayed the potential for conflict with business and PODEMOS over an income tax (2007: Herbas, Pimentel), a third informant simply reiterated that the government had no intention of creating an income tax, thereby dismissing the issue as irrelevant (Ramírez 2007), and another informant left no opportunity to ask about anticipated business-PODEMOS reactions by resolutely declaring that an income tax was neither necessary nor appropriate (Executive Advisor 2007). MAS perceptions aside, it is likely that economic elites would have deployed their sources of instrumental power against reform. However, economic elites' instrumental power did not play a central role in keeping reform off the agenda via anticipated reactions.

Three other factors explain the government's lack of initiative on progressive direct taxation. First, the income tax remained discredited given association with former president Sanchez de Lozada, neoliberalism, and the IMF (Chapter 8). MAS politicians showed little interest in income or property taxes and did not associate these policy tools with redistribution (2007 interviews:

Pimentel, Executive Advisor, Ramírez, Torrico). Many still misinterpreted the individual income tax as a tax on wage earners rather than a tax on rich Bolivians. Two informants asserted that Bolivia already had an income tax (the ineffective RC-IVA), indicating limited understanding of the technical issues (2007 interviews: Pimentel, Ramírez).[1] Those who were more open to the idea of progressive income taxation nevertheless observed that memories of the tax protest remained strong: "There is still trauma from 2003" (interview, Herbas 2007).[2]

Second, MAS prioritized more radical redistributive policies and a broader transformative agenda instead of progressive taxation. Foremost among these policies was land reform, which MAS informants viewed as more effective than taxation not only for promoting social justice, but also for generating revenue, on the premise that breaking up large landholdings would increase productivity (2007 interviews: Ramírez, Pimentel). Moreover, land reform entailed observable transfers of tangible assets from the "oligarchy" to the government's peasant constituencies. Land reform had the potential to generate greater popular support than progressive taxation, which entails less visible, multistage transfers from rich to poor. Tax payments cannot be directly observed, and the connection between elite taxation and popular-sector benefits is not always obvious.[3]

Income and wealth taxation also took a backseat to other elements of Morales's transformative agenda, including reforming the constitution to end Bolivia's historic socioeconomic and political exclusion of indigenous peoples (interview: Pimentel 2007; Gamarra 2008) and centralizing power to facilitate longer-term reforms (Madrid 2011: 256). In these areas, MAS was willing to take on major political battles with economic elites. Constitutional reform absorbed much of the government's attention from 2006 to 2009; opposition parties and wealthy eastern *media luna* departments resisted virulently (Lehoucq 2008). Facing declining instrumental power in national politics with the rise of MAS and the government's growing use of constitutionally questionable tactics for marginalizing the opposition in Congress, *media luna* elites redoubled their efforts to secure regional autonomy as protection from MAS's redistributive ambitions (Eaton 2007). Business associations played a major

---

[1] Similarly, an Executive Advisor (2007, interview) asserted that Bolivia's tax system was already equitable and progressive.

[2] Technocrats concurred that the greatest political challenge entailed precluding popular opposition (Chapter 8).

[3] A Finance Ministry informant (A 2007) expressed similar views: "Saying let's expropriate property from people who have more than one home – that is popular – that rich person who has more than one home, why do they need so many? I think that the government is aware of this.
    –*Expropriation is more visible?*
    –Exactly. The people see it and believe it. Whereas saying we're going to tax the rich, and the money will be given to the poor, yes, but it's more direct to say we're going to confiscate. That sells better."

role in organizing and financing massive pro-autonomy protests that they hoped would force Morales to concede to their demands; the government ultimately accepted important limitations on land reform (Eaton 2011).

Third, taxing hydrocarbon multinationals constituted a clear and politically appealing alternative to taxing Bolivian citizens that MAS embraced as a key component of its platform. In the words of MAS Senator Ramírez (2007, interview): "Our government does not intend to increase taxes on Bolivians' wages or patrimony. We have a new vision that more and better resources must come from natural resources." In May 2006, Morales increased royalties for the companies operating Bolivia's two largest gas fields to 82 percent and "nationalized" the hydrocarbons sector amid widespread popular approval, even among the *media luna* departments that generally opposed MAS's economic policies (Gamarra 2008: 129).[4]

Higher hydrocarbon-sector taxes, combined with booming international prices, alleviated Bolivia's revenue needs and financed redistributive spending initiatives[5] without need for new taxes. Total tax revenue increased from an average of 13.8 percent of GPD from 2000 to 2004 to 22.7 percent of GDP from 2006 to 2008. Taxes on hydrocarbons, most importantly the "direct tax" legislated in 2005, totaled 8 percent of GDP on average during the latter period, accounting for essentially all of the increase. This revenue dwarfed the 1–2 percent of GDP that previous governments had attempted to raise with taxes on individual income and wealth. Thanks in large part to the hydrocarbons tax, Bolivia achieved an unprecedented fiscal surplus of 4.6 percent of GDP in 2006 (EIU 2008). As in Chile from 2006 to 2010, the context of abundance reduced incentives to increase domestic taxes.

Instead, the government had strong incentives to revise the rules governing hydrocarbons-revenue allocation between national and subnational governments, a major point of contention with the *media luna*. MAS sought to recentralize this revenue; the 2005 law earmarked large percentages of the hydrocarbons tax to departmental and municipal governments, as well as universities and other entities, leaving a relatively small share for the national treasury. One MAS informant characterized these revenue-sharing provisions, which arose out of negotiations in congress and civil society pressure, as "a mistake," (interview, Torrico 2007). *Media luna* departments in contrast sought to retain a larger share of all tax revenue generated in their departments (PODEMOS 2005, Eaton 2007). In late 2007, the government nevertheless managed to recentralize 30 percent of hydrocarbons-tax revenue to fund old-

---

[4] The measures enacted did not entail traditional nationalization; rather, contracts were renegotiated on terms more favorable to the state (interviews: Mesa 2006, J. Torres 2007, Hydrocarbons-B 2007). Companies accepted the new contracts partly because they included new investment incentives and the possibility of recovering exploration costs (2006 interviews: Zaratti, G. Torres; Hydrocarbons-B 2007; Molina 2010).

[5] These included cash transfers, pensions, and energy subsidies for low-income sectors (interview: Cuevas 2007; Madrid 2011).

age pension increases (Arellano 2012, Eaton 2014). This revenue influx further obviated (short-term) need for domestic tax revenue.

By 2008, however, limitations of the resource-taxation model were hard to ignore, and business power resurfaced as a salient concern in policymaking. New investment was at a standstill (EIU 2008), and Bolivia failed to fulfill gas contracts signed with Argentina and Brazil (Molina 2010). Foreign investors' structural power did not immediately compel the government to reverse its policies. Declining investment may instead have encouraged more radical reforms to increase the state's role in the hydrocarbons sector and reduce reliance on private capital: in May 2008, the government forcibly acquired majority shares in the three major companies (Miranda 2009). By late 2011, however, structural power began to act in investors' favor. Government officials ascertained that the hydrocarbons regime had discouraged investment, particularly in exploration, and the Hydrocarbons Ministry drafted tax reform proposals intended to make the sector more attractive to foreign investors (Arellano 2012). However, the government recognized that the immense popularity of the prevailing hydrocarbons regime and the strength of its own rhetoric on this issue could make reform difficult (Arellano 2012). The government would have to walk a tax-reform tightrope similar to what its predecessors had confronted, facing potential opposition from mobilized masses on the one hand, and the consequences of business's structural power on the other hand.

There are two important exceptions to MAS's lack of interest in progressive domestic taxation. First, the government restricted a simplified tax regime for interdepartmental transport that had allowed large operations to avoid and evade corporate taxation. Previous governments had avoided this equity-enhancing, revenue-raising tax reform for fear of protest (2007 interviews: Finance Ministry-C, D, E). As expected, the transport sector did strike against the measure, but Morales held firm, and public opinion sided with the government (2007 interviews: Ramírez, Herbas, Finance Ministry-D, ASOBAN-C). Second, the government endeavored to increase taxation of the domestic mining sector, along with foreign-owned mines, in the context of booming metal prices. Mining-cooperative protests compelled the government to target large foreign-owned mines[6]; however, government informants believed the domestic mining sector also needed to pay higher taxes (2007 interviews: Ramírez, Torrico, Finance Ministry-E, Carrazana). Although transport operatives and cooperative miners may not be among the ranks of Bolivia's wealthiest economic elites, these tax initiatives certainly enhanced horizontal and vertical equity, and they provide concrete evidence of MAS's professed interest in broadening tax bases and incorporating evaders and avoiders into the tax net

---

[6] BBC, Feb. 8, 2007: "Bolivia miners call off protest." A November 2007 tax reform partially exempted cooperatives. www.cedib.org/wordpress/wp-content/uploads/2012/03/Las-reformas-al-codigo-minero.pdf

rather than creating new taxes (2007 interviews: Executive Advisor, Carrazana, Torrico, Pimentel, Ramírez, Herbas, Finance Ministry-E).

9.2 PIÑERA'S TAX INCREASES

Tax politics took unexpected turns in Chile after the 2009 election that brought the right to power for the first time since the transition to democracy. The Piñera administration confounded expectations by legislating a two-year corporate tax increase to fund reconstruction after Chile's 2010 earthquake, and then making the tax increase permanent in 2012. The 2010 reform entailed a moderate, expressly temporary deviation from business preferences in an exceptional context, whereas the 2012 reform was driven by a surge of protests demanding not only massive state investment in education, but also higher taxation of economic elites. Popular mobilization counterbalanced business power and altered business-right calculations, while a context of growing antibusiness public sentiment augmented pressure on the right to take defensive actions.

The 8.8-magnitude earthquake that devastated central Chile days before Piñera's inauguration created extraordinary revenue needs; earthquake damage was estimated at U.S.$30 billion.[7] Yet right-wing economists maintained that reconstruction could be financed entirely through borrowing and recourse to Chile's copper stabilization fund. As such, Piñera's decision to temporarily increase the corporate tax is remarkable.

Four main factors explain the 2010 reform. First, concern with consolidating public support in the context of damaging criticisms regarding Piñera's conflicts of interest as the country's president and its wealthiest businessman motivated the administration to deviate from the preferences of its core business constituency, as the right had occasionally done in the past when promoting business interests became an electoral liability.[8] The Concertación persistently denounced Piñera's candidacy as an inappropriate marriage of money and politics. Piñera responded by promising to sell his extensive holding in the airline LAN before assuming office. However, the process was not completed before the inauguration, and Piñera was accused of avoiding taxes on the sale of his remaining shares.[9] RN president Larraín identified Piñera's tardy divestiture as a major political mistake: "This gave the opposition a pretext to attack not only the government, but also Piñera's personal morality.... I advocated selling [LAN] much earlier.... Had that been done, Piñera would have won by half a million votes or more."[10] Critics within the right also called on Piñera to sell his television station, Chilevision, joining the Concertación in denouncing

---

[7] *El Mercurio*, March 12, 2010.
[8] That Piñera helped engineer RN support for the 1990 corporate tax increase makes the 2010 reform less surprising.
[9] *El Mostrador*, March 22, 2010.
[10] *El Mercurio*, March 29, 2010.

conflicts of interest surrounding presidential appointments to the state-owned television network.[11]

The government viewed increasing the corporate tax as a way to counteract the damage, by sending "a potent political signal that neutralizes the fear and rumors ... that Piñera's administration will be a government of big business."[12] A government informant confirmed that the measure served "political and electoral objectives" (Executive Advisor-C 2011). Polls indicated strong support for the corporate tax increase,[13] and advisors hoped the measure would win Piñera a public opinion boost. Strong electoral competition in a context of weak partisan affiliation likely augmented concern over public opinion. The percentage of voters not identifying with any major coalition increased sharply after 2005 to around 50 percent (Luna and Altman 2011: 15). Meanwhile, the vote-share gap between the center-left and right coalitions narrowed from 9.7 to 3.9 and 20 to 1.6 for the lower house and senatorial elections respectively from 2005 to 2009. Bachelet won the 2005 presidential election by 7 percentage points; Piñera won in 2010 by 4 points. As many authors argue, deviations from core-constituency preferences to cultivate electoral support are more likely when political challengers are strong.[14]

Second, business's instrumental power declined in the congressional arena given that the center-left won an absolute Senate majority. The corporate tax increase helped secure center-left votes for measures in the reconstruction package that reflected business-right preferences (interview: Executive Advisor-C 2011), including tax credits for private donations and reducing the "stamp tax" on loans and credits. Many Concertación politicians opposed these measures as regressive; several senators announced early on that they would condition support for donations credits on a corporate tax increase.[15] The donations credits and the stamp tax cut in turn tempered business antagonism. The corporate tax increase would raise an average of 0.25 percent of GDP for two years, but thereafter, the reform entailed a permanent annual revenue reduction of approximately 0.2 percent of GDP.[16]

Third, the extraordinary context of natural disaster disposed business to accept the measure. A business informant explained: "The damage was huge, it was an exceptional situation. That justified the tax increases" (interview, CPC-E 2011). Although some businesspeople remained unconvinced that tax increases were necessary given Chile's strong macroeconomic position, they recognized that resisting was impolitic (2011 interviews: ABIF, Mining-H, CNC), particularly with winter approaching and thousands homeless (Mining

---

[11] *El Mercurio*, April 13, 2010.

[12] *El Mercurio*, March 30, 2010.

[13] An *El Mercurio* survey reported 74 percent support among Santiago respondents (April 11, 2010).

[14] E.g., Murillo 2009, Jacobs and Shapiro 2000, Gilens 2012.

[15] *El Mercurio*, April 15, 2010.

[16] Author's calculations using Finance Ministry estimates.

Ministry 2011, interview). This reaction paralleled business acceptance of the 1990 tax reform, which also occurred under extraordinary circumstances that made increased spending imperative (Chapter 3). In both cases, business perceived that modest tax increases would serve the private sector's longer-term interests. In 1990, business calculated that accepting a corporate tax increase would legitimate the neoliberal model and promote social peace after the democratic transition; in 2010, business compromised in a time of dire need, recognizing that refusing to contribute would provoke widespread social censure that could create pressure to increase corporate taxation much more significantly.[17] Given these considerations, business did not deploy its sources of instrumental power against the reform.

Finally, the executive's credible commitment to raising the corporate tax for only two years contributed to business acquiescence. Concertación governments often legislated temporary tax increases and inevitably made them permanent thereafter, arguing that an abrupt revenue drop would jeopardize fiscal discipline. In contrast, the 2010 reform phased out the corporate tax increase; after one year at 20 percent, the rate would decrease to 18.5 percent in 2012 and return to 17 percent in 2013. The government's partisan stripes further alleviated business concerns; a government informant recalled: "They trusted that a right government would not extend the time period" (interview, Executive Advisor-C 2011).[18] Business informants identified the manifestly temporary nature of the tax increase as critical for business acceptance (2011 interviews: CPC-E, ABIF, Mining-H, CChC-D, SNA-B, CNC).

However, unforeseen developments forced tax increases back onto the agenda. The Chilean student movement staged a series of massive protests from May through October of 2011 that captured the world's attention. The largest of more than forty major demonstrations brought 100,000–200,000 people into the streets to demand a stronger state role in education, with the goals of improving quality, expanding access, and lowering the high cost of secondary and university education. The students' demands resonated with the public, whereas the government's ineffective response contributed to a precipitous decline in Piñera's approval ratings. Polls in September 2011 reported that 76 percent of respondents supported the students' demands; likewise, 76 percent disapproved of how the government had handled the conflict.[19] The government's approval ratings sunk to 22 percent in November while disapproval reached 62 percent (CEP 2012: 54); these figures were as bad as Fernández de Kirchner's ratings during the 2008 export-tax strike (Chapter 7).

The student movement broke new ground in Chile not only by staging the largest and most sustained episode of popular mobilization since the return

---

[17] This logic was particularly evident regarding a mining tax increase included in the 2010 reform (interview: Mining-G 2011).

[18] Flores-Macías (2013) describes a similar dynamic surrounding Colombia's wealth tax.

[19] www.adimark.cl/es/estudios/archivo.asp?id=130

to democracy, but also by raising the issues of inequality and progressive taxation. The students' demands were expansive; they framed problems with the educational system as symptomatic of a development model that perpetuated extreme inequality. In line with this diagnosis, when the government dismissed their calls for radical reforms as too costly, the students proposed taxing business and the rich more heavily (interview: Jackson 2012). Other civil society actors rallied to this demand. In August 2011, the labor federation staged a national strike in support of the students; taxing business and the rich was listed first among the unions' six motives for calling the strike.[20]

The student protests forced direct tax increases onto the government's agenda through multiple mechanisms. First, popular mobilization created major new revenue needs. By July 2011 it was clear to even the most ardent defenders of Pinochet's model that a return to social peace and recovery in approval ratings required (at a minimum) expanded state financial assistance for students. The government's first proposal (which failed to placate the students) included an educational fund of U.S.$4 billion. Although many within the government maintained that tax increases were not necessary to finance this new expenditure – most notably the finance minister[21] – others argued that given additional spending obligations incurred during the previous year, tax increases were advisable for fiscal discipline (interview, Executive Advisor-C 2012).

Second, as in Bolivia, popular mobilization removed regressive tax increases from the agenda. A government informant (Executive Advisor-C 2012) explained: "Social pressure was too strong…. In this context, the only possibility was to get money from business, not from the VAT or taxes that end up being regressive." Regressive tax increases may or may not have stimulated additional protests, as Bolivian governments had feared, but such alternatives clearly were not politically feasible given societal demands for equity-enhancing reform and the Concertación's Senate majority.

Third, popular mobilization raised the public salience of taxation, not only by generating widespread support for educational reforms that required investment of several percentage points of GDP, but also by demanding progressive taxation to fund this massive new expenditure. A Concertación deputy explained: "The students installed the idea that it was legitimate and necessary to look for more fiscal resources so that the state could meet its responsibilities," (interview, Auth 2012). Similarly, a Concertción senator noted that while education remained the more "popular" issue, "taxation today is much more present in the minds of average Chileans…. Before it was an issue that nobody talked about" (interview, Lagos-Weber 2012). In this context, political actors had electoral incentives to increase taxes to fund educational reform. The more conservative politicians within the Concertación who had previously shown little interest in direct tax

[20] "Las seis razones de la CUT para el Paro Nacional." July 2011, www.cutchile.cl
[21] *El Mercurio*, Sept. 11, 2011.

increases embraced proposals that would both raise significant revenue and enhance tax equity (2012 interviews: Lagos-Weber, Auth). Meanwhile, a minority within the right that had been more open to tax increases gained strength relative to the (still dominant) pro-business, antitax core.[22]

Fourth and relatedly, the student movement dramatically expanded the scope of tax proposals under debate, which in turn altered the government's strategic calculations. Whereas in previous years, few consequential actors suggested anything beyond raising the corporate tax to 20 percent and eliminating loopholes, center-left politicians and technocrats began to consider much more radical changes that entailed fundamentally altering the income-tax structure to fund investment in education (interview, Cieplan 2012). In April 2012, all four Concertación parties, the Communist Party, and the new left party MAS issued a joint proposal that included ending deferred taxation of reinvested capital income and gradually eliminating accumulated tax credits in businesses's FUT ledgers.[23] With the opposition rallying around tax reform as a core issue and a host of radical tax proposals under public debate, Piñera advisors argued that the government's best move was moderate reform in hope of diffusing pressure for radical reform (interview, Executive Advisor-C 2012).

Meanwhile, several high-profile business scandals enhanced political incentives for the government to deviate from its business constituency's tax preferences. News broke in June 2011 that the successful La Polar department store chain had illegally increased interest rates without informing customers. The story received extensive press coverage and produced a climate of hostility against big business. Antibusiness sentiments were stoked a year later when the tax agency announced it would pardon U.S.$118 million of fines accumulated by Johnson's department store. This decision was denounced as a subsidy for one of Chile's wealthiest businessmen, who subsequently purchased the company; the Piñera administration was still managing the political fallout in early 2013. Popular antagonism toward both economic and political elites was reflected in Piñera's persistently low approval ratings (CEP 2012).[24]

By September 2011, arguments circulated within the government that returning the corporate tax to 20 percent could both appease the student movement and rebuild support for Piñera by signaling sympathy with the populace rather than business.[25] Furthermore, ending the debate on tax reform before the 2013 presidential campaign, which could create even stronger pressure for far-reaching reform, became an increasingly pressing concern.[26]

---

[22] *Diario Financiero*, Sept. 9, 2011.

[23] See Chapter 3.

[24] By late 2012, Piñera's approval rate recovered to only 30 percent; disapproval remained at 51 percent.

[25] *El Mercurio* Sept. 10, 2011, *Mostrador* Sept. 22, 2011.

[26] The finance minister resisted the corporate tax increase on the basis that it could undermine growth, particularly given the uncertain course of the international economy (interview, Executive Advisor-C 2012). In this case, business's instrumental power via partisan linkages

After prolonged debate within the right and among the president's inner circle, Piñera proposed a bill to "perfect tax legislation and finance educational reform." This defensive initiative raised the corporate tax rate permanently to 20 percent and included measures to curtail income tax avoidance similar to those proposed by previous Concertación governments. These tax increases were partially offset by personal income tax cuts and a credit for educational expenditure, along with another stamp tax cut. Despite the latter measures, which appealed to business and the right, the bill would raise an estimated 0.4 percent of GDP, essentially all from direct taxes.[27] Negotiations with the UDI, which opposed several of the anti-avoidance measures, and the Concertación, which opposed top marginal income tax rate cuts, resulted in a compromise bill with a slightly lower anticipated direct tax revenue yield of 0.34 percent of GDP. This figure was significantly less than the 1990 reform, which increased direct tax revenue by 1.3 percent of GDP. Nevertheless, Piñera's 2012 reform was Chile's largest tax increase in the subsequent two decades.

Business associations disliked the corporate tax increase but quickly accepted the proposal. Business understood that the initiative was a consequence of the student protests and perceived little room to resist (2012 interviews: CPC-E, D, Executive Advisor-C). A significant current within the business sector hoped the tax increase would mitigate societal demands and contribute to social peace (interview: SOFOFA-A 2012).[28] Those who disagreed nevertheless felt the best possible outcome was rapid approval of the government's initiative, given that publicly debated alternatives entailed far greater tax increases (interview: LyD-B 2012). A private-sector informant colorfully remarked: "Today we have a festival of tax proposals, and those in the gallery that are receiving the most attention are those designed to raise the most money" (confidential interview, 2012). The respected think tank CEP proposed direct tax reforms that would raise 1 percent of GDP, while the opposition-party proposal would raise more than 2 percent of GDP from radical income tax revisions that business adamantly opposed.[29] The government initiative raised much less revenue, did not increase the corporate tax above 20 percent – the benchmark set by the Concertación's goal for the 1990 reform, which remained the second-lowest in

---

arguably enhanced structural power by ensuring that the appointed finance minister held highly orthodox views regarding the effect of taxation on investment. However, the political considerations previously discussed in Section 9.2 led Piñera to override structural power concerns.

[27] The government's direct-tax revenue estimate exceeded this figure by 0.3 percent of GPD due to overestimates of two income tax avoidance measures (Jorratt 2012), one of which was removed given UDI opposition.

[28] *El Mercurio* Sept. 24, 2011.

[29] Comparación de Propuestas Tributarias, Cieplan, May 2012; Reforma Tributaria de la Oposición, April 2012.

the region – and entailed no major changes beyond what business had already accepted (as temporary measures) in 2010.

The La Polar scandal further contributed to business quiescence. One informant emphasized business concern with improving its severely tarnished public reputation (CPC-D 2012); another noted that the scandal made the tax reform very popular (SOFOFA-D 2012); in this context, resistance would be counterproductive. In addition, many businesspeople professed sympathy with the students' financial plight and recognized that some educational reform was necessary; they thus condoned the ends to which their tax dollars would be applied, even if they believed tax increases were unnecessary (2012 interviews: CPC-E, SNA-C, SOFOFA-A). Once again, extraordinary circumstances that legitimated increased spending tempered business resistance to taxation.

The student movement significantly changed tax politics in Chile, wresting business of its remarkable influence over agenda formulation. The door has been opened to the possibility of major direct tax increases. Despite the Piñera government's hope of precluding further reform initiatives, informants across the political spectrum anticipated that taxation would be a central campaign issue in 2013 (2012 interviews: Macaya, Silva, Lagos-Weber, Auth). These anticipations proved correct – tax reform featured prominently in former present Bachelet's campaign platform. Shortly after Bachelet's inauguration in 2014, she sent a sweeping progressive tax-reform package to Congress that proposed not only raising the corporate tax to 25 percent but also broadening the personal income tax base to include accrued profits, a major institutional change that would dramatically increase taxation of Chile's wealthiest citizens. Taxation has thus moved from the realm of business-interest politics to the realm of electoral politics, not only because issue salience increased (Culpepper 2011), but more importantly because popular mobilization, with the disruption it entailed, counterbalanced business power and altered business-right strategic calculations. Societal pressure for both increased spending and progressive taxation, along with the greatly debilitated position of the right parties in Congress following the 2014 elections, may initiate a period of significant equity-enhancing policy change beyond what Chile's instrumentally strong business sector would otherwise accept.[30]

---

[30] As this book entered production, Bachelet's far-reaching 175-page tax-reform bill, which included multiple measures that past Concertación governments considered but judged politically infeasible, was under debate in Congress. While the administration will likely compromise to make a battery of anti-evasion measures and extensive new powers for the tax agency more palatable to business, the right, and conservative-leaning government coalition members, the central features of the reform could be approved if the government's majority in both houses of Congress holds strong and civil society pressure continues. Despite persistent lobbying, business accepted the reform's revenue target of 3 percent of GPD and significant modifications to income taxation as inevitable given the new political configuration.

9.3 PARTISANSHIP AND TAX POLICY

Many authors have argued that partisanship matters for economic policymaking and redistribution in Latin America, notwithstanding the homogenizing and constraining forces of globalization and capital mobility (Murillo 2009, Hart 2009, Huber and Stephens 2012). This book concurs with that thesis; explaining divergent tax policy outcomes requires close attention to domestic politics, and political parties matter for policy preferences and for business power.

Yet the cases in this book display more continuity than might be expected in tax policy agendas across partisan divides, and not in the direction that globalization-capital mobility hypotheses would predict, in that governments ranging from the ideological left to the center-right all proposed direct tax increases to meet the diverse revenue needs they confronted. This broad-ranging interest in, or recourse to, direct taxes arose partly due to the simple fact that consumption taxes were already high whereas extremely concentrated income and profits were under-taxed. Of course, the extent to which governments promoted direct tax increases and the fate of these initiatives depended on business power, one aspect of which involves partisanship: right parties whose core constituencies are economic elites do not favor significant direct tax increases. However, electoral concerns and popular mobilization in rare cases can compel the right to raise direct taxes, as occurred under Piñera in Chile.

The notable exception to this wide-ranging consideration of progressive direct tax increases is Bolivia's MAS, which dismissed income taxation as a neoliberal policy instrument. Indeed, progressive direct taxes are entirely compatible with neoliberalism, despite the Washington Consensus's preference for effecting redistribution on the spending side of the fiscal equation (Appendix 1.1). As such, taxation was important (if difficult to increase, given business power) for Chile's economically orthodox left, which sought to work within a market-friendly framework. But taxation was less relevant for Bolivia's heterodox left, which pursued radical redistributive policies and transformative agendas transcending neoliberal confines. Moreover, Bolivian citizens directly and negatively associate income taxes with neoliberalism and the IMF (although ironically, the personal income tax was eliminated during structural adjustment). Accordingly, even without ample natural-resource revenue, MAS probably would not have considered implementing an income tax.

Furthermore, this and previous chapters question several of Hart's (2009) hypotheses about the effects of partisanship on tax policy. His observation that the left prefers progressive direct taxes to regressive consumption taxes is certainly correct to first order. But it does not follow that when the left holds power, it "deemphasizes VAT and sales tax revenue and redistributes the tax burden toward the progressive personal income tax" (Hart 2009: 16). None of the left governments examined in this book, whether economically orthodox or heterodox, sought to reduce the VAT or add significant exemptions – they preferred to retain that revenue to support spending and/or fiscal stability. And they had different views on progressive direct taxes as discussed above. In addition, case evidence contradicts the statement that "increasing the rate of tax collection, cutting the cost of tax collection, and stymieing tax evasion are all distinctly rightist goals in South America's neo-liberal era" (Hart 2009: 19). Left governments promoted major anti-evasion reforms, including Lagos's 2001 reform in Chile and Kirchner's 2003 reforms in Argentina. Even Bolivia's interventionist left made steps toward reducing evasion by reforming the transport tax regime in 2006.[31] Moreover, Chile's right frequently opposed anti-evasion reforms, precisely because they entailed increasing the tax burden on economic elites.

---

[31] Subsequent initiatives sought to curtail customs-tax evasion associated with smuggling (Aug. 11, 2010: "Nueva Ley de Aduanas," www.fmbolivia.net/noticia15019).

10

Conclusions

The classic concepts of business' structural (investment) power and instrumental (political) power are critical variables that merit greater attention in contemporary political economy. These two types of power correspond to conceptually distinct means of influence. Structural power is rooted in the profit-maximizing behavior of individual firms and capital owners, which can have consequential aggregate economic effects. If policymakers anticipate that a reform will provoke reduced investment or capital flight through the market incentives it creates, they may rule it out for fear of harming growth and employment. In contrast, instrumental power arises from capacity to undertake political actions like lobbying or various forms of collective action. Sources of instrumental power that make such actions more likely to succeed include relationships with policymakers – like partisan linkages or recruitment into government – that enhance access and create bias in favor of business and economic elites more broadly, and resources like cohesion that help them pressure policymakers more effectively. Both structural power and instrumental power are variables that acquire different values in different contexts and across different cases.

When economic elites possess multiple sources of power, policymakers will take their interests into account more often and more extensively. Multiple sources of power correspond to multiple channels through which influence can flow; if any given source of power fails to achieve results in a particular circumstance, another may succeed. Moreover, while structural power and instrumental power are conceptually distinct, they can be mutually reinforcing; each may be stronger in the presence of the other. For example, structural power can be instrumentally enhanced; lobbying from a position of strong instrumental power may augment policymakers' concerns over potential disinvestment. Conversely, when economic elites have strong structural power, policymakers may grant them additional sources of instrumental power such as recruitment into government in order to reduce the likelihood of disinvestment. However, a single type or strong source of power may be sufficient to preclude or block reforms that economic elites oppose. Institutionalized sources of instrumental power like partisan linkages are particularly effective; they provide more consistent influence than noninstitutionalized relationships like informal ties or recruitment. Influence arising from the latter sources tends to be much more contingent and depends on the institutional environment and characteristics of the policymakers in question.

The structural and instrumental power framework provides strong leverage for explaining how, when, and to what extent economic elites influence policy in market democracies, as demonstrated through this book's analysis of tax policymaking in Latin America. Initiatives to tax economic elites following structural adjustment encompassed substantial cross-national variation in scope and fate, and in several countries, initiatives varied over time and across tax policy areas. In Chile, economic elites had multiple, highly institutionalized sources of instrumental power, including cross-sectoral cohesion and partisan linkages to right parties with significant representation in Congress. Strong instrumental power made it difficult for center-left governments to increase taxes and dissuaded policymakers from venturing to propose reforms they felt were important – even when structural power was weak. In Argentina, economic elites tended to be much weaker, and governments accordingly had greater leeway to tax income and profits. Business was highly fragmented, and economic elites lacked strong ties to parties in Congress. However, some sectors did have instrumental and/or structural power during delimited periods – particularly finance in the 1990s – that helped them block reforms with sector-specific impact. Bolivia is an intermediate case; economic elites' instrumental power was stronger than in Argentina but weaker than in Chile during the studied period. In contrast to Chile, business was not able to keep objectionable reforms off the agenda, but business had greater capacity than in Argentina to defeat initiatives later in the policy process.

Business power is not the only factor that influenced tax policy. When satisfying economic elites conflicted with electoral prerogatives, policymakers occasionally opted to please voters instead, even if economic elites had strong sources of power. However, given that public opinion on tax measures affecting economic elites is often tenuous and voter control over politicians' policy decisions requires multiple cognitive steps that can often be easily obstructed, electoral politics rarely drove significant deviations from the preferences of strong economic elites. In contrast, when popular sectors mobilized on tax issues, their demands were far more consequential.[1] In several cases, especially in Bolivia and in Chile with the student movement's recent ascendance,

---

[1] These findings agree with Garay's (2014) analysis of social policy in Latin America. She argues that expansion of benefits occurs through two paths: electoral competition and social mobilization, but reform tends to be more significant in the latter case. In contrast to taxing elites, however, social policy is more likely to engage voters and social movements.

widespread and disruptive popular mobilization compelled policymakers to take the demands of nonelite actors into account. On some occasions, popular mobilization counterbalanced or even overwhelmed substantial business power, although on other occasions, popular demands unintentionally advanced elite interests. Nevertheless, in almost all of the cases examined in this book, analyzing business power is critical for understanding political dynamics and reform outcomes.[2]

Government reform strategies affected the fate of tax initiatives as well, although their explanatory role was secondary to business power. This book identified six strategies for taxing economic elites that act through one or both of two mechanisms. First, they may cultivate public support, which puts electoral pressure on politicians who might otherwise defend economic elites. Second, they may temper antagonism on the part of those economic elites who will bear the tax burden, making them more likely to accept reform rather than using their instrumental power to resist or responding by reducing investment. Most of the strategies are intimately related to reform design, yet many also require concerted framing efforts. In contexts of strong business power, as in Chile, these strategies made feasible tax increases that might otherwise have failed. However, consistent with the above comments on the limited impact of public opinion, mobilizing public support tended to facilitate at most modest tax increases, even on high-salience issues. Likewise, tempering elite antagonism required significant concessions that eroded the revenue-raising capacity of tax increases. In contexts of weak business power, reform strategies helped governments legislate more substantial tax increases. In Argentina, for example, legitimating appeals and selective compensation tended to be more effective than in Chile. In two cases, however – Argentina's 2008 export tax increase and Bolivia's 2003 income tax proposal – government strategic errors contributed to reform failure.

The instrumental and structural power framework offers many advantages for analyzing policymaking in unequal democracies. First, it accounts for multiple means and mechanisms through which economic elites influence policy and can thereby explain a greater range of cross-national and within-country variation in the extent to which economic elites can defend their core interests than theories which focus on a single source of power – whether money, economic importance, or technical expertise. Likewise, delineating multiple stages and arenas of policymaking allows for more comprehensive analysis of how and when economic elites exert influence. Second, the framework provides a basis for systematically assessing elites' bargaining power with respect to state authorities, independently of policy outcomes. This approach helps avoid pitfalls of post hoc assessment that sometimes arise in fiscal-bargaining literature and strengthens causal analysis. Identifying specific sources of power – a credible threat of reduced investment in the case of structural power,

---

[2] An exception is Argentina's 2008 income tax reform, driven exclusively by union demands.

and relationships with policymakers and resources in the case of instrumental power – is particularly important in this regard. Third, distinguishing between instrumental and structural power and elucidating mechanisms that connect specific sources of power to influence is critical for selecting appropriate strategies and identifying propitious opportunities for increasing tax capacity in highly unequal societies, which is critical for stable economic growth as well as welfare-state development and redistribution.

It bears emphasizing that while this book focuses on taxation in Latin America, nothing in the instrumental and structural power framework is specific to either the policy area or the region. Prior research has investigated aspects of business power in relation to economic policy in Indonesia (Winters 1996), welfare-state development in the United States (Hacker and Pierson 2002), and international environmental regulation (Falkner 2009); business power is also emerging as a central concern in contemporary research on financial regulation and bank bailouts in developed democracies (Suarez and Kolodny 2011, Woll 2014, Culpepper and Reinke forthcoming). The theoretical clarifications and extensions elaborated in this book, especially with regard to operationalizing structural and instrumental power and analyzing the ways in which they aggregate and reinforce one another, could thus prove valuable for analyzing a wide range of political economy issues.[3] Policy areas that strongly affect core interests of business and economic elites are particularly appropriate for applying this framework. Analyzing instrumental and structural power is less likely to provide analytical traction, however, in countries where the state still dominates economic activity and the private sector remains small.[4]

10.1 BUSINESS POWER AND INFLUENCE

Several general insights on business power and influence emerge from this study of tax policymaking. In particular, the foregoing chapters highlight the importance of examining agenda formulation. As the case of corporate taxation in Chile illustrates, business influence over the reform agenda can be much more important than influence during subsequent stages of policymaking. Focusing on more visible aspects of business power, including lobbying after bills have been drafted, without ascertaining policymakers' actual preferences and the considerations that motivated them to propose or rule out particular reforms, may lead scholars to underestimate business influence. In the Chilean case, for example, overlooking agenda formulation could lead to the incorrect conclusion that marginal tax reform reflected minor compromise between government and

---

[3] Contemporary financial-sector literature could benefit from more systematically assessing the relative roles of banks' instrumental and structural power in shaping regulatory reforms and bailout design, as well as clearly specifying the arenas and stages of policymaking in which business influence operated.

[4] See Handley (2008) and Arriola (2013) on business in Africa.

business within the parameters of a strong consensus on appropriate policies, rather than significant business influence on an issue characterized by substantial latent conflict between these actors. While other authors have made similar points on the importance of agenda formulation,[5] contemporary scholarship would benefit from greater attention to how the scope of policies under debate is delineated and how policymakers decide which reforms to pursue.[6] Since policies deemed politically infeasible may not be publicly discussed, studying agenda formulation is not an easy task. However, interviews with policymakers and other actors involved in reform politics can provide valuable evidence for analyzing this critical stage of policymaking.

Further, I find that instrumental power can be as, or more significant than structural power for setting the agenda, an important possibility that most authors do not consider. Instrumental power does not come into play only after the executive has delineated the core features of a reform. Just as policymakers may rule out reforms because they anticipate reduced investment, they may also rule out reforms because they anticipate political resistance from business and business allies. The role that instrumental power can play in agenda setting has not been sufficiently appreciated partly because of a tendency to focus on observable actions (e.g., lobbying) instead of anticipated reactions, or even to equate instrumental power with observable actions. Distinguishing between actions and sources of instrumental power is a critical step for resolving this imbalanced perspective. Even if they are not actively deployed, economic elites' sources of power may deter policymakers from initiating reforms that run counter to elite interests. This scenario is most relevant in stable political systems where business has strong, institutionalized sources of instrumental power, as in Chile, such that it is easy for policymakers to anticipate reactions and assess the likely outcome of political conflicts that reform initiatives will stimulate. When elites' sources of instrumental power are less institutionalized, or when the political system is undergoing significant changes, greater uncertainty will prevail regarding anticipated outcomes. In these situations, policymakers may be more inclined to attempt legislating their preferred policies. Likewise, policymakers may be more likely to propose reforms that powerful economic elites oppose if popular-sector supporters are highly mobilized and capable of counterbalancing business power.

---

[5] Bachrach and Baratz 1970, Lukes 1974, Gaventa 1980, Korpi 1985, Hacker and Pierson 2002.

[6] This point applies even to innovative recent research on business lobbying and influence (Baumgartner et al. 2009). In examining the congressional agenda, they emphasize interest groups' goals and overt lobbying over policymakers' preferences and anticipations regarding interest-group reactions. This aspect of their research design could partly account for their surprising finding that business power in Washington is limited, although they do note that the wealthy tend to set the lobbying agenda even if they do not always achieve their goals (Baumgartner et al. 2009: 237, 257). Further, their study is not designed to systematically detect differences between interest groups' (or policymakers') ideal policy positions and those they publicly advocate given strategic considerations.

However, decisions will depend on policymakers' levels of risk aversion and the anticipated costs of political conflict and/or potential defeat. A related but distinct point regarding instrumental power also merits emphasis: while structural power clearly imposes limits on the extent to which market democracies can tax business and economic elites, instrumental power may prove even more constraining, keeping taxes well below any level that might begin to suppress investment.

Regarding the nature of structural power, this study emphasizes several important characteristics that are not always appreciated. First, business's structural power cannot be reduced to a sector's economic importance. Instead, structural power varies across distinct policy areas and reform initiatives. Some reforms create clear incentives to withhold or relocate investment; others do not, even if they affect the same sector or type of investors. Chapters 6 and 7 illustrated these points with regard to finance and agriculture in Argentina. Second, while capital mobility can be a key component of structural power, it does not ensure a credible disinvestment threat. Operationalizing structural power as capital mobility for large-N analysis, which is common in literature on taxation and globalization, can therefore be problematic. Important cases where structural power was weak despite high mobility include corporate taxation during substantial time periods in Chile and Argentina, and tax-agency access to bank information in Chile and post-2001 Argentina. Economic agents will relocate investment or shift into other types of production only if a reform significantly reduces profits relative to alternative options. Favorable policies in other areas may offset the costs of higher taxation; alternatively, high commodity prices may sustain profitability despite heavy taxation. Many other contextual factors can affect how investors respond to reforms. The difficulty of expanding tax-agency access to bank information in Argentina during the 1990s (Chapter 6) provides an excellent example of how country-specific factors shape structural power: the widespread fear that reform would trigger flight from the banks can only be understood in light of Argentina's historical experience of financial-sector instability and its proximity to a country with strict banking secrecy rules. Third, structural power ultimately depends on policymakers' perceptions regarding anticipated consequences of reform; technical experts often disagree about how private-sector agents will respond and what the aggregate economic effects will be. Likewise, structural power with respect to a previously enacted reform, and hence prospects for modifying or rescinding it, depend on policymakers' perceptions regarding that reforms' actual impact on investment. Even where disinvestment does occur, policymakers may disagree over how a particular reform contributed and what should be done to redress the situation.

In sum, structural power is a highly context-specific variable. Broad shifts over the past several decades in the relative weight of the state versus the private sector in economic activity and in the degree of global capital mobility have set the scene for structural power to play a more significant role in policymaking in Latin America and beyond, yet even in the neoliberal era, structural power it is not the monolithic force described in early business politics literature.

10.2 BUSINESS POLITICS AND THE "PUBLIC GOOD"

Prominent research views strong business organization and institutionalized government-business consultation as facilitating socially desirable outcomes, including good economic governance and transparency (Schneider 2004a, Handley 2008), strong direct-tax capacity (Lieberman 2003, Slater 2010), and equity more broadly (Weyland 1997, Martin and Swank 2012, Iversen and Soskice 2009). Authors argue that strong organization lengthens business's time horizons, shapes preferences in favor of social insurance policies, resolves collective-action problems that otherwise hinder state-building and provision of public goods, and facilitates cross-class bargains. Likewise, institutionalized government-business consultation is a key component of coordinated market economies, which produce greater equity than liberal market economies (Hall and Soskice 2001, Iversen and Soskice 2009). In developing countries, strong business associations may limit arbitrary state power, thereby promoting democracy (Schneider 2004a: 2467, Moore 2004: 312), and where business-government consultation is institutionalized, rent-seeking and corruption may be less pervasive (Arce 2005: 44, Schneider 2010, Handley 2008).

While not denying the possibility of these dynamics, this book emphasizes less salutary causal effects that can be associated with these factors. Strong business organization and institutionalized government-business consulta-tion – particularly where labor is weak or excluded from corporatist arrange-ments – may impede reforms that are crucial for equitable development and privilege business interests to the detriment of the quality of democracy, par-ticularly regarding dimensions of participation and representation (O'Donnell 2004, Diamond and Morlino 2004). Organization (a key component of cohe-sion) and institutionalized consultation are sources of power that enhance eco-nomic elites' ability to block redistributive reforms. In Chile, strong business organization and government-business concertation helped keep revenue-rais-ing, equity-enhancing tax reforms off the center-left's agenda for nearly twenty years. The critical issue of taxation – ironically a key policy area analyzed in formal models of democracy and inequality (Meltzer and Richard 1981, Boix 2003, Acemoglu and Robinson 2006) – was thereby largely removed from the realm of public debate. Limited tax revenue in turn constrained initiatives to expand redistributive social spending. In this context, popular frustration with democracy became widespread,[7] despite Chile's stellar record of growth and macroeconomic stability to which institutionalized government-business

---

[7] In 2008 Chile scored lowest among eighteen Latin American countries on the Latinobarómetro's index of political participation, and Chile had the highest percentage of citizens (27 percent) who viewed voting or protesting as ineffective for effecting change (Boas 2009). Recent scholarship

consultation arguably contributed (Schneider 2004a). While business has assumed a more flexible position regarding the Bachelet administration's far-reaching 2014 tax reform initiative, this change was largely driven by the ascent of the student movement, whose capacity for disruptive protest and demands for redistributive reforms altered business's strategic calculations.[8]

Strong peak associations also helped business fight redistributive policies in Bolivia. Beyond their successful resistance to income and wealth taxes, business associations played a leading role in the Santa Cruz-based "conservative autonomy movement," which sought to shield economic elites from President Morales's redistributive policies, particularly land reform (Eaton 2011, 2014). Among other concessions, economic elites secured grandfathered exemptions from limits on the admissible size of landholdings legislated by the national government. While it could be argued that Bolivia's business associations served the beneficial role of checking the authority of a government prone to circumventing established political institutions, land concentration is a longstanding problem that jeopardizes social peace and equitable development in Bolivia. Similarly, Guatemala's strong business peak association has long thwarted tax increases that are essential for promoting stable, inclusive development (Dosal 1995, Fuentes and Cabrera 2006, Sanchez 2009, Schneider 2012); popular sectors by contrast remain too fragmented and unorganized to participate meaningfully in politics (Schneider 2012).

To be sure, elite fragmentation does not guarantee that states will be able to build redistributive capacity and act autonomously of business interests.[9] Other sources of power beyond cohesion and government-business consultation must also be taken into account. This and related points are developed further in the next section with regard to the tax side of the redistributive equation. The point I wish to make here is simply that cohesion and institutionalized consultation are sources of power that can help elites defend their interests in ways that may not contribute to the broader public good, particularly in highly unequal societies.

10.3 ELITE COHESION AND TAXATION

A closer look at arguments linking elite cohesion to stronger and more progressive tax capacity clarifies how and why this book's perspective diverges from prior literature. Weyland (1997) and Lieberman (2003), among others

also highlights the Chilean party system's weak legitimacy and weak roots within society (Luna and Altman 2011).

[8] Weakened instrumental power given the right parties' significant loss of representation in Congress further motivated business's strategic acquiescence to redistribution.

[9] In Argentina and Brazil, for example, the fragmented private sector pays high taxes, but businesses also enjoy particularistic subsidies, protections, and rents. Assessing the state's overall redistributive capacity of course requires examining the net effect of both taxation and spending. I thank Ben Schneider for highlighting this point.

(Slater 2010), view direct taxation as a collective-action problem that can be resolved when elites are cohesive.[10] Drawing on Olson, Weyland (1997) argues that fragmentation discourages business from coordinating around shared, long-term interests in fiscal stability. In contrast, encompassing associations facilitate tax increases by helping business transcend narrow, short-term interests, streamlining bargaining, and making agreements enforceable, as argued in literature on corporatism (Schmitter and Lehmbruch 1979, Hall and Soskice 2001). Likewise, Lieberman (2003) argues that when elites are divided, each subgroup opposes taxation, perceiving that the benefits will accrue to others at its own expense. When elites share a common identity that promotes class cohesion, it is easier for governments "to provide bargains and credible commitments that will actually appeal to those upper-group interests," and prospects for cross-class bargains are improved (Lieberman 2003: 16).

The taxation as collective-action problem perspective rests on two assumptions. First, elites must perceive that they will benefit from the manner in which their tax dollars are spent. Second, they must agree that tax increases are critical for providing the desired collective benefits. When these conditions hold, classic free-riding problems may ensue where economic elites would like collective goods, but individuals or subgroups have incentives to avoid paying their due share. However, governments do not always use tax revenue in ways that benefit economic elites; redistributive spending is a key example.[11] Elites may sometimes perceive redistribution as in their longer-term interest, but cohesion alone is not a good predictor of elite reactions. Lieberman (2003: 17) himself notes that elite responses to tax initiatives will depend on "the objective circumstances in front of them." While a sense of common identity may certainly play a role in shaping elite reactions to taxation, I find that the details of the reform in question, its associated costs and benefits, and circumstantial factors that affect elites' strategic calculations play a more important explanatory role than their degree of cohesion. Further, economic elites do not always perceive taxation as necessary for providing desired benefits; they often argue that revenue can be obtained in other ways, including greater efficiency, reallocating resources, privatizing state assets, or borrowing. In such cases, elite resistance to taxation cannot necessarily be characterized as a free-rider problem or as an effort to shift the burden onto other societal groups. The scope of cases in which direct taxation can be treated as a collective-action problem is therefore limited.

Conceptualizing cohesion as a source of instrumental power accommodates a broader range of cases. Economic elites may decide to accept tax increases under certain circumstances; for example, when revenue will be used in ways

---

[10] For more general collective-action treatments, see Levi (1988), Bates (1989), Cheibub (1998), and Bergman (2009).

[11] Kurtz (2009), who emphasizes the importance of elite collective action for early state-building and taxation, also emphasizes the problem of guaranteeing that the benefits accrue to elites.

TABLE IO.I. *Elite Cohesion and Taxation*

	Lower Direct Taxation and/or Marginal Increases	Higher Direct Taxation and/or Substantial Increases
Cohesion	Chile 1991–2010 & Bolivia 2003–04 (this study) Guatemala & El Salvador, 1990s–2000s (Schneider 2012)	South Africa (Lieberman 2003) Chile 1990 (Weyland 1997) Colombia 2002–09 (Flores-Macías 2013) Guatemala 1930s (Schneider 2012)
Fragmentation	Brazil (Weyland 1996, 1997) (Lieberman 2003)	Argentina 1992–2008 (this study)

that promote elite interests, as emphasized in fiscal contract literature (Levi 1988) and recent research on Latin American state-building (Schneider 2012, Kurtz 2013), or when threats from below raise the perceived costs of recalcitrance (Acemoglu and Robinson 2006, Slater 2010). In these cases, cohesion may facilitate reform through the mechanisms discussed above. Yet cohesion does not necessarily predispose economic elites to accept higher taxation. And when they reject tax increases, cohesion strengthens their ability to block reform. Conversely, fragmentation does not necessarily hinder extractive initiatives. Even if fragmentation does predispose elites to reject tax increases as per the elite collective-action problem perspective, preferences alone cannot predict outcomes; elites must have sources of power with which to exert influence. In sum, we cannot predict whether economic elites will accept or reject tax increases or whether they will be able to influence policy outcomes by examining cohesion alone.

Table 10.1 illustrates that elite cohesion is neither necessary nor sufficient for building direct-tax capacity. The cases in the lower-left and upper-right quadrants are consistent with the argument that elite cohesion facilitates direct taxation. In the lower left, Brazil's regionally fragmented elites successfully resisted tax increases. In the upper-right cases, cohesive economic elites had incentives to accept tax increases. In South Africa, white elites accepted tax increases because the state served their interests; for example, direct taxation helped stabilize apartheid by financing eradication of white poverty and thereby undermining the potential for lower-class white solidarity with the excluded black majority (Lieberman 2003). Likewise, cohesive economic elites in Guatemala were willing to pay taxes in the 1930s to fund repression of mass uprisings that threatened their privileged status (Schneider 2012), and Colombia's cohesive economic elites accepted wealth taxes in the 2000s to finance counterinsurgency in a context of guerilla violence that threatened business interests (Flores-Macías 2013). And as discussed in Chapter 3, business in Chile accepted a corporate tax increase in 1990 given strategic calculations that the social spending it would finance would legitimize and thereby help consolidate neoliberalism (Boylan 1996, Weyland 1997).[12]

However, this book calls attention to cases in which fragmented elites were powerless to prevent direct tax increases, as in Argentina, and cases in which cohesive elites rejected and successfully prevented direct tax increases, as in Chile after 1990 and Bolivia in the mid-2000s. In Chile during the two decades following democratization, business had limited incentives to support redistributive spending in a context of remarkable political stability and popular demobilization. And in Bolivia, economic elites failed to view direct tax increases as in their interest, despite a context of tremendous social unrest. Likewise, Guatemala's strong cross-sectoral business association repeatedly blocked tax increases, while El Salvador's cohesive economic elites agreed to raise revenue primarily with indirect taxes, not progressive direct taxes (Schneider 2012). Understanding this diversity of outcomes requires examining the strategic considerations that shape how elites react to tax increases and analyzing all the sources of power that elites can draw on to influence policy decisions – including but not limited to cohesion.

Because Weyland and Lieberman do not examine cases in the upper-left and lower-right quadrants of Table 10.1, they do not identify cohesion as a source of power that can facilitate elite collective action against tax increases. Further, factors beyond elite fragmentation play a key role in precluding direct tax increases in Weyland's (1996) analysis of Brazil. First, his process-tracing narrative suggests that informal ties to decision makers – a source of instrumental power – helped business groups defeat initiatives to eliminate particularistic tax benefits and exemptions. Weyland (1996: 51, 59, 184–85) maintains that in Brazil, fragmentation created incentives for business to "penetrate the state apparatus" (i.e., to develop informal ties to state officials), and, accordingly, he tends to subsume the causal effects of informal ties under the consequences of business fragmentation. Yet business fragmentation does not always coincide with strong informal ties. Argentina is a case in point. During the period analyzed in this book, some sectors did have informal ties to executive authorities, yet others did not.

Second, fragmentation of state authority contributed significantly to the failure of progressive tax reform initiatives in Brazil: "Competing state agencies have often blocked reform measures in conflicts within the executive branch, subverted them by lobbying in congress, or corroded their implementation by wrangling over bureaucratic turf" (Weyland 1996: 59). In this context, Weyland identifies a dynamic whereby fragmented business interests conquered

---

[12] Chile's cohesive elites had incentives of distinct types to accept tax increases (of lesser magnitude) in 2010 and 2012 (Chapter 9).

a divided executive branch by seeking protection from captured agencies and exploiting bureaucratic rivalries. Weyland (1996) argues that business fragmentation contributed to fragmented state authority in Brazil. But just as business fragmentation may not coincide with informal ties to state officials, it need not imply that state authority is fragmented. Where business is fragmented but state authority on economic policy is concentrated within a single ministry, as in Argentina during the period studied in this book, a different dynamic may arise, in which a cohesive executive branch conquers divided business interests (Chapter 5, 7).

10.4 THE POLITICS OF POLICIES

The idea that different policies give rise to different politics is well established in political science, dating back to the classic works of Lowi (1964) and Wilson (1980). Market reform literature and recent work on business politics also stress that political dynamics vary across distinct policy arenas. However, in accord with policy feedback research, this book illustrates that the politics of policy change are even more variable than these literatures anticipate.[13]

Several typologies classifying the politics of policy change make specific predictions about tax politics. Taxation tends to be characterized by immediate, certain, and concentrated costs – especially when tax increases target economic elites. These characteristics set taxation apart from other policy areas like trade or capital account liberalization, where costs may be less concentrated and/or distributional effects may be difficult to discern (Schneider 2004b, Brooks and Kurtz 2007). Accordingly, taxing elites usually falls within the concentrated costs and diffuse benefits quadrant of Wilson's (1980) typology, which gives rise to "entrepreneurial politics" – politicians attempt to counter special interests by mobilizing public support that might not otherwise become manifest. Drawing on Wilson's work, Arce (2005) argues that tax reform stimulates business collective action, resulting in dilution of reform initiatives. Meanwhile, Schneider (2004b) identifies four types of reform coalitions showcasing different actors – electoral (voters), legislative (parties), distributive (organized interests), and policy (individuals in public and private sectors) coalitions – and posits that different reforms engage different coalitions. He theorizes that policies imposing clear costs on small groups – like taxation – involve primarily distributive and policy coalitions.

Yet even within the seemingly narrow policy domain of taxing economic elites, politics depend significantly on the details of which groups are affected, what sources of power they possess, and how governments endeavor to tax

---

[13] Murillo (2009) also finds significant variation within a specific policy arena: public utilities privatization and regulation. Brooks and Kurtz (2007) note variation within policy areas arising from domestic institutional and economic contexts but emphasize differences across policy areas.

them. Wilson's "entrepreneurial" politics may be relevant, yet mobilizing popular support is not the only possible approach – policymakers may also temper elite antagonism – and political dynamics depend on the particular mix of strategies employed as well as the underlying reform design.[14] Arce's (2005) framework, meanwhile, neglects variation in business's capacity for collective action; elites may not have sources of power with which to effectively resist policies they oppose. Regarding coalitional dynamics, although negotiating with economic interest groups (managing distributive coalitions) was critical in most of the cases examined in this book as Schneider (2004b) anticipates, engaging with parties (managing legislative coalitions) and voters (building electoral-coalitions) was also imperative.[15]

Culpepper's (2011: 180–85) political-salience/institutional-formality typology also makes concrete predictions about tax politics. He places taxation within the high-salience, formal-rules domain, where partisan representation in congress and public opinion determine reform outcomes. In contrast, the low-salience, formal-rules domain engenders "bureaucratic network negotiation," where politicians delegate authority to bureaucracies and expertise becomes the key source of business power. However, this book's cases do not conform to the typology. As predicted, political parties were often central tax policy actors. Yet business influence depended not just on how allied political parties reacted to reform, but also on other sources of power including cohesion, recruitment into government, and credible disinvestment threats. Furthermore, public opinion mattered only at the margins when business power was strong, even for manifestly high-salience reforms. Standard media-coverage indicators may be problematic for scoring the salience of tax increases,[16] but in one of the few patently high-salience reforms examined in this book – Chile's mining royalty (Chapter 4) – right parties defended economic elites' interests to a remarkable extent despite strong public opinion in favor of reform.[17] This book's least salient tax issue – tax-agency access to bank information in Argentina (Chapter 6) – evidences some aspects of "bureaucratic network negotiation";

---

[14] For example, legitimating appeals may exacerbate elite antagonism and stimulate overt political conflict, whereas compensation behind closed doors may mitigate business resistance.

[15] Schneider recognizes that his four coalition types are interconnected and calls for more analysis of the ways in which they interact.

[16] Culpepper (2011), Murillo (2009), and others use this approach. For tax reforms, however, establishing salience without opinion-poll data – which were rarely available in my cases – is difficult. Even if media coverage is heavy, average citizens may not understand, pay attention to, or have well-defined views on tax reforms that primarily affect economic elites (Bartels 2008, Graetz and Shapiro 2005). Politicians interviewed in Chile, where tax issues received extensive media coverage, often felt (nonelite) voters in their districts had little interest in tax reforms (interviews: 2005: UDI-A, Kuschel, Prat; 2006: Vierra-Gallo, Sabag, Silva; Garcia 2007; Macaya 2012).

[17] For the other patently high-salience tax issue – Bolivia's hydrocarbons reform – what mattered most was not public opinion but destabilizing popular mobilization.

tax-agency bureaucrats were central actors, and technical expertise was arguably relevant for business power in the 1990s. However, recruitment into government, informal ties, and a credible disinvestment threat contributed more significantly to nonreform.[18]

This book's finding of broad variation in the politics surrounding efforts to tax economic elites agrees with Pierson's (1993: 625) expectation that politics cannot be neatly categorized across aggregate policy types. Instead, a specific policy may stimulate multiple political responses that depend on the details of its design as well as manifold context-specific variables. Among other cases, Bolivia's income and wealth tax initiatives (Chapter 8) and Argentina's export tax increases (Chapter 7) illustrate these points. In the two Bolivian cases, reform design played a critical role in determining the intensity of opposition from economic elites and in activating or precluding opposition from mobilized popular sectors. Likewise, the novel design of Argentina's 2008 export tax increase helped spark producer protests, whereas previous increases were not effectively contested. Meanwhile, contextual factors in the form of accumulated grievances involving other policy areas contributed to conflict in the cases of Bolivia's income tax and Argentina's 2008 export tax increase.

These findings suggest that research on tax capacity would benefit from disaggregating taxation more extensively and conducting more comparative case studies, rather than focusing on aggregate revenue data or reform indices and relying on large-N analysis. Many authors distinguish among different types of taxes: easy versus hard to collect (e.g., Melo 2007), more versus less "earned" in terms of organizational effort and engagement with citizens (Moore 1998), or "taxes on capital" (corporate tax and employer social security contributions) versus "taxes on labor" (consumption, social security, and individual income taxes) (e.g., Wibbels and Arce 2003). These authors develop interesting hypotheses, yet their categories nevertheless lump together taxes that can generate very different political dynamics. For example, individual income taxes and consumption taxes not only affect different groups of taxpayers but also tend to stimulate distinct responses from business.[19] And administrative challenges of collecting taxes need not correlate with political challenges of legislating taxes. Taxes that are easy to collect can be difficult to legislate (Chile's copper royalty) or easy to legislate (Argentina's export taxes, 2002–08); taxes viewed as harder to collect may also be easy to legislate (Argentina's wealth tax) or difficult to legislate (Bolivia's wealth tax), depending on the power of economic elites and the factors that shape their strategic calculations.

---

[18] Culpepper (2011: 182) anticipates that interest groups will develop relationships with bureaucrats in this policy quadrant, but he does not treat informal ties or recruitment as sources of power distinct from technical expertise.

[19] Hart (2009) disaggregates taxes more extensively, but the large-N approach still misses broad within-category variation in political dynamics.

10.5 ON POLITICS AND EXPLANATION

Stepping back, the observation that politics is the art of the possible is particularly salient for taxing economic elites. This book has argued that what is possible in politics is contextual, contingent, and conditional. Social scientists do not always embrace this view; many might prefer parsimonious arguments and far-reaching generalizations. Yet there is no single explanation for policy dynamics and outcomes. Consider physics as an analogy: even in this hard science, a grand unified theory remains elusive after decades of search. If the behavior of something as elemental as an electron is ineluctably complex, it should not be surprising that the same is true of political interactions and policymaking processes. Economic elites have distinct power-resource profiles in different times and places, and the types and sources of their power, as well as the details of their strategic interactions with policymakers and other societal actors, matter for taxation and redistribution.

We can however systematize this political complexity within an explanatory framework that identifies these different types and sources of power and elaborates how and when economic elites will be more likely to shape policy outcomes. Economic elites may have multiple mechanisms for exerting influence in market democracies, and examining each of these mechanisms and causal pathways is important for explanation, even though the ultimate impact on policy outcomes can be similar across different cases. Moreover, while focusing on a single source of power may explain elite influence in multiple cases, there will inevitably be other cases in which that source of power provides at most an incomplete explanation. Physics shows that there are many different kinds of forces with different characteristics. While it is the aggregation of these forces that ultimately matters for particle trajectories, identifying, classifying, and understanding the distinct forces and their relative importance in different contexts is a crucial part of the analysis. Likewise, understanding and assessing multiple sources of power is crucial for analyzing the influence economic elites exert on policy change.

Appendix 1.1

Latin America's Tax Problem

Many Latin American countries enacted extensive market-oriented tax reforms during structural adjustment, from the late 1970s through the early 1990s. These "first generation" reforms established the efficient but regressive value-added tax (VAT) – a sales tax collected from businesses but ultimately paid by consumers – as the main revenue-raising engine. In Chile, Argentina, and Bolivia, VAT revenue as a percent of GDP reached European levels, around 7 percent of GDP, by the mid-1990s (Table 1.1.1).

However, total taxation remained low, not only compared to developed democracies, but also controlling for level of development. There is a positive empirical relationship between per capita GDP and tax revenue as a percent of GDP; most Latin American countries fall well below the worldwide regression line (Figure 1.1.1). Latin America's tax revenue shortfall arises primarily from under-taxation of income and profits (Table 1.1.2). On average, direct tax revenue in the 1990s fell below predicted levels by 3.4 percent of GDP (Perry et al. 2006: 96). Direct tax revenue shortfalls in Chile and Argentina exceeded 5 percent of GDP; Bolivia's shortfall reached 3 percent of GDP. Most of the direct tax revenue shortfalls are associated with individual income taxes (Sabaini et al. 2012, Mahon 2012), although there is also room to increase corporate taxation. In contrast to direct taxes, Latin America's revenue from consumption taxes (VAT and other sales taxes) on average fell squarely on the predicted regression line.

Tax systems not only failed to meet growing revenue needs following first-generation reforms, they also tended to be regressive.[1] In contrast, taxation in most European countries contributes directly to redistribution (Barreix et al. 2006: 52). Latin America's tax-equity problem arises from overreliance on consumption taxes, which tend to be regressive – the poor pay more taxes in

---

[1] Gaggero and Sabaini (2002), Barreix et al. (2006: 51), Jorratt (2009), Jiménez et al. (2010).

TABLE 1.1.1. *Average Tax Revenue (% GDP), 1995–1999*

	EU-15[a]	Latin America[b]	Chile[c]	Argentina[d]	Bolivia[e]
Total w/ Social Security	41	16	17	17	14[b]
Total w/o Social Security	29	13[f]	16	13	12
VAT	7.2	4.9[g]	8.0	6.9	6.6
Direct Taxes	15	3.0	3.6	3.0	2.3
Individual	11	0.9	1.2	1.1	0.4
Corporate	3.1	2.0[h]	2.3	1.8	1.8

[a] ECTCU 2006
[b] Sabaini 2005, excluding Haiti
[c] SII, DIPRES
[d] DNIAF
[e] SIN, 1996–1999 average
[f] 1995–2004 averages
[g] Includes other consumption taxes
[h] 2002 value

TABLE 1.1.2. *Differences between Actual and Predicted Tax Revenue (% GDP)[a]*

	Chile	Argentina	Bolivia	Latin America Median
Total[b]	−3.6	−12.3	−3.6	−4.0
Consumption Taxes	+2.9	−3.4	+1.5	−0.6
Direct Taxes	−6.4	−5.6	−3.0	−3.9
Individual	−4.0	−4.4	−1.5	−2.9
Corporate	−2.4	−1.2	−1.5	−1.0

[a] Based on average tax revenue, 1990s.
[b] Excluding social security taxes.
Source: Perry et al. 2006: 96.

proportion to their income than the rich because the poor spend a larger fraction of their income.[2] Direct taxes, in contrast, tend to be progressive. Personal income taxes place a much larger burden on the rich than on the poor because marginal tax rates generally increase with income brackets, and because thresholds exempt the vast majority of Latin American citizens, who have very little taxable income. Corporate taxes are less progressive than individual income taxes because the burden may be passed on to labor or consumers through wages and prices. However, capital owners are usually assumed to bear a substantial portion of the burden.[3] Piketty and Saez (2006: 33) emphasize that

[2] The VAT is less regressive in practice when the tax-evading informal sector contains primarily poor venders and consumers (Cossio 2006).
[3] Corporate tax incidence assumptions vary widely, from assigning the corporate tax entirely to capital owners, to dividing it equally among shareholders and labor income. Piketty and Saez

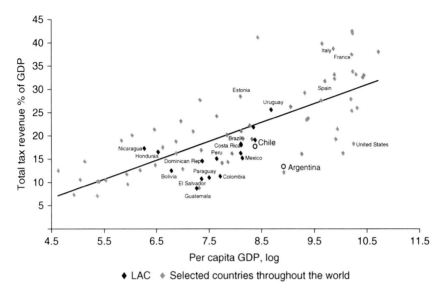

FIGURE 1.1.1. Average Tax Revenue, 1990s. Reprinted with permission from the World Bank: Perry, Guillermo, Omar Arias, Humberto López, William Maloney, and Luis Servén, *Poverty Reduction and Growth*, Washington, DC: World Bank, p. 95, copyright 2006. Circles superimpose tax-agency data for Chile and Argentina.
Sources: SII (2009), DNIAF (2012).

when capital income is very concentrated, the corporate tax "has a sizeable impact only in small groups at the top of the income distribution."

The international policy community in the 1980s and 1990s did not favor increasing direct taxes as a way to redress revenue shortfalls and inequality in developing countries. The prevailing view assumed that progressive direct taxation was administratively prohibitive, inherently inefficient, and irrelevant for redistribution. The standard prescription entailed raising revenue with the economically efficient VAT and redistributing through spending alone.

However, support is building for the alternative view that increasing direct taxation is imperative for development in Latin America (Perry et al. 2006, Barreix et al. 2006, IMF 2011: 40, Sabaini et al. 2012).[4] Three factors have contributed to this shift. First, tax administration improved dramatically in many countries that underwent structural adjustment. While taxing economic elites remains administratively challenging,[5] specialized large-taxpayer units, withholding regimes, third party reporting, and other innovations that curtail

(2006: 10) employ an intermediate approach: they impute the corporate tax to individuals in proportion to income from capital of all forms, including pensions.

[4] See also Woodrow Wilson Center conference report on Taxation and Equality in Latin America, May 24, 2011, www.wilsoncenter.org

[5] Tax havens present pending challenges.

TABLE 1.1.3. *Income Distribution, c.1999*

	Decile			
	1	2	9	10
Chile	1.2	2.3	15.5	45.1
Argentina	1.5	2.6	15.6	39.3
Bolivia	0.3	1.0	17.3	43.9
Latin America	1.0			43.2

Source: CEPAL: *Anuario Estadístico* 2006 (household surveys).

opportunities for evasion have made the task more feasible. My interviews with tax agency specialists indicate that taxing income and assets is less difficult than conventionally assumed for these reasons. In fact, VAT administration can be equally challenging in terms of informational demands and administrative capacity (Toye and Moore 1998).

Second, cutting-edge optimal-taxation research shows that progressive taxation does not necessarily incur large efficiency costs. Progressive taxation with high marginal rates can actually be optimal for raising revenue when income distributions are heavily skewed (Saez 2001).[6] Losses from evasion or avoidance can be curtailed by eliminating loopholes and exemptions that create inequities across different income types (Piketty et al. 2011: 8–9). The potential revenue yield of progressive income taxes in Latin America is significant, given extreme top income shares. According to household surveys, top deciles received on average 43 percent of national income in 1999 (Table 1.1.3). Moreover, income and profits are extremely concentrated within the top decile (Alvaredo 2010, Fairfield and Jorratt 2014).

Third, recent research shows that the redistributive impact of progressive direct taxation should not be ignored. Studies have found negative correlations between top income tax rates and top income shares in India, the United States, and France (Atkinson et al. 2010). In the United States, Saez (2004: 32) argues that tax cuts for the rich made possible a dramatic growth in top incomes since the 1970s. Further, Saez (2002: 3) finds that "progressive capital income taxation is much more effective than linear taxation to redistribute wealth." Likewise, Bird (2003: 40) observes that taxation is "one of the few ways in which the wealthy may be made less wealthy" in market economies. Focusing exclusively on targeted spending to the neglect of progressive direct taxation therefore unnecessarily curtails the redistributive potential of fiscal policy, which remains limited in Latin America (Goñi et al. 2011).

---

[6] Results depend on the shape of the top income distribution tail and earnings elasticities. See also Diamond (1998).

This book's focus on taxing economic elites contrasts with the welfare-state literature's emphasis on regressive consumption taxes (Steinmo 1993, Wilensky 2002, Kato 2003), which have been lauded as fiscally more lucrative and politically more feasible than progressive direct taxation. In light of this important literature, it is worth stressing that increasing direct taxation of economic elites is most relevant for countries with highly unequal income distributions and low income tax revenue, where "first-generation" tax reforms have already established broad-based value-added taxes. To emphasize this sequencing logic, I refer to initiatives that increase taxation of income, profits, wealth, and/or rents as "second-generation" tax reforms. Given Latin America's revenue shortfalls and extreme inequality, assessing the political feasibility of second-generation reforms and explaining variation in the extent to which such reforms have been enacted is of significant substantive importance, as well as theoretical interest.

It should be noted that the revenue data cited for Chile, Argentina, and Bolivia throughout this book come directly from tax-agency and Finance Ministry sources (SII, DNIAF, SIN). Data assembled by third parties including the IMF, OECD, and World Bank sometimes differ nontrivially. I judge tax-agency sources as more accurate, particularly since significant expertise is required to construct cross-nationally comparable revenue categories from these primary sources. The figures I report reflect in-depth consultation with tax-agency experts and generally coincide with those in CEPAL studies. For Argentina, I report taxes collected by the central state. Data from other sources may exclude revenue that is subsequently transferred to provinces according to revenue-sharing rules or may include revenue collected by all levels of government.

Appendix 1.2

Tax Revenue and Commodity Booms

Two of the countries in this study, Chile and Bolivia, have substantial mineral resources: copper and hydrocarbons respectively. Commodity booms in the 2000s exogenously increased direct tax revenue from privately owned resource sectors, as well as revenue generated from state-owned production. As rentier-state theories predict, these revenue influxes reduced government incentives to raise taxes. This book's primary concern is analyzing to what extent governments can increase taxation when revenue needs arise. Yet business power plays a key role in determining how much privately owned commodity sectors are taxed when revenue needs or social pressures put that issue on the agenda.

Before commodity booms reached full swing, Chile and Bolivia both legislated tax increases on their extractive sectors. Chile's reforms were modest, whereas Bolivia's were radical. Meanwhile, Argentina enacted significant tax increases on agro-exports; grains also experienced commodity booms in the 2000s. The empirical chapters argue that strong business power explains the modest nature of Chile's 2005 mining tax, whereas agricultural producers' remarkably weak power allowed Argentine governments to heavily tax agro-exports after 2001. Weaker business power in Bolivia compared to Chile facilitated the 2005 hydrocarbons royalty, but in this case, popular mobilization overwhelmed business power and led to radical reform.

Figure 1.2.1 shows combined direct tax and commodity tax revenue in the three countries. Argentina's direct tax and agro-export tax revenue exceeded Chile's direct tax and copper royalty revenue for all but one year in the series.[1] This comparison is partly motivated by the fact that experts consider

---

[1] The graph does not include revenue from Chile's publicly owned copper sector, which peaked at almost 6 percent of GDP in 2006. Most of this revenue is saved in a stabilization fund.

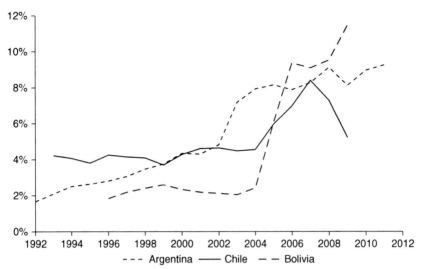

FIGURE 1.2.1. Direct Tax Plus Royalty or Export Tax Revenue (% GDP).
Sources: SII (2009); SIN (2006); DNIAF (2012).

Argentina's export taxes to be direct taxes on agricultural income (Cetrángolo and Sabaini 2009). Hydrocarbon royalty revenue pushed Bolivia's collections above the other two countries after 2006.

Figure 1.2.2 shows total tax revenue (2007–08) in relation to level of development. Argentina's revenue-raising progress is apparent: collections exceeded the worldwide regression line by 5.5 percent of GDP, whereas Chile remained 3.7 points below; on average Latin America fell 2.8 points below (Jiménez et al. 2010: 27). Examining central-state revenue only without social security contributions, Argentina falls below the regression line (lower solid circle), but the gap remains significantly smaller compared to Chile (open circle). Bolivia's tax revenue also exceeded expectations based on per capita GDP, thanks to hydrocarbons tax revenue.

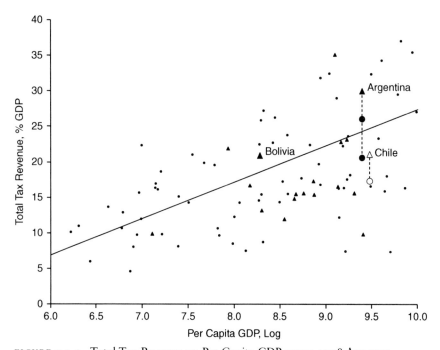

FIGURE 1.2.2. Total Tax Revenue vs. Per Capita GDP, 2007–2008 Averages.

Central government only including social security contributions, except for Argentina, Bolivia, Brazil, Chile, and Costa Rica (all levels of government); Triangles: Latin American countries.

Source: Database generously shared by Juan Pablo Jiménez, Juan Carlos Gómez Sabaini, and Andrea Podestá.

Large circles: central government collections 2007–2009; Argentina: with and without social security.

Sources: SII (2009); DNIAF (2012).

Appendix 1.3

Case Selection

Commonly cited case-selection strategies for qualitative research often prove infeasible in practice because they require information that is not available at the outset of research and/or cannot be obtained subsequently. Random sampling, advocated by Fearon and Latin (2008), requires full prior knowledge of the case population. Moreover, it may not be possible to gather adequate data for process tracing on the selected cases. Seawright and Gerring (2008: 295) elaborate a menu of purposive case-selection techniques for maximizing variation on key dimensions while maintaining representativeness within a broader population; however, their strategies also assume advance knowledge of the population, and they are relevant only "where data for key variables are available across a large sample." Such conditions did not apply for this study. Limited information on tax proposals was available outside the countries analyzed, and scoring key business power variables as well as evaluating the scope of tax proposals and concessions subsequently granted often involved extensive case analysis.

Therefore, in accord with the theory-building nature of my research, I employed a pragmatic, iterative approach to case identification and selection that proceeded in parallel with data gathering and analysis. This approach follows in the spirit of Glaser and Strauss' (1967) "theoretical sampling," which entails jointly collecting and analyzing data while developing and refining theory and concepts, which in turn shape subsequent decisions regarding data collection and case selection. Ragin (1997) describes a similar process, where the investigator compiles a preliminary list of comparable cases that is refined as concepts and theory evolve; the investigator continually assesses which cases will be most fruitful for theory building and/or testing and digs hard to uncover evidence on these cases if information is not readily available.

I define my case population to include (1) all major revenue-raising tax reform proposals, (2) proposals with lesser revenue capacity that would nevertheless increase the burden on economic elites, and (3) "nonreforms" where policymakers considered but decided against proposing initiatives to tax economic elites that they felt were important and appropriate. I identified all relevant proposals by reviewing legislative records and news coverage, and, most importantly, consulting with tax experts, policymakers, and business advisors in each country. I focused on proposals from the resultant lists that were most consistently identified by experts as major revenue-raising and/ or elite-targeted initiatives. I included additional cases that were precursors or subsequent amendments to these important reform proposals and/or that I later deemed analytically relevant for comparative purposes. I emphasized executive initiatives, which are much more consequential than congressional initiatives in the countries analyzed.

Identifying cases, gathering data on the surrounding policy processes, and selecting cases for closer analysis were ongoing aspects of research, in contrast to approaches that treat identifying the population and selecting cases as initial stages of fieldwork (Kapiszewski 2012).[1] While rigorous and systematic, Kapiszewski's (2012) methodology for triangulating among case lists produced from sources similar to those I employ would not have allowed enough flexibility for studying policymaking. First, key nonreforms, which are critical for analyzing agenda-formulation, came to light through interviews with high-level informants that were possible only after I established extensive contact networks during fieldwork. Second, policymaking is ongoing; newly generated cases present opportunities for testing and refining arguments developed from prior cases. Third, cases beyond those originally viewed as central may become relevant in light of new cases that emerge later in time. For example, I gathered information on agro-export tax policy during my core fieldwork in Argentina in 2006, but I did not view periodic export tax increases as key cases until the 2008 reform provoked protests (Chapter 7). This high-profile new case brought previous export tax increases into analytical focus by raising the question of why the 2008 reform failed whereas previous reforms were easily enacted. Finally, temporally new cases can reinforce the salience of previously identified theoretical categories. Piñera's 2012 tax reform in Chile (Chapter 9) provides a second instance of popular mobilization overwhelming business power, an analytical possibility I previously theorized based on Bolivia's 2005 hydrocarbons reform (Chapter 8). The Chilean example highlights that while empirically rare, this dynamic can be important for understanding critical moments of policy change.

Over the course of my research, I gathered data on a population of fifty-four proposed reforms – many of which were large tax reform packages – and six instances of nonreform. This book includes process tracing on multiple measures contained in twenty-six of these proposed reforms and all six nonreforms,

---

[1] Those strategies will be more appropriate for larger populations.

as well as two supplemental cases of tax cuts[2] that fall outside the defined population but illuminate aspects of my arguments. In some cases, I uncovered evidence directly substantiating my arguments, whereas in others, my inferences are necessarily more indirect given the less decisive nature of the evidence I was able to acquire. Following Bayesian prescriptions, I make the best inferences possible from available evidence whenever I deem the case analytically or substantively important.

The medium-N sample analyzed in this book displays substantial variation across multiple dimensions and variables of interest – an important goal for case selection. Regarding the type of tax instrument used to raise revenue from economic elites, the cases include direct taxes, indirect taxes, rate increases, base-broadening reforms, anti-evasion measures, and tax agency auditing powers. While I focus on direct taxes, including other types of taxes provides additional leverage for explaining the scope of the agenda, policymakers' choices, and the nature and extent of business influence. Regarding causal variables, the cases encompass all possible combinations of weak and strong scores on instrumental and structural power, as well as variation in the sources of instrumental power. Regarding procedural outcomes, I analyze proposals that were: considered but never initiated, initiated but withdrawn or rejected, initiated and enacted with modifications, and enacted without substantive changes.

To illustrate the relationship between the book's case sample and the broader population, I first define three case types based on their relationship to my theoretical framework. *Typical cases* illustrate my central argument that strong business power hinders taxation of economic elites beyond marginal reforms, whereas weak business power facilitates more significant tax increases. Most reform proposals in the population fall within this category (78 percent). *Extraordinary cases* entail situations where popular mobilization counterbalances business power, allowing significant tax increases despite otherwise strong business power. These cases are theorized within my explanatory framework, but they are empirically rare: the only instances across the three countries during the studied time period are Bolivia's 2005 hydrocarbons reform (Chapter 8) and Chile's 2012 corporate tax reform (Chapter 9). *Anomalous cases* diverge from first-order theoretical expectations because causal factors other than business power take precedence and/or circumstances lead actors to adopt unusual policy positions. Examples include Chile's 1990 reform (Chapter 3), where business accepted significant tax increases despite strong instrumental power, Argentina's 2008 agro-export tax strikes (Chapter 7), where a radical reform and government strategic errors provoked effective resistance from producers whose power was otherwise weak, and Bolivia's failed 2003 income tax (Chapter 8), where popular sectors acted as circumstantial elite allies. While anomalous, these cases do not contradict my

---

[2] Chile's 2007 accelerated depreciation initiative (Chapter 3) and Argentina's 2008 income tax cut (Chapter 5).

theoretical framework; a full explanation simply requires attention to unusual case-specific circumstances and contributing causal factors along with assessing business power. The relatively low frequency of extraordinary and anomalous cases within the population (13 percent) illustrates the broad causal leverage that analyzing business power provides.

Tables 1.3.1 and 1.3.2 illustrate that this book's purposive sample can be considered representative of types in the population – a second key objective of case selection – with "oversampling" of extraordinary and anomalous cases. The latter types allow refinement of theory and assessment of scope. Moreover, the anomalous cases mentioned above constituted major political events with important consequences for future policy decisions and thereby merit careful explanation on substantive grounds.

The twenty-eight proposed reforms that I do not extensively analyze in the book break down as follows. I lack sufficient information to reconstruct the policy process for seven proposals on which I gathered data. For an additional five reforms, I lack relevant evidence to inform or evaluate my arguments. In most of these twelve cases, proposal contents and outcomes appear consistent with my theoretical expectations. I excluded five typical cases after preliminary analysis, based on my judgment that intensive process tracing would not add significant new insights. I conducted more extensive process tracing on eleven additional typical tax increases (and two tax cuts) that do not feature centrally in the book for similar reasons – I deemed that they provided limited added value for illustrating and strengthening my causal arguments.

A few comments on my case types in relation to Seawright and Gerring's (2008) classifications are in order. My use of "typical" generally coincides with theirs; however, the cross-case relationship underlying this classification emerged only *after* extensive within-case analysis, not from identifying a regularity in a large-N dataset relative to a preexisting causal model. At first glance, my extraordinary cases and anomalous cases may appear similar to their "extreme" cases (a key variable assumes an unusual value relative to its distribution in the population) and "deviant" cases (outliers with respect to the cross-case relationship), respectively. However, there is no exact correspondence; several (but not all) of my atypical cases that are "extreme" with respect to popular mobilization are also "deviant" relative to the general relationship between business power and tax policy change (Table 1.3.3). In contrast to Seawright and Gerring's approach, my types are defined to illuminate distinct analytical dynamics within cases, not just variable scores. Moreover, my causal model embraces more complexity than the linear regression model Seawright and Gerring employ to define deviance. As such, the four "extreme" cases with popular mobilization sort into different types, depending on how this variable affects policy outcomes. Where popular mobilization counterbalances business power, these cases are extraordinary: rare but not theoretically surprising. Where popular mobilization instead furthers elite interests, these cases are anomalous (independently of

TABLE 1.3.1. *Population and Cases Analyzed*

	Population[a]	In-depth process tracing conducted:		
		Yes		No
		In book	Not in book	
Typical cases	47 (78.3%)	24	11	12
Extraordinary cases	2 (3.3%)	2		
Anomalous cases	6 (10.0%)	6		
Unclassified (insufficient information)	5 (8.3%)			5
Total	60 (100%)	32	11	17

[a] Reform proposals (may bundle multiple measures) and nonreforms (considered by executive but not initiated)

TABLE 1.3.2. *Population by Country and Case Type*

	Chile	Argentina	Bolivia	Total
Typical cases	20 (11)	24 (12)	3 (1)	47 (24)
Extraordinary cases	1 (1)	0	1 (1)	2 (2)
Anomalous cases	2 (2)	2 (2)	2 (2)	6 (6)
Unclassified (insufficient information)	0	1	4	5
Total	23 (14)	27 (14)	10 (4)	60 (32)

Note: Parentheses denote cases analyzed in this book.

whether outcomes are consistent with cross-case expectations based on business power scores); understanding these counterintuitive dynamics requires examining unusual contextual factors.

A final point merits mention: the number of analytical case studies in this book exceeds the number of reform proposals and nonreforms examined, because the unit of analysis may shift between a reform package that bundles together multiple tax initiatives, and subsets of those initiatives. When political dynamics and outcomes do not vary across a set of measures bundled into a single reform, I treat the aggregate reform as the unit of analysis. However, different measures within a larger reform package may not only provoke different reactions from political actors but also encounter distinct fates (e.g., some may be enacted while others may be rejected or withdrawn). A single reform package may therefore bifurcate into multiple units of analysis (see Chapter 8 on Bolivia's 2004 reform).[3] Further, I occasionally treat a single measure within

[3] These sub-units are not necessarily independent cases; features of the broader reform package may influence how actors respond to any given component.

TABLE 1.3.3. *Atypical Cases*

Type	Analytical Dynamic	Instances	N
Extraordinary	Popular mobilization counteracts business power[a]	Bolivia's 2005 hydrocarbons royalty[b] Chile's 2012 reform[b]	2
Anomalous	Business accepts substantial tax increases despite strong power	Chile's 1990 reform[b] Chile's 2010 reform[b]	3
	Radical reform design and strategic errors provoke effective contestation despite weak business power	Argentina's 1991 reform proposal[b] Argentina's 2008 export tax reform[b]	2
	Mobilized popular sectors act as circumstantial elite allies[a]	Bolivia's 2003 income tax initiative Argentina's 2008 income tax cut[c]	2

[a] Extreme cases (Seawright and Gerring 2008) regarding the value of popular mobilization (present as opposed to absent).
[b] Deviant cases (Seawright and Gerring 2008) relative to the general cross-case business power/tax policy change relationship.
[c] Case outside population but analyzed in book.

a reform package as a separate additional case to illuminate an aspect of my theory that is distinct from lessons drawn when analyzing the reform package as a whole. Consider Argentina's 1998 reform. The corporate tax increase, corporate assets tax, and tax on interest payments included in this reform together serve as a typical case of weak business power at the cross-sectoral level facilitating direct tax increases (Chapter 5). Yet the tax on interest, which engaged the powerful financial sector, also gives rise to a separate case study (Chapter 6) that demonstrates the role of government reform strategies in facilitating tax increases that might not otherwise be feasible.

Appendix 4.1

Chilean Case Universe

Tables 4.1.1 and 4.1.2 display revenue-raising and/or equity-enhancing tax reforms legislated in Chile between 1990 and 2010. The tables omit municipal-tax increases legislated by the national government.[1]

[1]   See Fairfield (2006).

TABLE 4.1.1. *Reform Strategies in Chile*

REFORM		TAX-SIDE STRATEGIES			BENEFIT-SIDE STRATEGIES	
		Attenuating Impact	Legitimating Appeals	Compensation	Emphasizing Fiscal Discipline	Linking to Social Spending or Popular Benefits[a]
AYLWIN	1990: CT, PIT & VAT increases	Temporary	Vertical equity	No direct tax increases for four years	Finances spending	Discourse: multiple social programs
	1993: Made 1990 CT increase permanent	NA	NA	Top PIT rate cuts; no direct tax increases for four years	Prevents fiscal deficit	NA
FREI	1995: Excise tax increases	NA	Vertical equity	NA	Finances spending	Contingent: pension increases
	1997: Made 1990 VAT increase permanent	NA	NA	NA	Finances spending	Inclusion: education reform (full school day)
	1998: Anti-evasion reform	Some measures temporary	Horizontal & vertical equity	Savings incentives	Finances spending	Contingent: pension increases

LAGOS	2001: Anti-evasion reform	Phased in	**Horizontal & vertical equity**	Sumptuary & capital gains tax cuts	Finances spending	Discourse: Lagos's program of government
	2001: CT increase	Phased in	Vertical equity	**Top PIT rate cuts**	Finances compensations	NA
	2003: VAT increase, excise taxes	**Temporary, phased in**	Vertical equity[b]	Tariff reductions (legislated separately)	Finances compensations & spending	**Discourse: health care, targeted social programs**
	2005: Mining tax	Phased in	**Nationalism**	Tax invariability clause	NA	NA
	2005: Eliminated 57 bis	NA	**Vertical equity**	NA	Finances spending	Inclusion: scholarships
BACHELET	2006: Made 2003 VAT increase permanent	NA	NA	NA	Finances spending	**Contingent: pension increases**
	2008: Restricted construction VAT benefit	Phased in	**Vertical equity**	**Contingent: gas & stamps tax cuts**	Finances compensations & popular benefits	**Contingent: gas tax cuts**

Note: Primary strategies in bold. CT: Corporate tax; PIT: Personal income tax; VAT: Value-added tax.

[a] See Chapter 2 on linking technique (discourse; inclusion in reform package; contingent on enacting tax measures).

[b] Although the VAT is regressive, the executive nevertheless advanced tax-side vertical equity appeals.

TABLE 4.1.2. *Expected Revenue Yield of Chilean Reforms*

Reform		% GDP
Aylwin	1990: CIT, PIT & VAT increases	~[2][a]
	1993: Made 1990 CIT increase permanent (& PIT cuts)	−0.2
Frei	1995: Excise tax increases	0.2
	1997: Made 1990 VAT increase permanent	No new revenue
	1998: Anti-Evasion Reform	< 0.14
Lagos	2001: Anti-Evasion Reform	0.9
	2001: CIT increase (& PIT cuts)	0
	2003: VAT increase	0.4
	2005: Mining tax	0.07 [0.5][b]
	2005: Eliminated 57 bis	0.02
Bachelet	2006: Made 2003 VAT increase permanent	No new revenue
	2008: Restricted home-construction VAT benefit (& stamp and gas tax cuts)	−0.04

Note: Square brackets denote actual, rather than expected, revenue yield.

Source: Author's calculations using Finance Ministry estimates provided to Congress.

[a] Marcel 1997.

[b] 2006 yield, given copper price increases.

Appendix 5.1

Expected Revenue Yield of Direct Tax Reforms

Tables 5.1.1 and 5.1.2 display expected-revenue estimates available while reforms were debated in Chile and Argentina. Where contemporary estimates could not be found but actual revenue yield could be identified, the latter appears in square brackets.[1]

Table 5.1.1 omits minimum taxable income and deduction increases to adjust Argentina's personal income tax for inflation from 2006 on; Chile's income tax is automatically inflation-adjusted. Various investment and industrial promotion incentives and other reforms with negligible or transitory revenue effects are also omitted. In addition to the measures listed, several important postcrisis "nonreforms" entailed significant revenue gains, including the government's decision not to allow an inflationary adjustment or an extension of carry-forward losses for the corporate tax, despite intense business lobbying (interview, Lavagna 2006). Sources for revenue estimates include news articles and government and congressional documents. Executive-branch estimates were selected whenever available.

Table 5.1.2 excludes tax cuts for small and medium-sized businesses, along with a few reforms with negligible revenue impact. Where reforms made previously legislated temporary tax increases permanent, I omit the associated revenue to avoid double-counting. Figures are my calculations based on Finance Ministry estimates reported to Congress.

[1] The tables exclude taxes on agroexports in Argentina and mining in Chile (see Appendix 1.2).

TABLE 5.1.1. *Expected Revenue Yield of Direct Tax Reforms in Argentina*

Reform			% GDP
Menem	1991	Wealth tax enacted	[0.05]
	1992	CT and PIT	1.75
	1995	Wealth tax	0.12
	1996	CT and PIT	0.35
	1998	CT and PIT	0.65
De la Rua	1999	PIT and wealth tax	0.55
	2000	Corporate interest tax phased out	−0.30
Duhalde	2002	Wealth tax	0.24
	2002	Anti-evasion	[0.06]
Kirchner	2003	Anti-evasion	0.34
Fernández de Kirchner	2007	PIT: Machinea's Table altered	−0.18
	2007	Wealth tax made more progressive	0
	2008	Wealth tax	0.04
	2008	PIT: Machinea's Table eliminated	−0.15
		Net sum	**3.5**

Note: CT: corporate tax; PIT: personal income tax.

TABLE 5.1.2. *Expected Revenue Yield of Direct Tax Reforms in Chile*

Reform			% GDP
Aylwin	1990	CT and PIT increases	[1.3]
	1993	PIT cuts	−0.2
Frei	1998	Anti-evasion	0.1
Lagos	2001	Anti-evasion	0.04
	2001	CT increase / PIT cuts	0
	2001	Capital gains	−0.03
	2005	Eliminated 57 bis	0.02
Bachelet	2008	CT investment credit	−0.02
	2008	CT investment credit	−0.01
		Net sum	**1.2**

Note: CT: corporate tax; PIT: personal income tax.

References

Acemoglu, Daron, and James Robinson. 2006. *Economic Origins of Dictatorship and Democracy*. New York: Cambridge University Press.

2008. "Persistence of Power, Elites, and Institutions." *American Economic Review* 948 (1): 267–93.

Acuña, Carlos. 1994. "Politics and Economics in the Argentina of the Nineties." In William Smith, Carlos Acuña, and Eduardo Gamarra, eds., *Democracy, Markets, and Structural Reform in Latin America*. Coral Gables: North-South Center Press, University of Miami.

1995. "The Industrial Bourgeoisie as a Political Actor: The Logic of Its Organization and Strategies in Argentina." Ph.D. dissertation, Department of Political Science, University of Chicago.

1998. "Political Struggle and Business Peak Associations." In Francisco Durand and Eduardo Silva, *Organized Business, Economic Change, and Democracy in Latin America*. Coral Gables: North-South Center Press, University of Miami.

Acuña, Carlos, and William Smith. 1994. "Political Economy of Structural Adjustment: The Logic of Support and Opposition to Neoliberal Reform." In William Smith, Carlos Acuña, and Eduardo Gamarra, eds., *Latin American Political Economy in the Age of Neoliberal Reform*. Coral Gables: North-South Center Press, University of Miami.

Administración Federal de Ingresos Públicos (AFIP). 2008. *Anuario Estadísticas Tributarias*. www.afip.gob.ar/estudios/anuario.asp

Adranaz, Martín, and Carlos Scartasini. 2011. "Why Don't We Tax The Rich?" IADB Working Paper 282.

Akard, Patrick J. 1992. "Corporate Mobilization and Political Power: The Transformation of U.S. Economic Policy in the 1970s." *American Sociological Review* 57, 5 (October): 597–615.

Alvaredo, Facundo. 2010. "The Rich in Argentina over the Twentieth Century." In A. B. Atkinson and T. Piketty, eds., *Top Incomes: A Global Perspective*. Oxford: Oxford University Press.

Ames, Barry, Miguel Carreras, and Cassilde Schwartz. 2012. "What's Next? Reflections on the Future of Latin American Political Science." In Deborah Yashar and Peter

Kingstone, eds., *Routledge Handbook of Latin American Politics*. New York: Routledge.

Angell, Alan, and Benny Pollack. 2000. "Chilean Presidential Elections of 1999–2000 and Democratic Consolidation." *Bulletin of Latin American Research* 19: 357–78.

Appel, Hilary. 2011. *Tax Politics in Eastern Europe*. Ann Arbor: University of Michigan Press.

Arce, Moisés. 2005. *Market Reform in Society*. University Park: Pennsylvania State University.

Arce, Moisés, and Roberta Rice. 2009. "Societal Protest in Post-Stabilization Bolivia." *Latin American Research Review* 44 (1): 88–101.

Arnold, R. Douglas. 1990. *The Logic of Congressional Action*. New Haven: Yale University Press.

Arellano, Javier. 2012. "Industrias Extractivas, Descentralización, y Desarrollo Local." Unpublished paper.

Arriola, Leonardo. 2013. *Multi-Ethnic Coalitions in Africa: Business Financing of Opposition Election Campaigns*. New York: Cambridge University Press.

Ascher, William. 1984. *Scheming for the Poor: The Politics of Redistribution in Latin America*. Cambridge, MA: Harvard University Press.

1989. "Risk, Politics, and Tax Reform: Lessons from Some Latin American Experiences." In Malcolm Gillis, ed., *Tax Reform in Developing Countries*. Durham: Duke University Press.

Asociación de Bancos de la Argentina (ABA). 2001a. "Percepción del Impuesto a las Transacciones Financieras." Buenos Aires, Argentina.

2001b. "Memoria Annual." www.aba-argentina.com

Atkinson, A. B., Tomas Piketty, and Emmanuel Saez. 2010. "Top Incomes in the Longrun of History." In A. B. Atkinson and T. Piketty, eds., *Top Incomes: A Global Perspective*. New York: Oxford University Press.

Auyero, Javier. 2000. "The Logic of Clientelism in Argentina: An Ethnographic Account." *Latin American Research Review* 35 (3): 55–81.

Bachrach, Peter, and Morton Baratz. 1970. *Power and Poverty*. New York: Oxford University Press.

Barnett, Michael, and Raymond Duvall. 2005. "Power in International Politics." *International Organization* 59: 39–75.

Barr, Robert. 2005. "Bolivia: Another Uncompleted Revolution." *Latin American Politics and Society* 47 (3): 69–90.

Barreix, Alberto, Jerónimo Roca and Luiz Villela, eds. 2006. *La Equidad Fiscal en los Países Andinos*. Washington, DC: DFID, IADB, CAN.

Bartell, Ernest. 1992. "Business Perceptions and the Transition to Democracy in Chile." Working Paper 184, Kellogg Institute, University of Notre Dame.

Bartels, Larry. 2008. *Unequal Democracy*. Princeton: Princeton University Press.

Basinger, Scott, and Mark Hallerberg. 2004. "Remodeling the Competition for Capital: How Domestic Politics Erases the Race to the Bottom." *American Political Science Review* 98 (2): 261–76.

Bates, Robert. 1989. "A Political Scientist Looks at Tax Reform." In Malcolm Gillis, ed., *Tax Reform in Developing Countries*. Durham: Duke University Press.

Bates, Robert, and Da-Hsiang Donald Lien. 1985. "A Note on Taxation, Development, and Representative Government." *Politics and Society* 14 (1): 53–70.

Baumgartner, Frank, Jeffrey Berry, Marie Hojnacki, David Kimball, and Beth Llech. 2009. *Lobbying and Policy Change*. Chicago: University of Chicago Press.

Becerra, Martín, and Guillermo Mastrini. 2009. *Los Dueños de la Palabra*. Buenos Aires: Prometeo.

Bell, Stephen. 2012. "The Power of Ideas: The Ideational Shaping of the Structural Power of Business," *International Studies Quarterly*, 56: 661–73.

Bell, Stephen, and Andrew Hindmoor. 2014. "The Structural Power of Business and the Power of Ideas: The Strange Case of the Australian Mining Tax," *New Political Economy* 19 (3): 470–86.

Bennett, Andrew. 2010. "Process Tracing and Causal Inference." In Henry Brady and David Collier, eds. *Rethinking Social Inquiry*. 2nd ed. Lanham: Rowman and Littlefield.

Bennett, Andrew, and Jeffrey Checkel, eds. 2014. *Process Tracing in the Social Sciences: From Metaphor to Analytic Tool*. New York: Cambridge University Press.

Bergman, Marcelo. 2009. *Tax Evasion and the Rule of Law in Latin America*. University Park: Pennsylvania State University Press.

Bird, Richard. 2003. "Taxation in Latin America." ITP Paper 0306, Rotman School of Management, University of Toronto.

Birney, Mayling, Ian Shapiro, and Michael Graetz. 2008. "The Political Uses of Public Opinion." In Ian Shapiro, Peter A. Swenson, and Daniela Donno, eds., *Divide and Deal*. New York: New York University Press.

Block, Fred. 1977. "The Ruling Class Does Not Rule." *Socialist Revolution* 33: 6–27.

Blyth, Marc. 2002. *Great Transformations*. New York: Cambridge University Press.

Boas, Taylor. 2009. "Varieties of Electioneering: Presidential Campaigns in Latin America." Doctoral dissertation, University of California, Berkeley.

   2013. "Mass Media and Politics in Latin America." In Jorge Domínguez and Michael Shifter, eds., *Constructing Democratic Governance in Latin America*, 4th ed. Baltimore: Johns Hopkins University Press.

Boeninger, Edgardo. 2005. "Economia Política de la Reforma de la Salud." In Hector Sanchez Rodriguez and Favier Labbé, eds., Reforma de Salud en Chile. Santiago, Chile: Duplika Ltda.

Boix, Carles. 2003. *Democracy and Redistribution*. New York: Cambridge University Press.

Bonvecchi, Alejandro. 2010. "The Political Economy of Fiscal Reform in Latin America." *IDB Working Paper* 175.

   2011. "Del Gobierno de la Emergencia al Capitalismo Selectivo." In Andrés Malamud and Miguel de Luca, eds., *La Política en Tiempos de los Kirchner*. Buenos Aires: Eudeba.

Boylan, Delia. 1996. "Taxation and Transition: The Politics of the 1990 Chilean Tax Reform." *Latin American Research Review* 31 (1): 7–31.

Brooks, Sarah, and Marcus Kurtz. 2007. "Capital, Trade, and the Political Economies of Reform." *American Journal of Political Science* 51 (4): 703–20.

Bull, Benedicte. 2008. "Policy Networks and Business Participation in Free Trade Negotiations in Chile." *Journal of Latin American Studies* 40: 195–224.

Calvo, Ernesto, and Victoria Murillo. 2012. "Argentina: The Persistence of Peronism." *Journal of Democracy* 23 (2): 148–61.

Cámara Chilena de la Construcción (CChC). 2005. "IVA a la Vivienda." *Fundamenta* 23. Santiago, Chile.

Cámara de Industria, Comercio, Servicios, y Turismo de Santa Cruz (CAINCO). 2003a. "Universalidad Tributaria y Formalidad Económica." DOC-CEBEC/02/03. Santa Cruz, Bolivia.

2003b. "Análisis del Proyecto de Ley del Nuevo Código Tributario Boliviano." Santa Cruz, Bolivia.

2004a. "Proyectos de Ley: Impuesto Complementario al Impuesto a la Propiedad de Bienes Inmuebles e Impuesto a las Transacciones Financieras." Santa Cruz, Bolivia.

2004b. "La Presión Tributaria en Bolivia." Santa Cruz, Bolivia.

Campbell, Angus, Philip Converse, Warren Miller, and Donald Stokes. 1960. *The American Voter*. New York: John Wiley.

Campello, Daniela. 2009. "Between Votes and Capital: The Politics of Redistribution in Less Developed Democracies." Conference paper, LASA, Rio de Janeiro.

Forthcoming. *The Politics of Market Discipline in Latin America*. New York: Cambridge University Press.

Carey, John. 2002. "Parties, Coalitions, and the Chilean Congress in the 1990s." In Scott Morgenstern and Benito Nacif, eds., *Legislative Politics in Latin America*. New York: Cambridge University Press.

Carey, John and Matthew Shugart. 1995. "Incentives to Cultivate a Personal Vote: A Rank Ordering of Electoral Formulas." *Electoral Studies* 14 (4): 417–39.

1998. *Executive Decree Authority*. New York: Cambridge University Press.

Castiglioni, Rossana. 2005. *The Politics of Social Policy Change in Chile and Uruguay*. New York: Routledge.

Centro de Estudios de la Realidad Contemporánea (CERC). 2004. "Informe de Prensa, Encuesta Nacional, Abril 2004." www.cerc.cep.cl

Centro de Estudios Públicos (CEP). 2008. "Estudio Nacional sobre Partidos Políticos y Sistema Electoral." March–April. Santiago, Chile.

2012. "Estudio Nacional de Opinión Pública No 68." Santiago, Chile.

Cerda, Rodrigo, and Felipe Larraín. 2005. "Inversión Privada e Impuestos Corporativos: Evidencia para Chile." *Cuadernos de Economía* 42: 257–81.

Cetrángolo, Oscar. 2007. "Búsqueda de Cohesión Social y Sostenibilidad Fiscal en los Procesos de Descentralización." Santiago, Chile: CEPAL.

Centrángolo, Oscar, and Juan Carlos Gómez-Sabaini. 2009. "La Imposición en la Argentina." *Serie Macroeconomía del Desarrollo* 84. Santiago, Chile: CEPAL, GTZ.

Cheibub, José Antonio. 1998. "Political Regimes and the Extractive Capacity of Governments." *World Politics* 50 (3): 349–76.

Chibber, Vivek. 2003. *Locked in Place: State-Building and Late Industrialization in India*. Princeton: Princeton University Press.

Chile Transparente. 2008. "Financiamiento Político en Chile." Working paper #4. Santiago, Chile.

Ciappa, César Marcelo. 2005. "Indicadores de Rentabilidad en el Sector Agrario Argentino." Federación de Centros y Entidades Gremiales de Acopiadores de Cereales; Facultad de Ciencias Económicas Universidad Nacional la Plata. Working Paper.

Coelho, Isaias, Juan Carlos Gómez-Sabaini, Paulo Medas, and Pablo Serra. 2004. "Bolivia: Hacia Un Sistema Tributario Más Eficiente y Justo." International Monetary Fund.

Collier, David. 2011. "Understanding Process Tracing." *PS: Political Science and Politics* 44 (4): 823–30.

Collier, David, Henry Brady, and Jason Seawright. 2010 "Sources of Leverage in Causal Inference." In Henry Brady and David Collier, eds., *Rethinking Social Inquiry*, 2nd ed. Lanham: Rowman and Littlefield.

Collier, David, Jody LaPorte, and Jason Seawright. 2012. "Putting Typologies to Work: Concept Formation, Measurement, and Analytical Rigor." *Political Research Quarterly* 65: 217–32.

Conaghan, Catherine, and James Malloy. 1994. *Unsettling Statecraft: Democracy and Neoliberalism in the Central Andes*. Pittsburgh: University of Pittsburgh Press.

Comisión Económica para América Latina y el Caribe (CEPAL). 2006. "Anuario Estadístico de América Latina y el Caribe." Santiago, Chile. www.cepal.org

Confederación de la Producción y el Comercio (CPC). 2000. "Posición de la CPC en Relación al Proyecto de Ley que Modifica la Legislación Tributaria." September. Santiago, Chile.

2001. "Posición de la CPC en Relación al Proyecto de Ley que Modifica la Legislación Tributaria." March. Santiago, Chile.

2007. "Alfredo Ovalle: Discusión en Torno a la Depreciación Acelerada." June 24. www.cpc.cl

Coppedge, Michael. 1997. "A Classification of Latin American Political Parties." Kellogg Institute Working Paper #22, University of Notre Dame.

2007. Party Ideology Dataset.

Corrales, Javier. 1998. "Coalitions and Corporate Choices in Argentina, 1976–1994." *Studies in Comparative International Development* 32 (4): 24–51.

Cossio, Fernando. 2005. "Análisis de un Potencial Impuesto al Ingreso Personal en Bolivia." La Paz: Fundación Jubileo.

2006. "Informe de Equidad Fiscal de Bolivia." In Alberto Barreix, Jerónimo Roca, and Luiz Villela, eds., *La Equidad Fiscal en los Países Andinos*. Washington, DC: DFID, BID, CAN.

Culpepper, Pepper. 2011. *Quiet Politics and Business Power*. New York: Cambridge University Press.

Culpepper, Pepper, and Raphael Reinke. Forthcoming. "Structural Power and Bank Bailouts in the United Kingdom and the United States." *Politics and Society*.

Dahl, Robert. 1961. *Who Governs? Democracy and Power in and American City*. New Haven: Yale University Press.

De Riz, Liliana, and Catalina Smulovitz. 1991. "Instituciones y Dinámica Política: El Presidencialismo Argentino." In Dieter Nohlen and Liliana de Riz, eds., *Reforma Institucional y Cambio Político*. Buenos Aires: CEDES, Editorial Legasa.

Di Gresia, Luciano. 2004. "Efectos Económicos y Fiscales de la Eliminación de las Retenciones a las Exportaciones." Working paper. Buenos Aires, Argentina.

Diamond, Larry, and Leonardo Morlino. 2004. "The Quality of Democracy." *Journal of Democracy* 15(4): 20–31.

Diamond, Peter. 1998. "Optimal Income Taxation." *American Economic Review* 88: 83–95.

Dirección de Presupuestos (DIPRES). 2009. "Estadísticas de las Finanzas Públicas." Santiago, Chile (www.dipres.gob.cl).

Dirección Nacional de Investigaciones Y Análisis Fiscal (DNIAF). 2012. "Presión Tributaria." www.mecon.gov.ar

2011. "Gastos Tributarios." www.mecon.gov.ar

Domhoff, G. William. 1967. *Who Rules America?* Englewood Cliffs, NJ: Prentice-Hall.

1990. *The Power Elite and the State: How Policy is Made in America*. New York: A. de Gruyter.

Dosal, Paul. 1995. *Power in Transition: The Rise of Guatemala's Industrial Oligarchy*. Westport, CT: Praeger.

Drake, Paul. 1978. "Corporatism and Functionalism in Modern Chilean Politics." *Journal of Latin American Studies* 10, 1 (May): 83–116.

Dunkerley, James. 1984. *Rebellion in the Veins*. London: Verso.

Dunning, Thad. 2008. *Crude Democracy*. New York: Cambridge University Press.

Easter, Gerald. 2008. "Capacity, Consent, and Tax Collection in Post-communist States." In Deborah Bräutigam, Odd-Helge Fjeldstad, and Mick Moore, eds., *Taxation and State-Building in Developing Countries*. New York: Cambridge University Press.

2012. *Capital, Coercion, and Postcommunist States*. Ithaca: Cornell University Press.

Eaton, Kent. 2002. *Politics and Economic Reforms in New Democracies*. University Park: Pennsylvania State University Press.

2005. "Menem and the Governors: Intergovernmental Relations in the 1990s." In Steven Levitsky and Victoria Murillo, eds., *The Politics of Institutional Weakness: Argentine Democracy*. University Park: Pennsylvania State University Press.

2007. "Backlash in Bolivia: Regional Autonomy as a Reaction to Indigenous Mobilization." *Politics and Society* 35 (1): 71–102.

2011. "Conservative Autonomy Movements: Territorial Dimensions of Ideological Conflict in Bolivia and Ecuador." *Comparative Politics* 43 (3): 291–310.

2014. "Recentralization and the Left Turn in Latin America: Diverging Outcomes in Bolivia, Ecuador, and Venezuela." *Comparative Political Studies* 47 (8): 1130–57.

Economic Intelligence Unit (EIU). 2004. "Country Report: Argentina." December. eiu.com

2008. "Country Profile: Bolivia." eiu.com

Estevez-Abe, Margarita, Torben Iverson, and David Soskice. 2001. "Social Protection and the Formation of Skills: A Reinterpretation of the Welfare State." In Peter Hall and David Soskice, eds., *Varieties of Capitalism*. New York: Oxford University Press.

Etchemendy, Sebastián. 2011. *Models of Economic Liberalization*. New York: Cambridge University Press.

Etchemendy, Sebastián, and Ruth B. Collier. 2007. "Down but Not Out: Union Resurgence and Segmented Neocorporatism in Argentina." *Politics and Society* 35: 363–401.

Etchemendy, Sebastián, and Candelaria Garay. 2010. "Between Moderation and Defiance: The Kirchners' Governments in Comparative Perspective (2003–2008)." In Steve Levitsky and Kenneth Roberts, eds., *The Resurgence of the Latin American Left*. New York: Cambridge University Press.

Evans, Peter. 1995. *Embedded Autonomy: States and Industrial Transformation*. Princeton: Princeton University Press.

1997. "State Structures, Government-Business Relations, and Economic Transformation." In Sylvia Maxfield and Ben Ross Schneider, eds., *Business and the State in Developing Countries*. Ithaca: Cornell University Press.

Faguet, Jean Paul. 2012. *Decentralization and Popular Democracy.* Ann Arbor: University of Michigan.

Fairfield, Tasha. 2006. "Taxing Elites in Chile: Policy Formulation, Coalition Building, and Opposition." LASA, Puerto Rico, March 15–18.

2010. "Business Power and Tax Reform: Taxing Income and Profits in Chile and Argentina." *Latin American Politics and Society* 52 (2): 51–71.

2011. "Business Power and Protest." *Studies in Comparative International Development* 46: 424–53.

2013. "Going Where the Money Is: Strategies for Taxing Economic Elites in Unequal Democracies." *World Development* 47 (2013): 42–57.

Fairfield, Tasha, and Michel Jorratt. 2014. "Top Income Shares, Business Profits, and Effective Tax Rates in Contemporary Chile." Revised from ICTD Working Paper 17. http://eprints.lse.ac.uk/56016

Falkner, Robert. 2009. *Business Power and Conflict in International Environmental Politics.* Basingstoke: Palgrave Macmillan.

Falleti, Tulia, and Julia Lynch. 2009. "Context and Causal Mechanisms in Political Analysis." *Comparative Political Studies* 42: 1143–1166.

Fearon, James, and David Laitin. 2008. "Integrating Qualitative and Quantitative Methods." In *The Oxford Handbook of Political Methodology,* eds. Janet M. Box-Steffensmeier, Henry E. Brady, and David Collier. Oxford: Oxford University Press.

Fishman, Robert. 2011. "Democratic Practice after the Revolution." *Politics and Society* 39 (2): 233–67.

Flores-Macías, Gustavo. 2013. "Financing Security through Elite Taxation." *Studies in Comparative International Development.* Published online.

2012. *The Left and Economic Reforms in Latin America.* New York: Oxford University Press.

Fox, Elizabeth, and Silvio Waisbord, eds. 2002. *Latin Politics: Global Media.* Austin: University of Texas Press.

Frieden, Jeffry. 1991. *Debt, Development, and Democracy.* Princeton University Press.

1999. "Actors and Preferences in International Relations." In David A. Lake and Robert Powell, eds., *Strategic Choice and International Relations.* Princeton, NJ: Princeton University Press.

Fuchs, Doris. 2007. *Business Power in Global Governance.* Boulder: Lynne Rienner Publishers.

Fuentes, Juan Alberto, and Maynor Cabrera. 2006. "El Marco Institucional de la Política Fiscal Guatemalteca antes del Pacto Fiscal del 2000." *Revista de la CEPAL* 88: 153–65.

Gaggero, Jorge, and Juan Carlos Gómez Sabaini. 2002. *Argentina: Cuestiones Macrofiscales y Políticas Tributarias.* Buenos Aires: Fundación OSDE-CIEPP.

Gallo, Carmenza. 2008. "Tax Bargaining and Nitrate Exports: Chile 1880–1930." In Deborah Bräutigam, Odd-Helge Fjeldstad, and Mick Moore, *Taxation and State-Building in Developing Countries.* New York: Cambridge University Press.

Gamarra, Eduardo. 1997. "Hybrid Presidentialism and Democratization: The Case of Bolivia." In Scott Mainwaring and Matthew Shugart, eds., *Presidentialism and Democracy in Latin America.* New York: Cambridge University Press.

2003. "The Construction of Bolivia's Multiparty System." In Grindle, Merilee and Pilar Domingo, eds. *Proclaiming Revolution: Bolivia in Comparative Perspective.* Cambridge, MA: Harvard University Press.

2008. "Evo Morales and Democracy." In Jorge Domínguez and Michael Shifter, eds., *Constructing Democratic Governance in Latin America*. 3rd ed. Baltimore: Johns Hopkins University Press.

Gamarra, Eduardo, and James Malloy. 1995. "The Patrimonial Dynamics of Party Politics in Bolivia." In Scott Mainwaring and Timothy Scully, eds., *Building Democratic Institutions: Party Systems in Latin America*. Stanford: Stanford University Press.

Garay, Candelaria. 2007. "Social Policy and Collective Action: Unemployed Workers, Community Associations, and Protest in Argentina." *Politics and Society* 35: 301–28.

2014. "Including Outsiders: Social Policy Expansion in Latin America." Unpublished manuscript.

Garrett, Geoffrey and Deborah Mitchell 2001. "Globalization, Government Spending, and Taxation in the OECD." *European Journal of Political Research* 39: 145–77.

Garretón, Manuel Antonio. 2000. "Atavism and Democratic Ambiguity in the Chilean Right." In *Conservative Parties, The Right, and Democracy in Latin America*, ed. Kevin Middlebrook. Baltimore: Johns Hopkins University Press.

Gaventa, John. 1980. *Power and Powerlessness*. Oxford: Clarendon Press.

Gehlbach, Scott. 2008. *Representation through Taxation: Revenue, Politics, and Development in Postcommunist States*. New York: Cambridge University Press.

Gelleny, Ronald, and Matthew McCoy. 2001. "Globalization and Government Policy Independence: The Issue of Taxation." *Political Research Quarterly* 54 (3): 509–29.

George, Alexander, and Andrew Bennett. 2005. *Case Studies and Theory Development in the Social Sciences*. Cambridge, MA: MIT Press.

Gervasoni, Carlos. 2010. "A Rentier Theory of Subnational Regimes." *World Politics* 62 (2): 302–40.

Gibson, Edward. 1992. "Conservative Electoral Movements and Democratic Politics." In Douglas Chalmers, Maria Campello de Souza, and Atilio Borón, eds., *The Right and Democracy in Latin America*. New York: Praeger Publishers.

1996. *Class and Conservative Parties*. Baltimore: Johns Hopkins University Press.

Gibson, Edward, and Ernest Calvo. 2000. "Federalism and Low Maintenance Constituencies." *Studies in Comparative International Development* 35 (3): 32–55.

Gibson, Edward, Ernesto Calvo, and Tulia Falleti. 2004. "Reallocative Federalism: Legislative Overrepresentation and Public Spending in the Western Hemisphere." In Edward Gibson, ed. *Federalism and Democracy in Latin America*. Baltimore: Johns Hopkins University Press.

Gilens, Martin. 2012. *Affluence and Influence*. Princeton: Princeton University Press.

Giraldo, Jeanne. 1997. "Development and Democracy in Chile." In Jorge Dominguez, ed., *Technopols*. University Park: Pennsylvania State University Press.

Glaser, Barney, and Anselm Strauss. 1967. *The Discovery of Grounded Theory: Strategies for Qualitative Research*. Chicago: Aldine Publishers.

Goertz, Gary, and James Mahoney 2012. *A Tale of Two Cultures: Qualitative and Quantitative Research in the Social Sciences*. Princeton: Princeton University Press.

Goñi, Edwin, Humberto López, and Luis Servén. 2011. "Fiscal Redistribution and Income Inequality in Latin America." *World Development* 39 (9): 1558–69.

Graetz, Michael, and Ian Shapiro. 2005. *Death by a Thousand Cuts*. Princeton: Princeton University Press.

Hacker, Jacob, and Paul Pierson. 2002. "Business Power and Social Policy: Employers and the Formation of the American Welfare State." *Politics and Society* 30: 277–325.

2005. "Abandoning the Middle: The Bush Tax Cuts and the Limits of Democratic Control." *Perspectives on Politics* 3 (1): 33–53.

2010. "Winner-Take-All-Politics: Public Policy, Political Organization, and the Precipitous Rise of Top Incomes in the United States." *Politics and Society* 38 (2): 152–204.

Hacker, Jacob, Paul Pierson, and Kathleen Thelen. 2013. "Drift and Conversion: Hidden Faces of Institutional Change." Presented at the American Political Science Association conference, Chicago, Aug. 29–Sept. 1.

Haggard, Stephan, and Robert Kaufman, eds. 1992. *The Politics of Economic Adjustment*. Princeton: Princeton University Press.

2008. *Development, Democracy, and Welfare States: Latin America, East Asia, and Eastern Europe*. Princeton: Princeton University Press.

Haggard, Stephan, Sylvia Maxfield, and Ben Ross Schneider. 1997. "Theories of Business and Business-State Relations." In Sylvia Maxfield and Ben Ross Schneider, eds., *Business and the State in Developing Countries*. Ithaca: Cornell University Press.

Hall, Peter. 2010. "Historical Institutionalism in Rationalist and Sociological Perspective." In James Mahoney and Kathleen Thelen, eds., *Explaining Institutional Change*. New York: Cambridge University Press.

Hall, Peter, and David Soskice. 2001. *Varieties of Capitalism*. New York: Oxford University Press.

Hall, Richard, and Alan Deardorff. 2006. "Lobbying as Legislative Subsidy." *American Political Science Review* 100 (1): 69–84.

Hall, Richard, and Frank Wayman. 1990. "Buying Time: Moneyed Interests and the Mobilization of Bias in Congressional Committees." *American Political Science Review* 84 (3): 798–820.

Handley, Antoinette. 2008. *Business and the State in Africa*. New York: Cambridge University Press.

Hart, Austin. 2009. "Death of the Partisan? Globalization and Taxation in South America, 1990–2006." *Comparative Political Studies* 43 (3): 1–25.

Heredia, Mariana. 2003. "Reformas Estructurales y Renovación de las Élites Económicas en Argentina." *Revista Mexicana de Sociología* 65 (1): 77–155.

2004. "Emergencia y Consolidación del Liberalismo Tecnocrático." In Alfredo Pucciarelli, ed., *Empresarios, Tecnócratas y Militares*. Buenos Aires: Siglo Veintiuno.

Heredia, Blanca, and Ben Ross Schneider. 2003. "The Political Economy of Administrative Reform in Developing Countries." In *Reinventing Leviathan*, Blanca Heredia and Ben Ross Schneider, eds., Coral Gables: North-South Center Press, pp. 1–29.

Hirchman, Albert. 1970. *Exit, Voice, and Loyalty*. Cambridge, MA: Harvard University Press.

1973. *Journeys toward Progress*. New York: Twentieth Century Fund.

Huber, Evelyne, and John Stephens. 2012. *Democracy and the Left*. Chicago: University of Chicago Press.

Hughes, Sallie, and Chappell Lawson. 2004. "Propaganda and Crony Capitalism: Partisan Bias in Mexican Television News." *Latin American Research Review* 39, 3 (October): 81–105.

Humphreys, Macartan, and Alan Jacobs. 2014. "Mixing Methods: A Bayesian Integration of Qualitative and Quantitative Inferences." Working paper.

Huneeus, Carlos. 2003. "A Highly Institutionalized Party: Christian Democracy in Chile." In Scott Mainwaring and Timothy Scully, eds., *Christian Democracy in Latin America*. Stanford: Stanford University Press.

Inclán, Carla, Dennis Quinn, and Robert Shapiro. 2001. "Origins and Consequences of Changes in U.S. Corporate Taxation, 1981–1998." *American Journal of Political Science* 45 (1): 179–201.

International Monetary Fund (IMF). 2011. Regional Economic Outlook, Western Hemisphere: Shifting Winds, New Policy Challenges. October.

Iversen, Torben. 2005. *Capitalism, Democracy, and Welfare*. New York: Cambridge University Press.

Iversen, Torben, and David Soskice. 2009. "Distribution and Redistribution." *World Politics* 61 (3): 438–86.

Jacobs, Lawrence, and Robert Shapiro. 2000. *Politicians Don't Pander*. Chicago: University of Chicago Press.

Jacobs, Lawrence, and Joe Soss. 2010. "The Politics of Inequality in America: A Political Economy Framework." *Annual Review of Political Science* 13: 341–64.

Jiménez, Juan Pablo, Juan Carlos Gómez Sabaini, and Andrea Podestá. 2010. *Evasión y Equidad en América Latina*. Santiago, Chile: Cepal/GTZ.

Jones, Mark. 2002. "Explaining the High Level of Party Discipline in the Argentina Congress." In Scott Morgenstern and Benito Nacif, eds., *Legislative Politics in Latin America*. Cambridge University Press.

Jones, Mark, and Wonjae Hwang 2005. "Provincial Party Bosses: Keystone of the Argentine Congress." In Steven Levitsky and Victoria Murillo, eds., *The Politics of Institutional Weakness: Argentine Democracy*. University Park: Pennsylvania State University Press.

Jorratt, Michel. 2009. "La Tributación Directa en Chile." Serie Macroeconomía del Desarrollo, 92. Cepal: Santiago, Chile.

   2012. "Análisis del Proyecto de Ley de Ajustes Tributarios." Presentation to Congress. Santiago, Chile.

   2013. "Gastos Tributarios y Evasión Tributaria en Chile." In José Pablo Arellano and Vittorio Corbo, eds., *Tributación para el Desarrollo: Estudios para la Reforma del Sistema Chileno*. CEP/CIEPLAN. Santiago: Uqbar Editores.

Kapiszewski, Diana. 2012. *High Courts and Economic Governance in Argentina and Brazil*. New York: Cambridge University Press.

Kapiszewski, Diana, and Matthew Taylor. 2008. "Doing Courts Justice? Studying Judicial Politics in Latin America." *Perspectives on Politics* 6 (4): 741–67.

Kaplan, Stephen. 2013. *Globalization and Austerity Politics in Latin America*. New York: Cambridge University Press.

Karcher, Sebastian, and Ben Schneider. 2012. "Business Politics in Latin America." In Deborah Yashar and Peter Kingstone, eds., *Routledge Handbook of Latin American Politics*. New York: Routledge.

Karl, Terry. 1997. *The Paradox of Plenty*. Berkeley: University of California Press.

Kato, Junko. 2003. *Regressive Taxation and the Welfare State*. New York: Cambridge University Press.

Kaufman, Robert. 2009. "The Political Effects of Inequality in Latin America: Some Inconvenient Facts." *Comparative Politics* 41 (3): 359–79.

Kingstone, Peter. 1999. *Crafting Coalitions for Reform*. University Park: Pennsylvania State University Press.

Korpi, Walter. 1985. "Power Resources Approach vs. Action and Conflict: On Causal and Intentional Explanations in the Study of Power." *Sociological Theory* 3 (92): 31–45.

2006. "Power Resources and Employer-Centered Approaches in Explanations of Welfare States and Varieties of Capitalism." *World Politics* 58 (2): 167–206.

Kurtz, Marcus. 2009. "The Social Foundations of Institutional Order." *Politics and Society* 37 (4): 479–520.

2013. *Latin American State-Building in Comparative Perspective*. New York: Cambridge University Press.

Lagos, Martín. 2002. "La Crisis Bancaria Argentina, 2001–2002." Asociación de Bancos de la Argentina. Buenos Aires, Argentina.

Latinobarómetro. 2008. *Informe*. Santiago, Chile.

2009. *Informe: ¿La Democracia está Más Madura?* Santiago, Chile.

Lazarte, Jorge. 2005. *Entre Los Espectros del Pasado y Las Incertidumbres del Futuro*. La Paz, Bolivia: ILDIS / Plural Editores.

Lehoucq, Fabrice. 2008. "Bolivia's Constitutional Breakdown." *Journal of Democracy* 19 (4): 110–24

Levi, Margaret. 1988. *Of Rule and Revenue*. Berkeley: University of California Press.

Levitsky, Steven. 2001. "Organization and Labor-Based Party Adaption: The Transformation of Argentine Peronism in Comparative Perspective." *World Politics* 54 (1): 27–56.

2003. *Transforming Labor-Based Parties in Latin America*. New York: Cambridge University Press.

Levitsky, Steven, and Victoria Murillo. 2005. "Building Castles in the Sand? The Politics of Institutional Weakness in Argentina." In Steven Levitsky and Victoria Murillo, eds., *The Politics of Institutional Weakness: Argentine Democracy*. University Park: Pennsylvania State University Press.

2008. "Argentina: From Kirchner to Kirchner." *Journal of Democracy* 19 (2): 16–30.

Levitsky, Steven, and Kenneth Roberts. 2011. "Introduction: Latin America's 'Left Turn': A Framework for Analysis." In Steven Levitsky and Kenneth Roberts, eds., *The Resurgence of the Latin American Left*. New York: Cambridge University Press.

Lieberman, Evan. 2003. *Race and Regionalism in the Politics of Taxation in Brazil and South Africa*. New York: Cambridge University Press.

Lindblom, Charles. 1977. *Politics and Markets*. New York: Basic Books.

1982. "The Market as Prison." *Journal of Politics* 44 (2): 324–36.

Lorenzini, Pablo, Jorge Insunza, Carlos Montes, José Miguel Ortiz, Alberto Robles, Raúl Súnico, and Eugenio Tuma. 2006. "El Sistema Tributario Chileno: Ideas Para un Rediseño." Santiago, Chile.

Lowi, Theodore. 1964. "American Business, Public Policy, Case-Studies, and Political Theory." *World Politics* 16 (4): 677–715.

Lukes, Steven. 1974. *Power, a Radical View*. London: Macmillan.

Luna, Juan Pablo. 2010. "Segmented Party Voter Linkages in Latin America: The Case of the UDI." *Journal of Latin American Studies* 42 (2): 325–56.

2014. *Segmented Representation: Political Party Strategies in Unequal Democracies.* Oxford: Oxford University Press.

Luna, Juan Pablo, and David Altman. 2011. "Uprooted but Stable: Chilean Parties and the Concept of Party System Institutionalization." *Latin American Politics and Society* 53 (2): 1–28.

Madrid, Raul. 2011. "Bolivia: Origins and Policies of the Movimiento al Socialismo." In Steve Levitsky and Kenneth Roberts, eds., *The Resurgence of the Latin American Left.* New York: Cambridge University Press.

Mahon, James. 1996. *Mobile Capital and Latin American Development.* University Park, PA: Pennsylvania State University Press.

2004. "Causes of Tax Reform in Latin America, 1977–95." *Latin American Research Review* 99, 1 (Feb.): 3–30.

2012. "Tax Incidence and Tax Reforms in Latin America." Washington, DC: Wilson Center Update on the Americas.

Mahoney, James, and Kathleen Thelen, eds. 2010. *Explaining Institutional Change.* New York: Cambridge University Press.

Manley, David. 2012. "Caught in a Trap: Zambia's Mineral Tax Reforms." Institute for Development Studies: ICTD Working Paper 5.

Mainwaring, Scott, and Timothy Scully. 1995. *Building Democratic Institutions: Party Systems in Latin America.* Stanford: Stanford University Press

Mainwaring, Scott, and Matthew Shugart. 1997. *Presidentialism and Democracy in Latin America.* New York: Cambridge University Press.

Mainwaring, Scott. 1999. *Rethinking Party Systems in the Third Wave of Democratization: The Case of Brazil.* Stanford: Stanford University Press.

Marcel, Mario. 1997. "Políticas Públicas en Democracia: El Caso de la Reforma Tributaria de 1990 en Chile." *Estudios Cieplan* 45: 33–84.

Mares, Isabela. 2003. *The Politics of Social Risk: Business and Welfare State Development.* New York: Cambridge University Press.

Marfán, Mauel. 1998. "El Financiamiento Fiscal en los Años 90." In René Cortázar and Joaquín Vial, *Construyendo Opciones*, Santiago: Cieplan.

Martin, Cathie Jo, and Duane Swank. 2012. *The Political Construction of Business Interests.* New York: Cambridge University Press.

MAS. 2005. "Programa de Gobierno 2006–2010." La Paz, Bolivia.

Maxfield, Sylvia. 1991. "Bankers' Alliances." *Comparative Political Studies* 23 (4): 419–58.

1997. *Gatekeepers of Growth.* Princeton: Princeton University Press.

Mayorga, René Antonio. 2004. "La Crisis del Sistema de Partidos Políticos: Causas y Consecuencias. Caso Bolivia." Working paper.

2005. "Bolivia's Democracy at the Crossroads." In Frances Hagopian and Scott Mainwaring, eds., *The Third Wave of Democratization in Latin America: Advances and Setbacks.* New York: Cambridge University Press.

McCarty, Nolan, Keith Poole, and Howard Rosenthal. 2008. *Polarized America.* Cambridge, MA: MIT Press.

McGuire, James. 1995. "Political Parties and Democracy in Argentina." In Scott Mainwaring and Timothy Scully, eds., *Building Democratic Institutions: Party Systems in Latin America.* Stanford: Stanford University Press.

2010. *Wealth, Health and Democracy in East Asia and Latin America*. New York: Cambridge University Press.

Melo, Marcus. 2007. "Institutional Weakness and the Puzzle of Argentina's Low Taxation." *Latin American Politics and Society* 49 (4): 115–48.

Meltzer, Allan, and Scott Richard. 1981. "A Rational Theory of the Size of Government." *Journal of Political Economy* 89 (5): 914–27.

Miliband, Ralph. 1969. *The State and Capitalist Society*. New York: Basic Books.

Mills, C. Wright. 1956. *The Power Elite*. Oxford: Oxford University Press.

Ministerio de Hacienda. 2005. "Exposición Sobre el Estado de la Hacienda Pública." Santiago, Chile.

2008. "Verdades y Mitos en Torno a una Reforma: Franquicia del IVA a la Construcción de Viviendas." Santiago, Chile.

2010. "Estado de la Hacienda Pública." Santiago, Chile. www.hacienda.cl

Miranda, Carlos. 2009. "Los Hidrocarburos en el Contexto Regional." In Fernando Candia and Napoleón Pacheco, eds., *El Péndulo del Gas*. La Paz: Fundación Milenio.

Molina, George Gray. 2010. "The Challenge of Progressive Change under Evo Morales." In Kurt Weyland, Raul Madrid, and Wendy Hunter, eds., *Leftist Governments in Latin America*. New York: Cambridge University Press.

Moore Mick. 1998. "Death without Taxes." In Mark Robinson and Gordon White, *The Democratic Developmental State*. Oxford: Oxford University Press.

2004. "Revenues, State Formation, and the Quality of Governance in Developing Countries." *International Political Science Review* 25 (3): 297–319.

Morrison, Kevin. 2009. "Oil, Nontax Revenue, and the Redistributional Foundations of Regime Stability." *International Organization* 63 (Winter): 107–38.

Morrow, James. 1999. "The Strategic Setting of Choices." In David A. Lake and Robert Powell, eds., *Strategic Choice and International Relations*. Princeton, NJ: Princeton University Press.

Murillo, Victoria. 2009. *Political Competition, Partisanship, and Policy Making in Latin American Public Utilities*. New York: Cambridge University Press.

Mustapic, Ana. 2002. "Oscillating Relations: President and Congress in Argentina." In Scott Morgenstern and Benito Nacif, eds., *Legislative Politics in Latin America*. New York: Cambridge University Press.

Navarrete, Bernardo. 2005. "Un Centro Excéntrico: Cambio y Continuidad en la Democracia Cristiana." *Política: Revista de Ciencia Política, Universidad de Chile* 45: 109–46.

Nelson, Joan. 1990. *Economic Crisis and Policy Choice*. Princeton: Princeton University Press.

Newell, Peter. 2009. "Bio-Hegemony: The Political Economy of Agricultural Biotechnology in Argentina." *Journal of Latin American Studies* 41: 27–57.

North, Douglass. 1990. *Institutions, Institutional Change, and Economic Performance*. New York: Cambridge University Press.

O'Donnell, Guillermo. 1978. "State and Alliances in Argentina, 1956–1976." *Journal of Development Studies* 15 (1): 3–33.

2004. "Human Rights, Human Development, and Democracy." In Guillermo O'Donnell, Jorge Cullell, and Osvaldo Iazzetta, eds., *The Quality of Democracy: Theory and Applications*. Notre Dame, IN: University of Notre Dame Press.

Olson, Mancur. 1965. *The Logic of Collective Action.* Cambridge, MA: Harvard University Press.

Organization for Economic Cooperation and Development (OECD) 2000, 2007. "Improving Access to Bank Information for Tax Purposes." www.oecd.org

2009. "A Progress Report on the Jurisdictions Surveyed by the OECD Global Forum in Implementing the Internationally Agreed Tax Standard." www.oecd.org

2012. "OECD Economic Surveys: Chile 2012." OECD Publishing.

Ostiguy, Pierre. 1997. "Social-Cultural Bases of Political Identity in Argentina." Conference paper, LASA: Guadalajara, Mexico.

2009. "The Argentine Political Space." Working Figure.

Otto, James. 2000. "Mining Taxation in Developing Countries." Colorado: Colorado School of Mines.

Otto, James, Craig Andrews, Fred Cawood, Michael Doggett, Pietro Guy, Frank Stermole, John Sterole, and John Tilton. 2006. "Mining Royalties." World Bank.

Pacheco, Napoleón. 2004. "Evaluación de la Capitalización Frente a los Objetivos y Expectativas." In Zaratti, Francesco, ed., *A 10 Años de la Capitalización: Luces y Sombras.* La Paz, Bolivia: Creativa.

Perry, Guillermo, Omar Arias, Humbero López, William Maloney, and Luis Servén. 2006. *Poverty Reduction and Growth.* Washington, DC: World Bank.

Pierson, Paul. 1993. "When Effect Becomes Cause: Policy Feedback and Political Change." *World Politics* 45 (4): 595–628.

1994. *Dismantling the Welfare State? Reagan, Thatcher, and the Politics of Retrenchment.* New York: Cambridge University Press.

Piketty, Thomas, and Emmanuel Saez. 2006. "How Progressive is the U.S. Federal Tax System?" NBER Working Paper 12404.

Piketty, Thomas, Emmanuel Saez, and Stefanie Stantcheva. 2011. "Optimal Taxation of Top Labor Incomes: A Tale of Three Elasticities." NBER Working Paper 17616.

Poder Democrático Social (PODEMOS). 2005. "Programa de Gobierno 2006–2010." La Paz, Bolivia.

Pollack, Marcelo. 1999. *The New Right in Chile.* London: Macmillan Press.

Polsby, Nelson. 1968. "Book Review: Who Rules America? By G. William Domhoff." *American Sociological Review* 33 (3): 476–77.

Posada-Carbó, Eduardo, and Carlos Malamud, eds. 2005. *The Financing of Politics: Latin American and European Perspectives.* London: Institute for the Study of the Americas.

Posner, Paul. 2004. "Local Democracy and the Transformation of Popular Participation in Chile. *Latin American Politics and Society* 46 (3): 55–81.

Pribble, Jennifer. 2013. *Welfare and Party Politics in Latin America.* New York: Cambridge University Press.

Przeworski, Adam, and Michael Wallerstein. 1988. "Structural Dependence of the State on Capital." *The American Political Science Review* 82 (1): 11–29.

Ragin, Charles. 1997. "Turning the Tables: How Case-Oriented Research Challenges Variable-Oriented Research." *Comparative Social Research* 16: 27–42.

Richardson, Neal. 2009. "Export-Oriented Populism: Commodities and Coalitions in Argentina." *Studies in Comparative International Development* 44: 228–55.

Roca, José Luis. 1999. *Fisonomía del Regionalismo Boliviano.* La Paz: Plural.

Roemer, John. 1999. "Does Democracy Engender Justice?" In Ian Shapiro and Casiano Hacker-Cordón, eds., *Democracy's Value*. New York: Cambridge University Press.

Rodrik, Dani. 1997. "Sense and Nonsense in the Globalization Debate." *Foreign Policy* 107: 19–36.

Rodríguez, Javier, and Nicolás Arceo. 2006. "Renta Agraria y Ganancias Extraordinarias en Argentina." Centro de Estudios para el Desarrollo Argentina, Working Paper 4.

Ross, Michael. 2004. "Does Taxation Lead to Representation?" *British Journal of Political Science* 34 (2): 229–49.

Sabaini, Juan Carlos Gómez. 2005. "Evolución y Situación Tributaria Actual en América Latina." Santiago, Chile: CEPAL.

2010. "El Rol de la Política Tributara para el Fortalecimiento del Estado en América Latina." Draft paper. Santiago, Chile: CEPAL.

Sabaini, Juan Carlos Gómez, Juan Pablo Jiménez, and Darío Rossignolo. 2012. "Imposición a la Renta Personal y Equidad en América Latina." Santiago, Chile: CEPAL/GIZ.

Saez, Emmanuel. 2001. "Using Elasticities to Derive Optimal Income Tax Rates." *Review of Economic Studies* 68: 205–29.

2002. "Optimal Progressive Capital Income Taxes in the Infinite Horizon Model." NBER Working Paper 9046.

2004. "Reported Incomes and Marginal Tax Rates, 1960–2000." NBER Working Paper 10273.

Saez, Emmanuel, Joel Slemrod, and Seth Gieretz. 2012. "The Elasticity of Taxable Income with Respect to Marginal Tax Rates: A Critical Review." *Journal of Economic Literature* 50 (1): 3–50.

Salman, Ton, and Ximena Sologuren. 2011. "Anti-Elites as New Elites: Complexities of Elite Performance in Baffled Bolivia." *Comparative Sociology* 10: 614–35.

Samuels, David. 2001. "Money, Elections, and Democracy in Brazil." *Latin American Politics and Society* 43 (2): 27–48.

Sanchez, Omar. 2009. "Tax Reform Paralysis in Post-Conflict Guatemala." *New Political Economy* 14 (1): 101–31.

2011. *Mobilizing Resources in Latin America*. New York: Palgrave Macmillan.

Schamis, Hector. 1999. "Distributional Coalitions and the Politics of Economic Reform in Latin America." *World Politics* 51: 250.

2002. *Re-Forming the State: The Politics of Privatization in Latin America and Europe*. Ann Arbor: University of Michigan Press.

Schmitter, Philippe, and Gerhard Lehmbruch, eds. 1979. *Trends towards Corporatist Intermediation*. London: Sage Publications.

Schneider, Aaron. 2012. *State-Building and Tax Regimes in Central America*. New York: Cambridge University Press.

Schneider, Ben Ross. 1997. "Big Business and the Politics of Economic Reform: Confidence and Concertation in Brazil and Mexico." In Sylvia Maxfield and Ben Ross Schneider, eds., *Business and the State in Developing Countries*. Ithaca: Cornell University Press.

2004a. *Business Politics and the State in Twentieth-Century Latin America*. New York: Cambridge University Press.

2004b. "Organizing Interests and Coalition in the Politics of Market Reform in Latin America." *World Politics* 56 (3): 456–79.

2010. "Business Politics in Latin America: Patterns of Fragmentation and Centralization." In David Coen, Graham Wilson, and Wyn Grant, eds. *Oxford Handbook of Business and Government*. Oxford: Oxford University Press.

2013. *Hierarchical Capitalism in Latin America*. New York: Cambridge University Press.

Schneider, Ben Ross, and David Soskice. 2009. "Inequality in Developed Countries and Latin America: Coordinated and Hierarchical Systems." *Economy and Society* 38 (1): 17–52.

Schrank, Andrew. 2007. "Asian Industrialization in Latin American Perspective." *Latin American Politics and Society* 49 (2): 183–200.

Seawright, Jason, and John Gerring. 2008. "Case Selection Techniques in Case Study Research A Menu of Qualitative and Quantitative Options." *Political Research Quarterly* 61(2): 294–308.

Sehnbruch, Kirsten. 2007. "The Sorcerer's Apprentice." *Berkeley Review of Latin American Studies* (Spring). Center for Latin American Studies: pp. 6–9.

Servicio de Impuestos Internos (SII). 2000a. "Propuesta de Reforma al Impuesto a la Renta." Santiago, Chile.

2000b. "Plan de Lucha Contra la Evasión." Santiago, Chile.

2003. "Antecedentes de la Tributación Minera en Chile y su Fiscalización." Santiago, Chile.

2005. "Informe de Gasto Tributario." Santiago, Chile.

2009. "Serie Ingresos Tributarios en Moneda Nacional." Santiago, Chile (www.sii.cl).

Servicio de Impuestos Nacionales (SIN). 2006. "Recaudación por Fuente de Ingreso, Gestiones 1996–2006." La Paz, Bolivia.

Shapiro, Ian. 2006. "On the Second Edition of Lukes' Third Face." *Political Studies Review* 4: 146–55.

Sharman, J. C. 2008. "Power and Discourse in Policy Diffusion: Anti-Money Laundering in Developing States." *International Studies Quarterly* 52: 635–56.

Shliefer, Andrei, and Daniel Treisman. 2000. *Without a Map: Political Tactics and Economic Reform in Russia*. Cambridge, MA: MIT Press.

Siavelis, Peter. 2000. *The President and Congress in Postauthoritarian Chile*. University Park: Pennsylvania State University Press.

2002. "Exaggerated Presidentialism and Moderate Presidents." In Scott Morgenstern and Benito Nacif, eds., *Legislative Politics in Latin America*. New York: Cambridge University Press.

2005. "Los Peligros de la Ingeniería Electoral." *Política: Revista de Ciencia Política, Universidad de Chile* 45: 9–28.

Sidicaro, Ricardo. 2002. *Los Tres Peronismos*. Buenos Aires: Siglo Veintiuno.

Sigmund, Paul. 1977. *The Overthrow of Allende and the Politics of Chile, 1964–1976*. Pittsburgh: University of Pittsburgh Press.

Silva, Eduardo. 1996. *The State and Capital in Chile*. Boulder: Westview Press.

1997. "Business Elites, the State, and Economic Change in Chile." In Sylvia Maxfield and Ben Ross Schneider, eds., *Business and the State in Developing Countries*. Ithaca: Cornell University Press.

1998. "Organized Business, Neoliberal Economic Restructuring, and Redemocratization in Chile." In Francisco Durand and Eduardo Silva, eds.,

Organized Business, Economic Change, and Democracy in Latin America. Miami: North-South Center.

2002. "Capital and the Lagos Presidency: Business as Usual?" *Bulletin of Latin American Research* 12 (3): 339–57.

2009. *Challenging Neoliberalism in Latin America.* New York: Cambridge University Press.

Skocpol, Theda. 1992. *Protecting Soldiers and Mothers.* Cambridge, MA: Harvard University Press.

Slater, Dan. 2010. *Ordering Power: Contentious Politics and Authoritarian Leviathans in Southeast Asia.* New York: Cambridge University Press.

Smith, Mark. 2000. *American Business and Political Power.* Chicago: University of Chicago Press.

Snyder, Richard, and David Samuels. 2004. "Legislative Malapportionment in Latin America." In E. Gibson, ed., *Federalism and Democracy in Latin America.* Baltimore: Johns Hopkins University Press.

Sociedad de Fomento Fabril (SOFOFA). 2002. "Ministros de Estado Informan Resultados del Trabajo en Conjunto con la SOFOFA." Santiago, Chile. www.sofofa.cl

Spiller, Pablo, and Mariano Tommasi. 2000. *Las Fuentes Institucionales del Desarrollo Argentina.* Buenos Aires: Editorial Universidad de Buenos Aires.

Stallings, Barbara. 1978. *Class Conflict and Economic Development in Chile, 1958–1973.* Stanford: Stanford University Press.

Steinmo, Sven. 1993. *Taxation and Democracy: Swedish, British, and American Approaches to Financing the Modern State.* New Haven: Yale University Press.

Suarez, Sandra and Robin Kolodny. 2011. "Business Interests and the Politics of Financial Deregulation in the United States." *Politics and Society* 39 (1): 74–102.

Swank, Duane. 2006. "Tax Policy in an Era of Internationalization." *International Organization* 60: 47–882.

Swenson, Peter. 2002. *Capitalists against Markets.* New York: Oxford University Press.

Tarrow, Sidney. 1994. *Power in Movement.* New York: Cambridge University Press.

Taylor, Matthew. 2009 "Institutional Development through Policymaking." *World Politics* 61 (3): 487–515.

Teichman, Judith. 2001. *The Politics of Freeing Markets in Latin America.* Chapel Hill: University of North Carolina Press.

2009. "Competing Visions of Democracy and Development in the Era of Neoliberalism in Mexico and Chile." *International Political Science Review* 30 (67).

Thacker, Strom. 2000. *Big Business, the State, and Free Trade: Constructing Coalitions in Mexico.* New York: Cambridge University Press.

Thelen, Kathleen. 2004. *How Institutions Evolve.* New York: Cambridge University Press.

Timmons, Jeffery. 2005. "The Fiscal Contract: States, Taxes, and Public Services." *World Politics* 57: 530–67.

2010. "Taxation and Credible Commitment: Left, Right, and Partisan Turnover." *Comparative Politics* 42 (2): 207–28.

Toye, John, and Mick Moore 1998. "Taxation, Corruption and Reform." *European Journal of Development Research* 10 (1): 60–84.

Valdés, Juan. 1995. *Pinochet's Economists*. Cambridge: Cambridge University Press.

Van Cott, Donna Lee. 2005. *From Movements to Parties in Latin America*. New York: Cambridge University Press.

Van Evera. Stephen. 1997. *Guide to Methods for Students of Political Science*. Ithaca, NY: Cornell University Press.

Viguera, Aníbal. 2000. *La Trama Política de la Apertura Económica en la Argentina*. La Plata, Argentina: Universidad Nacional de La Plata.

Vogel, David. 1987. "Political Science and the Study of Corporate Power: A Dissent from the New Conventional Wisdom." *British Journal of Political Science* 17 (4): 385–408.

1989. *Fluctuating Fortunes: The Political Power of Business in America*. New York: Basic Books.

Weyland, Kurt. 1996. *Democracy without Equity: Failures of Reform in Brazil*. Pittsburgh: University of Pittsburgh Press.

1997. "Growth with Equity in Chile's New Democracy?" *Latin American Research Review* 32, 1: 37–67.

2002. *The Politics of Market Reform in Fragile Democracies: Argentina, Brazil, Peru, and Venezuela*. Princeton: Princeton University Press.

2006. *Bounded Rationality and Policy Diffusion*. Princeton: Princeton University Press.

2009. "The Rise of Latin America's Two Lefts." *Comparative Politics* 41 (2): 145–64.

Wibbels, Erik, and Moisés Arce. 2003. "Globalization, Taxation, and Burden-Shifting in Latin America." *International Organization* 57: 111–36.

Wilensky, Harold. 2002. *Rich Democracies: Political Economy, Public Policy, and Performance*. Berkeley: University of California Press.

Williams, John, and Brian Collins. 1997. "The Political Economy of Corporate Taxation." *American Journal of Political Science* 41: 28–44.

Wilson, J. Q. 1980. "The Politics of Regulation." In J. Q. Wilson, ed., *The Politics of Regulation*. New York: Basic Books.

Winters, Jeffrey. 1996. *Power in Motion*. Ithaca: Cornell University Press.

2011. *Oligarchy*. New York: Cambridge University Press.

Wolf, Sonia. 2009. "Subverting Democracy: Elite Rule and the Limits to Political Participation in Post-War El Salvador." *Journal of Latin American Studies* 41: 429–65.

Woll, Cornelia. 2014. *The Power of Inaction: Bank Bailouts in Comparison*. Ithaca: Cornell University Press.

Woodruff, David. 2005. "Boom, Gloom, Doom: Balance Sheets, Monetary Fragmentation, and the Politics of Financial Crisis in Argentina and Russia." *Politics and Society* 33 (1): 3–46.

Yadav, Vineeta. 2011. *Political Parties, Business Groups, and Corruption in Developing Countries*. Oxford: Oxford University Press.

Yashar, Deborah. 2005. *Contesting Citizenship in Latin America*. New York: Cambridge University Press.

Zaratti, Francesco, ed. 2004. *A 10 Años de la Capitalización: Luces y Sombras*. La Paz, Bolivia: Creativa.

Zucco, Cesar. 2007. "Where's the Bias? A Reassessment of the Chilean Electoral System," *Electoral Studies* 26 (2): 303–14.

Author's Interviews

Argentina

142 interviews conducted with 116 informants: 51 private sector; 17 legislators, 17 Economy Ministry, 16 tax agency, 4 other executive-branch informants, 9 economists, 2 other.

Interviews cited (conducted in Buenos Aires unless otherwise specified):
Abad, Alberto. Tax Agency Director (2002–08). Nov. 17, 2006; July 23, 2008.
AEA. High-level informant, Asociación Empresaria Argentina. July 21, 2006.
AFIP-A. High-level Tax Agency informant. Aug. 17, Nov. 9, 2006; July 21, 31, 2008.
AFIP-B. High-level Tax Agency informant. July 12, Nov. 14, 2006.
AFIP-C. High-level Tax Agency informant. July 19, Aug. 4, 2006.
AFIP-D. High-level Tax Agency informant. June 30, July 25, 2006.
AFIP-E. High-level Tax Agency informant. June 30, July 25, Nov. 14, 2006.
AFIP-F. High-level informant, large contributors unit. Oct. 27, 2006.
Alchouron, Guillermo. SRA president (1984–90), Acción por la República Deputy, 1999–2007, Budget and Finance Committee member. July 25, 2008.
Artana, Daniel. Chief Economist, FIEL. June 27, 2006.
Baglini, Raul. UCR senator (1985–93, 1999–2003). Sept. 13, 2006.
Bolsa Cereales. Agro-industrial association staff member. Nov. 2, 2006.
Capitanich, Jorge. PJ/FPV senator (2001–07); Senate Budget and Finance Committee president. Aug. 3, 2006.
CONINAGRO. Agricultural cooperative association staff member. Aug. 11, 14, 2006.
CRA-A. Confederaciones Rurales Argentina, staff member. Aug. 25, 2006.
CRA-B. Confederaciones Rurales Argentina, provincial leader. July 31, 2008.
Economy Ministry-A. Treasury Secretary (1996–99). Aug. 8, 18, Oct. 23, 2006.
Economy Ministry-B. Subsecretary of Tax Policy (1996–99). Sept. 4, 2006.
Economy Ministry-C. Vice Minister (1996–98). Aug. 28, 2006.
Economy Ministry-D. High-level informant. Aug. 11, 2006.
Economy Ministry-E. Tax policy advisor. June 23, Nov. 15, 2006.
Economy Ministry-F. Economic advisor. June 13, Nov. 20, 2006.
Economy Ministry-G. High-level Subsecretariat of Public Revenue informant. Aug. 10, 2006.
Exporter-A. Tax advisor, Argentine Oil Industry Chamber (CIARA). Oct. 26, 2006; July 30, 2008.
Exporter-B. High-level Argentine Oil Industry Chamber (CIARA) informant. Aug. 16, 2006; July 18, 2008.
Exporter-C. Agro-export sector informant. July 9, 2008.
FAA. Director, Federación Agraria Argentina. July 28, 2008.
Fernández, Roque. Economy Minister (1996–99). Aug. 29, 2006.
Finance-A. Banking association informant (ABA). Sept. 6, 2006; July 22, 2008.
Finance-B. Banking association informant (ABA). Sept. 12, 2006; July 24, 2008.
Finance-C. Banking association informant (ADEBA). Oct. 18, 2006; July 22, 2008.
Finance-D. Banking association informant (ABA). Oct. 19, 2006.
Finance-E. Former banking association (ABA) advisor. Oct. 18, 2006.
Lamberto, Oscar. PJ deputy (1985–2007), Budget and Finance Committee member, Treasury secretary (2002). Oct. 19, 2006.

Lavagna, Roberto. Economy Minister (2002–05). Dec. 1, 2006.
Machinea, José Luis. Economy Minister (1999–2001). April 4, 2007. Santiago, Chile.
Miceli, Felisa. Economy Minister (2005–07). July 22, 2008.
Sabaini, Juan Carlos Gómez. Tax expert. Secretary of Public Revenue (1999–2001). May 18, 24, July 6, Aug. 31, Nov. 23, 2006.
SRA-A. Staff member, Sociedad Rural Argentina. Aug. 15, 2006; July 17, 2008.
SRA-B. Former Sociedad Rural Argentina tax advisor. Sept. 5, 2006.
SRA-C. Staff member, Sociedad Rural Argentina. July 21, 2006; July 21, 2008.
SRA-D. Staff member, Sociedad Rural Argentina. July 21, 2006; July 25, 2008.
SRA-E. Staff member, Sociedad Rural Argentina. July 21, 2006.
Tomada, Carlos. Minister of Labor. Nov. 23, 2006.
UIA-B. Former industrial association president and COPAL president. Aug. 24, 2006.
UIA-B. High-level industrial association informant. July 26, 2006
Zavalia, Eduardo. President, Sociedad Rural Argentina (1990–94). July 25, 2008.

Bolivia

88 interviews conducted with 82 informants: 37 private sector; 18 legislators or party members, 7 Finance Ministry, 7 tax agency, 10 other executive-branch informants, 3 other.

Interviews cited:

ASOBAN-A. Banking association informant. Feb. 26, 2007. Santa Cruz.
ASOBAN-B. Banking association informant. March 8, 2007. La Paz.
ASOBAN-C. Vice President, CAINCO; Vice President, banking association. Feb. 22, 2007. Santa Cruz.
CADEX. General manager, Exporter's Chamber. Feb. 21, 2007. Santa Cruz.
CAINCO-A. Staff member, industry and commerce association. Feb. 13, 2007. Santa Cruz.
CAINCO-B. President, industry and commerce association. Feb. 16, 2007. Santa Cruz.
CAINCO-C. President, industry and commerce association (2001–05). Feb. 21, 2007. Santa Cruz.
CAO-A. President, Eastern Agricultural Chamber (1998–2000); Vice President, Comité Pro Santa Cruz. Feb. 13, 2007. Santa Cruz.
CAO-B. General manager, Eastern Agricultural Chamber. Feb. 15, 2007. Santa Cruz.
Carrazana, Tito. MAS senator. Feb. 7, 2007. La Paz.
CEPB. President, Private Entrepreneurs' Confederation. Dec. 15, 2006. La Paz.
CNCB. Staff member, National Commerce Chamber. March 15, 2007. La Paz.
CNI. Executive secretary, National Industries Chamber. Dec. 12, 2006; March 13, 2007. La Paz.
COB. Executive secretary, Bolivian labor union. March 8, 2007. La Paz.
Cuevas, Javier. Finance Minister (2004). March 9, 12, 2007. La Paz.
Executive Advisor. Advisor to President Morales. March 6, 2007. La Paz.
FEPB-LP. President, La Paz Private Entrepreneurs' Federation. March 6, 2007. La Paz.
FEPB-SC-A. Former vice president, CAINCO; former president, Santa Cruz Private Entrepreneurs' Federation. Feb. 14, 2007. Santa Cruz.
FEPB-SC-B. President, Santa Cruz Private Entrepreneurs' Federation (2001–03). Feb. 16, 2007. Santa Cruz.

FEPB-SC-C. President, Santa Cruz Private Entrepreneurs' Federation. Feb. 12, 2007. Santa Cruz.

Finance Ministry-A. Minister of Finance (2002–03). Feb. 8, March 5, 2007. La Paz.

Finance Ministry-B. Vice Minister of Tax Policy (2002–03). Dec. 13, 18, 2006; March 15, 2007. La Paz.

Finance Ministry-C. Advisor, Vice Ministry of Tax Policy. (2003). Jan. 12, Feb. 21, 2007. Santa Cruz.

Finance Ministry-D. Former Vice Minister of Tax Policy, international tax consultant. March 10, 2007. La Paz.

Finance Ministry-E. Vice Ministry of Tax Policy informant. Dec. 13, 2006; March 6, 2007. La Paz.

Herbas, Gabriel. MAS deputy, Finance Committee president. March 8, 2007. La Paz.

Hydrocarbons-A. President, Bolivian Hydrocarbons Chamber. Feb. 15, 2007. Santa Cruz.

Hydrocarbons-B. Company informant. Feb. 14, 2007. Santa Cruz.

Hydrocarbons-C. Company informant. Feb. 14, 2007. Santa Cruz.

Jemio, Luis Carlos. Finance Minister (Dec 2004–June 2005). Dec. 18, 2006. La Paz.

Justiniano, Guillermo. Minister of Sustainable Development (2002–03). Feb. 17, 2007. Santa Cruz.

Mesa, Carlos. Bolivian President (2003–05). Dec. 15, 2006. La Paz.

Nogales, Xavier. Hydrocarbons Minister (2004). March 12, 2007. La Paz.

Ortiz, Oscar. PODEMOS senator; former general manager, Industry and Commerce Association (CAINCO). Feb. 16, 2007. Santa Cruz.

Pimentel, Jose. MAS deputy, Economic Development Committee. March 13, 2007. La Paz.

Ramírez, Santos. MAS senator. March 13, 2007. La Paz.

Sanchez de Lozada, Gonzalo. Bolivian President (1993–97, 2002–03). Oct. 26, 2010. Telephone interview.

Soruco, Norah. Former MIR deputy. Feb. 27, 2007. Santa Cruz.

Torres, Guillermo. Hydrocarbons Minister (2004–05). Dec. 12, 2006. La Paz.

Torres, Juan José. Former MIR deputy. March 15, 2007. La Paz.

Torrico, Gustavo. MAS deputy. March 6, 2007. La Paz.

Vaca Diez, Hormando. Former MIR senator. March 3, 2007. Santa Cruz.

Zaratti, Francesco. Hydrocarbons sector expert. Dec. 12, 2006, La Paz.

Chile

216 interviews conducted with 161 informants: 41 private sector; 38 legislators or party members, 21 Finance Ministry, 10 tax agency, 21 other executive-branch informants, 16 economists, 14 other.

Interviews cited (conducted in Santiago unless otherwise specified):

ABIF. Banking sector informant. Jan. 5, 2006; April 25, 2011; 2012.

Agostini, Claudio. Economist, Universidad Alberto Hurtado. Aug. 19, Sept. 30, 2005.

Aninat, Eduardo. Finance Minister (1994–99). March 5, 2007.

Auth, Pepe. Fundación Chile 21; PPD deputy (2010–14). Sept. 30, 2005; June 25, 2012.

Bitar, Sergio. PPD senator (1994–2002); Minister of Education (2003–05). March 25, 2007.

Boeninger, Edgardo. Minister of the General Secretariat of the Presidency (1990–94); PDC senator (1998–2006). Nov. 14, 2005.

CChC-A. Construction association staff member (2002–06). Nov. 23, 2005.

CChC-B. Construction association staff member and two tax consultants. Dec. 6, 2005; Jan. 3, 2006.

CChC-C. Former president, Construction Association. Dec. 16, 2005; Aug. 4, 2008; May 12, 2011.

CChC-D. Construction Association staff member. Aug. 13, 2008; May 3, 2011; July 5, 2012.

CEP. Centro de Estudios Públicos investigator. Nov. 15, 2005; March 23, 2007.

Cieplan. Concertación think tank: two former-government fiscal policy experts. July 10, 2012.

CNCC. General manager, National Chamber of Commerce. May 6, 2011.

Coloma, Juan Antonio. UDI senator (2002–) and party president (2008–12). April 4, 2011.

CPC-A. President, Production and Commerce Confederation (2000–02). Dec. 13, 2005; June 28, 2012.

CPC-B. General manager, Production and Commerce Confederation (2000–05). March 12, 2007.

CPC-C. Tax committee member, Production and Commerce Confederation. Oct. 7, 2005.

CPC-D. General manager, Production and Commerce Confederation (2006–09). Aug. 4, 2008; July 5, 2012.

CPC-E. General manager, Production and Commerce Confederation (2010–). April 26, 2011; June 26, 2012.

CPC-F. Guzmán. President, Production and Commerce Confederation (1990–96). Dec. 29, 2005.

Dittborn, Julio. UDI deputy, Finance Committee member. Nov. 15, 2005.

Escalona, Camilo. PS senator and party president (2006–10). March 12, 2007; Aug. 7, 2008.

Etcheberry, Javier. Tax-agency director (1990–2002). Dec. 12, 2005; June 26, 2012.

Executive Advisor-A. Lagos administration. Oct. 21, 2005.

Executive Advisor-B. Lagos administration. Nov. 23, 2005.

Executive Advisor-C. Piñera administration. April 27, 2011; June 26, July 11, 2012.

Eyzaguirre, Nicolás. Finance Minister (2000–05). March 25, 2007.

FDD. Fundación Democracia y Desarrollo. Santiago, Chile. Telephone interview. 2012.

Ffrench-David, Ricardo. PDC economist, CEPAL. Sept. 5, 2005.

Finance Ministry-A. Economist, Lagos administration. Oct. 14, 2005.

Finance Ministry-B. High-level informant. Oct. 13, 25, 2005.

Finance Ministry-C. High-level informant. Oct. 17, 24, 2005; Jan. 31, 2006.

Finance Ministry-D. High-level informant. Nov. 25, 2005.

Finance Ministry-E. High-level informant. Aug. 13, 2008.

Finance Ministry-F. High-level informant. March 10, 2007; Aug. 7, 2008.

Finance Ministry-G. Former Finance Ministry informant. April 17, 2007.

Finance Ministry-H. Finance Ministry economist (2000–02). Oct. 18, 2005.

Finance Ministry-I. Budget Director (1997–2000). Oct. 19, 2005.

Finance Ministry-J. High-level informant. May 5, 2011.

Foxley, Alejandro. Finance Minister (1990–94); PDC senator (1998–2006). Jan. 19, 2006.

García Ruminot, José. RN senator (2002–). March. 17, 2007.

Gazmuri, Jaime. PS senator (1990–2010). Jan 31, 2006; Aug. 6, 2008.

Insunza, Jorge. PPD deputy (2006–10). March 10, 2007.

Jackson, Georgio. Student movement leader. July 11, 2012.

Jorratt, Michael. Tax agency studies division (1991–2006), international consultant. Multiple interviews, 2005–08, 2010–11.

Kuschel, Carlos Ignacio. RN deputy (1990–2006). Dec. 21, 2005.

Lagos, Ricardo. Chilean President (2000–06). Sept. 20, 22, 28, 2006; April 28, 2011; July 10, 2012; May 30, 2014.

Lagos Weber, Ricardo. PPD senator (2010–). July 9, 2012.

LyD-A. Economist, Libertad y Desarrollo (UDI think tank). Nov. 25, 2005.

LyD-B. Libertad y Desarrollo informant. April 2, 2011; June 25, 2012.

Macaya, Javier. UDI deputy (2010–). July 3, 2012.

Marcel, Mario. Budget Director, Finance Ministry (2000–06). Dec. 28, 2005; Jan. 5, 2006; March 24, 2007.

Marfán, Manuel. Sub-Secretary of Finance (1994–99), Finance Minister (1999–2000). Oct. 25, 2005, Dec. 12, 2005; Feb. 8, 2006; July 4, 2012.

Matthei, Evelyn. UDI deputy (1994–98), senator (1998–2011). Jan. 27, 2006, Aug. 6, 2008.

Mining-A. Mining-sector informant. Jan. 18, 2006.

Mining-B. Mining-sector informant. Dec. 7, 2005; May 2, 2011; July 6, 2012.

Mining-C. Mining-sector informant. Dec. 29, 2005.

Mining-D. Mining-sector informant. Nov. 30, 2005.

Mining-E. Mining-sector informant. May 13, 2011.

Mining-F. Mining-sector informant. March 13, 2007.

Mining-G. Mining-sector informant. April 29, 2011

Mining-H. Mining-sector informant. May 2, 2011; July 4, 2012.

Mining-I. Mining-sector informant. May 5, 2011.

Mining-J. Mining-sector informant. May 9, 2011.

Mining Ministry. Government informant. April 28, 2011.

Montes, Carlos. PS deputy (1990–). Dec. 17, 2005; March 23, 2007; Aug. 6, 2008; May 27, 2011; July 9, 2012.

Novoa, Jovino. UDI senator (1998–) and party president (2004–06). May 11, 2011.

Prat, Francisco. RN senator (1990–98), UDI senator (1998–2002). Nov. 28, 2005.

Private Sector-A. Tax consultant. Sept. 6, 2005.

Sabag, Hosain. PDC senator (1990–). Jan. 3, 2006.

SII-A. Tax agency informant. Nov. 30, 2005.

SII-B. Tax agency informant. Oct. 27, 2005.

SII-C. Tax agency informant. March 23, 2007.

Silva, Exequiel. PDC deputy (1994–2006). Jan. 23, 2006.

Silva, Ernesto. UDI deputy (2010–). May 4, 2011; June 27, 2012.

SNA-A. President, agricultural association. Dec. 7, 2005.

SNA-B. President, agricultural association. May 6, 2011.

SNA-C. Agricultural association informant. June 27, 2012.

SOFOFA-A. High-level industry association informant. Dec. 15, 2005; July 26, 2012.

SOFOFA-B. Industry association staff member. Nov. 18, 2005.

SOFOFA-C. Former industry association president. Dec. 28, 2005.

SOFOFA-D. Industry association staff member. June 28, 2012.

UDI-A. UDI Deputy (1998–2010). Dec. 23, 2005; March 13, 2007.

UDI-B. Former campaign advisor to Joaquín Lavín. Nov. 16, 2005.

Ulloa, Jorge. UDI deputy (1990–). May 4, 2011.

Velasco, Andrés. Economist, Bachelet campaign advisor and Finance Minister (2006–10). Sept. 13, 2005.

Viera Gallo, José Antonio. PS deputy (1990–98), senator (1998–2006). Jan. 16, 2006.

Zaldívar, Andrés. PDC senator (1990–2006, 2010–), senate president (1998–2004). March 26, 2007; May 9, 2011; July 10, 2012.

Index

CPSIA information can be obtained at www.ICGtesting.com
Printed in the USA
BVOW03*1607260715

410205BV00004B/28/P